(1901)

£5

Dr.

IN SEARCH OF
COLUMBUS

IN SEARCH OF COLUMBUS

BY

HUNTER DAVIES

Colombo '92

SINCLAIR-STEVENSON

First published in Great Britain by
Sinclair-Stevenson Limited
7/8 Kendrick Mews
London sw7 3HG, England

Cataloguing in Publication Data for this title
is available from the British Library

ISBN 1 85619 067 6

Photoset by Rowland Phototypesetting Limited
Bury St Edmunds, Suffolk
Printed and bound in Great Britain by
Clays Limited, St Ives plc

CONTENTS

	Acknowlegements	vi
	Introduction	vii
1	*Birth and Youth in Genoa*	1
2	*Genoa Today*	12
3	*Portugal*	25
4	*Portugal Today: Lagos, Lisbon and Madeira*	44
5	*Spain*	56
6	*Palos Today*	71
7	*The First Voyage, Palos to Bahamas*	80
8	*Bahamas Today*	103
9	*First Voyage – from the Bahamas, via Cuba and Hispaniola, to Spain*	118
10	*Seville Today*	144
11	*Second Voyage*	152
12	*Haiti Today*	176
13	*The Third Voyage*	191
14	*Venezuela Today*	203
15	*The Third Voyage: 1498–1500*	217
16	*The Dominican Republic Today*	226
17	*The Fourth Voyage*	236
18	*Jamaica Today*	250
19	*The Death of Columbus*	257
20	*Spain Today – Gomera and Valladolid*	271
21	*Columbus Today*	279
	Bibliography	296
	Chapter Notes	299
	Index	304

ACKNOWLEDGEMENTS

I WOULD like to thank all those experts, academic and lay, in Europe and the Americas, who helped so much over the last four years by making free their knowledge and possessions and all those I met along the way who offered hospitality and comfort.

In particular: Rosario Parra Cala, Director of the Archivo General de Indias, Seville; Dr Aldo Agosto, Director of the Archivo di Stato, Genoa; Dr Kathleen Deagan, University of Florida; Foster Provost, Duquesne University; Alfredo Jimenez Nunez, Cultural Director, Expo 92, Seville; Eduardo Garrigues Lopez Chicheri, Spanish Institute, London; Prof. Angel Sanz, Valladolid University; Francesca Vego, Venezuelan Ambassador, London; Professor A B Chiarelli, University of Florence; Dr Charles Hoffman, University of Northern Arizona; Carey Robinson, National Trust, Kingston, Jamaica; Peter Barber, British Museum.

Not forgetting: in Madeira, Peter and Brenda Brainch, Mrs Georges Welsh, Heather Woods, Ricardo Barbeito; in Seville, Jock Wallace, Marianne; in Madrid, Aurora and Colin Grove; in London, Paco Pena; in San Jose, California, Dr John Davies; in Washington, DC, John Kelly, Francisco Martinez – Avarerz of the 500 Commission; in the Bahamas, Jose Gomez, Paul Bower and their families, Basil Albury at the Ministry of Tourism; in Jamaica, Sam and Lee Hart, Sheila and Kenneth Kennedy, Jean and Oliver Cox, Martin and Jane Reid at the British High Commission; in the Dominican Republic, Maureen Tejeda, the Hon British Consul, Bernardo Vega, Dr Perez Memen at the Museum of Dominican Man; in Haiti, Dr William Hodges and staff at the Hospital le Bon Samaritan, John Aldis, Elizabeth Abbott Namphy, Chantal Wichert, Albert Manganes; in Venezuela, Jesus Rubio and family of Vencemos, Charles Walsh, Clive Bashleigh, Bill Quantrill of the British Embassy.

Introduction

CHRISTOPHER COLUMBUS was born in Genoa in 1451.

There are three simple facts in that simple little sentence, modest enough morsels of information, plain statements which we all carry around with us, like telling the world our name and place and date of birth, passport fodder which we can fill out in our sleep. But what agonies, what arguments, have taken place over the last 500 years to enable me now to come out, matter of fact, with these, well, matters of fact.

In 1892, at the time of the 400th anniversary celebrations of the Discovery of the New World, that simple statement contained two facts still in dispute. Different experts had different years for Columbus's birth, based on their different bits of evidence. Differing claims were also being made for a variety of birthplaces. In 1939, Salvador de Madariaga produced a book which maintained Columbus was a Spanish Jew, a view, as I discovered on my travels, still believed in some remoter parts of the world, but now dismissed by all the leading scholars.

In 1988, a Portuguese lecturer put forward a theory, after extensive research, that Columbus was born in Portugal and originally called Zarco, only changing his name later to Columbus. I have read the relevant chapters in his book and he does have one interesting theory – that Columbus was an occasional spy for the King of Portugal. This would help to explain some minor mysteries in his life, but he has produced no proof for Columbus's birth in Portugal. There have been other books, over the centuries, which have maintained he was born in Corsica, in Turkey, in Spain and even in England.

It is, today, universally agreed that the man we know as Columbus was born in Italy (at least what we now call Italy) and that his family's home was in Genoa (though they moved around the city and environs) and that he was born there in 1451 (the month is not known).

All this concern about the basic facts might suggest that we know little about the life of Columbus. The opposite is the case. I have been overwhelmed in the last five years by the enormous amount of material. In Italy, for example, there are ten volumes of contemporary documents relating in some way to Columbus. In Seville, there is a whole library devoted to the Indies. In Port au Prince, Haiti, that tragic country, I stood in amazement and gaped at the anchor from the *Santa Maria*. When you consider that these papers, these objects, have survived 500 years, then it is remarkable.

By comparison, we know next to nothing about the life of Shakespeare, have no letters by him, nor any contemporary descriptions of him, yet Shakespeare lived some hundred years later and he was in the business of putting pen to paper, while Columbus put ships to sea. Over the age of twenty-one, we can almost date the life of Columbus, month by month, and then, from 1492 onwards, it can often be done day by day. The reason is that, when Columbus achieved fame, it was instant world fame, at least in that section of the world which considered itself the seat of modern civilisation.

The problems concern his early years. Facts are few, but the legends are endless. For centuries, children in Spain, and in the USA, have been fed Columbus stories, wholesome moral tracts, patriotic tales, which have varied with the times, and with the patriotic needs. His personality is ever-changing, as is his portrait. Today, in the picture books, he varies between Rambo and Robert Redford, depending on the market. Now and again there is a striking similarity to how we imagine Jesus Christ.

I have attempted to untangle the facts from the fiction, peeling back the layers, trying to find out why and when certain stories first appeared, discovering how they developed and improved over the centuries. Many can be traced back directly to Columbus, telling nice tales about himself in later life, while fudging some of the truth. In my search for the facts about Columbus I think I know now which are irrefutable, based on documents which exist. When it is a supposition, my own or someone else's, I plan to make that clear. I have taken a vow, one of several, not to adorn a fact with 'probably' or 'must have'. Fine sentiments. Let us hope I stick to them, though it will be very difficult, as I will undoubtedly have to simplify and omit.

One has to simplify because the agreed facts are now too extensive, and increasingly specialist. I have met and talked to scholars on my travels round the world who are working ceaselessly to perfect and publish their slice of the Columbus story for 1992, examining minute slivers, often totally unaware of what is happening, what is being discovered, elsewhere in the Columbus world. Since the death of Samuel Eliot Morison, the American historian, there is no expert who can boast that he or she carries around the complete and up-to-date Columbus story in their head. There is just too much to know, to read, to keep up with. In preparation for 1992, there have been six learned bulletins I know of, some monthly, some annual, appearing in six different countries, which list the academic work being done in each country. Reading these bulletins is a formidable task in itself.

The most distinguished modern expert on Columbus is Paolo Emilio Taviani, an Italian senator as well as scholar. His major work appeared not long ago, *Christopher Columbus: The Grand Design* (published in English in 1984). It is almost 600 pages long and the notes to each chapter take up as much space as the chapters themselves. And yet this magnificent work of scholarship finishes on Columbus's departure in 1492 – just when, so most people would assume, the story is about to begin.

I have to simplify because I plan to include the whole life story in one volume, covering the major, recorded events and developments. And I aim to tell that story, as far as possible, in chronological order, not skipping ahead, not letting out information before it happens. I am assuming everyone knows Columbus sailed the ocean blue, in fourteen hundred and ninety-two, but that even so-called educated people have little idea what went before, or came afterwards.

The facts about Columbus basically depend on three types of primary sources. They must be mentioned now, as I will be referring to them continually when the book begins. Firstly, there are in existence around thirty major contemporary Columbus documents and letters. Some are very long, almost book-length, others are notes scribbled in the margins of books, but enough to show Columbus's thought process. Not all these documents are in Columbus's hand, but they can be considered first-hand in that they are printed versions of letters he actually wrote (the originals having disappeared), or are copies of letters and documents, done by people who had Columbus's originals in front of them at the time. These then are the Columbus Documents (not to be confused with documents written by other people, giving their views on the same events).

Secondly, we have two complete books, written by contemporaries, people who were there and had access to what happened. One is the biography of Columbus written by his son Fernando, whom I refer to throughout as Ferdinand. (There, I've broken one of my vows. Now you know he had a son.) Ferdinand, as a little boy, went on one of the voyages. (Now you know there was more than one voyage.) He had his father's letters and family documents to work from, but this biography of his father was not published till much later, for reasons which will be explained. Ferdinand's biography is vitally important but, as with all such examples of filial piety, it cannot always be said to be totally objective. The other book is by Bartolome de Las Casas, a Spanish bishop, a contemporary who produced a *History of the Indies*, based on his own first-hand experiences and also on logs and letters written by Columbus which he had in his possession. We have to rely on Las Casas, and on Ferdinand, that they did not fabricate, or interpolate, when quoting or paraphrasing Columbus's own words, but no scholar has ever cast doubt on either of them. Unlike Ferdinand, Las Casas also clearly states his own opinions and feelings and is violently opposed to the Spanish Establishment. It is a marvellous piece of political invective, not just a historical document, and makes a perfect counterpoint to Ferdinand's account.

Thirdly, amongst the primary sources, is a mass of contemporary, or near-contemporary, descriptions by people who were there, who met Columbus, who went on his voyages, who set down their own opinions and memories of these great events. There are about thirty major examples of these, plus hundreds of minor references, growing all the time, as dusty records in local archives can still produce a chance fact in some legal document or financial transaction, not apparently connected with Columbus, but which can throw light on some aspect of his life and times.

The reason for this mass of primary material, for the wealth of verbatim accounts by Columbus and others which have survived for 500 years, is due to one fact. If he had sailed forty years earlier, very little documentary evidence would have survived. In 1456, when Columbus was a child aged five, Gutenberg produced his version of the Bible. Printing changed the world of communications. By the time Columbus returned from the New World, Europe no longer needed street gossip to pass on news. There were printed copies of Columbus's letters available in the capital cities of Europe within weeks of their being written and received; pirated, no doubt, but how fortunate we have them. The original copies, meant for the eyes of the King and Queen, have in most cases disappeared, but thanks to the magic of print the same words live on, for us all to study. And to enjoy. It is fascinating to consider the speed of all this, happening 500 years ago, and equally fascinating to discover such good writing and marvellous descriptions.

I have also been in search of Columbus today. The view of what happened 500 years ago is different from a view taken 400 years ago, or from how it will look when the 600-year mark is up. It is not just a matter of new material appearing, but that we, the lookers and seekers, even when turning over the same old embers, are different. We reflect ourselves, our situation, our perspective, seeing strengths which were formerly dismissed as weaknesses, values which we now think worthless. The past does not change. We do.

I tried to imagine, on my travels, Columbus coming back today to the places he 'discovered'. (We will leave discussions of the word 'discover' till later.) How amazed he would be to find countries he left with whites speaking Spanish now run by blacks speaking French (Haiti) or blacks speaking English (Bahamas). I wanted in each place to know what happened in the 500 years since he left, and have tried to tell that story, as briefly as possible, and to discover what each country thinks of him today, whether they are pleased and proud, dismissive and resentful, or bored and uninterested.

The book, therefore, has become two books – a combination of past and present. In alternate chapters, I break off from the fifteenth-century story, leaving it at a suitable and sometimes an exciting point, to jump 500 years forward, describing the same places today. I also wanted to describe where the relics of Columbus, from documents and letters to houses and statues, can be seen today. I often feel cheated when academics do not reveal the provenance of their sources, how exactly to gain access to those letters, the key of the door, the person to speak to; or indeed the places they failed to find, the buildings locked or knocked down when they eventually got there, the trials and tribulations of being a searcher, if not always a researcher.

In all my own travels I was eager to discover what each country associated with the life of Columbus is doing about 1992. If anything. The simple answer is that every country, every place, is doing something, as we shall see. They might violently disagree today on his actions, and some certainly do not revere him, but no one is ignoring the 500th anniversary of his arrival. The common denominator is that they are turning it to their own advantage, from the USA to Spain, from San Salvador to Porto Santo. They are celebrating themselves.

The year 1992 will see the biggest celebrations for any single event the world has ever known. Is this a wild exaggeration, a ridiculous claim? I witnessed many of the bicentennial celebrations in the USA in 1976, which were most exciting, but it was a regional not a global event. The French Revolution celebrations of 1989 were also exciting, but equally local. It is true that 1992 will still be localised, with certain countries missing out completely. It might, for example, not be much of an Anglo–Saxon event. There will be those in Germany or Great Britain who will be unaware of any excitement, or think that 1992 refers only to some changes in the European Common Market. The 500th anniversary of the Discovery of the New World will naturally be proclaimed loudest in those countries with a strong Hispanic element, Latin America, the USA and the Caribbean, or in those European countries connected with Columbus, such as Italy and Spain, but the celebrations will still have a global importance.

The importance of what Columbus did, or caused to happen, is still with us. No other single person can be said to have changed the nature of the globe. Before him, there was no New World. That divide, between Old and New, East and West, has dominated the history of the last 500 years. It is still with us. While American and Russian warlike confrontations seem, for the moment, less threatening, an American-versus-European economic struggle could well arise. Just as it did 500 years ago.

But my search for Columbus has not been political. I have been seeking out the man: who was he, what did he do, and what happened afterwards?

I

Birth and Youth in Genoa

CHRISTOPHER COLUMBUS was born in Genoa in 1451, as we all now agree, but he was not born Christopher Columbus. That is the English-speaking world's version, taken from a Latin translation, and he himself would hardly have recognised it.

In modern Italian, he is known as Cristoforo Colombo, and, if any birth certificate should turn up, that would roughly be the spelling, though it might well have been the more Latinised Cristoforus Columbus. In Portuguese, he is always known as Cristovão Colombo. In French he is Christophe Colomb. In Spanish he is Cristobal Colon, a name you meet all over Latin America, in towns and squares, and it is surprising that the English language did not take on Colon rather than Columbus. In Russia, where every school child learns about him, he is called Hristofor Koloomb, which is itself a variation on the French variation.

All variations are interesting, but then Columbus himself found his own name endlessly fascinating. In Italian, 'Colomba' means dove. Very significant, so he thought, the Dove of Peace, bringing goodness to the world. Christopher also has hidden meanings. Lurking inside you can find a member of Christ, or you can see St Christopher, the saint who carried Christ over deep water and became the patron saint of all travellers. Ferdinand, in his biography, believes, as did his father, that his name was a 'secret providence' from God.

Columbus changed the spelling of his name as he changed countries, much as immigrants do to this day, not necessarily to disguise their roots but to ease their passage, allow themselves to

slip more easily on to new tongues. Columbus added to confusion
about his origins by not wishing to give out too many details, at
least in his early life; and then, in later life, he gave out details
which were often contradictory. In one of his own letters, accepted
as genuine, he states that on his first voyage (1492, no argument
about that) he had been twenty-three years at sea and that he had
first gone to sea at the age of fourteen. *Ergo*, he must have been
born in 1455. But, on another occasion, he said he had been at sea
forty years, having started aged ten, which led several authors to
deduce he was born in 1442. 'About the year 1435' was the date
accepted by Washington Irving, the American writer, and the first
person in English to tackle his whole life. His book came out in
1828 and remained the standard work for many decades.

Columbus could have got his years at sea wrong, or been exaggerating, or counting in the years while he waited to go to sea, or
perhaps an unknown hand or printer made a mistake in copying
out the date. It is a problem with all letters, or with all history
come to that, if you decide to rely on just one piece of evidence to
prove a certain date.

The confusion has in recent years been resolved by a series of
documentary evidence coming to light. In 1931, a legal paper, dated
October 31, 1470, was found which refers to Christopher Columbus
as being aged nineteen. Then another turned up, dated August 25,
1479, a deposition concerning a law suit, which declares that
Columbus is then aged 'around twenty-seven'. In all, there are now
over one hundred documentary references to Columbus and his
family, if merely in passing, recording the fact of his existence in
a certain place at a certain time, written in impartial, impersonal
legal prose. In those days, you went to a local notary for many
reasons, not just over a disagreement, and the notary would record
the facts of the matter. Together, these documents conclusively
prove that 1451 was the year of Columbus's birth. The exact
day and month, however, is never mentioned. Internal evidence
suggests it was between August 25 and October 31.

All these documents come from Genoa. In later life, Columbus
made no secret of connections with that city, boasted it was his
home town, was grateful to those local businessmen who had helped
him. Whether he was born in Genoa, or in a village nearby, is still
not certain.

Italian scholars have traced his family in Genoa and in the
surrounding area, and can go back many generations, and there is
now little mystery about his lineage, nor the slightest sign of any

Jewishness. The houses and streets where his family lived would have made this impossible in the fifteenth century. The main 'proof' of the Jewish theory is his devotion to the Old Testament and his apparent name changes, suggesting that he was trying to hide his real identity to avoid persecution as a Jew.

His roots were humble, which was one reason for rarely referring to them. Later he liked to pretend there had been admirals in his family, all spurious, while Ferdinand goes back further and suggests they were descended from a Roman Consul called Colonus, again without any proof, though it was a legend the whole family enjoyed believing. Very often, great men make their humble origins even humbler, exaggerating the bare feet, the coal in the bath, the dry crusts, but Columbus chose to polish up his background, wanting to believe he did have aristocratic connections, which no one so far has managed to find. He probably felt the need for extra dignity when dealing with the aristocracy.

Columbus's father was Dominico Colombo, a weaver, and his mother Susanna, née Fontarossa, the daughter of a weaver. Both families can be traced back into the hill villages behind Genoa, in the region known today as Liguria. Dominico was born in Quinto, then a village just outside Genoa, but now part of the city. Around the age of twenty-two, Dominico moved into the walled city, in an area where other woolworkers lived, known as the Vico dell' Olivella. It is thought very likely Columbus was born there, though on the other hand his mother could well have moved out to Quinto for the birth, to be with the women of her family during her confinement.

Columbus was the first of their five children. The second child, Giovanni, is thought to have died young. There was one daughter, Bianchinetta, who married a local cheesemaker and lived and died, as far as is known, in Genoa. Then there were two more sons, Bartolmeo (Bartholomew) and Giacomo (usually known as Diego), the baby of the family, seven years younger than Columbus.

Dominico appears to have been slightly more than an artisan woolworker, and aspired for a time to be a minor merchant with his own shop and business; then things went wrong and he was involved in other occupations, including acting as keeper of one of the gates to the city. This appointment was in return for political services, a little perk for supporting one of the two political parties then struggling to control Genoa. He backed the Fregosos, who in turn drew support from the French (the Anjou dynasty), while their rivals had Spanish support (from the House of Aragon). It was a dangerous game to play in fifteenth-century Genoa, especially as the Fregosos were soon to lose their power. His father's political activity, however limited and localised, might well have been a reason why Columbus kept his background quiet when he went out into the world.

Taviani has tracked down seventy-seven references to Dominico in the Genoese and Ligurian notarial records, an unusual amount for a humble weaver; but it reflects his various occupations, his political activities and his legal disputes. In February 1470 he had moved for some reason to another town nearby, Savona, working as a weaver and innkeeper, but six months later he was back in Genoa with his son Christopher, according to a document dated September 22, 1470, the first known reference to Columbus.

This particular document is also interesting because it reveals that Dominico had been arrested – and put in prison. The case revolved round a dispute over the ownership of some land. Dominico was soon released, declared innocent, but he had to pay a 35 lire fine.

Life with Dominico was clearly eventful, with his numerous changes of habitat, perhaps to keep ahead of his debts or his enemies, and at times positively exciting, even dangerous. He was ambitious, an entrepreneur in the making, sailing close to the wind with some of his deals, which now and again came to grief. He was active in the weavers' guild, and at one time represented their interests, which would indicate he had the respect of the local weaving community. At his most successful, he owned two houses and some land, but in the end he died in poverty, looked after by his daughter and her husband, the cheesemaker. As for the life and character of his wife Susanna, not enough is known, except that she brought some property to the marriage and that she stuck by her husband to the end.

From all these assorted scraps about Dominico, some Italian writers have suggested he was a megalomaniac who happened to be cursed with an evil spell, which was why things never went right for long. Naturally, they have looked for similar traits in his son.

Genoa was part of a City State, an independent and separate power, one of many in what is now Italy. The Republic of Genoa was as rich and powerful as its great rival Venice and together they had fought over and shared the major part of the Mediterranean sea routes and trading colonies. Around the time of Columbus's birth, Genoa claimed land on the mainland of Italy as far as Pisa, the island of Corsica, several islands in the Aegean such as Lesbos and Chios, a great part of the island of Cyprus, and even lands and settlements around the Black Sea.

The wealth and power of Genoa stemmed from its magnificent natural harbour. According to one theory, it is the reason for Genoa's name, coming from the Latin 'janua', meaning door, in this case a doorway leading to the sea. Another theory says the name comes from Janus, the two-headed god, facing both the land and the sea. The latter has traditionally been preferred by Genoa's enemies, as they like to imply that the Genoese are two-faced.

The harbour was vital in Roman times and later during the Crusades when Genoese merchants grew fat on hiring out shipping and lending money. They invested in trade and banking and Genoa became one of Europe's chief financial centres. By 1300, it had a population estimated at 50,000, one of the biggest in the known world, defended by strong city walls and boasting several magnificent palaces. It was a cosmopolitan city, with many foreign communities, and Genoese merchants constantly travelled back and forward to their various colonies and possessions.

The most important bank was the Banco di San Giorgio, named after the patron saint of Genoa, St George, adopted by the city in 1190. As in England, the emblem is a red cross on a white background, and the slain dragon, a symbol of heresy, figures prominently. The Bank of St George grew to such wealth and influence that Machiavelli described it as 'a state within a state'.

Genoa had produced two Popes, though one ruled for only thirty-nine days and was known as the Miser. This was Adrian V, elected in 1276. The other was Innocent IV who became Pope in 1243. Genoa had produced several explorers, notably the Vivaldi brothers, and it was also visited by Marco Polo, originally from Venice, who dictated one of his diaries there.

While Columbus was growing up, the main direction of Genoese trade was drastically changing, thanks to the fall of Constantinople in 1453 to the Turks. This city had been partly governed by Genoa, so enabling them to exert power in the Black Sea, sometimes known as Genoa's Lake, giving her merchants free access to the Orient. Genoese merchants had dominated the Eastern trade in gold, silver, furs, silks and spices. This trade was particularly important to Europe as spices were used to make food palatable, to ferment and improve the taste of wines and beers, for use in medicines, and to disguise the bad odours of medieval plumbing. Once the Turks controlled the eastern end of the Mediterranean, Genoa lost its Levantine possessions, though it retained Chios. It began to look more to the West, to Europe and the Atlantic for its trade and wealth.

Outside Italy, Portugal was becoming the new power in Europe. The Portuguese had finally thrown out their Moslem invaders in 1267 and, as a unified nation, had begun a policy of exploration and expansion. Their neighbours in Spain were still divided and still in Moorish hands. England was preoccupied with the Wars of the Roses, Dark-Age intrigues and civil disruption, and there was no interest in international expansion until the Tudors came to power in 1485. In France, the influence of the House of Burgundy was at last diminishing, but the country was still rent by various local disturbances.

The leading City States of Italy were not only rich and powerful, economically and politically, despite their relatively small home regions, but were the intellectual and artistic centres of Europe. Columbus grew up at the height of the Renaissance, primarily associated with the nearby City State of Florence, though its effects spilled out throughout Italy and all Europe. Scientists and geographers, artists and writers, were investigating new methods and ideas, seeking to discover new solutions. They were as interested in new lands on the planet as in new planets in the sky. It is astonishing to realise just how many great men, whom we now called geniuses, were contemporaries or near-contemporaries of Columbus, and who lived and grew up just a few hundred miles away: in particular Leonardo da Vinci, Michelangelo, Raphael. Leonardo was just a year younger than Columbus. In 1492, he was designing a machine which could fly.

By the age of fifteen, Columbus, on his own evidence, had already gone to sea, if not as a full-time sailor, then on several voyages, presumably locally. It is difficult to decide what sort of education he had, if any. Ferdinand boasts that his father had the benefit of a university education, surprisingly for a weaver's son in the fifteenth century. And a good university at that. 'He learned his letters at a tender age at the University of Pavia to understand the geographers, of whose teaching he was very fond.' Alas, a host of scholars over the centuries have been through the matriculation records of the University of Pavia and so far there has not been a sign of a C. Columbus.

There were, however, guild schools in Genoa at the time, and a successful or ambitious weaver such as Dominico could have managed the modest fees, in his more affluent moments, so Columbus might well have learned the rudiments of reading and writing at a

young age, though there is no proof of this either. It is assumed he
spoke the local Genoese dialect, still strong today so that other
Italians find it hard to understand, but then Italians always maintain
they cannot understand people from the next town.

As to why and how he first went to sea, that again is a matter of
conjecture, though it has not stopped authors, and even academics,
over the centuries from painting vivid pictures. Samuel Eliot Morison is a total romantic as far as Columbus the mariner is concerned,
and as an ex-admiral himself it is understandable. He describes 'the
dreamy little boy' as being besotted by the sea from a young age,
excited by his first trips, coming ashore and trying to swap treasures
with other boys so that he can have a jack-knife. Even Taviani,
normally very dry and factual in his accounts, obsessed by the
documents, lets himself wax lyrical. He states that 'from adolescence
Christopher was determined to go to sea'. This would seem obvious
enough, knowing as one does what happened later, but there is no
proof. It could simply have been a reaction to his father, determined
to make him an apprentice weaver, which made the young
Columbus decide to get away, anywhere, rather than stay
at home. He was looking for a job, something to do. Perhaps it was
only later that he fell in love with the sea. In history, and in
biography, we like to see patterns and plans, when very often it
was mere chance.

There is also a problem, for those who insist on painting touching
scenes of our sea-struck young hero, wandering round the harbour
at Genoa, staring longingly at the horizon, of describing exactly
what he looked like. Did he have piercing blue eyes? Or deep
brown sensitive eyes? Perhaps an open freckled face? At the Great
Exposition in Chicago in 1892, to celebrate the 400th anniversary,
there were seventy-two portraits of Columbus on show. In some
he has a moustache, in others he is clean-shaven. His hair appears
long, and also short, his face both thin and fat, his eyes blue and
brown, his hair blond and dark, sometimes bobbed, while at other
times it billows out behind. No two paintings are alike, for the
simple reason that none of these portraits was done from real life.
The most 'contemporary' portrait was not painted until a couple of
decades after his death.

We have to rely on written descriptions, such as they are. Ferdinand's description of him is generally accepted, as other contemporary writers point to similar features. 'He was a well built man of
more than average stature, the face long, the cheeks somewhat
high, his body neither fat nor lean. He had an aquiline nose and

light-coloured eyes; his complexion was light and tending to bright red.' This is Columbus in middle age, as remembered by his son, but Ferdinand does add a sentence about his father's earlier days. 'In his youth, his hair was blond, but when he reached the age of thirty, it all turned white.' So we can allow the piercing light eyes, possibly even blue, though that is not stated, to go with his fair complexion. Unusual for an Italian, or a Jew for that matter, though not rare. Genoa was a cosmopolitan city.

The age at which he went to sea is in doubt, as Columbus confused the matter in his own statements. Perhaps he was ten when he made his first-ever boat trip, while it was not until fourteen that he considered going to sea full-time. Columbus later liked to give the impression that, once he started, he very quickly jumped to captaining ships, as if he had been some sort of officer cadet, on a special training scheme. Sailors have always started young. Drake went to sea at twelve, as did Nelson, but they began, even as boys, as proper professionals, on a career structure. Columbus acquired his merchant seamanship gradually, and haphazardly.

My feeling, from reading the known details of his early voyages, from the age of fourteen, is that he began as little more than a message boy, sent on little errands along the coast by his father, bringing back raw wool, or delivering material. In between times, he probably stayed on shore, helping his father in other ways. In his later teens and early twenties, he slowly developed as an agent in his own right, representing other merchants, taking and delivering, then negotiating his own deals, buying and selling, looking for opportunities in all the ports and places he visited. The documents which survive refer to these minor deals, trading agreements, arguments over goods not arriving or not being paid for. These are the known facts, which make clear his occupation. What we do not know is how he learned navigation.

It is hard to envisage today how he managed this big jump, especially if we imagine him starting as a passenger, as opposed to a sailor, a young commercial traveller going about his business, who somehow acquires considerable navigational skills. No doubt the demarcation lines were not at all clear-cut. Possibly you could work your passage, helping out in return for a free ride. Whatever his status on these early trips, he did show a natural aptitude and was quickly giving advice, directing the helm, working out how best to use the winds, understanding the waves and the weather.

On these early voyages, along the Ligurian coast, Columbus was in boats which hugged the local shores. In 1474, aged twenty-three, he went on a much longer, more adventurous voyage, right round the foot of Italy, round Greece, and into the Aegean, to the island of Chios, just off the shores of Turkey, reputed to be the birthplace of Homer. He is thought to have sailed on a tall, three-masted ship called the *Roxana*, some thirty metres high, and for much of the way they were in open sea. Such a voyage required constant observation and analysis, of the sea and the sky; all of which Columbus enjoyed.

Today, Chios is part of Greece, but then it was a Genoese colony, though later to fall into Moslem hands. It was Columbus's first experience of being in the Orient, or so it seemed to him. The voyage obviously made a big impression, as he mixed with Arabs and Greeks, saw new landscapes, smelt the spices of the Orient, imagined Jerusalem and the Holy Land, not far away, waiting to be recaptured for Christianity from infidel hands.

Columbus stayed on Chios for a year. He might even have been planning to remain there for good, to seek his fortune and not return to Genoa. He started dealing in mastic, an aromatic resin used in perfumes and medicines, still a major product of the island, exported in wooden barrels. The Genoese controlled most of the market, which was highly lucrative. Columbus hoped to do well but matters did not work out, and eventually he returned home.

It is clear from this incident that Columbus considered himself something of a merchant-adventurer, looking for any likely opportunities. When he was back in Genoa, he was willing to be hired by the powerful Genoese banking and merchant firms, like the Spinolas and the DiNegros, to go on business voyages for them.

There was also a spell when he appears to have acted as little more than a pirate. One particular event, described by both Ferdinand and Las Casas, happened before his stay in Chios. The politics are complicated, but it concerned a raiding party organised by the King of Anjou to capture some ships off Tunis belonging to the King of Aragon. Genoa was at that time hostile to Aragon, so it can be made to sound like a patriotic gesture, but Columbus was basically a hired navigational hand.

The point of the story, as told by Ferdinand, is not the politics, or the piracy, but to repeat a ruse of which his father was clearly proud. While they were near Sardinia, the crew of the ship containing Columbus (and he tries to give the impression he was in charge) took fright and refused to go any further. Columbus tried to persuade them on, but failed, so he agreed to turn back, saying he would head instead for Marseilles. He swung the compass round, did a few turns, but only pretended to retreat, carrying on instead. The end result of the voyage is not described. Columbus was using the incident to illustrate his wonderful powers of seamanship, able to fool even the most experienced old salts.

For his first ten years since going to sea, from the age of fourteen to twenty-four, Columbus was therefore keen to try his hand at many things, from business speculations to mercenary work, taking longish voyages when they came up, or willing to settle ashore if the opportunities looked good.

In the summer of 1476, when he was aged twenty-five, Columbus set off with a commercial fleet, heading for the Atlantic, his first trip due west, as far as is known. It was a convoy of five Genoese ships, financed by the Spinolas, bound for England. The ships were armed, with canons and smaller firearms, as of course there was always the possibility of pirates. They sailed safely through the Straits of Gibraltar and worked their way along the Algarve coast of Portugal, but near Cape St Vincent they were attacked by French corsairs. Genoa was at peace with Portugal, and with France, so the French ships might well have been pirates, or perhaps the Genoese ships themselves started the firing. Whatever the cause, by the evening of August 13, 1476, a full-scale sea battle had commenced.

There were four, possibly five, pirate ships, and as the battle raged they became so entwined with the five commercial vessels that the Genoese were able to throw barrels of burning oil over the pirates. In the end they all caught fire. Four pirate ships went down, along with three Genoese. Men in armour drowned at once. Others burned to death. In all, 500 men lost their lives.

Columbus was on one of the ships which sank. Most of the sailors on board were from Savona, near Genoa, the town where Columbus's father had lived for a while. Nearly all of them perished. When the news eventually reached Savona, a contemporary report declared that 'the women made a world out of their tears'.

Columbus found himself in the water amidst the wreckage, clinging to a spar. According to Ferdinand, he was a 'prodigious swimmer' and he managed somehow to struggle six miles or so to reach the shore near the fishing port of Lagos.

He later described it as a miracle, and so in a way it was. He was certainly fortunate to survive, and to find himself washed up in what just happened to be the leading maritime nation. He arrived in Portugal in a state of collapse, with no money, no possessions, knowing nobody, but it was in Portugal that story really begins. He never returned to live in Genoa. The Genoa chapter of his life was over.

Genoa in the 15th Century.

2

Genoa Today

Colombo '92

I STARTED writing letters to Genoa a whole year before I arrived, wanting to arm myself with people to talk to and places to see, both those connected with the past and those involved with the 1992 celebrations, wishing to maximise my time in Genoa and miss nothing of interest which might be considered, however remotely, part of the Columbus Trail. This was to be my master plan, before visiting all the many countries ahead, in the Old World and the New World.

In London, the Italian Embassy referred me to the Italian Institute of Culture and from them I eventually got a list of very impressive-sounding officials and addresses in Genoa. I wrote to them all – to the Province of Genoa's Columbian Celebration Office, the Municipality of Genoa '92 Exhibition Organisers, the Columbian Civic Institute. I asked them the same things – could I have the names of any Columbus places to see, especially the so-called Columbus House, any archives, remains or memorabilia which can be inspected? Total silence. So I wrote again. Please, just any help at all, any advice, any leaflets. Not one reply. I was very depressed. If this happens when I write simple letters to Italy, one of the world's more civilised countries, what will happen when I try to make contact in Haiti?

I rang Genoa's only five-star hotel, the Colombia, for the name as much as anything else, and got a recorded message, saying it was closed, for alterations. So I picked a three-star hotel from a guide book as it looked central, handy for the Old City and quite near the place marked 'Casa Colombo'. Two days before I left, I got a 'phone call from one of the addresses I had written to, at the Town Hall in the Via Garibaldi. So my letters had not been falling off the edge of the planet, disappearing into Ultima Thule. The only trouble, said the voice on the 'phone, was that she was on the '92 Scientific Commission, so she would be no use to me. Don't go away, I yelled, just as she was about to hang up, please, please, I implore you, can you find a 'phone number for the Casa Colombo? It took ages, but she eventually gave me a name and number.

I do not think I have ever arrived in a place less prepared. If you write in advance, you are normally overwhelmed with brochures and appointments are easily fixed, as every city has officials whose job it is to look after visiting writers and journalists. I had been through Genoa twice in the past, but neither time did I need official help. This time I noticed that the airport has a name – Cristoforo Colombo. How had I missed it before? I got a taxi into town and was appalled by the first sight of my hotel. The entrance was in an alley, the two men at reception, smoking heavily, looked very sinister. They had no knowledge of my name or my booking. I produced a letter confirming my booking, and eventually one of them gave me a key and left me to make my way along cardboard corridors to my room. It had obviously been broken into at one time and the door not properly repaired.

There were no messages for me, although in my third batch of letters I had given the name of my hotel. I tried to have a shower, but could get no water. I sat looking at the telephone, wondering what to do. I rang the number I had been given for Casa Colombo, but it turned out to be a government office and no one there knew how to contact the curator. I was passed from department to department, endlessly being told to hang on, while a taped tune was played in my ear. It was 'Greensleeves'.

Eventually I got through to the press office and asked a woman if she had got any of my letters. She said yes, and then she laughed. Could I come and talk to her tomorrow, or to anyone? After some discussion, we agreed on a time, but she could not promise to be there, at that place and time. Roll on Haiti.

I went for a walk around the local streets, wondering what to do. I had an address for the History of Spaghetti Museum, which sounded interesting, but the guide book said it was open only 'on request'. I thought about visiting Mazzini's house, or looking for Paganini's violin. I studied some graffiti which said 'Doria Merda', thinking at first it might refer to another of Genoa's heroes, Admiral Doria, before deciding it was common or garden football abuse.

Genoa had that week been promoted to the first division, joining their local rivals, Sampdoria.

On my walk, I kept an eye out for any fair-haired, laughing, mischievous children, but everyone seemed swarthy, stunted, depressed, miserable. I was hoping for a café, or a simple restaurant, but could find neither. I stuck to the main streets, avoiding all the narrow dark alleyways, even though I told myself that many of them would not have changed much since Columbus's time, so really I should explore them. I felt safer on the streets, despite the ugliness of the dark and grimy buildings. Now and again through a doorway I caught sight of an inner courtyard, and a hint of marble and trees, but mostly the city seemed drab and deprived.

I came to the remains of the old walls of the city, the Porta Soprana, near where Columbus's father once lived, but could see no sign of the Columbus House. I walked through the gates and found myself amidst huddles of suspicious-looking young men, some lying on walls, or on the ground, menacing but motionless. I could not decide whether they were drunk, drugged or just dazed by life. It felt eerie and dangerous. I'll do without a meal, I thought.

Back in my hotel room, I sat idly turning over the pages of the 'phone book, staring at the yellowing walls, the bumpy bed, the broken shower. What a beginning to my Great Adventure. I was certain that out there, in this city of almost one million souls, there were people just dying to talk to me, to tell me what they knew about Columbus. Some are being paid to talk to me, dammit. But how do I reach them? It's not as if I'm going to expose them, reveal any dirty linen, dig out criminal activities. I'm here to help their city, pass on any good news, as we all get ready to celebrate 1992.

My gaze fell upon section C. I narrowed my eyes, moved my lips, and began counting the number of people in the Genoa 'phone book named Colombo. It came to 194 in all. Then I counted up the most common first names. Carlo and Maria were the joint winners, with seven each, followed by Giovanni five, Giuseppe and Ricardo four each. There was not one Dominico, as in Columbus's father, or a Bartolomeo, like his brother. But there was one Cristoforo Colombo. Well, material was thin, so, before I could stop myself, I had dialled his number.

'*Parla Inglese?*' I asked.

There was a long pause, then a pleasant, calm voice replied, in very good English, 'Yes, I do.'

'Are you Cristoforo Colombo?'

Another long pause.

'No,' said the voice, then he hung up.

Idiots must ring him all the time. Drunks at parties. Lonely foreigners stuck in hotel bedrooms. If so, how does he feel and what will he do in 1992? Change his name? I could have asked him some good questions. Should I try again? Oh, I'm not that desperate. So I went to bed. What else was there to do. I did not sleep, of course, in that horrible room with the broken door. I lay and thought about the first Christopher Columbus. He certainly had the right idea. He got out of Genoa, as quickly as he could.

When Columbus left Genoa it was still a proud and powerful city state. Despite the rise of the Turks in the East, it went on developing smoothly and naturally as a financial centre; and for the next hundred years, throughout the whole of the sixteenth century, it had enormous wealth and influence. Its bankers were everywhere, in England, France, Spain and Portugal, and it financed whole kingdoms as well as private enterprises. Genoa richly deserved its ancient title – La Superba.

In the seventeenth and eighteenth centuries, however, Genoa became caught in the cross-fire between the emerging European super-powers. At various times it was bombarded by the French, to whom it eventually lost its last Mediterranean colony, Corsica, and was then occupied by the Austrians. It managed to remain an independent nation until 1796, when Napoleon arrived. His troops were eventually expelled in 1814, but the Congress of Vienna gave Genoa to the Kingdom of Sardinia. That was the end of Genoa as an independent state and republic. It was reduced to a mere dukedom.

Genoa played a crucial part in the unification of Italy. Mazzini was Genoese and Garibaldi sailed from Genoa to Sicily in 1860 with his army of liberation. Once unification came, Genoa had a second flowering as an industrial centre, becoming Italy's leading port and a centre for steel, railways and manufacturing. This industrial strength continued till the Second World War, and its revolutionary tradition was repeated in an insurrection against the Germans in 1945. But, since then, Genoa has been in industrial decline. What went wrong?

In the rest of Italy, they make faces when Genoa is mentioned. The Ligurian coast still has some famous and fashionable holiday resorts, but few people want to visit or live in Genoa itself. Milan and Turin are now the prosperous, vibrant industrial centres. They moved smartly into the new industries, such as cars, aeroplanes,

clothes, computers, while Genoa was left behind, with only its past
to boast about. Some people blame the unions for ruining the docks
with their restrictive practices, others point to bad management.

In Italian folklore, the Genoese are known as stingy, the Aber-
donians of the nation. They are considered tight-fisted and greedy.
Was this trait in Columbus? Did it explain the family legal rows
about money? All generalisations, of course, and hard to believe
they can be stretched back over 500 years.

Next day, I set off for my tentative appointment, looking forward
to visiting the Columbus celebrations office. Or one of them. I had
a list of seven in all, with similar titles, which could explain why I
had never persuaded one of them to reply. Genoa is a city with a
town hall and a council structure. It is also a province, with
provincial offices. And it is also the capital of the region of Liguria,
with its own regional administration. Everything is triplicated, as
they all insist on their Columbus committees.

I walked from the old gates down towards the harbour, the route
which Columbus took many times as a boy. In the Via San Lorenzo
I went into the Cathedral, large and ill-lit, in the Italian fashion,
more like an empty railway station. I noticed an English bomb-shell
on display near a doorway, the relic of an attack on the city in the
last war.

I knew where the harbour must be, and could follow the street
map clearly, so I walked expectantly, hoping for a splendid view,
as the physical situation of Genoa is so naturally magnificent, with
its massive bowl of a harbour, and the town rising steeply up the
hillside. In the many engravings and paintings which have been
done over the centuries, right back to Columbus's day, it always
looks utterly dazzling.

Alas, I could not even catch a glimpse of a boat. In a mad
burst of civic self-destruction in 1965, the city fathers built a
vast overhead freeway, right round the whole of the harbour,
the Strada Sopraelevata Aldo Moro. It dominates all views, a
concrete monster in the sky, cutting off the town from its pride,
its joy, ruining the connections, destroying all aesthetics. Going
under it, and across a busy road, I did eventually reach some
harbour buildings and piers, jutting out into the dirty, sludgy
water, but they were mostly derelict or disused, and I soon gave
up. It was all too depressing.

It took some time to find the Palazzo Serra Gerace, where many
of the Columbus '92 offices are located. It faces the harbour and is a

sixteenth-century building, dull on the outside, but very handsome inside. Genoa Council has bought it and recently renovated the main rooms, ceilings and decorations.

I was slightly later than I had intended, delayed by negotiating the concrete monster, and the woman who said she might see me was busy, showing a party round the building. She could not talk to me, but I was invited to tag on behind. There were about twenty local girls in the party, rather cowed-looking students, self-conscious, badly dressed. (Elsewhere in Italy, most young people are obsessed by clothes, but street styles in Genoa were non-existent. I might as well have been in Moscow.) They were being led from room to room, having the ceilings and paintings explained, so that in 1992 they can act as guides for visitors. Some of the rooms, still heavy with gilt and brocade, were being used as offices by various important bureaucrats. They each had the latest plastic, see-through, highly modern desk, mostly cleared of papers so as not to spoil the line, with ingenious lamps on long metal stalks.

I followed the tour for half an hour, trying to get a word with the leader, but she said she was still too busy. In the end she handed me over to a boy assistant, wearing a Lisbon tee-shirt, and he took me to a store-room and piled me high with Columbus '92 literature, the stuff I had asked for a whole year previously.

I left, staggering under my load, and found a café where I studied the lovely graphics, felt the thick paper, admired the expensive colour, the luxurious lay-out. The most important event planned for 1992, so I discovered, is an international shipping exhibition, 'Christopher Columbus: Ships and Sea'. This will take place in the port, round the piers where I had just walked. It will cover five hectares of a 'unique historic and scenic area with great environmental interest'. I must have missed it, too busy cursing the noise from the fly-over. There was obviously a huge amount of work to be done before it opens, on May 15, 1992, and four million visitors arrive from around fifty countries, so they hope. The Italian pavilion will be a real ship, built for the exhibition, some 200 metres long, with enough dining space for banquets of 200.

Reading all the purple prose, feeling the full-colour architectural plans, I sensed that the exhibition space devoted to ships and navigation in 1492 is likely to be rather less extensive than the 1992 displays. There is going to be a lot of hard selling done on behalf of today's cargo handling, container ships, oil tankers, underwater technology, hovercraft, hydrofoils and other modern wonders. The clear message is hurrah for Genoa, such a marvellous modern port, a perfect place to do business in.

I suppose it is hard to blame them. This might be their last chance to bring prosperity to Genoa, along its ancient maritime lines, before it is finally and perhaps humiliatingly forced to search for a new role in life. The bankers of Columbus's day managed it when their old colonies diminished. Will the present city fathers engineer another economic miracle?

The brochures listed various cultural exhibitions which will be mounted in the city during 1992, including one scheduled for the Casa Colombo. On the 'phone, I had failed even to get the address of this enticing-sounding building. This time the site was arrowed, so off I rushed, clutching the map, wondering how I had missed it. It is in the Piazza Dante, through which I had walked before, on the way to the Porta Soprana.

I soon found out why it is not listed in any of the city's museum or gallery guides, or why there is no 'phone number. At first glance, it looked like a lock-up garage. Closer to, it appeared to be a bomb-damaged gable-end of a row of artisans' cottages, left behind from the war, waiting for a bulldozer to finish it off. Visitors must wonder why it is there, amidst the traffic, surrounded by office blocks, banks, insurance companies, cluttering up the square. You have to work hard to discover its identity, as it is partly covered in ivy and the explanatory plaque is high up. And in Latin.

The garage-like doors at the front were securely locked, so I went round to the back and stared through a little window. I could see one room at ground level, with another upstairs, bare and unfurnished, with crumbling plaster. There was another inscription on an inside wall, this time in Italian, which I took to say that Columbus's father had his dwelling and wool shop here.

Many writers over the years have described this modest dwelling as the birth house, which is not correct. The present building dates only from the seventeenth century, replacing an earlier house which was destroyed in a siege. Most experts, including Taviani, agree, however, that Dominico did live in a house on this site, when Columbus was a little boy, though whether it was here that he was born is unknown.

A cobbled path goes up from the little house through the Old Gates, the Porta Soprana, so there is a genuine historic atmosphere about the site; and, if you look in the right direction, shield your eyes and avoid the yellow taxis screeching by and ignore the roar of the orange buses, you can imagine that little boy, fair-haired or not fair-haired, leaving his house to go through the gatehouse to the Old City.

At the side, slightly behind, is a small patch of grass, a desperate sylvan touch, with inside some miniature ecclesiastical cloisters. They look totally false, straight from Disney World, wrapped up each evening and put away. They are real, but have been moved, remains from the old St Andrew's church. (Porta Soprana is a derivation of St Andrew.) I asked a passer-by to take my photograph, standing in front of the house, but he refused, as did two others. Genoese are said to be suspicious and unwelcoming, as well as mean. Eventually I did get someone to snap me, proof that I was there, outside if not inside Columbus's House. Then I went back to my hotel, determined to make one last effort to find a curator and a key.

I rang lots of likely numbers before deciding to try what I thought might be the highest local authority, the Ligurian regional offices. I got through to the Tourist Promotional Department and finally secured an appointment with a Dr Luigi Borsadoli. He would see me later that day, and would in the meantime find out about the Casa Colombo.

His office was in a modern concrete block, in the Via Fieschi, which took some finding as I could not get the hang of the system of street numbering; there seemed to be so many numbers, in red and in black lettering. Then I had to find the front door, also hidden away, and get through security. Most buildings in Italy, official or private, are heavily protected these days, because of possible terrorist attack. Aldo Moro, after whom that flyover is named, was one of those killed by urban terrorists.

Dr Borsadoli, wearing casual clothes, designer trousers and a fashionable shirt, and smoking heavily, was in a large basement office. He was full of apologies. For two hours he had been on the 'phone, but had failed to find the curator. He promised by 9.30 the next morning he would be able to arrange entry for me. In the meantime, he gave me a book about Columbus, which I might find interesting.

I got lost coming out, then the lift broke down, but a young man helped me. He had just been to England on holiday and all he wanted to talk about was London Green. I thought at first he meant the Prime Minister's conversion to ecology, but in fact he meant Green Park, and all the other parks, how wonderful they were. It was not until then that I realised how tree-less and park-less Genoa is, another element in its overall drabness.

In my hotel bar, about the size of a table, drinking white wine, the colour of Genoa harbour water, I settled down to read the Columbus book. It was written by Lia Peirotti Cei, and obviously aimed at teenage readers. There was an introduction by the President of the Ligurian Region, attributing Columbus's genius, and his stubbornness, to his birth place. 'It was in Genoa that his character was formed, here he learned the art of navigation, and from the Italian cultural scene of the time he absorbed his scientific convictions with regard to the world being round.' Good patriotic stuff. It's a shame there's so little proof.

The first chapter of the book describes Columbus, aged thirteen, as a 'tall thin youth with reddish hair', sitting in Genoa harbour, desperate to be taken on board a ship. He goes home and his mother gives him his favourite dish, eel pie, and he tells her he's going to sea. His father is furious, but agrees to let him go, and all his family come to see him off, bringing him presents. 'Oranges and lemons, ship's biscuits, a cap and a woollen scarf for the cool nights, and a pair of new sandals.' More literary licence, but very touching. There are no illustrations, alas. I would like to have seen how modern Italian artists view Columbus. I went to bed, making a vow to buy a children's book on Columbus in every country I went to.

At 9.30, my friendly Dottore rang. Some bad news, he said. He had been unable to find anyone to open up the Casa Colombo. But some good news. He had arranged for me to see the Columbus documents in the Archivo di Stato di Genova, the state archives. I would never find the building, so he would meet me in the Via San Lorenzo and take me there.

We went down an alley and entered through a side-door, into what had obviously at one time been a palazzo. Perhaps I had been missing many fine buildings in Genoa, not knowing how to get inside them. We passed various reception desks, up stairs and along corridors, and came at last to a display room, laid out with exhibition cases, each one containing a Columbus document. There were sixty-three in all, beautifully arranged, well-mounted, with neatly typed explanations, all in modern Italian. Almost all the originals are written in Latin.

I felt genuinely thrilled. This was where the most important Columbus research has emanated from in the last hundred years, the painstaking search for local documents which has resulted in proof of his birthplace and family background. I wondered if anywhere else round the world I would see as many original

Columbus documents in one place at one time, so I savoured the sight, before examining each one. It was luck that I had got inside, and it seems a shame the general public do not seem to know more about this room. During the morning I spent there, I saw only one person, a Professor of Transport from Genoa University, who was waiting to see the Director of the Archives, to interest him in a scheme to put the documents on computer.

The earliest document is dated February 21, 1429, and records the fact that Dominico, Columbus's father, then aged eleven and living with his family in Quinto, just outside Genoa, is being taken on as an apprentice to a certain weaver who will teach him the craft for the next six years. The next twenty-six documents are related to Dominico and are mostly legal, to do with debts and disputes over property, but they furnish important dates and addresses, showing how he moved around.

In one of them, dated September 14, 1465, I learned that Dominico had at one time been in the cheese business, which was new to me, as the document is not mentioned in Taviani. It is yet another example of the changes in his life, as he struggled to make a living. The document explains that Dominico has lost his employment as a gatehouse-keeper, and owes money, so he is being allowed to go into partnership with a cheese-seller.

The first document to mention Christopher Columbus by name is number 27, dated September 22, 1470. This is in connection with Dominico's brief imprisonment, for debt. In appointing a judge to arbitrate for the family, it names Dominico's father as Giovanni and his son as Cristoforo. This document was actually signed in the building where it now resides, formerly the Palazzo di Serravalle, used then as a court. It is in good condition, with few stains or holes, clear enough to read, if you have the Latin, but the handwriting is not very neat. In those days, the best and neatest copy was given to the client, while the notary kept a rougher copy for the records, and these are the ones which have survived. (The practice today is the opposite – the client gets a copy, while the lawyers keep the best.)

Document number 30, dated October 31, 1470, is also very important, as this is the one which gives Columbus's age as nineteen, and so enables us to estimate that 1451 was his year of birth. This document does have a hole in it, but not in a vital part. There is a clear watermark in the paper, still shining through, which appears to be in the shape of a pair of scissors.

The most important of all documents is number 44, dated

August 25, 1479. It provides another cross-reference to Columbus's age, this time twenty-seven, but also records his last known visit to Genoa and where he had come from, explaining an important event in his later life. It is twelve pages long and much better written than most of the other documents.

I was examining it, and some other documents, when the Director of the Archives appeared, Doctor Aldo Agosto. 'Yes,' smiled Dr Agosto, as I was struggling to decipher some handwriting. 'The notaries did write very hurry scurry.'

Dr Agosto explained that they now have 170 Columbus documents in all. He is reproducing them in a new book, due out soon, and he later took me into his office to show me the proofs, promising to send me a finished copy to help my researches.

He spent some time explaining to me the significance of a letter, written much later by Columbus, in Spanish with Italian overtones, in which he is offering money to the City of Genoa. Dr Agosto laughed as he translated it, and the Professor of Transport joined in, but I did not quite understand their mirth. Apparently Columbus was furious that his first letter to Genoa had not been answered. (I know how he felt.) In a second letter he moans that it is typical of bureaucracy and he does not know why he ever bothered making his kind offer. '*Che chi serve al commun non serve a nessun.*' This is the phrase which amused them. It is still used, apparently, in Italy. Roughly translated it means that a person who does good for the community is wasting his time.

There was also much laughter over a 1496 document referring to Columbus's cousins who are planning to share the expenses for a trip from Genoa to see Columbus, now famous, obviously hoping to get some money from him. I like to see academics happy in their work.

The last few letters on display are copies only, the originals being locked up in Genoa Town Hall, and my new friends did not fancy my chances of seeing them. They are written by Columbus, much later, and end with his special signature, one he created for himself. No one has successfully worked out what it means, but Dr Agosto gave me his explanation (which we will come to later).

There are places in Genoa I failed to get into, such as the Naval Museum at Pegli, which was closed, and might have been interesting, or the Town Hall which has the originals of several of Columbus's letters and an urn containing some of his ashes. (I did turn up, but no one on the door knew anything about it.) I did, however, see the large and impressive statue of Columbus, outside the Principe station.

I also think I picked up a feeling of the Genoese character, which might or might not turn out to be significant in explaining Columbus's later actions. It was summed up in an article by a distinguished Genoese journalist, Dr Piero Ottone, in one of the official publications I was given, *Genoa: towards 1992*.

He tells two stories about the Genoese reputation for being stingy. One is about a rich local businessman, old Mr Piaggo, who regularly took coffee with a friend in a bar in Portofino. On the way out, Mr Piaggo always called for the bill for his own coffee, not wanting to run the risk of paying for his friend's. In the other story, two Genoese meet and discuss the death of a common friend, a Mr Parodi. 'I'm so sorry Parodi's died,' says one. 'I can't believe it.' The other pauses and eventually replies, 'He must have got something out of it . . .'

Dr Ottone says these stories reflect national stereotypes, but they are generalisations, no truer than saying 'Germans are cruel, the English are hypocrites, the Italians are cowards'. He then argues that the Genoese are not in fact mean, but thrifty, and not crafty, but flexible. At heart, what they really are is proud. That was what spurred them on to their great discoveries and achievements, though they have had nothing to be proud of for a long time.

They are also fiercely independent, and this could be a cause of their present problems, with endless arguments about different urban proposals, development plans, new industries, tourist initiatives. 'Maybe now the plans for the Columbus celebrations run the risk of failing because of the conflicts between entrepreneurs, trade unions and politicians.'

He asked a Roman what he considered the most important element today in the character of Genoese. 'Their disagreement' was the answer. 'They are proud people, who are reluctant to compromise.' Does that sound like Columbus?

It is dangerous to trace character back to place, or even to someone's family background, and who knows what part environment and what part genes play in any one person. Columbus left Genoa at twenty-five, and there were many other influences in his life, still to come.

Italians generally are of course proud of Columbus, and get upset when the rest of the world does not realise he came from Genoa. This rather explains why they sometimes overdo the Genoese connections. In one of the booklets I was given, it states that before he left Genoa 'Columbus was already the greatest sailor of all time'. He has also passed into the Italian language. As English people say, 'Queen Anne's just died,' when someone makes a totally obvious remark, Italians say, 'And Columbus discovered America.'

In the end, I left Genoa feeling slightly happier than when I arrived. I had imagined a little of the historic atmosphere around the old walled city where he once lived, inspected some vital documents, and I did finally see an Italian with blond hair – called Colombo. Not in the flesh, but on television in the hotel bar. Angelico Colombo. He was a footballer.

3

Portugal

COLUMBUS CLAMBERED ashore near the Algarve fishing port of Lagos, on the southern coast of Portugal, in mid-August 1476. The sea is the Atlantic, with real tides and very cold water in winter, but in August it is relatively warm, as warm as it ever gets. If the battle took place off the coast at Cape St Vincent, the Land's End of mainland Europe, he must have drifted and swum, clinging to his bit of drift-wood, for between ten and fifteen miles.

He was just another shipwrecked mariner. There were a few others, saved from the same disaster, but no details are known. Lagos was accustomed to sailors arriving from the sea, speaking of their miraculous salvation, from shipwrecks caused by the hand of God, or by pirates and men of war. Their own local fishermen took risks every evening when they set out to bob up and down all night long in their little sardine boats.

Lagos was also something of a naval dockyard, from where Portuguese explorers sailed for distant parts, and then, if they were lucky, to where they limped back again. Gil Eanes sailed from Lagos just forty-three years earlier to navigate down the coast of Africa. Would Columbus have heard of him? Would he have realised that his own fateful shipwreck took place almost opposite that point on the Algarve coast where Henry the Navigator established a school of navigation which changed the whole face of European exploration? If he had learned all he needed to know about navigation in Genoa, and was already the greatest sailor ever, as some modern Genoese fondly imagine, then he would certainly have done so. Most educated people had heard of Henry the Navigator.

But Columbus, aged twenty-five when he arrived by chance in Portugal, was probably still semi-literate.

He was a foreign-speaking shipwrecked mariner, with no money and no possessions. Presumably, being a good Catholic, he paid homage at some church for his miraculous escape, then rested at some seamen's hostel, till he decided what to do next. The sea battle is well documented, and we have Columbus's own memories of how he struggled ashore, but Lagos understandably has no record of his stay. Columbus next appears in Lisbon. It is unlikely he got there by land, as the routes over the Monchique mountains are poor to this day. More likely he got a boat, working his passage round to Lisbon, or perhaps his Genoese masters laid on transport for those who had survived.

Landing in Portugal was fortunate for Columbus. Portugal was establishing itself as the leading naval and colonial power in Europe, and Lisbon was one of the most exciting cities to live in, both intellectually and economically. While Genoa was feeling the effects of the Turkish encroachment in the East, and beginning to lose possessions and spheres of influence, Lisbon was expanding in all directions. It could see no obstacle which its men of vision and action could not overcome. Looking out from Lisbon you see only open seas. In the Mediterranean, there were battle clouds, and Moors on almost every horizon.

At the beginning of the fifteenth century, the Iberian peninsula contained four Christian kingdoms. In what we now call Spain, there were Castile, Aragon and Navarre, three separate Christian states, divided by various internal political disputes. But one large part of Spain, Granada, was still in Moorish hands.

The fourth Christian country was Portugal which had freed itself from the Saracens in 1267 and was now ruled by a strong monarchy, the House of Aviz. King John I, founder of the Aviz dynasty, had defeated Castile in battle and secured peace with them in 1411. The old rivalry with England had ceased under a treaty of 1441, still today in force, the longest-surviving international friendship treaty in the world. Throughout the whole of the fifteenth century, Portugal was a united kingdom, hardly touched by civil disturbance.

King John married Philippa of Lancaster, daughter of John of Gaunt, a union which helped his relationship with England, and also produced six sons, the third of whom was Henry, known to the world as the Navigator. As a young prince of twenty-one, he had taken part in a battle on the North African coast, storming a Muslim fort, and defeating the infidel. Spurred on by this success, he planned a proper crusade, to capture Gibraltar, but while the expedition was getting underway King John cancelled it.

Prince Henry returned to Lisbon, supposedly sulking. Instead of rejoining the court, and taking his part in governing the country, he retreated to the southern tip of Portugal, to a point near Cape St Vincent, said to have mystic significance, known for centuries as Promentorium Sacrum, or Sacred Promontory, which the Portuguese translated into Sagres. He devoted the rest of his life to intellectual and spiritual matters at Sagres. When he died in 1460, still a virgin, so it was said, he was found to be wearing a hair shirt.

'Navigator' was a partial misnomer, as he himself did not do any navigating, or go on any further expeditions, but he did more for navigation than anyone else who has ever lived. He created at Sagres what was essentially a University of the Sea. He hired the best brains of the age, regardless of whether they were Christian, Jew or Moslem, and set them to work to solve the problems of the sea, of the stars, of the oceans, and how to understand and conquer them. And he acted on their recommendations, building instruments they had designed, and then boats, particularly the famous caravels, especially designed to manage shallow inshore waters as well as open seas. The normal cargo boat which sailed the Mediterranean, and on which Columbus had arrived, was square-rigged, in Portuguese called a barca, and built to carry as much as possible. More cargo meant bigger profits. They were clumsy and slow boats, unless they had the wind behind. The caravels were smaller and narrower with lateen sails, slanting and triangular, which were ideal for tacking against the wind. A barca was not able to sail very close to the wind, and could end up taking almost twice as much in time and distance to cover the same route.

The important cargo being carried by Henry's caravels was news. It could be taken on a few sheets, even in the head of one man, but it was vital for the information to return, otherwise the whole journey had been pointless; so seamen who went on caravels knew they had a very good chance of coming home. Lagos became the centre for the building of Henry's caravels and it was from there they set out to make scientific tests, examine plants and animals, chart seas and gulfs. At Sagres, just along the coast, the experts would then analyse the results and cartographers would draw maps, ready for the next expedition. He was running a research and development institute, backed by the Government. In this case, he and his family were the Government.

Every year, new expeditions would leave Lagos, mainly into the Atlantic and down the coast of Africa. It was the exploration which excited Henry, the prospect of new lands, new problems, new challenges. He had sent off fifteen expeditions with the aim of rounding the coast of West Africa before Gil Eanes managed it, conquering not just the barrier of reefs and treacherous seas, but a barrier of fear, as the ordinary seamen had begun to think the feat was impossible.

Each Portuguese expedition erected a stone monument on the beach, a 'padrões', surmounted by a cross, to mark the point they had reached; then, the following season, the next expedition would try to locate it, and then do better. By the time Henry died, the Portuguese had reached the Congo; his African work was carried on by King John II, whose sailors went further and further down the land mass, hoping to reach the bottom.

Henry's explorers also discovered many islands. Madeira was found in 1420, and claimed for Portugal, one of three important groups of islands which Portugal had colonised by the time Columbus reached Lisbon. The other two were the Azores, colonised in the 1430s, and the Cape Verde Islands, right down the coast of Africa, which were discovered in 1454. The Canaries had been taken by Spanish explorers.

While the advance parties went south from Lagos on exploration missions, the bulk of the trading boats and the merchants, the colonisers and officials, left from Lisbon, the capital. Columbus arrived in a city pulsating with enormous activity, wealth and opportunity. Fleets of boats constantly left for the new lands, carrying supplies, men, arms, horses, as well as bangles and bracelets, hawks' bells and glass beads which could be traded with the primitive peoples of the new lands. The boats would then return laden with gold, ivory, pepper and Negro slaves.

Lisbon was a cosmopolitan city, with a strong Genoese community, and it was there Columbus settled, meeting up with his brother Bartholomew. The date of his arrival is not known, and it is just possible that Bartholomew was already there, which would explain why Columbus headed for Lisbon in the first place. Bartholomew had a job which reflected the prevailing nature of the Portuguese economy at the time – he was a chartmaker. Columbus occasionally helped in this business, making and selling maps, as well as books on exploration.

It seems clear that Columbus now started a definite policy of self-education, reading books and pamphlets on exploration, making notes in the margins of those he had studied. He tried to learn Latin, as well as Portuguese, and went back to the classics, to the early scientists and philosophers, the Greeks and Romans, struggling to become a good Renaissance man. Columbus also reverted to his old job, as a seaman-merchant, again employed by the Genoese banking houses. He went on his first trip in late 1476, not long after he arrived in Portugal. Taviani thinks this might well have been a continuation of the delayed journey from Genoa, the one which ended in the sea battle, as the same bankers were backing it and the destination was England.

He arrived in London and then went on to Bristol. In subsequent letters and memories, Columbus often talked about his days in England, comparing landscapes and customs. No one, so far, has found any records of his stay there, but by his own account it was quite extensive as he then signed up for at least one voyage from Bristol, sailing north to Iceland, presumably with a Bristol crew and boat. The voyage to Bristol had been to load wool, for his Genoese masters, but now he was on a fishing trip. It obviously fascinated him, and Ferdinand describes it in some detail. His father had never sailed in such northern waters before, nor seen shoals of herring, cod and salmon, all rather different from the sardines, tuna and anchovies of the Mediterranean.

Ferdinand dates his arrival in Iceland as February 1477. Many experts now do not believe he ever got there. Would any British fishing fleet venture to Iceland at that time of the year? Records have been searched, and 1477 turns out to have been a particularly mild winter, but there is only Columbus's word for it that he got that far. One of the things he specially remembered from his Icelandic trip was a great tidal wave, 'with a flow 26 fathoms high', an amazing sight he had never witnessed before. This is more likely to have been the Avon, in Bristol, a tidal phenomenon, and one of course not known in the Mediterranean. Perhaps he only got as far as the north of Scotland, or Ireland, confusing Ireland with Iceland. This is one problem with all Columbus's memories of his early years. It is remarkable and invaluable to have any, and so carefully recorded, but he is recalling them in later life, by which time a great many more voyages had been made. However, there seems no doubt he visited England, and did some cold water sailing.

He was back in Lisbon by the end of 1477 and the following year he went on a trip to warmer southern waters, to Madeira, again working for a Genoese master, this time DiNegro. He was supposed to pick up a cargo of sugar in Funchal, and then deliver it to Genoa, but there was some sort of mix-up. He never received the cash to buy the sugar, only a promissory note, and the merchants in Funchal refused to let him have any credit, so he arrived in Genoa without the sugar. The row ended in court with Columbus demanding payment for having hired the boat.

The details of the dispute do not really matter – though it indicates he had prospered enough as an agent to hire a ship – but the existence of this legal document is vital. For a start, it pinpoints exactly where he was at a certain time, namely a court in Genoa on August 25, 1479. (This is assumed now to have been his last-ever visit to Genoa.) It gives his age as twenty-seven, another indication of his year of birth. He states, in his legal submissions, that he is a resident of Lisbon, proof of his adoption of Portugal as his new home. He also adds that he is returning to Lisbon the next morning, 'di cràstino de mane'.

It is safe to assume the reason why he was returning so quickly to Portugal, because we know what happened a few months later. Columbus got married. No marriage documents have so far been discovered, but the wedding is well described by both Ferdinand and Las Casas. It occurred in September or October 1479, by which time Columbus was twenty-eight.

His bride was Felipa Moniz Perestrello, a Portuguese lady of good breeding, in fact of aristocratic birth, according to Ferdinand. At the same time, Ferdinand makes it clear that Columbus himself was a bit of a catch. 'As he behaved very honourably and was a man of handsome presence and one who never turned from the path of honesty, a lady named Dona Felipa Moniz, of noble birth and a superior of the Convent of Saints, where he used to attend Mass, had such conversations and friendships with him that she became his wife.'

On first reading, this might give the impression he had married a nun, but the convent in question appears to have had a school for young ladies and Felipa was some sort of teacher. On second reading, the notion of 'conversations' is interesting, if elliptical, and one wonders how intimate these conversations were, and also why Fernando stresses Columbus's honesty and his honour. And, as he was so handsome, perhaps he had 'conversations' with quite a few girls?

Las Casas spells it out more clearly. Columbus 'had relations with her, so she had to marry him'. He also adds that he knew quite a few of these girls, but Felipa was the one he married.

The facts about her family have been well established. Her

mother's family, Moniz, was Portuguese, going back a long way, and did have some aristocratic connections. Her father, Bartholomew Perestrello, had distinguished himself in the service of Henry the Navigator and been rewarded with the Governorship of Porto Santo, in the Madeira islands. His surname reveals his Italian antecedents, though he himself had been born in Portugal. Perhaps these Italian connections helped Columbus to be accepted into the family in the first place.

All the same, if the family was so noble, as Ferdinand maintains, why did they allow a daughter to marry this nobody from Genoa? Unkind people over the years have suggested that Felipa was ugly and on the shelf. There is a hint that she was older than Columbus and, at twenty-eight, he himself was comparatively old to get married. It has even been suggested she was illegitimate. And, according to Las Casas's description, she was also of course pregnant.

It seems more likely the family had fallen on relatively hard times. Her father had been dead for twenty years and possessions and privileges had been sold off. Her brother-in-law had now acquired the Governorship of Porto Santo. Columbus presumably seemed a suitable husband, despite the fact that he had been in the country only two years, was still an immigrant, with no family, apart from his brother, and had no possessions. He certainly gained by the marriage. Ferdinand indicates he was proud of his wife's social status and connections, and marriage to her entitled him to certain residential qualifications. It also gave him somewhere to live. Soon after the marriage, he and Felipa moved to Madeira, first to Funchal and then to Porto Santo. This was Columbus's home for the next two years, from 1480 to 1482, and it was during this time their son Diego was born. (There are no birth documents, so there is always the chance he was born in Lisbon, then brought to Madeira.)

Porto Santo is a very small island, just nine miles long, a few miles away from the bigger island of Madeira. It was the end of civilisation, as the Portuguese knew it, over 1,000 miles south of Lisbon, 500 miles west of Morocco. Porto Santo had been uninhabited, as was Madeira, when the first Portuguese arrived in the 1440s.

Madeira proved to be rich, with fertile, sub-tropical slopes, covered in forests. The Portuguese word for wood is 'madeira', hence the name they gave the island (the wine came much later). The forests were burned down in a fire which is said to have raged for seven years, then sugar plantations were established which

proved very successful. There was a rush of planters and speculators, merchants and traders, hoping to make their fortunes
quickly. One of the speculators was Columbus himself, engaged on
that sugar deal which went wrong.

Porto Santo never experienced the same economic boom, being
too dry and arid, too flat and infertile, despite attempts to establish
crops and settlements. Bartholomew Perestrello, when he was sent
by Henry the Navigator to settle the island, left Lisbon with a
pregnant rabbit, kept in a cage on board. At sea, she gave birth,
which all the sailors thought was a propitious sign, convinced their
enterprise too would flourish and multiply. The rabbits were let
loose on the island, and multiplied so quickly that in two years they
had eaten all the young plants. Bartholomew and the first settlers
were so depressed they gave up and came home to Portugal,
but Prince Henry urged them to return, this time conferring the
Governorship of the island on Perestrello and his descendants. He
lived there till his death in 1457.

Columbus and his wife and son moved into the Governor's
quarters on Porto Santo. From there he made trips across to
Funchal, on business, and sometimes much longer voyages, continuing his main activity as a sailor-merchant. He went on one
particularly long voyage, probably in 1483, down the African coast,
as far as Guinea, where Portugal was establishing a fortified trading
post. On this enterprise he described himself as the captain, so
possibly he hired the boat. This Guinea trip made a great impression
on him, one of those he never forgot in later life. He saw tropical
vegetation at first hand, experienced the slave trade and was fascinated by the Portuguese search for gold. He could now boast, as
he did, that he had sailed all the 'known' seas, from Iceland in the
far north down to the African equatorial waters.

While not at sea, he returned to his wife and child in Porto Santo,
wandering the beaches, staring out at the horizon. There was not
much else to do in Porto Santo, compared with the excitements of
Lisbon, or of Genoa.

Columbus's thoughts are worth speculating on at this apparently
quiet period in his life, despite the lack of any written evidence, for
he was about to do something unexpected. He was about to take
his first tiny step on to the world stage. In 1484, he put forward a
proposal, in person, to King John II of Portugal.

Until now, the facts about Columbus's life have depended on his
own memories, mostly passed on by Ferdinand, or the circumstan-
tial evidence thrown up by chance documents later found in Genoa

and elsewhere. A royal audience, even one of dozens in a day, means that you are recorded, your name and number goes down in the royal record books. You are part of court history.

Columbus's proposal to the King of Portugal was very simple. 'Buscar el Levante por el Poniente.' In other words, he wanted to sail to the Levant, or the East, by going west. Trade with the East, as we have seen, was once again being hindered by the rise of Islam. Columbus was proposing therefore to sail due west, the other way, right out across the Atlantic, and end up in the East, creating a new route to all its riches. Simplistic, perhaps, rather than simple.

Where on earth had he got this notion from? Did he steal it? Was it in a book he read? Or could he possibly have worked it all out for himself? It is hard to fathom, considering how little we know so far about his life and education and experience.

That big question can still not be answered, even after 500 years. Ferdinand, who must have constantly asked his father, found it very difficult to explain, and ended up writing pages and pages on the conundrum, eventually listing three major reasons, plus numerous sub-divisions. Other experts have added to the list, suggesting other influences, pointing out parallels, drawing different conclusions, but still there is not one simple explanation, agreed by all. Columbus, and Ferdinand, could not put it in a nutshell, so why should we?

There are many touching legends about other, later incidents in Columbus's life, most of them still repeated and illustrated in children's books in Italy and Spain, but this vital moment in history is totally obscure. Perhaps there was no one moment; instead it was a series of stray strands which gradually came together.

Most educated people in fifteenth-century Europe accepted, of course, that the world was a globe. The Greeks had first propounded the theory, and it was now generally believed. If, therefore, you could somehow move round the globe, you would end up where you began. No one had done it, however, so no one knew what was out there, or whether you might drop into some huge hole along the way, fall off the edge, or be burned to death.

But where had he got it from? Columbus was proposing, so he thought, a worked-out, scientific method of achieving this aim. It seems to me, reading all the accounts, that seven assorted strands of evidence and influence and hypothesis had come into his life, and into his mind, since settling in Portugal.

1: PERSONAL OBSERVATIONS

Columbus was by now aged thirty-three. He had been at sea for around twenty years, depending on whether he started at ten or fourteen. He had sailed into Turkish waters, south almost to the Equator, and north to somewhere near Iceland. His mileage must have been extensive, enough already to take him several times round the globe. He had acquired great navigational skills, by trial and error, doing and observing, long before he started to read and study. Such a person is likely to have worked out for himself that the world is round, without benefit of Greek philosophers and scholars. The rise and fall of the stars, in which Columbus was deeply interested, provided a clue. Any sailor, with his eyes and mind open, knows that you see the top of a mast first, before you see the hull below, just as on the horizon you see the mountain peaks of a distant island, before the land appears, a sure sign that the surface of the world must be curved. If it were flat, we would see the shore at the same time as the mountain tops. Columbus would have observed, living on Porto Santo, that the sun goes down two hours earlier each day than in Genoa. He would have seen birds, migrating across oceans, heading for somewhere, some place. On his own, he could well have worked out the idea of a global world.

'He believed that since all the water and land in the world form a sphere,' says Ferdinand, 'it would be possible to go around it from east to west until men stood feet to feet, one against the other, at opposite ends of the earth.' But how?

2: FAMILY CONNECTIONS

Not his parents in Genoa, with whom he seems to have had no contact ever again, nor his brother Bartholomew, though they remained close, but the new family he had married into, the Perestrellos. His father-in-law had been a sailor and explorer, and had served under Henry the Navigator. Although he had been dead twenty years by the time Columbus married his daughter, his exploits lived on in the family, as did his papers. Ferdinand relates how Columbus's mother-in-law came to live with them, when he moved to Porto Santo, and handed over to Columbus all her late husband's charts, maps, notes, manuscripts, many of which were original copies of those produced by the cosmographers at Sagres.

It is not known how important they were, or exactly what was in them, but Ferdinand stresses the effect they had on Columbus. 'Be that as it may,' writes Ferdinand, 'one thing led to another and starting a train of thought, while living in Portugal he began to speculate that if the Portuguese could sail so far south, it should be possible to sail westward, and that it was logical to find land in that direction.'

So these family papers might have hinted at how the ocean could be sailed. Or did the Columbus family deliberately over-emphasise them, in order perhaps to hide other sources? Whatever their ultimate importance, Columbus always said they had helped to fire his imagination.

3: SAILORS' TALES

Many of these date back to Columbus's time in Porto Santo, when he was supposedly wandering on the beaches, picking up strange-shaped bits of wood, exotic plants, seeds, branches, looking out west and wondering where they might have come from.

Moving up the scale a bit, Ferdinand repeats a tale of two corpses who were washed ashore, 'that seemed to have very broad faces, of a shape different from those of Christians'. Best of all perhaps is the incident, sworn to be true since 1535 when it first appeared in a book about Columbus by Oviedo (an enemy of Columbus's), about the day on Porto Santo when Columbus was walking a deserted shore and found a ship on some rocks. Its mast was broken, the hull smashed, all the sailors had died, except for the helmsman. Columbus drags him from the wreck, and takes him to his home. The man blurts out a tale of a land out there, on the other side of the ocean. Columbus asks him to draw a map, which the man starts to do, but, before he can finish it, he dies in Columbus's arms . . .

Not even a 1940s B movie would have dared include that scene. Who would believe it? Even Oviedo himself, having related it, said he personally did not think it happened, a ploy used by journalists ever since, enabling them to tell a lurid tale, then distance themselves from it. Since 1535, it has of course appeared in countless books as a true story.

It is probably unfair to include here those people now believed to have actually crossed the Atlantic, such as the Norsemen in the eleventh century who reached Vinland, or St Brendan, the sixth-century monk who is claimed to have got there even earlier.

This field of speculation is vast, growing all the time, and very controversial, but there are no written records.

At the time Columbus lived, these sailors' tales, legendary and historical, were being taken seriously. The Dark Ages were dark because it was a time when knowledge was lost, Greek philosophy forgotten, Roman inventions ignored, life became inward-looking. With the Renaissance, men looked out once again, eager to accept legends, as well as to explore life, the Universe, everything.

4: SCIENCE

Science, in its original sense, means knowledge. The scientific knowledge Columbus was looking for came mostly from the study of ancient writers. Ferdinand is vague on the sequence of events, inferring that Columbus used books to confirm what he had already begun to think. A few decades earlier and he would have found it almost impossible to obtain such books, as they were transcribed in writing by monks. Now, with the advent of printing, great men and institutions in most cities had their libraries. So could lesser men, if they saved their money. We know that Columbus did have his own copies of the classic books of the Ancient World.

Ptolemy was still considered the Father of Geography, despite being a second-century Greek. He stated not only that the world was round, and divided into 360 degrees, but that each degree on the globe measured fifty miles. (The reality is sixty.) This fact was vital to all Columbus's thinking and planning.

Ptolemy also asserted that the world was half land and half water, something Columbus did not want to hear, as it made his proposed crossing too long. So he turned to other philosophers and mathematicians, such as Aristotle, Strabo, Pliny, Marinus and Seneca. Most of them estimated that the ratio of land to sea on the globe was greater, usually about five-eighths land to three-eighths water.

As he read these authors, Columbus often noted down his comments in the margins. In one book, referring to Aristotle, he scribbled: 'The master of scholasticism tells us the world's waters are few and they are joined together, the space that they occupy is quite small. One can easily cross from Spain to the Indies.' In another book, he mused: 'Between the edge of Spain and the Indies, it is short and can be crossed in a matter of days.'

The exact figures on which Columbus was working have become confused over the centuries. Different translators have found them hard to transcribe, as different nations and different languages have used different measurements. Miles have been mistaken for leagues, nautical lengths mixed up with land lengths. The main point which concerned Columbus was to prove that the sailing distance round the globe was not as far as some people maintained, so the less sea and more land the better.

It has also to be realised that Columbus was thinking about the possibility of literally circumnavigating the globe, going west from Europe direct to the Indies, by which he meant Japan and China, perhaps then coming back via India. There was nothing known in between Europe and Japan, just sea: hence, the shorter the sea distance, the quicker the journey.

Columbus worked on his figures, using estimates from selected scientists, and decided that the distance was just 2,400 sea miles. With the most modern ships, such as the speedy Portuguese caravels, taking a route he had worked out, using winds and stars he had observed, he was confident it was possible. In reality, the distance is more like 10,000 miles, but Columbus maintained he had Science on his side.

5: RELIGION

It is often hard to appreciate now, but cartographers with a scientific bent, and seamen who had personally sailed thousands of ocean miles, still accepted most Old Testament descriptions of the World and its Creation as being gospel truth. The Garden of Eden was placed on maps as a geographical reality, with the four great rivers flowing from it, the Euphrates, Nile, Ganges and Tigris. Noah's Ark was believed to exist, somewhere. Hell was down below, and was likely to be hot. Maps themselves, such as the Mapa Mundi, were decorative religious objects, meant primarily to show the Holy Land, with other places optional. They illustrated the Bible, rather than geography. The medieval mind could accept both physical and metaphysical explanations, knitting them together, and did not see any contradiction. After all, no one had been round the globe, so everything might be true.

Columbus knew his Bible, as his later letters fully illustrate. He knew the Prophet Esdras who said that God created the world six parts land and one part water. Theology believed that the known world was in fact the whole world. There was just one massive land mass – Europe, Africa and Asia – with the Mediterranean in the middle, as the name suggests. The outer limits were a bit sketchy, but could be guessed at. On the outside was a bit more water, but not much, often known as the Ocean Sea. It seemed to make sense, looking out from this land mass, that the world was only one-seventh sea. It was believed that St Augustine was correct when he said Christ's teachings reached 'the whole world'.

Columbus therefore supported his scientific arguments with 'facts' from the Bible. He also persuaded himself that Biblical prophecies would prove correct. 'And his dominion shall be from sea to sea, and from the rivers to the ends of the earth': so it says in Zachariah chapter 9, verse 10, words which are repeated in Psalms 72, verse 8.

Who might take the Word from sea to sea, be the Great Navigator, going from west to east as God's Messenger? Columbus himself, of course.

6: CONTEMPORARY ACCOUNTS

Columbus's favourite book, judging by his numerous references to it, was *Imago Mundi*, an explanation of the world, written by Cardinal Pierre d'Ailly (1350–1420), one-time Rector of the Sorbonne in Paris. He summed up the main wisdoms of the Ancients, which no doubt saved Columbus the effort of reading them individually. He too believed that the width of the Ocean Sea was relatively narrow.

The Venetian Marco Polo's adventures had a great impact on Columbus. They were best-sellers in the late fifteenth century, although his travels had taken place a century earlier. He maintained he had seen palaces with gold roofs in India and China and had reached the court of the Great Khan or Kubla Khan, an exotic and all-powerful Christian monarch, who held sway in the East.

There were many other published descriptions of travels in the Orient which excited the imagination of Europeans. One popular book was *The Travels of Sir John Mandeville*. It was assumed at the time that he must be an Englishman, from his name, but the book is now thought to have been written, or imagined, by a physician from Liège.

Ferdinand mentions both Marco Polo and Mandeville as being on his father's reading list. At the time, their stories were taken as totally true, the fruit of real explorations. Marco Polo did of course travel to the East, though his tales were later exaggerated by other people. His measurements for China made it much bigger than it really is, thereby leaving the Ocean Sea smaller. It was a theory that appealed to Columbus.

7: TOSCANELLI'S LETTERS

Paolo Toscanelli (1397–1482) was a Florentine astronomer, geographer, mathematician, physicist, a complete Renaissance man. In Florence, as in Genoa and Venice, people were worried about the advance of the Turks in the Eastern Mediterranean, and the consequent damage to their merchant trade. Toscanelli turned his brain to how this state of affairs could be combated, and suggested a route which would avoid the Mediterranean, by sailing west to China.

Toscanelli was an intellectual. He never actually explored anywhere, but he read all the books, did his research, worked out his figures, drew his own charts. Around June 1474 he suggested, through an intermediary, Canon Martins of Lisbon, that the King of Portugal should mount a voyage westwards, to reach Japan. Nothing appears to have been done about this letter, which lay unacknowledged in the royal archives.

Seven or eight years later, while he was based in Porto Santo, this correspondence 'came to the notice' of Columbus. Ferdinand quotes it, word for word, but does not explain how it fell into Columbus's possession. Columbus wrote to Toscanelli, and got a letter back, which again Ferdinand quotes. In this, Toscanelli says he is very pleased to hear that Columbus plans to sail from west to east, how it will give him 'most lofty fame amongst Christians' and provide 'all manner of spices and jewels in great abundance'. This letter gives no details, but says that a map is enclosed with a route 'which would appear more clearly upon a sphere'. This map has disappeared but Las Casas, in his account, boasts that he actually handled it and says it marked out spaces, or degrees, between Lisbon and China, each of which measured 250 miles.

This correspondence is puzzling. Firstly, we do not know how Columbus saw a copy of the original letter. Had he a friend at Court, through his family connections? It is hard to imagine, as by now the Perestrellis were impoverished and living in a remote part of the Portuguese empire. Perhaps Toscanelli, having failed with the King, told other people. Or he might have published a copy of his letter.

It is easier to understand why Toscanelli replied to Columbus. He was an old man, well over eighty, soon to die. Perhaps he was touched that someone should finally have seized upon an idea he had conceived some ten years earlier.

The correspondence must have mattered to Columbus, otherwise Ferdinand would not have published in his biography the two vital letters (to the Lisbon canon, and to Columbus). But did it create the master-plan, or just encourage it? Those who assume that Columbus, a self-educated merchant-sailor, could not possibly himself have devised the scheme point to Toscanelli as being the most important factor. Others, like Ferdinand, believe it was one of several influences. Whether Columbus worked it all out for himself, or borrowed the idea from elsewhere, two elements made him rather different from those who had considered it in the past. Firstly, Columbus had a route in his head, which he kept secret. Secondly, he became an obsessive. He was instantly a man possessed, trapped by a vision, by a mania, which made people who met him stop and think and wonder if there might after all be something in this wild scheme.

It is not known how Columbus managed to secure his audience with the King of Portugal. His in-laws might have helped, but it is just as likely that it was the power of his own personality, knocking at enough doors, convincing enough people that he should be given a proper hearing.

King John II of Portugal, great-nephew of Henry the Navigator, succeeded to the throne in 1481. He too was passionately interested in expanding the Portuguese empire, and had far more money and resources than Prince Henry ever possessed. Trade with the West African coast was now well-established and the names the Portuguese gave to each new settlement indicated its particular riches – the Gold Coast, Pepper Coast, Ivory Coast, Slave Coast. The main object was still to reach down the entire length of Africa, and find if there was a route round the bottom. King John was also pushing into the interior, into Sierra Leone, even reaching Timbuctoo, hoping to establish contact with the famous Prester John, another legendary figure, as well-known as Kubla Khan in the East, the Christian ruler of a distant land, somewhere in the heart of Africa. If only contact could be made with him, then, together, they could finally rout the infidel from the Holy Land.

Columbus was allowed to explain his plan in person in 1484. Ferdinand says that the King 'listened attentively' to Columbus because 'of the strong arguments the latter advanced'. The official court historian agrees that the King found Columbus an impressive speaker, but rather 'vainglorious in boasting his merits' and 'very full of fantasy and imagination as to this Cipango island' (or Japan, which was where Columbus hoped to land in the East).

The King decided to take advice from a small committee, comprised of a bishop and two scientists. One scientist was Jewish and held the post of Royal Doctor, the other was an astronomer. They did not take long to reject Columbus's plan.

The most obvious reason for the rejection was that the proposal was unrealistic. They did not accept his facts and figures about the voyage, or how long it would take to get to his destination, or where he would land. They considered his geography as about as reliable as Marco Polo's. They were of course totally correct in thinking this.

The other reason is that Portugal was much more committed elsewhere. Ferdinand admits the King was 'cool towards the project because of the discovery and conquest of the west coast of Africa'. It would have needed much stronger arguments and better evidence to induce him to invest money in a different scheme, especially as the person putting it forward, an unknown, untried foreigner, struck many of them as not just a fantasist but a boaster and braggart.

Columbus compounded the bad impression he gave by adding certain conditions, listing the rewards he wanted to receive, should his voyage succeed. Ferdinand does not give the details, but makes Columbus's conditions sound fairly reasonable. 'Being a man of noble and lofty ambition, he would not covenant save on such terms as would bring great honour and advantage, in order that he might leave a title and estate befitting the grandeur of his works and his merits.'

Las Casas describes the conditions much more fully. At first glance, they are hardly believable. Columbus was demanding an hereditary Lordship and to be made Admiral of the Ocean Seas. He would be Viceroy and Governor of all the lands he might discover. He would be entitled to one-tenth of all revenues from these lands, whether in gold or silver, or in trade. And so on. It was hardly surprising that Columbus was dismissed so quickly.

Perhaps his strategy was to make himself sound as important as possible, and therefore be taken more seriously. In one way, his demands can be seen as pure pathos, rather than exorbitant. He had hung around at Court, knocking at back doors, being mocked, as Ferdinand admits, before being admitted. What he most wanted in life was a title, to be on an equal footing with all those superior aristocrats. But there is an even simpler explanation – greed. Columbus was convinced he was correct, that he would succeed, so he wanted the biggest possible reward.

While telling him to his face that his project was doomed, the Portuguese 'secretly sent a caravel to attempt what Columbus had offered to do, thinking that if those lands were discovered, they would not have to give the rewards demanded'. This is Ferdinand's account of what happened next. It is believed that a Portuguese expedition, some time later, did set off west from the Azores, but it returned after forty days, having found nothing.

The rebuff at court marked the end of Columbus's life in Portugal. He had been there over eight years, during which time he had acquired a wife and family, a great deal of scientific and classical knowledge, a wide experience of sailing most of the known seas, and an obsession which was eating into his heart.

In 1485, he decided to leave Lisbon. Ferdinand says that the Portuguese expedition had now returned, and the whole idea of sailing west was being derided. 'When Columbus learned of this, he formed such a hatred of that city and nation that he resolved to depart for Castile with his little son Diego.' In passing, Ferdinand adds that 'his wife had meantime died'.

This is the first, and only time, that the death of Columbus's wife is mentioned. It is not clear when it occurred, or whether it was in Lisbon or Porto Santo. Some have suggested it happened in child-birth. Las Casas gives no more details, except to say that 'God made him free of his wife'. It might, therefore, have been a contributing factor in making him give up Portugal, now that his Portuguese wife was dead.

There is a further mysterious fact added by Ferdinand. 'He secretly departed from Portugal with his little son Diego, fearing that the King might seek to detain him.'

This statement has puzzled many people. One explanation is that he had run up debts, now that his wife had died, in addition to all the expenses he had incurred while at Court. Or he might have been involved in some minor legal dispute, and so wanted to avoid any appearance before a notary. The King himself is mentioned, which suggests a more serious crime. Was he considered a state criminal, a spy perhaps? Did they think that he had stolen some of their secrets while at Court? Or did they not want him to leave with his own secret plans, which they had supposedly turned down?

His departure was sudden, and possibly suspect, and has been the source of many stories over the centuries. In most picture-books about Columbus, there is usually a drawing of poor but brave Columbus, clutching the hand of his little four-year-old son Diego, departing into the unknown, saddened and humiliated.

There was nothing further to keep him in Portugal. He had no money, no property, no wife, no backers, no prospects, no hopes. It was time to move on.

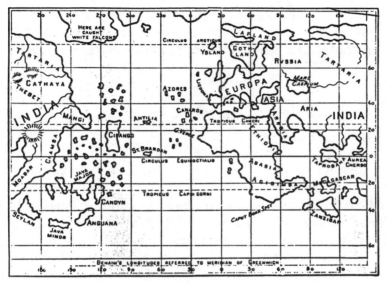

Martin Behaim's view of the world, 1490, as adapted on a Mercator projection.

4

Portugal Today: Lagos, Lisbon and Madeira

THERE IS no statue of Christopher Columbus in Portugal today, which is strange, considering that many people, when asked about his origins, often guess that he was Portuguese, or at least that he was working for the Portuguese, when he made his discoveries. It was in Portugal that he first thought of his grand design, yet in that country he matters relatively little.

'Christopher Columbus is not part of Portuguese history,' so replied the Cultural Counsellor at the Portuguese Embassy in London, when I wrote to him about any Columbian relics I might look at in Portugal. 'He succeeded as a great navigator at the service of the King of Spain (our mistake). Therefore there are no statues of Columbus in Portugal, as far as I know . . .'

The main reason is very obvious, if you happen to be Portuguese. They have their own native-born navigators, many more than Spain, or Britain or France, men who were responsible for changing our knowledge of the world. It can be argued that several of them were far cleverer, more knowledgeable, more daring than, and just as important as, Columbus himself. It was the Portuguese who opened up the Atlantic in 1420; who first crossed the Equator and, thanks to Henry the Navigator, sent a stream of explorers down the coast of Africa; who produced Bartholomew Dias, Cabral, Vasco da Gama and Magellan, all world figures, heroes to engender pride. And the present-day Portuguese certainly are proud.

Since 1988, Portugal has been busy celebrating all their achievements, in the plural, marking in turn the anniversary of each event, under the direction of the National Board for the Celebration of Portuguese Discoveries. It will go on doing so for several years yet. The rest of the world has, alas, been paying little attention. Since the sixteenth century, Portugal has not exactly been a world leader. It is a small country, with a population of only ten million, economically the poorest in Western Europe.

I have owned a little house in the Algarve region of Portugal since 1968. I remember going to see the lawyer in Lagos who was handling the sale and staring at a huge map of the world on his wall. Great parts of it were splattered in red and I thought at first it must be the British Empire, on a map put there to amuse his British clients. It turned out to be the Portuguese Discoveries. It was a brand-new map, yet most things on it were as they had been around five centuries ago. Then I met a Professor of Portuguese from London University. He said it was sad how Portugal had declined. Every Portuguese learns at school about their nation's great achievements, and feels proud, till they come abroad and find that no one else seems to have heard of the names. To cheer himself up, he tries to make regular trips to Brazil. Simply landing in such a vibrant, architecturally exciting place like Rio or Saõ Paulo was enough to puff out his patriotic chest and allow him to bask in the sound of Portuguese being spoken, his language, spawned by his people, even though he well knows that Brazilians today have no great love for Portugal, any more than the old Spanish colonies love and admire present-day Spain.

I never realised, back in 1968, that it was Lagos where Columbus landed, washed up from his shipwreck. The latest research suggests that the actual beach where he came ashore was Porto de Mos, just a couple of miles to the west of Lagos, and one of the very few undeveloped stretches of golden sand left in the Algarve, without a hotel or even an apartment block. We like to call it 'our' beach. When we first arrived, it was totally empty all day long, except on Sundays when a few local peasant families would come down from the hills. Young men crippled from fighting pointless colonial wars in Africa would sit and stare at the sea. Old women in black would hitch up their skirts for a delicate paddle. These scenes have gone, life has moved on, and the Algarve become affluent. But this particular beach still feels 'Portuguese'.

There is nothing to record that Columbus landed at Porto de Mos, or thereabouts. Recently, I asked a few Portuguese regulars if they were aware of the Columbus connection and they stared at me in amazement. They denied he had anything to do with the Algarve, or even with Portugal.

In Lagos itself, there are no traces or references to Columbus. There is a Rua Vasco da Gama, a Praca Gil Eanes, and the main avenue along the river front is called Avenida dos Descobrimentos (or Discoveries). Henry the Navigator is of course much in evidence. His handsome statue guards the harbour, with a splendid square in front, done out in a black-and-white cobbled design, in the Portuguese fashion. A palace in which he once lived is now a hospital.

Lagos was already a thriving port well before Columbus arrived. Its town walls date back to Roman times and there are Moorish influences in the churches and the chimneys, but it was Henry's ship-building work which put it on the map. Lagos also became the site of Europe's first slave market, though the inhabitants do not like to talk much about that. It was the capital of the Algarve until the eighteenth century; an honour that now belongs to Faro. But Lagos is still a thriving fishing port, with ancient buildings and battlements. It feels slightly old-fashioned, despite the summer tourists, and unlike Albufeira it has not yet been overwhelmed by modern life.

Sagres, where Columbus did not, as far as we know, go, but from where most nautical wisdom came in the fifteenth century, is just twenty miles further west along the Algarve coast, the Land's End of Europe. You can drive there in just over half an hour from Lagos, and all the way see the landscape changing, from lush Mediterranean vegetation to Hebridean barrenness. Every year, the tourist industry gobbles up another undeveloped little village, another empty stretch of sand, but Sagres's time has not quite arrived. The harbour is attractive enough, but the little settlement itself is bleak, a series of wind-swept, primitive concrete blockhouses, more like a war-time military establishment than a possible tourist trap. There is a large Pousada or state-run hotel and a good restaurant, A Tasca, with marvellous views over the bay.

What most tourists come to visit is the Fortress of Sagres. It was re-built in the seventeenth century, but inside you can clearly see Henry's College of Seamanship, his house, the monastic rooms for study and his chapel. There is usually a little display and film show telling the world, in various languages, about the glories of Portugal. You can examine the giant compass, laid out in stone, on which Henry is reputed to have made his calculations.

Why did he not create his centre of excellence in Lisbon, much more central? Or in Lagos, where his caravels were actually being built? A visit to Sagres suggests he was a cerebral prince, determined to get away, to find himself and the secrets of the oceans, drawing inspiration from nearness to nature and the elements. Out on the wild rocks, away from the simple habitations, you can understand why the ancients thought Sagres did have sacred significance. Sagres does not, however, feel or sound particularly sacred today, least of all to the Portuguese; Sagres is the name of one of the nation's best-selling beers.

There is not a lot to detain the Columbus-searcher in Lisbon today. The old Genoese quarter is no more, except for one supposedly Genoese-style whitewashed palace. According to Taviani, there are still several Genoese-related names lurking in the Lisbon telephone directory, such as Spinola, Doria, Centurione, Pardodi, Pessagna and Gaggeiro. It is not clear in which church Columbus actually got married, or where he lived, or where he and his brother had their map-making business. Old Lisbon has been virtually destroyed over the centuries, from the earthquake in 1755 to the fire of 1988, and many ancient buildings have now completely gone.

After mainland Portugal, I therefore set off for Madeira, so important in the Columbus saga, hoping for stronger relics, a clearer sense of his existence, perhaps some clues to his character.

Madeira is still Portuguese, now legally part of Europe, since Portugal joined the Common Market. It was the sugar trade which took Columbus there in 1478 and, until very recently, sugar was still thriving. The last refinery closed in 1985, when it became cheaper to import sugar, but the businesses it had spawned over 500 years, such as Madeira wine and Madeira cake, continue to flourish and have made the island's name known throughout the world. Most of the old families who grew rich on sugar have successfully moved on to other enterprises. Many of these families were originally British, Blandy, Leacock, Hinton, all still going strong, their names cropping up all over the island.

Madeira is perhaps best known today as a tourist island. For the last hundred years or so, it has been attracting the quality from Europe for their winter holidays, originally providing a long stopover for the nineteenth-century passenger ships, en route to South Africa, South America or the Far East. It has a healthy climate, lush landscape, with a profusion of flowers all the year round. For a small island, just 36 miles by 14 miles wide, it has a large population, some 300,000, with about a third of those living in the capital, Funchal. Inland, it is all steep mountains, which dominate the island, rising straight from the coast. The roads are circuitous and steep, so a journey which looks easy on the map can turn out to take hours, if not days, giving the impression of a much larger island.

I booked myself into Reid's, one of the world's leading hotels, created by a Scotsman, William Reid, who arrived on the island in 1836 with £5 in his pocket. The hotel opened in 1891 and in 1937 it was bought by the Blandy family. The guest list over the years is impressive, ranging from Winston Churchill, Lloyd George, Bernard Shaw, most of the crowned heads of Europe, to Gregory Peck and Roger Moore. Reid's has a reputation for being old-fashioned and formal, insisting on suits, collars and ties being worn after seven in the evening.

It was the week before Christmas and the lights throughout the town were turned on, the best I have seen anywhere, decorating all the main streets, the handsome Portuguese colonial public buildings and the entire length of the harbour and marina. Funchal is a well-preserved period town, and Columbus would recognise the Portuguese architecture, the squares and churches, the colours, the cobbles, the Portuguese gardens.

The street where he lived, the Rua Esmeralda, is still there, in the old quarter, but the original house was knocked down some time ago. I became very excited when we passed a shop called Perestrello, till I looked up my notes and saw that, in Portuguese history books, Columbus's wife's family is usually spelled with only one l in their name (as opposed to two in Italian and in English). All the same, I liked to think they must somehow be related, and marked it in my mind as the first sighting of a Columbus connection. It turned out to be a photographic shop, hardly relevant to Columbus. Photography, though, has a long history in Madeira, thanks to the tourist industry. One of the oldest studio photographers in all Europe, Vincente, opened in Madeira in 1863. His studio closed in 1972, but it has recently been re-opened as a most attractive photographic museum, containing photographs of buildings dating back to Columbus's day.

The day after I arrived, I walked slowly into town and made a surprising discovery. I was taking a short cut through a park, beside the Governor's pink-washed palace, coming first to two old steam engines, rather strange on an island which never had railways, when

I chanced upon several statues. One was of a naked man with his hat on, apparently throwing something. It was called 'The Sower', and clearly meant to be agricultural. On the edge of the park, there is a fine statue of Prince Henry, in full regalia. Then behind him, on the crest of the hill, in amongst the flower gardens, beside an old chapel, I found Cristovão Colomb, the object of my quest. He looks very important, with a sword in his left hand and a scabbard across his knees. In the other hand he seems to be holding a scroll, with a map between his legs. He stares magisterially out across the bay of Funchal. Had I come across Portugal's only statue of Columbus? I immediately wrote a postcard to the Cultural Minister in London. (He had meant mainland Portugal, not the old colonies, or so he said.)

I then visited the Cathedral, Portugal's first overseas Cathedral, which looked fairly modern on the outside, with overtones of an Austrian *Schloss* around its spire. It is one of several fifteenth-century buildings in Funchal built in the early Gothic style. It is always assumed Columbus worshipped here during his stay, which is not quite possible, as it was not begun till 1485, though he probably did so on a return trip to Madeira in 1498. 'In the town he was well received and fêted,' according to Las Casas, 'for he was well known there, having been a resident for some time. He stayed there six days and loaded up with water, wood and other stores.'

Inside the Cathedral, I thought at first a service was about to start, as people were standing on all sides, then I realised they were queueing patiently for the confessional boxes, three on either side. Each time someone finished and left the little grille, they were stared at, expectantly, questioningly. I counted the number of people waiting to confess their pre-Christmas sins, forty-eight in all, forty-two of them women.

Outside the main door, there were three little urchins, playing cards for money, shouting and squabbling. Two of them had incredibly blond but filthy hair. You see a lot of fair hair and blue eyes in Madeira, the bequest of a British garrison stationed on the island for many years during the Napoleonic wars.

I then went to see the Director of Madeira's Tourism and Cultural Board, João Goncalves Borges. He was grey haired and distinguished, and was soon to retire. I told him I was in Madeira on the Columbus trail, but he either misunderstood, or had decided there were more important things I should know, for he proceeded to give me a long lecture on Madeira's climate, complete with maps, the pens and ornaments on his desk representing the various winds and mountains. But what about Columbus? He then moved on to the history of the sugar trade. In passing, he said the reason Henry the Navigator was so clever was that he was half-English. 'Well that's what my wife always maintains. She's half-English.'

We eventually arrived at the Perestrello family, into which Columbus had married, and he offered me an interesting explanation of their name. As we know, they were a family of sea-faring people, originally from Italy. He suggested they had sailed '*per estrelli*', by the stars, hence their surname. He also told me that Columbus's father-in-law, the first Governor of Porto Santo, had the right to cut off anyone's hands if they misbehaved. 'A later Governor cut off someone's more personal part, after he had had an affair with the Governor's daughter.'

His own feeling about Columbus was that, while he was in Portugal, he was up to no good and usually in trouble with the law. 'And he was also probably Jewish.' I asked for his evidence. ' Why did he take all those Hebrews with him? I read somewhere that all his sailors were Jewish.' I said that was pure folklore, but I would look into it.

Government officials in Madeira had recently decided they should do something to celebrate 1992, though they were still not sure what. Unlike mainland Portugal, they do have definite places associated with Columbus, which might entice a few tourists. After much telephoning, two men were brought in who had just been appointed to a five-man committee for 1992, a pre-committee committee, to make suggestions rather than to do anything, as yet. They were both school-teachers, one of them now retired. The younger was called Dr Nelson Verissimo. Nelson is a fairly common christian name in Madeira, and in Brazil, thanks to the racing driver Nelson Piquet. I suggested it might originally have come from the English admiral, but they all said that Nelson was not English, never, it had always been a pure Portuguese name.

Their only plan, so far, for 1992, was to mount some sort of exhibition connected with Columbus, but the problem was the lack of anything to exhibit. 'All that's left is the Columbus window, and that's in someone's garden.'

Could it be something I might actually be able to see? After a lot more telephoning, I got a car and sped up the mountainside behind Funchal, clutching the name and address of a Mrs Georges Welsh, Quinta da Palmeira. I was not sure of her nationality, just that she was rather old, not very well, but had agreed on the telephone that I could come and look at her Columbus window.

Her house was enormous, a tropical stately home, with a long rather overgrown driveway and massive grounds, covered with palm trees, hence the name of the house, plus other exotic trees, bushes, and, here and there, little brick-laid English garden paths and bowers. The shutters were closed and the house looked empty. I knocked for some time before an old Portuguese maid in uniform appeared. I explained my purpose, in my best kitchen Portuguese, and she pointed down a path into the garden, and said I would find the window there.

It was about thirty feet high, a real stone window, minus glass of course, but with all its arches, stone ornaments, window seats, gargoyles, buttresses intact. I stood and looked through it, down over the town of Funchal, wondering how and when it had been moved into the garden.

I went back to the house and knocked again. The maid took even longer coming, but eventually allowed me into a large, circular entrance hall and told me to wait. I admired some old paintings, a clock and a huge pale mauve orchid in an ornamental pot, about the size of a small tree. I had become accustomed to orchids and flowers everywhere in Madeira, even though it was mid-winter, but this was the biggest I had seen.

I heard tap-tapping down a long corridor and an old lady slowly appeared, walking by herself, but using two sticks, while the maid followed, ten steps behind, as if in a dream. I tried to help her descend a couple of marble steps into the hall, but she ignored me, making her own way to a chaise-longue where she carefully sat down, got out some cigarettes and lit one. Only then, at last, did she turn to stare at me. Then she beckoned for me to sit beside her.

I apologised in Portuguese for interrupting her, then I admired the orchid, in English, not sure of the Portuguese for orchid. She smiled and said it was laelia superba. Her accent was decidedly English-sounding. She turned out to be from New Zealand, born eighty-seven years ago in Christchurch, and originally called Theo Beswick. She said her father spent most of his life telling people how to pronounce his surname. It rhymes with Keswick. At the age of seventeen, she had come with her mother to London, which led to a holiday in Madeira with a friend of her mother's who had taken a house in Funchal for health reasons. In Funchal, she met the man she was to marry, Georges Welsh, from an old Anglo–Madeiran wine and sugar family. She was now a widow. Her son was in the travel business.

She remembered the Columbus window being put up in the garden the year she got married, 1930, and the complications when it was discovered it had been erected back to front, with the stone window seats on the outside, rather than the inside. One is supposed to stand 'inside it', looking out over the Bay of Funchal. Her husband made the workmen re-construct it the right way round. She did not know at what stage it was taken from Columbus's house, the one where he is said to have lived in Funchal. It now looks as if it has been in her garden for ever, overgrown with vines and flowers. 'When I married, we had twelve gardeners. Now we manage with one and a half.'

I said it must seem strange, looking back on her life. How could she have imagined, as a little girl growing up in New Zealand, that she would end up in Madeira, living for sixty years in this fairy-tale, tropical mansion. She lit another cigarette, one of many, as she chain-smoked throughout our chat. 'I have never been back to New Zealand,' she said. 'I think now it would be a mistake, don't you?'

I explained that her Columbus window appeared to be Funchal's only Columbine artefact, and that the city fathers hoped to use it somehow in 1992. She had not heard about any of their plans so far, but she would try to help.

Porto Santo is totally different from Madeira. It is much smaller for a start, just nine miles long by three miles wide, flat and barren, with no mountains, no lushness; but it has what Madeira lacks, a beautiful golden sandy beach, seven miles of it, unspoiled, not built on, running the length of one side of the island. The other, northern, coast is rockier and much windier. It also has a massive air-strip, out of all proportion for such a small island, which is used as the refuelling base for planes leaving Funchal. The latter's airport is very small, a handkerchief hemmed in by frightening mountains. The larger planes need to be light to take off, so they do a ten-minute flip to Porto Santo, then fill up with enough fuel to take them on to Lisbon or London.

There were only three battered taxis at the little airport, which were taken by the time I had got my bearings, and were speeding off along a dusty track, about to leave me on a deserted air-strip. Then one did a U-turn and returned. The passenger, a school-teacher, coming home from Funchal for the holidays, had realised I must be a visitor and would be going to the Porto Santo Hotel, which was on her route.

As we passed along the sea-front, she pointed out the boarded-up summer homes belonging to well-off Madeirans. Porto Santo has a resident population of under 4,000, but in the summer this swells to 10,000 when whole families decamp for the season, making the most of Porto Santo's splendid beach, the safe clean swimming and the idyllic pace of life.

Columbus's house is in the island's capital, Vila Baleira, which comes from the word for whale, though no one can ever remember a whale being seen near Porto Santo. The town is really a big village, with a few shops, cafés, banks and government offices. I noticed a pension called Residencial Cristovão Colomb, and a Bazar Colombo, but Columbus himself merits only one reference in a 128-page Portuguese guide to Porto Santo. He is referred to as the 'navegador' (not 'Discoverer', as he is usually described in Spanish or Italian) whose claim to local fame is that he married Perestrello's daughter.

Casa Colomb is next-door to the parish church. The church itself was erected between 1420 and 1446, when Columbus's father-in-law and the first settlers arrived on the island, but was mostly rebuilt in the seventeenth century. It is thought that the Casa was built around the same time, used as the Governor's house, and this was where Columbus lived with his wife and baby son. Until recently, part of it was the island prison, and the other part the priest's house.

It was awash with workmen when I arrived, though on close inspection not many of them were doing much work. The foreman explained that it was a big house, for Porto Santo, good enough for a Governor's family to live in. He pointed out a handsome fireplace, done out in tiles, an old doorway which he had discovered when taking down a wall, and an old wooden spiral staircase which was full of woodworm and had to be removed. Apart from that, he thought most of the present building was nineteenth-century. They were rebuilding seven rooms, to become a Columbus museum, in time for 1992, so he hoped.

In the church, Nossa Senhora da Piedade, they were getting ready for Christmas. Round the nativity scene were little pots of emerald-green plants. I thought at first it must be some semi-tropical growth, which I would not be able to identify, but on closer inspection I saw it was common or garden cress. Early in December every year, local school-children are given seeds, such as cress or wheat, which they plant in jars or any other receptacle they can find; then, as the seeds sprout, they are used to give colour to the Christmas decorations.

I went into the chapel of the church, the oldest section, dating back to Columbus's time. Diego, assuming he was born in Porto Santo, would have been baptised here. On that return visit to the island, in 1498, Las Casas says 'he heard Mass and found the whole island in an uproar and all the haciendas, furniture and cattle under guard for fear of the French'.

Porto Santo was often left to its own devices, and defences, once the Portuguese realised there was very little to protect. During the first flush of settlement, considerable effort was put into agriculture, but the elements eventually defeated them. Now most of the farms lie barren, the soil eroded. The few cows are kept constantly indoors. Plastic-covered greenhouses are used for vegetables. There is a reservoir, but it is rarely full, even in winter. A new desalination plant has helped, but more is needed. Five hundred years later, Porto Santo's main problem is still lack of water.

There is serious unemployment on the island, especially amongst young people. Most of the work, around seventy per cent, is Government-created, and concentrated at the airport, the new harbour, or the town hall. Young girls go off to Jersey to work for six months at a time in the hotels. Young men emigrate to places like South Africa.

Before I left Porto Santo, travelling this time by boat, I went for a walk in a little public garden near the old pier and there I found my second Columbus statue on Portuguese soil, a rather modernistic version, done in 1982. It shows Columbus from the waist up, his left hand clutching his breast, apparently in some form of supplication. His hair is long and flowing, and there is a necklace on his bare chest. I could see no symbolic additions to mark him as the Great Discoverer, no maps or scrolls.

The sea was totally calm as I set sail on the *Independencia*, a modern catamaran, built in Norway. It holds 244 passengers and can do the forty-mile trip to Funchal in one and a half hours. It was practically empty.

Once we were well clear of the island, I asked a sailor if I could meet the captain. Eventually my request was passed on and I was ushered into the presence.

I asked Captain Caldeira if he admired Columbus, sailing these dangerous seas, up to 3,000 metres deep, without any mechanical aids. 'I think of him constantly. I've got a little sailing boat myself, so I know what's it like in these seas.'

On my last day in Madeira, I made contact with a Portuguese family I had been trying to reach all week, the Barbeitos, a noted name in the Madeira wine trade. I was trying to contact Manuella

Barbeito, as I had been told her late father had owned a very large collection of Columbus books and material. She had 'flu, but her son Ricardo agreed to see me. His grandfather had indeed left 30,000 books, the earliest dated 1516, but they were all locked away for the winter. He had recently spent three months of his summer holidays trying to catalogue them, but had not yet finished. He estimated around a thousand concerned Columbus, in a variety of languages. The family is hoping to convert an old wine cellar into a Columbus museum and library.

He told me about a new Columbus book, written in Portuguese, by Mascarenhas Barreto, a lecturer in art history, and called *Christopher Columbus: Portuguese Spy in the Service of King John II*. The book alleges that Columbus was born in Portugal, in a village called Cuba in the province of Alentejo, and that he was originally called Fernando Zarco, changing his name later to Columbus. 'The names Columbus gave the places he later discovered in the New World all came from the area of the Portuguese village where he was born, so the author maintains. He also states that Columbus was a cousin of King John and a member of an order of Knights of Christ.' The book's main thesis, hence its title, is that Columbus was not just Portuguese, but a Portuguese spy. This would explain why Columbus was able to leave Portugal so easily, despite the charges against him. King John wanted Columbus to interest the Spanish Court in his plan to sail west, which John had officially rejected, in order to deflect Spanish ambitions from the south, round Africa, an area where Portugal was so active.

It was satisfying to discover, as I left Madeira, that Columbus is not totally forgotten in Portugal today. I had seen two statues of him, visited the house where he lived, and heard an explanation of why he made that sudden departure to Spain. I do not believe a word of it. However, Columbus did leave Portugal in a hurry, for reasons which are still mysterious.

5

Spain

EVERY SPANIARD knows the scene. It is a dark and stormy night, sometime in 1485, and a poor tattered traveller arrives at the door of an isolated monastery called La Rabida near the little port of Palos in the south of Spain. By his side is his son, Diego, five years old. They have journeyed a long way and are hungry and homeless. The man is a widower, his wife having recently died, and he is very despondent, rejected and forlorn, ejected from another country, all his great hopes apparently destroyed.

He knocks at the door and begs for a glass for water, a bed for the night. He is taken in, washed and fed, given a bed, and the Father in charge of the monastery takes his confession. Gradually, he hears that this stranger has a vision, a call from God to take the Word to the heathen, in the form of a mission to cross the unexplored Ocean Sea to the west and to reach the Indies.

The friars are clever men, interested in science, like good Renaissance people, and one of them happens to have some important connections. I will help you, my son, he says. And so he does. It all comes to pass. The world is changed. The rest is history.

This touching scene is usually nicely illustrated. You see variations of it everywhere, in paintings, tapestries, tiles, plates, as well as verbally evoked in poems, novels, plays, songs and operas, all over the Spanish-speaking world, from Madrid to Mexico. North Americans should also be well aware of this legendary incident, as it appears on one of their most famous postage stamps, the 30-cent Columbian stamp of 1893. It shows Columbus with the friars, telling them his vision, with the caption, 'Columbus at La Rabida'.

Perhaps the most attractive thing about this story is that it is true. Admittedly the documentary evidence for the stormy night and the tattered clothes is less than conclusive. But the glass of water is correct. A witness who swore he saw it happen gave a description, under oath, in 1515.

What precisely Columbus's motivation was in going to Palos, or indeed to Spain, is still something of a mystery. There were a number of likely countries he might have chosen, in order to put forward his idea. And, in Spain, there were hundreds of better-situated, more important places to head for than Palos de la Frontera, right on the southern strip of Castile, stuck between Portugal to the west and the Moslem-held Kingdom of Granada to the east.

Other countries were definitely in his mind. Ferdinand describes how before Columbus left Portugal he sent his brother Bartholomew off to England. 'He had no Latin but had much skill and experience in navigation and made excellent sea maps and globes.' His instruction was to engineer an audience with Henry VII, the first Tudor monarch, recently crowned, and to secure his backing for a voyage west to the Indies. Columbus himself headed for Spain, Portugal's chief maritime rival.

It is presumed he went there by sea. Going by land would have been dangerous, if, as he said, the King of Portugal thought to apprehend him. The Spanish Court often met at Seville or Cordoba, both in the south, so, if the trip was spontaneous and unplanned, he might well have taken the first available boat in that general direction, sailed round to the south of Spain, then landed at Huelva, the nearest big port. Once at Huelva, he might have looked around for a Franciscan monastery in which to lodge, and been told by chance about the one at Palos. As a youth in Genoa he was brought up amongst Franciscans.

It is more likely he had planned where to go, and that it was family connections which took him to Huelva, for that was the home of a sister of his dead wife, married to a local man. Columbus hoped he might be able to leave young Diego with his aunt, which is what he very soon did, according to Taviani, while Columbus himself stayed on at the monastery of La Rabida, talking to the friars.

Travellers were traditionally taken in, given a simple cell for the night, but he was fortunate to encounter a friar who was also an astrologer and cosmographer, Father Antonio Marchena, who was delighted to discuss Columbus's views on the universe, the stars, the seas, and how to cross them. It was, however, unusually good luck that the Prior of the monastery, Father Juan Perez, had been a confessor to the Queen and was still retained as one of her chaplains. Father Perez pointed out that, under an old Spanish custom, any commoner could petition the monarch, or send a closed letter to Court, which would certainly be answered.

Finding the Court in Spain in the late fifteenth century was not an easy affair. It moved from city to city, and it was presided over by two monarchs. Columbus was at least fortunate that he arrived at a time of unity and peace, thanks to the marriage in 1469 of these two monarchs, Queen Isabella of Castile and Leon and King Ferdinand of Aragon. They held power over most of what we now call Spain, except for Granada in the deep south, which was still held by the Moors.

Queen Isabella was born in 1451, the same year as Columbus. She also had fair hair and blue eyes, another coincidence, often commented on. In Castile, she had to fight off rivals and win battles of succession, before and after her marriage. At the time of Columbus's arrival in Spain, she was aged thirty-four, secure politically and a powerful personality. She was deeply religious, convinced she had a duty to God to protect the Catholic Church.

The movement for religious purity started in Spain around 1481, rather quietly at first, to encourage and establish religious conformity, as a means of unifying the whole country behind the 'Catholic Monarchs', as they were always known, a title approved by the Pope himself. It was therefore anti-Jewish and anti-Islam, and all persons were banned from public position who did not profess to be Christians. Only later did the persecutions start with the establishment of the Inquisition.

Ferdinand of Aragon, one year younger than his wife, had spent most of the first ten years of their marriage endlessly departing on campaigns to subdue the nobles, leading his troops into battle and settling disturbances. Neither he nor Isabella came to their marriage, at the respective ages of eighteen and nineteen, with much money, so it was vital to control the financial power of the local lords and take hold of the economy. Ferdinand was a man of action, fond of archery, hunting and other sports, less well educated than his wife. She had intellectual pretensions he did not share, surrounding herself with artists and men of letters, taking up the study of Latin at the age of thirty, helping to found schools and hospitals.

In the earlier years of their marriage, Ferdinand had several mistresses and fathered at least two illegitimate daughters. Isabella herself was always beyond reproach, though she retained a fondness for fine clothes and jewels. Now that they were in their thirties, what had begun as a political match seemed to have grown into a happily married union. Ferdinand had become colder and more remote, though he was still as brave and athletic as ever, and many people found him impenetrable, whereas Isabella seemed more attractive, more dazzling as she grew older. They had five children, the last of whom, Catherine of Aragon, the future wife of Henry VIII of England, was born in 1485, the year Columbus came to live in Spain. Their oldest, Isabella, was by then fifteen, their only son and heir Juan was seven, Juana was six and Maria three.

Columbus arrived in Cordoba in January 1486 and presented himself to the royal officials, asking for an audience. He had with him a letter of introduction written by the Duke of Medina Celi, a contact of the Prior of La Rabida. Alas, his research on royal manoeuvres was not totally up to date. The King and Queen were elsewhere. They had gone to Madrid, to try to raise money and resources for a major campaign that was being planned. It was hoped to organise an army of some 50,000 to fight the biggest battle so far against the Moors of Granada. It would be a pan-European fight on behalf of Christendom. French horsemen had promised to come. Archers from England were on their way.

Don't you know there's a war on? Columbus was doubtless told that several times. It was as if at the height of the Battle of Britain, a polar explorer had approached Churchill with a plan to reach the South Pole.

Columbus stayed at Court for three months, making contacts, making himself presentable, waiting for their Majesties. Isabella was personally involved in the war effort, interested in the lines of supply and in establishing a military hospital. The Catholic Monarchs finally returned to Cordoba on April 28, and Columbus was seen by them not long afterwards, a remarkable fact, considering his project and who he was.

Columbus's first meeting with Isabella, in early May 1486, in the great hall of the Alcazar in Cordoba, is another incident which has grown in detail and importance over the years, inspiring many artists. Isabella is supposed to have been immediately taken with this tall, handsome, exciting foreigner. It is even suggested there was a sexual attraction. Las Casas is at the root of this gossip, saying that Isabella was impressed by Columbus's 'passionate eloquence' and was moved to 'confidence and sympathy' when he spoke about the mission which God had given him.

Isabella and Ferdinand listened to the explanation of his project, then they did what so many monarchs, presidents or prime ministers have done over the centuries when faced with a difficult decision. They set up a Commission.

Ferdinand went straight off to war, storming the Moors' stronghold at Loja. After a long and bloody battle, the Christians were victorious and took the town on May 28; their bishops immediately reconsecrated the mosques as Christian churches. On hearing the news, Isabella went barefoot to the Cathedral in Cordoba to give thanks to the Almighty.

The Royal Commission set up to look into Columbus's plan contained scientists and theologians, under the guidance of Talavera, one of the most learned men in the kingdom. The future Archbishop was an all-purpose adviser, sorting out internal tax difficulties, going to Portugal on royal missions, solving the problem of the Canaries which now acknowledged complete Spanish domination.

The Columbus Commission moved round the country, with the Court, and periodically examined various expert witnesses, but for most of the time nothing seemed to happen at all. Their first official reply to Columbus came after a year, in the spring of 1487, and it said very little. The project was not totally rejected, but it was found wanting in many respects. It was made clear that the Court had more important business, such as the continuing war in Granada.

How did Columbus survive all this time? Where did he live, where did he work, what did he do for money?

Many aristocratic ladies found him attractive and the names of some he became friendly with are known, such as Beatriz de Bobadilla, a lady-in-waiting to the Queen and one of her childhood friends. The woman he is definitely known to have become intimate with was, however, of much lower birth, Beatrice Enriquez. He met her in Cordoba, her home town. She had been orphaned at an early age and brought up by relatives. She was aged only twenty, while Columbus was nearly thirty-seven. She could read and write, unusual for a girl of her background. Taviani thinks Columbus met her through the Genoese community in Cordoba, but then Taviani sees Genoese connections in so many places.

Beatrice gave birth to Columbus's son in 1488. He was named Ferdinand, after the King, a diplomatic gesture. Columbus always acknowledged he was the father and Ferdinand is usually referred to as the natural son, while Diego, now around eight years old, was the legal son. Ferdinand it was who grew up to write his father's biography. It is not known why Columbus never married Beatrice. Perhaps she was too low-born, or had no money or connections. He continued to consider himself a devout Catholic, despite this apparent fall from grace, and still faithfully attended Mass.

As for his employment, there is evidence that he tried to do some bookselling and map-making, as in Portugal, but little came of it. There is no sign at all that he went back to sea, or even considered doing so, which is strange, as this had been his life-time's occupation up to then. Instead, he was determined to hang around the Court, waiting for the sign, waiting for destiny to call him, which was what he believed would eventually happen.

He was not without hope. In May 1487, he received the first of several monetary hand-outs from the Court, even though the Commission had still not agreed to back his plan. It showed that someone somewhere was taking his project seriously. It also tied him to the Spanish Court, putting him in their debt, not able to negotiate elsewhere. (Bartholomew, last heard of heading for England, seemed to have disappeared.)

On May 5, 1487, the Court records that Columbus received 3,000 maravedis as reimbursement for his expenses in Cordoba. On July 3, he got another 3,000. On June 16, 1488, he received 17,000. In a period of just over a year, he had been given 25,000 maravedis, a generous enough sum to live on. An ordinary seaman of the day was paid 12,000 maravedis a year while an experienced helmsman would get 24,000. It was enough for Columbus not to need to go to sea.

After that, however, the payments appear to have ceased. Columbus was on his own, kept alive by his own convictions, borrowing from friends, one assumes, taking any odd bits of work, looking for any further patrons who might help him.

Columbus made contact again with Portugal, which is surprising, unless you believe he was secretly working for that country all along. It could well have been news of his Portuguese contacts leaking out which caused his payments from the Spanish Court to be stopped. He certainly received a letter from King John of Portugal himself, promising that if he came to Portugal he would not be 'arrested, detained, accused, cited or prosecuted in any suit, civil or criminal'. Such an all-embracing laissez-passer might indicate that whatever had occurred four years previously must have been of a serious nature. Or, if one continues with the conspiracy theory, they may simply have wanted to see him again, to question him about what was really happening at the Spanish Court.

Columbus was in Lisbon in December 1488. Once again, fate and history seemed to be against him. He had chosen the worst possible time to persuade the King of Portugal to back his proposal to sail west to the Indies. Columbus arrived in time to observe, as an unknown member of the public, the moment when Bartholomew Dias sailed into the Tagus, returning from his triumphal expedition round the southernmost cape of Africa.

For many decades, since the days of Prince Henry the Navigator, it had been Portugal's aim to get round the bottom of Africa. Dias's voyage was the latest in a very long line. He had set off from Lisbon in August 1487 in two caravels plus a heavier supply ship, carrying the little stone columns which would mark their progress down the coast. They had many dramatic adventures, sailors died, they were attacked by natives, the supply ship became so worm-eaten it had to be burned. In the end, they were blown round the bottom in a violent storm. Dias wanted to continue and head for India, but his crew refused, and so did his captains. He made them sign a form, at the point of a sword, to say it was their decision to turn back, not his.

His arrival back in Lisbon, after a voyage of sixteen and a half months, was an occasion for great national celebration. Ptolemy had been proved wrong. He had believed there was a huge land bridge from the bottom of Africa across to India, making the Indian Ocean a land-locked sea. Now the sea route was clearly navigable and India was in Portugal's grasp. King John could foresee wonderful international links with Prester John in Africa, then with the Grand Khan in China. The riches of the East were there to be taken. However, he was less pleased when he heard the name Dias had given to the bottom bit of Africa, Capo Tormentosso, the Bay of Storms. He re-christened it the Cape of Good Hope.

We have Columbus's written word that he was in Lisbon on that very day. In the margin of his copy of the *Imago Mundi* he had scribbled that he was there when Dias returned. He also added that his brother Bartholomew was with him. This would appear to mark the return of Bartholomew from England, though the exact dates are not known.

According to Ferdinand, his uncle had fallen into the hands of pirates on the way to England. When he eventually got to London, he fell sick, ran out of money, and spent many months trying to organise an audience with the English Court. 'Eventually he obtained interviews with the King Henry VII, after he had gained some renown through his maps. He presented the King with a map of the world on which were written some verses which I found among my uncle's papers.' An interesting aside, though no one in the English archives has found any evidence of Bartholomew's maps, or of his proposals. The King was interested in the plan to sail west, says Ferdinand, but that was as far as it ever got.

Columbus returned from Lisbon to Spain, still obsessed by his plan, knowing that both England and Portugal were not receptive, Spain was preoccupied with its war but he was ever-hopeful that some country, somewhere, some day, would put up the money.

Why did he not turn to private enterprise? Could he not have asked the Genoese bankers to back him? Or borrowed money on his own account? This is to misunderstand the nature of the times, and of his project. Kings ruled the waves, or maintained they did, so freelances would be little more than pirates. Columbus envisaged not just a Royal Voyage, which would result in a shower of honours and titles for himself, but a Holy Roman Expedition, for Christendom, converting all the new peoples he might come across. He wanted it to be legal and above board, and he wanted it to make him incredibly rich. Only monarchs could give that sort of backing and protection.

None the less, when it appeared no monarchs were interested, he was forced to consider some lesser people, and at least two Spanish grandees were approached, both on the recommendation of the Prior of La Rabida. The order is not clear, nor is it known if he was discussing his project with them before or during his various royal negotiations.

He had serious discussions with the Duke of Medina Celi, one of the richest men in Spain, who later (in a letter written in 1493) boasted that he had for a while supported Columbus, put him up at his house, was willing to pay for his ships, but thought in the end the Monarchs should do so, as it was 'a job for the Queen, our Lady'. So he passed him on.

Thanks to this and other recommendations, Columbus secured a second audience with Isabella. It was in the summer of 1489, while Ferdinand was off at the war. Isabella saw him alone and again she seemed interested, but could promise nothing. He must be patient. The war in Granada was more important. But he was reinstated as a semi-official Court follower, fed and watered by various members of the household, and from time to time given money to pay his debts.

During all this time the Commission was supposedly still reconsidering his case. They had as good as dismissed it once, but were persuaded to consider it again. Columbus was eventually called before them and cross-examined, line by line, on his enterprise. His figures and estimates of the voyage and the distances were basically those he had put to the Portuguese Court, and as before the much better-educated, more knowledgeable experts soon picked holes in his arguments. The Ocean Sea was far bigger than he maintained. Working one's way down a very long coast, as the Portuguese had recently done, was clearly possible, but they argued that no ships would survive in the uncharted open sea long enough to cross it, far less to return.

There were also theological problems. St Augustine had said the rest of the world was uninhabited. God would not have allowed any humans not to be revealed to us. So what was the point of looking for new peoples and lands? And also, if you went too close to any unknown area, it might contain Hell, and you would certainly burn. Columbus replied that he had been down towards the Equator, and no ships and no man had ever burst into flames. But, they countered, no one has been due west, out across the Ocean Sea. Who knows what will be there?

Much of the cross-examination was Aristotelian in its basis. The burden lay with the protagonist to provide evidence and build up an intellectual argument inside a logical framework. Columbus, not having a classical education, was ill-equipped. Theological confrontations were equally hard. Columbus might have chosen suitable extracts from the Bible to prove his case, but the bishops confronting him could provide counter-evidence, or different, more learned interpretations. If Columbus argued too strongly it might be dangerous. After all, denying the Gospels could be heresy. And heretics were not wanted in Spain.

Most of the scientific arguments were clear-cut, still easy to understand to this day, based on estimated global measurements and distances, and on the whole the Commission's experts were right and Columbus was wrong. But underlying all the disputations was the medieval mind, which is much harder to appreciate today. His judges were the most learned men in Christendom, but they could still tie themselves in knots trying to visualise how a man, once he had journeyed round the globe, stood up. Surely he would be upside down? And, on the return journey, would it not therefore be harder, as it would be uphill?

Some members of the Commission were willing privately to give

Columbus the benefit of the doubt, swayed by the fact that her Majesty had agreed to see him again and was providing financial support. But these people were in the minority, and in the end, when the vote was taken, they did not speak in his favour. The Talavera Commission came out with its unanimous conclusion in 1490. The answer was no. They considered there was no scientific justification. The theological foundations were weak. The ultimate hypothesis was madness. All the calculations contained colossal errors.

Columbus had managed to achieve a fair and thorough hearing from the two nations, Spain and Portugal, most likely to back him. He returned to Palos, having nowhere else to go, to decide what he would do with the rest of his life. His intention appears to have been to say farewell to the Fathers at Palos who had helped him, pick up Diego, then move on, destination unknown.

Once again, however, Father Marchena the astronomer and Father Perez the Prior begged him not to give up, to try one last time. Father Perez offered to use his good offices again, appealing to all his friends at Court, including the Queen herself. The Marquesa de Moya, with whom Columbus had been friendly, is also said to have put in a good word for him.

The result of all this was that Columbus was called before the Court in January 1492. He was to be examined this time by a full meeting of the Council of Castile, headed by Talavera, but including on this occasion three archbishops, fourteen bishops, nine dukes and assorted lords, all assembled to decide the 'difficult enterprise' of Columbus.

At Cordoba and at Salamanca, when the Commission had previously pronounced, the result each time had been one hundred per cent against him. This time there was a minority opinion in favour, but the majority was still overwhelmingly opposed to Columbus.

Columbus believed this was the end. Isabella had done her best. He had been judged by the highest in the land. After six long years of struggles and intrigues, plans and plots, it appeared all over. He got ready to leave Santa Fé for good, on a mule, heading for La Rabida, determined to depart from Spain for ever.

Now we come to the point where history turned in his favour: 1492 would never have lingered so significantly in Western minds for so long were it not for the fact of another event which also happened in that year, an event hardly remembered today, outside Spain. In January 1492, just as the Council had finished their deliberations, there came some momentous news. After over 700 years of occupation, the Moors had been ousted. The final battle in Granada had been won. Spain was now a united Christian country.

The mood was suddenly one of celebration. All the dignitaries at Court prepared for the triumphal entry of the Catholic Monarchs into the city of Granada. There was a feeling of release, of hope, of expansion. The minority who had voted for Columbus were encouraged by the good news; they felt more kindly towards such new ventures, even when these were not entirely scientifically sound.

What had really annoyed Columbus's opponents was not simply his shaky grasp of science but what they considered his intolerable demands. Once again, he wanted a percentage of all the treasures found, plus royalties on the trade. He was willing to put up one-eighth of the cost of the ships himself, borrowing the money of course, in return for an eighth of the returns. As before, he wanted to be called Admiral of the Ocean Sea and Viceroy-Governor. This was a title already in existence, held by the King's uncle. The Court considered it the height of impertinence. It was one of the elements in Columbus's case which had always worked against him. Each time, it had been Columbus's personality, and not his project, which failed him.

Unknown to Columbus, as he left Santa Fé, the new mood at Court was already beginning to take effect. Luis de Santagel, the King's treasurer, had suddenly concocted a scheme whereby the enterprise would be far less expensive than everyone had assumed.

Santagel was of Jewish origin, like so many of the Court's best brains, but a *converso*, one who had turned Christian. He calculated that the whole project could be done for two million maravedis. He then announced he would personally raise half that sum. Columbus had already said he would provide a share, and he knew others who would come in as well, so that left really very little for the Crown to put up. And he had a further scheme to deal with that problem. Isabella was so overcome and excited by this new, positive approach, that she offered to pawn her jewellery.

And so we reach another touching scene, one that has also appeared in countless paintings and stamps and illustrations. It is the shot where the Queen hands over her jewels. She never did pawn them, however; perhaps it was only ever meant as a symbolic gesture, even a joke. All she did was offer them, according to both Ferdinand and Las Casas, to fit out a fleet. Santagel is supposed to have replied that it would not be necessary. 'I would be happy to surrender to her Highness a trifling service by lending her the money.'

It was of course the victory in Granada which had brought about this reversal. Attitudes suddenly changed. The other members of the Council, who had voted against Columbus, now looked at the whole project in a different light. Portugal had lavished millions on its expeditions, which had seemed at the time just as illogical as Columbus's, yet they had paid off. If this one failed, what had they got to lose, now that Santagel had worked out there need not be much state money invested?

The matter of the titles still troubled them. But, there again, why not consider all that as hypothetical, at this stage? If he never returned, it would all be forgotten. If he did return, claiming his pot of gold, then they would see.

Talavera was caught rather off-balance by the Council's new mood. 'If I insist on rejecting the enterprise, and Columbus goes off to another Nation, what great remorse it would be for me, having deprived my Sovereigns of such glory and riches.' All the same he wanted his objections noted, to keep his intellectual conscience clear, though he decided to vote for the venture, if it were organised with financial prudence. And so, in a matter of a couple of days, perhaps even that day, the decision was reversed.

A messenger was sent after Columbus. He caught up with him just four miles outside of Santa Fé, which shows how sudden the Council's change of opinion had been. He was commanded to return and meet the Queen, before a smaller meeting of the Council, to agree on the details.

On April 17, 1492, the first of the so-called Capitulations were signed, articles of agreement between the Crown and Columbus, setting out the conditions on which they would back his attempt to Buscar el Levante por el Poniente. Columbus had achieved all his ambitions, and all his demands.

On May 23, 1492, a royal proclamation was read out at the Church of St George in Palos. Columbus was present, and his friend Father Perez, as well as several royal and legal representatives. The proclamation decreed that three ships were to set out from Palos across the Ocean Sea, under 'the command of Don Cristobal Colon'.

Henceforth, Columbus appears in documents as Cristobal Colon, the Spanish version of his name. He now considered himself a

Spanish citizen, with the blessing of the Crown. Note also that he is called 'Don'. He had been promised, in the Capitulations, that he would rise to real glory, should his mission succeed, and become an hereditary admiral, but he had already been promoted. Not yet a lord, more a gentleman, in the old English manner, a courtesy title, like 'Esquire'.

The voyage was to start from Palos, another interesting point. Certainly it was a port that was convenient for the southern Atlantic, but no more so than several others, and it was quite small, compared with Cadiz, further along the coast. The most important reason why Palos had been chosen was due to the acute financial and political brain of Santagel. He discovered that the town was guilty of some offence against the Crown. The details are not known, but it could have been failure to provide the right amount of men or money or taxes during the campaign against the Moors. Whatever the crime, the penalty dreamt up by Santagel was that the town of Palos should provide two of Columbus's three boats, and fit them out at its expense.

Columbus already had one boat organised. It was owned by Juan de la Cosa, whom he had met some years earlier, during his negotiations with the Duke of Medina Celi. Cosa had been interested in the voyage at the time, but the plans had all collapsed. Now he was willing to provide his boat, the *Gallega*, and join the expedition as master. It would be the flagship of the little fleet. Columbus decided to re-christen it – the *Santa Maria*.

He now waited for the two other ships to be provided, fast, light caravels, as instructed by the Crown. Columbus wanted such boats for exploration, speed, and manoeuvrability, following the pattern of Dias and the other Portuguese mariners. They eventually appeared, but without crews. No one wanted to sail with Columbus. And why should they? The local sailors did not know Columbus. He was a foreigner, with no proven record, and this voyage sounded highly dangerous, even ridiculous, despite royal backing.

A further royal proclamation was issued to help Columbus in getting a crew together. It was announced that all criminals, or those about to be tried, would be granted instant release, if they signed on for the expedition. It was a considerable inducement, but still they did not flock. Prison sounded safer than the Ocean Sea.

Once again, the fathers of La Rabida came to Columbus's assistance. They offered to introduce him to Martin Alonso Pinzon, a local captain, who was about to return from a short voyage, unloading sardines in Rome. Pinzon was very experienced and greatly respected in Palos and the surrounding area. Like Columbus, he had sailed the Mediterranean in his youth, and been down the African coast to Guinea. But he had done better than Columbus. He owned one ship and regularly hired others.

Columbus met him and explained the whole project, laying out the letters from the Catholic Monarchs, his Capitulations, and even some of his own charts which it is said he had shown no one before. Pinzon was impressed. He understood the theory behind the expedition, and how it could be managed, far more quickly than all the academic and theological experts. He brought along his brother Vincente, also a master, and the two of them agreed to join the expedition, as captains of the two caravels. It was said, later, that they too had been considering such a voyage, which was why they joined it so easily.

Once it was known that the Pinzon brothers were going, there was little trouble hiring a crew. And there was no need to use criminals. That was another legend which grew up, that Columbus's little fleet was full of convicts. In fact only four of those who got ready to sail from Palos, during the summer of 1492, had a criminal record.

At long last, Columbus had succeeded. He had spent sixteen years wandering round Europe, since his shipwreck off Lagos, an outsider and a commoner. It was eight years since he had first dreamt up his Grand Design, during which time he had suffered endless humiliation and rejection, debasing himself before royal courts, being laughed at in the streets, treated like an idiot and a fool, an impostor and fantasist. He had finally triumphed over all his enemies and achieved his goal. His project was officially and royally accepted.

Without the Pinzon brothers coming forward at the last moment, the voyage would not have started when it did. Without the support of the friars at La Rabida through all those years Columbus might well have given up. And, of course, if Isabella had not always believed in him, nothing in Spain would have been possible. Further back it has to be remembered that those years in Portugal had formed the basis of his whole plan.

None the less, it seems abundantly clear that only one person made the whole thing happen – Christopher Columbus. He had laboured and struggled, fought and dreamt, finally overcoming every obstacle. It had taken him virtually a lifetime, but he had triumphed.

In the summer of 1492, as he made ready his ships in Palos, he was about to celebrate his forty-first birthday. The average life-span for a man in the fifteenth century was thirty-seven. By the standards of the day, he was not just middle-aged, but an old man. What he had done already in his life was remarkable. Yet he was only at the beginning . . .

Columbus bidding farewell to Ferdinand and Isabella at
Palos, 1492. (From Theodore de Bry, 1594)

6

Palos Today

Colombo '92

ANDALUCIA IS a large region, roughly equivalent to the old Roman province of Baetica, and includes Granada, the last piece of Spain to be removed from Moorish hands. It is still the most Moorish of all the Spanish regions. The name comes from Al-Andulas, which was what the Arabs originally called all the natives of the Iberian peninsula. Apart from Granada, Andalucia includes the provinces of Seville, Cadiz, Cordoba, Malaga, Jaen, Almeria and Huelva. I was heading for Huelva, in which Palos resides, driving due south from Seville in a hired car down the N49, supposedly a motorway, but with a disagreeable habit of narrowing to almost nothing and a distinct lack of road signs.

Spain is a geographical entity, just as Columbus left it, and it is again a kingdom, as it was in his day. The regional differences and stereotypes are much the same, at least in popular mythology. Castilians still consider themselves to be pure Spaniards, speaking the best Spanish, while the rest of the nation reckon they are simply avaricious and mean. The Basques are thought to be lumpen, who indulge in vulgar activities like sausage-eating and rock-throwing. The Gallegos, from Galicia, are like the Irish or the Poles, the butt of silly jokes. Andalucians are dismissed as lazy, lying about in the sun, boasting and bragging, not producing very much.

Most Spaniards, however, are aware of Andalucia's past. During those glorious years of the Spanish Empire, from the sixteenth to the nineteenth century, the New World was organised from Andalucia, the ships setting out for the Americas from its ports, the coffers of Seville collecting most of the profits. Thanks to

Columbus, Andalucia is still known to Spanish schoolchildren as the Cradle of the Discovery. Today, the Spanish of Latin America is spoken with an accent which is said to have Andalucian rather than Castilian overtones, traceable back to those original sailors who set off from Palos, in 1492.

I had no idea what to expect. Would Palos be a deserted village today, or lost under high-rise developments, turned into a mini-Benidorm or Torremolinos? It does not appear on the main Spanish tourist maps, so I assumed it must still be fairly small, whatever garb it now wears, whatever occupations the locals now follow.

I came to Huelva first, the local big town, capital of the province, but hurried through it, wanting to get to Palos, some nine kilometres further on, before darkness fell. Eventually I hit the coast road. It was horrendous. I do not think I have seen an uglier stretch of industrial wasteland, caused not by Victorian depredations, the result of once-proud heavy industries, as in Genoa, but by up-to-date modern despoliation. There were huge refineries, pumping out poison, waste tips stinking and reeking, stagnant canals, smouldering chimneys. I took back any thought about Columbus feeling at home in modern Spain. On the map, perhaps. In the flesh, he would be appalled.

The worst of the horrors disappeared from sight once I turned slightly inland, following a road sign saying La Rabida which led me through pine trees and olive groves. I realised that Palos was never strictly a seaport, on the coast itself, but a harbour tucked away on the banks of the broad estuary, where the Rio Tinto meets the Rio Odiel, two huge fingers of water, which then become the real sea, though the estuary is broad enough for the biggest boats.

The Monasterio de Santa Maria de La Rabida was just as I expected, as I wanted it to be, as it has appeared in countless engravings and drawings over the centuries. It is still a modest, white-washed building, with the same red-tiled roof, standing alone on a sandy hill. And, now that I stood reading its full name for the first time, I wondered if that was why Columbus changed the name of the boat, the one he re-christened *Santa Maria*.

The Hostaria is alongside, built in the same style, with the same roof, and blends in so well with the monastery that they appear to be one building, set in their own grounds. The gardens have been landscaped, with neat flower beds, hedges, paths and monuments. In the middle is a massive column put up in 1892 to mark the 400th anniversary, decorated at the bottom with stirring scenes from the

Discovery story. The top was in scaffolding, perhaps being cleaned for 1992. The gardens are perhaps too neat, smacking of municipal gardening. The fifteenth-century monks would surely not have been as fastidious.

I checked into the Hostaria, and was shown up to the first floor. My room was dark, with the blinds and shutters closed, and felt stuffy and unused, as if no one had slept there for some time. I threw open the windows, and the light flooded in, giving sudden life to a dead room. I found myself equally lit up by the view. I was looking directly over the estuary, hardly a mile away. I allowed myself the luxury of breathing in deeply and thinking that from this very spot there must have been locals, even some of those friars, watching for three little ships about to set sail.

Next morning, I was up early and went straight next-door to the monastery. It was not yet open, so I waited in a little entrance portico, hidden behind a red brick arch. It felt very secluded, cool in the heat of the day, giving shelter in inclement weather. If anyone had been following Columbus from Portugal, sent to keep an eye on a suspicious character, he would have felt safe here already, protected by the friars. Yet the building did not seem particularly holy. No signs from outside of a church spire, a cross, a belfry, monastic windows, nothing to indicate a place of worship. It could well have been a private residence, an exclusive villa in the hinterland of the Algarve, or even the Costa del Sol.

I could read around me various bits of graffiti, dug into the wood, which I traced with my fingers – Pepe, Jose, Silva, the occasional date. No obscenities. No football slogans. Just their names. In Genoa, or in London, holy places are not safe from vandals, and there would have been many more expletives.

The door suddenly opened and an old man beckoned me in. There was no entrance fee. I asked if he spoke English, but he shook his head. Just Castilian. He took me into a large, cool room, surrounded by murals, and pointed to a doorway in the corner, indicating the direction I should go next, in order to tour the monastery, then he disappeared. I studied the murals, done by Daniel Vasquez Dias, showing the usual Columbus scenes – Columbus talking to the friars, the boats departing – which appeared suitably worn and faded, though they were done in 1930. They seemed rather amateurish, almost primitive.

I moved on and came to an internal courtyard, bright and colourful after the sombreness of the first room, filled with flowers in full bloom, hydrangeas, little palm trees, trailing vines, hanging baskets, all carefully and artistically arranged. A discreet notice on a wall said this courtyard had been part of the Hospederia, the little lodgings where Columbus had stayed. The rooms themselves had been destroyed in an earthquake in 1755, the earthquake which ruined Lisbon. I walked round the courtyard, going into side-rooms and down corridors, several of them containing portraits and murals of Columbus. In one of them he appeared to be in a nightshirt, dark-bearded. In others his hair was shorter, very blond, sometimes even yellow.

Upstairs, I came to the Chapter House, a well-known setting in the Columbus saga, for it was here that he sat with the friars and first propounded his theories, capturing their interest and help. On the walls, I noticed some portraits of the Pinzon brothers, just as prominent as those of Columbus, with their elaborate coats of arms. There was also a portrait of Juan de la Cosa, owner of the *Santa Maria*. It seemed strange they should be given such prominence, as most people in the outside world have long forgotten the part they played, until I remembered they were locals, born or brought up in these parts.

Little explanatory notes were stuck under various portraits, all hand-written, rather shakily, poorly framed, as if the absentee owner had done them for his own amusement, then gone off somewhere, content for anyone to wander round and look at his treasures. It was genteelly attractive, with a pleasant absence of regimentation, or security, and for an hour I was totally on my own, able to amble around at will, in silence, except for some faint French voices in the distance.

The oldest part of La Rabida is the Mudejar cloisters which date back to the fifteenth century. The red brick and the red tiles have delicately faded over the centuries, while the mortar in between has turned almost white, giving a two-tone, checkered, Moorish effect. In the refectory, where Columbus ate, the heavy wooden tables had been laid out with ancient-looking plates and jugs, purely for display. On the wall was a thirteenth-century crucifix.

On my wanderings round the monastery, I had hoped for a glimpse of a monk, to catch the swish of his robes, the soft tread of a sandal. I had been told in the hotel, if I had understood correctly, that there were still ten or so monks attached to the monastery, but I saw no sign of them. I did eventually come to a chapel, deep inside the monastery, rich and rather ornate, which felt more like a place in use, rather than a museum. I sat for a while, getting used to the semi-darkness, looking up at three little windows which let in the gentlest of light.

Was Columbus ever tempted to remain here, for ever? He was deeply religious, so he always avowed, and often dressed monastically. La Rabida must have been an attractive place, for solace and rest and contemplation, after his adventures, and his failures, in Portugal. He became very friendly with the friars, who made him feel at home. Yet he had hardly settled here before he was off again, some inner force driving him back to a life of intrigue and manoeuvre, on the fringes of the Court, begging favours and introductions. And every time he came back here, it was to plan the next stage.

My tour of La Rabida ended in a little souvenir room, carefully positioned to capture the tourists, and immediately I was back in the real world. It was filled with the noisy French children whose voices I had heard earlier. They had presumably skipped the monastery itself and gone straight for mammon, pushing and shoving to buy Columbus postcards, pens, model ships, jewellery, ornaments. Affecting an air of studious detachment, I waited until they had all gone, then I followed suit, buying all the books and pamphlets I could find on La Rabida's history. I even bought a rather charming bust of Columbus. All the books were in Spanish. There was nothing in English, German or French.

The monastery and little hotel are isolated, in their own sylvan setting. I had to drive a couple of miles inland, further up the estuary, to reach Palos itself, or Palos de la Frontera, as it should properly be called, a settlement of some 5,000 inhabitants.

The first impression was how sleepy and cut off it was. Then, as I walked through the streets, I was struck by the cleanliness and plushness, baskets of flowers everywhere, the pavements spotless, gutters immaculate, council workmen at every corner, weeding and tending and hosing. Could it be an Andalucian Stratford-upon-Avon, or a Portofino, kept olde worlde and pristine in order to extract admiration plus cash from the visitors? Yet there seemed no signs at all of anyone catering for the tourist trade, and I was stared at from corners and doorways as I wandered round, as if they were not used to visitors.

I was walking back along the main street when I looked up and discovered it was called Fray Juan Perez, after the Father Superior of the monastery. I then came to a house beside the parish church which had a plaque announcing: 'A los Pinzons codescubridores con Colon del Nuevo Mondo.' Even my pidgin Spanish was sufficient to work out that this, controversially, was honouring the Pinzons as co-discoverers.

Outside the church, I noticed a small monument to the gallant sailors who set off in 1492. It was on the exact spot where they had been recruited, an historic location. I paused, before reading all the names inscribed on the monument. I wished I could pinpoint the origins of every surname, as I might be able to do with a similar list of British names, and identify those with say a Scottish, a Welsh or a Cornish background. So I contented myself with a quick count. It came to thirty-five in all.

Then I remembered that there were ninety men on those three little ships. Why were only thirty-five remembered here? I read the inscription again, very carefully, and realised the connection. Only those from around Palos have their names inscribed. Even Columbus himself is not listed. Palos, then and now, is strictly concerned with its own sons. On the face of it, a mysterious gesture, almost of revenge. For what?

I tried to get into the church, where the famous proclamations were read out, but it was securely locked. I walked across a little empty square and stopped the first workman, one of dozens I had seen already. He was busy watering an already-cleansed and purified and perfectly watered pavement. Slowly, he put down his hose, leaving it on at full pelt, wasting thousands of gallons, and walked across to the church. He banged again, waited, then shook his head and returned to his work. I watched him struggle to pick up the gushing hose, handling it like a demented serpent.

I went back down the main street and into the main square, rather pretty, with a little arcade at the side. At the far end, dominating the square, I spied a statue. Could it be Columbus at last? Certainly not. It was Palos's real hero, Pinzon. I stood back, to get a better view, and finished off the last two shots in my film. Some starlings flew above my head, swooping and diving, then disappeared into their nests under the eaves of a café. I sensed that the old men at the tables had been carefully watching me, perhaps surprised by someone standing in the middle of the square, in the heat of the midday sun; or quietly pleased that a visitor should want to photograph the blessed Pinzon. I ordered a beer and sat down amongst them, staring into their faces, hoping to unwrap and unravel 500 years, wondering how many of their forebears were in this square, or outside the church, when the call came. Some of them might well have had distant relations who set off on the three ships, for distant parts.

Thirty-five such men came from Palos. And so did the fresh water for the three ships. That was my next aim, to track down its source, known as the Fontilla. It was not all that easy to find as I kept on being directed to little local fountains, in people's back-yards, or to taps in the street. The original Fontilla is just outside the town, in a neat public garden. It dates back to Roman times, so it was already an ancient well when Columbus lived here. The night before he and his men sailed, in the summer of 1492, water was drawn for all three ships. I looked down. Empty. It had been bricked up.

I went in search of real water, the port of Palos, heading through the empty, silent, well-scrubbed side-streets in the direction of the estuary. On the way, I stopped and watched two workmen putting up some flimsy, home-made wooden scaffolding, so rickety it seemed impossible it could support itself, far less a new building. One was singing at the top of his voice. I could still hear him, several streets later. Then it was silent again, till two teenage girls passed me, both clapping. It was a rhythmic, exuberant clapping. They were not singing, or even humming, but hearing in their heads some passionate song which had taken over their minds and their bodies, a flamenco dance perhaps, which they were beating out together, totally absorbed, their hands like cymbals, finishing on a huge crescendo. The echo was still in my ears long after they had disappeared.

I found myself in the middle of nowhere. The houses had petered out. The village was well behind me. Ahead I could see a scrubby hillside sloping before me, with a few scrawny horses grazing. No signs of any buildings or harbour. The river must have changed course over the centuries. Palos village is now a good half-mile from the estuary. It was never a real seaport. Now it is not even a port.

Very disappointed, I came back into the main street, passing the Pinzon monument again, heading for my rented car, which I had parked near the church. I saw a chemist at last, the first I had noticed, and bought a film for my camera. When I came out, I looked up and saw the name of the shop. 'Drogueria Colon'. Not completely forgotten after all.

I drove back along the coast road to Huelva, averting my eyes from the industrial horror, and as I approached the city, crossing a long causeway over an arm of the estuary, I suddenly saw Columbus towering over me. How could I have missed him on the way out? He stands astride an enormous concrete obelisk, at least a hundred feet high, semi-abstract in design, but clearly meant to be the Great Discoverer. In a postcard I later bought, he appears to be totally isolated, surrounded by palm trees and an azure sea. In reality, he is on a narrow spit of land, jutting into the estuary, while all around him is industrial squalor.

I pulled off the dual carriageway at the end of the causeway, looking for somewhere to park, so that I could have a closer look at this impressive, modernistic monument. I drew in beside some horse-drawn caravans, assuming at first it might be a gypsy site, till I noticed how beautifully dressed everyone was, the adults and the children, in classic flamenco-style clothing. The men were in leathers and broad black hats, the women in colourful frills and flounces; the horses were equally well groomed. I could see about a hundred people in all, resting in the shade, under the trees, a stage army of costumed Spaniards, waiting for the next splendid scene to be shot in some highly expensive heritage film.

It was a pilgrimage. They were all en route to some holy shrine, one of many pilgrimages which can be seen every spring, winding its way across the Andalucian countryside. They normally take three days, some going on horseback, some walking, some travelling inside the wagons. The better-off have their attendants in tow, to change the horses, bring fresh clothing and food. The cheats turn up late, arriving in their cars, joining at the last minute, pretending they have travelled the whole pilgrimage trail.

I got talking to a group of them and admired their clothes, the decorated wagons, the handsome horses, and asked if I could take some photographs. They immediately jumped up, dragging in their friends from other groups, and posed proudly for me. Then they insisted I stood amongst them in their finery, while someone took me, with my camera. There was a lot of shouting and yelling in the distance. The caravan was about to move on. People were being called from a nearby café. They looked strange in their elaborate clothes, compared with the scruffy lorry-drivers. As they came out, joining the other pilgrims, they dusted themselves down, smoothed their dresses, tidied their hair, then called their dozing children from under the trees.

I paused for only an hour or so in Huelva, failing to find a monastery I was looking for, where Columbus once stayed, but I noticed once again the Pinzon presence. One of the main avenidas is named after him. I also saw a Mendez Nunez Street, in honour of another of Columbus's sailor heroes. Just outside the city, I came across the pilgrims again. They were in long straggling lines beside the road, stretching for miles, keeping to the fields where possible.

They looked happy and content, if not quite as exuberant as during their refreshment stop. Almost all the way to Seville I kept seeing trickles of similar pilgrims.

Columbus went on such pilgrimages, as did most Spaniards, especially sailors. They would very often make a vow while at sea, praying for a safe delivery during a storm, promising to do penance, should the good Lord deliver them; then afterwards they would trail long distances across the countryside, sometimes in bare feet or a hair shirt, to give thanks at a special shrine or chapel.

Contemporary reports, of the kind of penance Columbus endured on his return to Palos, make them appear very harsh, but now I had another view. Pilgrimages can be fun. Certainly safer and easier than going on a voyage.

RECUERDO DEL
MONASTERIO DE SANTA·MARIA DE LA RÁBIDA
SOUVENIR

7

The First Voyage, Palos to Bahamas

Colombo '92

FAMOUS PEOPLE in reality often turn out to be far less imposing than their image on the screen or in photographs. In fact we almost expect them to be smaller than we expect them. Does the same apply to famous objects? If we could see today those three little ships which set sail from Palos in 1492, they would strike us as faintly ridiculous, if not unbelievable. How could they have done it, when they were so small, so fragile, so insignificant? All three could easily be fitted on to a modern tennis court.

Yet there were ninety people on board Columbus's three ships – eighty-seven of whose names have been recorded. This is astonishing, when you consider it was in some ways just another trip. Scores of voyages into the unknown had been made from the Iberian peninsula over the previous hundred years, involving men who have for ever remained unknown. Enormous research has of course been done since 1492 on Columbus's first voyage, but the names must have been recorded at the time, otherwise they could not subsequently have been found. Royal patronage helped the detectives. All crew members were put on the royal payroll for the duration of the voyage, so their names, and wages, were duly noted down.

Alas, details of the three boats are not quite as exact. Their measurements are roughly agreed upon, and there is little doubt about their overall size, but there are no plans or precise drawings. That fine reproduction of the *Santa Maria* in Barcelona harbour, and the other modern versions which are to be built, and sailed, in 1992, are all based on guesswork. Intelligent, well-researched, informed, painstaking, and loving guesswork, but they are no more 'authentic' than those seventy portraits of Columbus.

There was a wood engraving, entitled the *Santa Maria*, as early as 1494, which would strike most people as unarguably authentic, and it has been reproduced thousands of times since. Samuel Eliot Morison ruined its reputation by pointing out that the same engraving appeared in a booklet published in Mainz in 1486, six years before the *Santa Maria* got her name.

Shipbuilders at the time did not always need drawings, preferring to construct a boat as they went along. No one seems to have sketched them when they were finished, or even on their voyages. Columbus promised the Queen and King he would keep detailed notes, which he did, and now and again he added rough maps to his daily notes, but none of the surviving memorabilia, from him or anyone else, contains a drawing of the boats, or a full description, with measurements. The images of them we now know and recognise have been built up from internal evidence, from descriptions of the voyage, from repairs that had to be made, the problems of sailing them, and from what is known of ships of the period.

The result is that most experts agree that the *Santa Maria* was approximately seventy feet in length and around a hundred in tonnage. This was not her basic weight, but the weight in tuns of wine which she could carry, fully laden, according to the Portuguese method of calculation. She had three masts, the main one in the middle being taller than the boat was long, giving her a top-heavy, uneven look. Columbus himself was not enthusiastic about the *Santa Maria*, thinking her clumsy. She became the flagship of the little fleet simply because she was the biggest, but he would really have preferred all three to be 'carabelas' or caravels. *Santa Maria* was often referred to as a 'nao', a common or garden ship, normally used for cargo. She had been built in the north, in Galicia, hence her previous name, *La Gallega*.

Pinta and *Nina* were both caravels, smaller, faster, sleeker, the sort which the Portuguese had used to explore the African coast. *Pinta* was about the same length as the *Santa Maria*, but thinner, carrying just sixty tons and only twenty-six men. Her official name, under which she was registered, is not known. It was the tradition of the time, as with pedigree dogs today, for a ship to have two names. The formal one was often religious, named after a saint, like *Santa Maria*, while the other was a nickname, given by the sailors. *Santa Maria* was often referred to by members of the crew as 'Naughty Mary'. *Pinta* would appear to have been a nickname, and it has been suggested that it stood for 'Painted One', a rough maritime usage for whore.

Nina was marginally smaller than *Pinta*, holding just twenty-two men. Her official name was *Santa Clara*. Her pet name, possibly came from the owner and master, Juan Nino. *Nina* came to be Columbus's favourite ship of the three.

The three ships were made of wood, with iron bolts holding them together. Underneath, the bottom was covered in pitch which had to be scraped every few months to remove the barnacles. All wooden boats let in water and constant pumping was needed to eliminate the bilge, otherwise it turned sour and stank. When the crew were not pumping, they were attending to the sails, their most important job. There were three main sails on each boat, either large and square, or lateen (meaning triangular), as well as other smaller ones. It was a massive manoeuvre, raising and altering the sails and supports, which was why so many crewmen were needed.

Each boat was single-decked, despite some fanciful illustrations of the *Santa Maria* which have appeared over the centuries making her look like a Spanish galleon, with rows of galleries and decks. The crew slept on the deck as best they could, which was no easy task on the *Santa Maria* as the deck was strongly curved so that water would run away. The hatch was considered best, as it was just about the only flat surface. Columbus, as Admiral, did have his own small cabin, as did the captains of the other two ships. The sails were white, some painted with a cross. Columbus also took with him a special banner with the letters Y and F, standing for Ysabella and Ferdinand.

The ships carried a little rowing boat each, for landing or emergencies, awkward to haul aboard, so in calm waters they pulled it behind them. Each ship was lightly armed, with a canon apiece, which could fire stone balls, plus a few primitive muskets. They were obviously equipped for exploration, not conquest, with just enough arms to repel passing pirates.

Columbus was captain of the *Santa Maria*, as well as Admiral of the little fleet, and as captain he was ultimately responsible for everything and everyone on board, seamen and civilians. Martin Alonso Pinzon was captain of the *Pinta* and Vincente Yanez Pinzon of the *Nina*.

Next in importance was the master, usually the owner of the boat, and always an experienced seaman. (The captain could well be a civilian.) The master took direct responsibility for all the mariners, stowing cargo and supplies, getting the boat underway, managing the sails. The third most important officer was the pilot, or First Officer as he might be called on a British or American ship. He was second in command of the men, but also took charge of navigation and kept a daily record of their position. The boatswain was akin to a Chief Petty Officer, making sure the men carried out instructions, the pumps were in working order, the boat clean and no rats were eating the stores or nibbling the sails.

Amongst the mariners, several were listed first as having special duties, chosen for their crafts and skills, such as carpenters, painters, tailors, surgeon-barbers, caulkers. After that came the ordinary seamen, named, but given no special functions. On *Santa Maria*, there were sixteen ordinary seamen, plus ten boys, or grumets as they were known. On *Pinta*, there were eleven seamen and eight boys; on *Nina*, nine seamen and seven boys.

The total wages for the entire crew came to 250,000 maravedis a month. The captains got 2,500, the masters and pilots 2,000, the boatswain 1,500, seamen 1,000 each and boys 666. Some of their pay was doled out in advance, but most of it was kept to be paid on return to Spain. It is impossible to give realistic modern equivalents of the maravedi. Don Quixote paid Sancho Panza 26 maravedis a day, just a bit less than one of Columbus's seamen, who got around 33 a day, but more than a ship's boy, at 22 a day. On shore, you could buy a cow for 2,000 maravedis, a pig for 400 and a bushel of wheat for 73. The crew's pay was nothing special, considering the danger, and was roughly the going rate for the time.

There were also several civilians on board, some of whose functions are not quite clear. Each ship had a marshal, in charge of justice and punishment. On the *Santa Maria* the marshal was Diego de Harana, a cousin of Columbus's mistress Beatrice, mother of his son Ferdinand. Perhaps he was brought along as an ally, in case Columbus became isolated in any quarrels. The crew lists do show strong family connections, with three Pinzons, three Ninos, and of course all the men from Palos.

Santa Maria, as flagship, carried two royal officials. Rodrigo Sanchez de Segova was comptroller, there to keep track of expenses and make sure the Crown got its proper share of any gold or other discoveries. Pedro Guttierrez is described as 'butler of the king's dais'. He was not Columbus's servant, as he had his own cabin steward. He could possibly have been a spy, sent by the Court to report back, or just a gentleman adventurer.

On board *Santa Maria* was one other interesting civilian passenger, Luis de Torres, listed as the interpreter. He was a 'converso', a converted Jew, who could speak Hebrew and Arabic, the only known Jew on board, thus dispelling all those Portuguese rumours. It was felt he would be invaluable should they meet any important personages on their journey. When they reached Japan, for example, and encountered the Grand Khan, it would be useful to converse in Arabic, thought to be the mother of all languages. The Grand Khan was believed to rule a vast Christian kingdom in the East. Whichever European country formed a link with him could control a very lucrative trade, and also be able to counter the threat from Islam. Moreover any Catholic monarch would of course be honoured by a grateful Pope. Columbus therefore carried with him a letter addressed to the Grand Khan from Isabella and Ferdinand. It was assumed one great ruler would be respectful of another and understand such diplomatic niceties. Columbus also had a form of passport, with a blank page where he might fill in the names of any countries he chanced to visit.

The total complement of ninety, seamen and civilians, comes from Columbus's son Ferdinand. That is the figure he mentions. Recent research has identified to eighty-seven names, so there are three still unknown. The crew list for *Pinta* includes a steward, who would be in charge of food and supplies, but no such person has so far been found for either *Santa Maria* or *Nina*, which would explain two of the missing names. It is also thought *Nina* would have had an extra seaman.

Judging by their names, all but five of the eighty-seven known members of the expedition were Spanish. Two, including Columbus, were Genoese, one was Venetian, one Calabrian, one Portuguese. About ten of the Spaniards came from the north of Spain, from Galicia, and were presumably original crew members of *Santa Maria*. The largest group, as we know, were local, from Palos, Moguer and Huelva.

No one was deemed to be a passenger. Even if the King's butler was doing some spying, that was still a function. Everyone on board had a job to do. There were no farmers or soldiers, or women. Nor was there a priest, which is perhaps more surprising. They were sailing under the aegis of the Catholic Monarchs and, like all sailors of the time, were deeply God-fearing, observing their devotions at set times during the day, but it was left to the captains to conduct prayers and worship.

They took on board enough food and stores and fresh water

to keep them going for up to a year, not an exceptionally long period. The Portuguese had often gone away for up to eighteen months.

Finally, each crew member confessed his sins and was absolved. Then, in the early hours of August 3, 1492, the little fleet left the harbour at Palos and slipped into the Rio Tinto estuary.

The date was significant. The final day for all Jews to leave Spain had ended only a few hours earlier, on August 2; the royal decree expelling them had been signed by the same royal secretary who had authorised Columbus's privileges (he himself was a 'converso'). Every Jew had been given four months either to convert or to leave. Their time was now up. All the ports of Spain were in utter chaos (it is estimated that around 800,000 Jews left the country in 1492) and refugees swarmed the quaysides, begging for space on already-overcrowded boats, selling what they could to pay their way. Rabbis read from the sacred scrolls, then departed with the refugees.

The expulsion of the Jews would explain why Columbus had such trouble getting a boat to his liking, and was forced to take *Santa Maria*; and why he did not leave from Cadiz, a much bigger and better-equipped port of embarkation. In Cadiz that previous day, 8,000 Jews had crammed themselves into all available boats. Columbus waited for the morning of August 3, till the harbour was empty, the seas quieter, the weeping and wailing over.

Columbus does not describe in his Journal the sight of these departing Jews, but he does refer to them obliquely, establishing the date of his departure as 'after all the Jews had been exiled from your realms and dominions'. They were mainly heading for North Africa, as most European countries were Catholic.

Columbus's Journal, as it is usually known, gives a day-by-day description of the voyage. Sometimes there are just a few words about the direction and the winds, while at other times there are fulsome descriptions of events, his thoughts and worries, scientific and geographical observations. The original Journal, in his handwriting, does not exist. It was written for the Court, addressed to their Majesties, but was somehow lost at a later stage, either by accident during packing and unpacking as the Court moved to a new location, or deliberately stolen by some enemy. However, two copies at least were known to have been made. Las Casas had one in front of him when he did his *History of the Indies* and he quoted long passages from it. Ferdinand, while writing his father's biography, also used a copy. Cross-references make it clear they

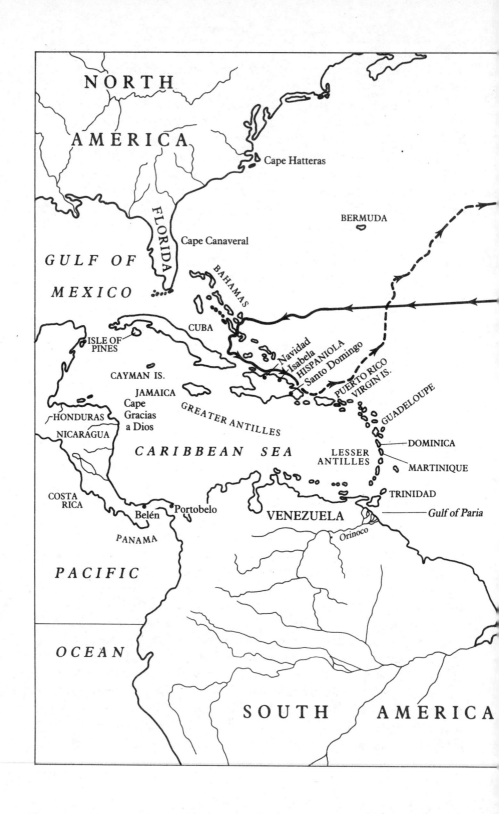

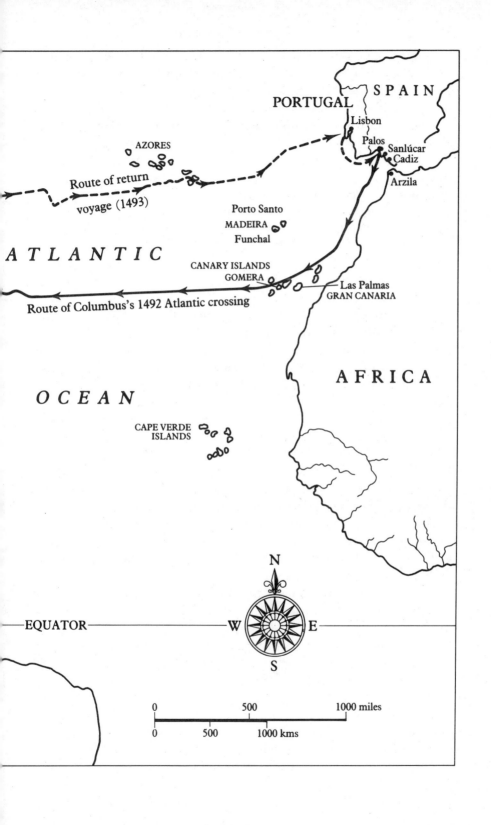

PORTUGAL

SPAIN

Lisbon

Palos

Sanlúcar
Cadiz

Arzila

AZORES

Route of return
voyage (1493)

Porto Santo
MADEIRA
Funchal

ATLANTIC

CANARY ISLANDS
GOMERA

Las Palmas
GRAN CANARIA

Route of Columbus's 1492 Atlantic crossing

OCEAN

AFRICA

CAPE VERDE
ISLANDS

N

EQUATOR

W

E

S

0   500   1000 miles

0   500   1000 kms

were working from the same story, and no one has ever doubted its veracity. There have of course been umpteen translations over the centuries, with more planned for 1992. They will always result in slight differences, depending on varying interpretations of certain fifteenth-century words no longer in use, and the desire to turn it all into modern, understandable prose. There is also the possibility that there were original mistakes made by Las Casas and Ferdinand in copying out passages, getting numbers wrong in some cases, or writing east when it should clearly be west.

The very first words in the Journal, for August 3, 1492, are few and decidedly clipped. 'We departed Friday, the 3rd day of August, 1492, from the bar of the Saltes at 8 o'clock. We proceeded with strong variable winds until sunset towards the South 60 Roman miles, which are 15 leagues; afterwards to the SW and S by W which was the course for the Canaries.'

This handful of simple words has not hindered commentators and biographers over the years from improving the romance and the colour of that first day. Morison describes the water as being 'like a mirror of burnished steel'; and, when they pass La Rabida, he maintains that, as it was the hour of prime, Columbus's crew paused to listen over the waters to the sounds of the friars chanting. He even quotes several verses of the Latin hymn they were using that night, then Columbus removes his hat to listen while his crew cross themselves. This is all highly imaginative, though improbable. Columbus could well have been in his cabin while they passed La Rabida, and heard nothing. The crew might have been busy with the sails, getting ready for the strong, variable winds.

On the fourth day out, August 6, there is the first mishap. *Pinta*'s rudder develops problems and jumps out of its gudgeons. Columbus, in his report, suspects sabotage, and even names the guilty man, Cristobal Quintero, owner of the *Pinta*, who is travelling as an ordinary seaman, not as the master. He had caused problems before departure, moaning and groaning, and clearly disliked going on the voyage, but Columbus feels confident that *Pinta*'s captain, Martin Alonso Pinzon, being 'a man of real power and ingenuity', will sort things out; which he eventually does. High praise, coming from Columbus.

Things then settled down into a routine. Life on board ship in 1492 revolved round the four-hour watches, around the clock, the clock being the half-hour glass, the only means of telling the time apart from the sun. It contained enough sand to run from top to bottom in half an hour. It was made of glass, usually from Venice, and as it was rather fragile lots of spares were carried (Magellan had eighteen on his flagship). It was the duty of one of the ship's boys, the grumets, to turn the glass the second it was finished; Columbus often feared the grumets had become slack. A whistle signalled the half-hour, then every eight changes a new watch came on, the old crew going off for a rest or for food.

The staple diet was wine and hard-baked biscuits, or hard tack as later sailors called it. Spanish mariners did not drink beer, unlike their northern counterparts, and tea and coffee had yet to be discovered. They had one hot meal every day, around eleven in the morning, cooked in olive oil. This could be salt beef, sardines or anchovies kept in barrels of salt. The hard tack was baked fresh when needed, from salted flour. The food generally was as good as any peasant on shore might expect, after a hard day in the fields, and quite varied, considering there was no refrigeration and everything was heavily salted to preserve it.

Columbus in a letter to the King and Queen listed the sort of produce he would need. 'Victualling will be done in this manner: one third good biscuits, well seasoned but not old, or the major part will be wasted; one third part salted flour, salted at the time of milling; and a third part of wheat. Further, there be wanted salt meat, oil, vinegar, cheese, chickpeas, lentils, beans, salt fish, fishing tackle, honey, rice, almonds and raisins.' Note the fishing tackle. Most sailors dangled a few lines from the side of the boat, hoping for a catch. (They also dangled their bottoms from the side, as there were no latrines on board. They sometimes did this in port, which led to complaints of indecency from local priests.) Cooking was carried out on an open fire, a box set up in a sheltered spot on deck, with sand on the floor. It was vital that at dusk every ember was extinguished; another task to keep the ship's boys on their toes.

During the early days of the voyage, some rearrangements were made to the sails. *Santa Maria* was found to be very slow, which meant that *Pinta* and *Nina* got far ahead, sometimes out of sight. The two caravels, with their traditional lateen sails, could run very close to the wind. They were re-rigged square, like the *Santa Maria*, to slow them down and keep them at the same pace as the flagship.

Columbus records these changes in his Journal, along with the direction and distance covered, and all the natural signs which a good sailor should note, the stars, the wind, the flights of sea birds, but he also made a lot of scientific calculations and astronomical measurements, as much to impress the sailors with his genius as anything else. Latitude was estimated by checking on the pole star and the sun by the use of an astrolabe, originally developed by the Arabs and perfected by the Portuguese, or a quadrant. Morison maintains it was a common quadrant which Columbus employed on his first voyage. This was a piece of wood, a quarter of a circle in shape, marked with degrees, along which you looked at the sun or the stars, with a plumb line indicating your latitude. You needed clear weather, or amazing eyesight, and a calm steady sea, but even then it was a hit and miss affair, but Columbus loved the quadrant and recorded many celestial observations. Longitude was a different problem. No method of calculating this exactly would be discovered for another 250 years. You therefore had to estimate distance sailed and direction taken, then work out longitude by what sailors called dead reckoning.

Columbus did have a compass, which gave him direction, and was his most important tool. This was suspended in a box in front of the helmsman and at regular intervals the pilot would check it against the pole star. He would follow the directions given to him by Columbus, noting any deviation due to winds, and would record the time. As most sailors were illiterate, there were several ways of keeping these compass records, in order that the next watch would know what was happening. One system involved pegs on a peg-board, moving them around during the four-hour watch.

The half-hour glass gave you time, after a fashion, the compass gave you direction, but how could you work out how far you had come, and how far there was still to go? That was the vital missing link. There was no accurate way of measuring speed or distance in the fifteenth century. When Columbus recorded the number of leagues sailed each day, this was purely his own estimate. It was not for another century that the 'chip log' method became widely used. All this entailed was lowering overboard a length of knotted line with a piece of wood at the end, allowing it to trail for half a minute, calculating by the hour glass. This measured how fast the boat was travelling, hence the term knots for miles per hour at sea.

Columbus has often been called the greatest navigator who ever lived, and this assessment is entirely credible, considering he was acting almost wholly on intuition and experience. His instruments were strictly limited. In a great many portraits of him he sits with his charts at the table, an astrolabe before him and one hand on a globe. There is no evidence he used an astrolabe on this voyage, and he never had a globe. None the less, he was in the end only nine per cent out on his distances as we measure them today.

The nature of his charts is not known either. Maps of the known world did exist, with places like Cipanga (Japan) marked in, but all fairly rough, as much fantasy as fact. More local maps, covering the Mediterranean, were tried and tested, and so now were the waters around Madeira, the Canaries, the Azores and the African coast. On the first stage of his journey from Palos, Columbus was in well-charted waters. Did he have a secret map of the new places he was heading for, as some have alleged? He did, though, have one secret, which he kept to himself before departure. This was the route he was planning to take. There was no mention of it in all the proposals put to their Catholic Majesties, or before that to the King of Portugal.

He gives it away in that first day's record in his Journal, which of course was private, for his own eyes. The rest of his crew did not know the direction he was going to take, though he must have given the two other captains some details once they set off. He was heading 'SW and S by W' because his intention was not to cross the Atlantic directly, but to start by aiming due south, down the coast of Africa for some 660 miles, and only then would he head west. His first port of call, as he revealed in his log, was therefore the Canaries.

Many maritime experts have applauded this as his master-stroke, praising him for having somehow discovered for himself and worked out how to use the trade winds, which at the right latitude would blow him straight across the Atlantic. No one else in recorded history had ever successfully taken this route. It is assumed that he had become aware of the trade winds during his years in Madeira. This was the knowledge he kept to himself, not wanting others to copy his secret route.

On the other hand, it could be argued that it was sensible to head first for a staging post, even off the obvious route, before hitting the open, uncharted sea. Madeira was out of the question, and the Azores, as they were in Portuguese hands. The Canaries were the most suitable, being Spanish. And, in most charts of the time, the Canaries were reckoned to be on the same latitude as Japan, his ultimate destination. Once you got there, you could head straight west. By doing that, you would, by chance, pick up those favourable trade winds, without knowing they were there. So was it partly luck?

There was a further attraction offered by the Canaries, one which helps to explain some rather strange behaviour when Columbus did reach the islands. He had to stop to get *Pinta*'s rudder mended, and take on some fresh supplies, not in themselves very time-consuming activities. Yet he tarried twenty-five long days in the Canaries. Why did he not get the work done quickly and set off at once? After all, he had laboured and schemed for over eight years to be allowed to make this voyage. Why such an enormously long delay? The answer would appear to be quite simple: a woman.

Columbus's movements in the Canaries are complicated, and there are many missing days in his Journal, but Ferdinand states that they left *Pinta* at Grand Canary, to be repaired, while the *Santa Maria* and *Nina* moved on to a much smaller, less fertile island, Gomera. On this little island, Columbus proceeded to hang around for eleven days, apparently doing nothing. Columbus's log records the same movements, but only Ferdinand offers an explanation. They were waiting for the return of 'Doña Beatriz de Bobadilla, mistress of the island'. She was known to Columbus from her days at Court, an attractive woman aged around thirty, with good connections. Las Casas and another contemporary account make everything much clearer by saying that Columbus was in love with her.

On the twelfth day of hanging around, Columbus eventually learned that she had gone to Grand Canary, so he set off there, but just missed her. He did pick up *Pinta*, her rudder repaired, but then he decided to pursue Beatriz back to Gomera. 'His people were much annoyed by this,' writes Ferdinand, as well they might have been. His given reason, in his Journal, is that Beatriz had a boat he was thinking of hiring. No one now believes that. At the time, the men probably did not believe it either.

In the end, Columbus and the desirable Beatriz had four days together. And why not? She was a widow and he was a widower, albeit with a mistress by whom he had had a son. It is comforting to think of him having one final, passionate embrace, before setting off into the unknown, perhaps for ever. It makes a change from some of the more puritanical portraits of Columbus, which would lead us to believe he was a religious fanatic, for ever in a hair shirt, possessed by a vision which left no time for ordinary, human life. We have no evidence of any love-making. Columbus restricts himself to observing that there were other very respectable Spaniards also being entertained by Beatriz. He name-drops, adding that her son became the first Count of Gomera, and says that the conversation included stories of land to the west of the Canaries, where the sun sets.

At last, on September 6, they got ready to leave the harbour at

Gomera. No sailor had absconded, or asked to leave. All ninety were back on ship, suitably refreshed. As they left, news came through that three Portuguese caravels had been spotted off the island of Ferro, looking for Columbus, either to attack him or to find out which route he was taking. In the Journal, Columbus, or the Admiral, as Ferdinand and Las Casas refer to him from now on, reflects that the King of Portugal is obviously envious that he has gone over to Castile. They do some bobbing and weaving for a couple of days, to avoid the Portuguese, before finally leaving the Canaries on September 8.

Columbus's Journal, as we will continue to refer to it, does move between the first and third person, because it is taken from the versions recorded by Ferdinand and Las Casas, based on the original. Sometimes they are obviously paraphrasing, referring to what the Admiral has written, but at other times they quote him, word for word.

On September 9, there is a most revealing note in the Journal. 'He made that day 15 leagues, and decided to reckon less than he made, so that if the voyage were long, the people would not be frightened and dismayed.' The next day, they made 60 leagues, 'but he reckoned only 48 leagues, in order not to frighten the people'. In other words, Columbus was fiddling the log. His Journal was private, so he could record in it his real measurements, but he was publicly telling the crew much smaller distances. Why?

He had quickly discovered they were making even better progress than he had anticipated. The trade winds were sweeping them straight across the Atlantic and it was proving to be a remarkably easy voyage. So far. In one twenty-four-hour spell, they covered 174 miles. Columbus realised that the main problem could be psychological, not physical. If the crew knew just how many hundreds of miles they had already travelled, they would naturally soon be struck by the obvious thought – how do we get back, against these winds? Better to let them think they had not travelled so far.

On September 19, just two weeks out of Gomera, he asked the pilots on the two other ships to estimate how far they had come. The pilot on *Nina* reckoned 440 leagues. *Pinta* thought 420. Columbus on the *Santa Maria* gave his public estimate as 400. The true distance that day, according to Morrison, who followed the same route, was 398 leagues, or 1,261 miles. Columbus's 'false' figures which he gave out were in fact almost exactly right. It was his 'correct' reckoning that was nine per cent out.

Everyone was remarkably cheerful, pleased by their good progress and the fine weather. 'Like April in Andalucia', writes Columbus on September 16. 'The sea is as smooth as in the river at Seville,' he records on September 18. They come across floating weed in which they find a live crab and Columbus states that this is a sure sign of land and they can only be 80 leagues from some shore. They spot a whale, another sign of land, so he maintains, and some birds which he alleges fly out to sea in the mornings only, looking for food: yet further proof. He points out a man-of-war bird which he says eats the vomit of another bird called the booby, something he had noticed when sailing in the Cape Verde Islands. (Today's naturalists say it is their excrement that is eaten, not the vomit.) The weather remains excellent, so calm that the men go swimming.

A slight breeze gets up against them on September 22, which pleases the Admiral, as he hopes the men will realise there will be winds to take them home, but they are soon being blown forward again at a great rate. To distract them, Columbus continues to point out signs of land, though no actual land is seen. On September 23 he records for the first time that the men are actively grumbling, maintaining there will be no wind to blow them back to Spain.

Ferdinand uses more emotive words, saying that some of the men had 'grown frightened at finding themselves so far from land without seeing the prospect of aid'. A line is dropped to test the depth of the ocean. It runs out at 200 fathoms, without reaching the bottom. Morison estimates that at this stage, just halfway across, the sea bottom is in fact about 2,300 fathoms.

'As these signs proved fruitless,' writes Ferdinand, 'the men grew more restless and fearful. They met together in the holds of the ships saying that the Admiral in his mad fantasy proposed to make himself a Lord at the cost of their lives, or die in the attempt . . . If the Admiral would not turn back, they should heave him overboard and report in Spain that he had fallen in accidentally while observing the stars . . . Since the Admiral was a foreigner without favour at Court and whose views had been rejected by many wise and learned men, none would speak in his defence and all would believe what they said.'

From this description, it would seem that Columbus had almost a mutiny on his hands. Las Casas is not quite so explicit and Ferdinand was perhaps interpolating his own account, adding in things he heard later, but there is no doubt Columbus was having trouble with the crew, alternately threatening them with punishment, then soothing them by convincing them land was near.

He was also having more technical arguments with the pilots. In his own mind, he wanted to keep on heading due west, the route he had set himself, rather than be side-tracked by any of the dots on his chart off the coast of Japan, which presumably meant islands. They must now be near some of them, yet it was strange they were never seen. He was sufficiently concerned on September 22 to pass one of his charts over to the *Pinta* and let Martin Alonso Pinzon have a look. This is unusual for Columbus, to let anyone else study his beloved charts. (Las Casas thought this might be the famous one, drawn by Toscanelli, but Morison thinks not.) Pinzon still had it after three days, so Columbus asked him to return it.

At sunset on that same day, September 25, Pinzon appeared on his poop deck and shouted across to the *Santa Maria* that he had sighted land. 'The Admiral went down on his knees to give thanks to the Lord and Martin Alonso said the Gloria in excelsis Deo with his people. Those on *Nina* all climbed the mast and into the rigging and declared it was land. The Admiral thought so too and declared it was 25 leagues away.'

Martin Alonso Pinzon immediately claimed the 'largesse', a prize of some 10,000 maravedis which the Queen and King had promised to the first person sighting land; worth winning, as such a sum would take an ordinary seaman almost a year to earn. But, by the next day, they realised it was all a mistake. 'What they had supposed to be land,' writes Ferdinand, 'was nothing more than squall clouds, which often resemble land.'

And so it was back to encouraging the sailors by further optimistic signs, spotting and catching birds, some of which Columbus maintained were land birds. A pelican was seen. Then a seaman managed to kill a flying fish with a harpoon. A ship's boy on one of the caravels brought down a petrel by hitting it with a stone.

They also saw a lot of floating weeds, which cheered them at first, as they thought it was another proof of land nearby, but when it became extremely thick they feared it would enmesh and trap them. It proved, however, quite easy to sail through, to their relief. This was the first recorded sighting of the Sargasso Sea.

On October 1, Columbus ordered another estimate of the distance travelled so far. *Pinta*'s pilot reckoned 634 leagues, *Nina* said 540, while Columbus gave his official distance as 584 leagues. As Ferdinand points out, Columbus's true estimate, from his secret records, was 707 leagues. He must therefore have begun to be seriously worried. He had originally told the seamen that the total distance to Japan would be 750 leagues. His official reckoning still gave him some leeway, but his 'true' distance was now almost up.

The cry of 'Land ahoy' was becoming increasingly frequent, especially on *Santa Maria*, as the more enthusiastic believed every good sign they were told, much to Columbus's annoyance. In the end, he issued a new order that anyone making a claim which was not substantiated within three days would lose his reward, even if it later turned out to be true.

At sunrise on October 7, *Nina*, which had been sailing ahead, still being faster than the *Santa Maria*, fired a gun and raised a flag to the masthead, an agreed sign that land had been sighted. By the evening, nothing had materialised.

Columbus then gave an order that all ships must stay together at sunrise and sunset. These were the two best times for sightings, when the haze was least, so Columbus explained. He clearly did not want the two caravels having an unfair advantage by getting ahead. (When they were all together, *Santa Maria*, having the highest mast, had the best viewpoint.)

Later that day, Columbus agreed to alter course from due west, deciding to go 'WSW for two days'. He was now obviously keen to find any land, however small, despite his avowed intention of aiming for the 'mainland', which he was convinced was straight ahead. The slight deviation was to follow a flight of birds, which they definitely felt were heading to roost on dry land. 'The Admiral knew that most of the islands the Portuguese held they had discovered by birds.' Three days later, there was nothing in sight and the complaints were coming loud and strong again.

Columbus himself was clearly wavering, by agreeing to change course for no logical reason, and it looks as if the loudest complaints were on his own ship, the *Santa Maria*. Morison suggests that Columbus lost his nerve at this point, which united the northern Spaniards on board against him. There is no evidence of this, but it would explain his sudden change of course. (If he had kept his nerve, and continued due west, instead of turning slightly south, he would have hit Florida within a few days.)

Once again, Columbus tried to cheer the men up, telling them about the riches in store in the Indies. And, anyway, there was no use complaining. 'He had come to go to the Indies, and so had to continue until he found them, with the help of Our Lord.'

On October 11, they came across the most convincing signs of land so far. *Pinta* picked up a cane and a little stick, 'fashioned so it appeared with iron'. On *Nina*, they fished out a little branch, covered in dog roses. Land *must* be very near this time. 'With these signs, everyone breathed more freely.'

Columbus prayed with his men that night and joined in their 'Hail Marys', thanking God for having brought them safely so far, urging the night watch to keep a very sharp look-out. He announced that he would personally give a silk doublet to the first person who spotted land, over and above the royal reward.

That very night, two hours before midnight, Columbus himself, standing on the sterncastle, saw a light. 'It was so uncertain a thing that he did not wish to declare it as land.' So he did not announce it publicly, but called the two royal officials on board to come and look. The King's butler rushed over and said yes, he could see it, but the Royal comptroller said he could see nothing. 'He was too slow in coming to the place from which the light could be seen,' asserts Ferdinand, loyally.

Some time before dawn on October 12, a canon was fired by *Pinta*, sailing two leagues ahead, which of course it should not have been doing. A seaman on board, Rodrigo de Triana, acting as look-out, had been the first to exclaim, 'Tierra, Tierra!' Immediately everyone on board *Pinta*, including Pinzon, awoke and started cheering. In the distance, despite the darkness, they could make out a white cliff. On *Santa Maria*, Columbus agreed this, at long last, was land. Very sensibly, he gave the order for all three ships to lower their sails and wait till the day had properly broken.

While they waited, Columbus convinced himself that he had been right after all, when he had seen that light, and became determined to claim the reward. To cheat a poor seaman out of the honour, and the reward, reflects poorly on Columbus, not quite the moral, upright figure usually portrayed by Ferdinand. 'It was not he [the seaman] who received the 10,000 maravedis from the Catholic Sovereigns, but the Admiral, who had first seen the light in the darkness, signifying the spiritual light with which he was to illuminate these parts.' Even Morison, who usually sees Columbus as a hero, agrees that Columbus had just imagined the light. He estimates land was all of thirty miles away at that stage, and even the sharpest-eyed fisherman could not have seen it. The real first sighting of the New World was by Rodrigo de Triana. (He, alas, disappeared very quickly from world history. He was later said to have fled to North Africa, where he became a Moslem and died a disappointed man.)

At daybreak, everyone could clearly see a large island, about fifteen leagues in length, says Ferdinand, full of green trees and inhabited by a multitude of people who rushed forward to stare at the boats, thinking they were animals. Columbus headed for the island in his barge, followed by the Pinzons in theirs. They all stepped ashore, Columbus broke the Royal standard and the two captains displayed banners. They knelt on the ground and gave thanks to the Lord, and Columbus took possession of the island in the name of the King and Queen.

Columbus then had himself sworn in as Admiral and Viceroy and ordered all the Christians, in other words the Spaniards, to swear obedience to him as representative of Ferdinand and Isabella. In the native tongue, the island was known as Guanahani, but Columbus re-christened it San Salvador, in honour of their safe arrival from the sea.

It was thirty-six days since they had left the Canaries. For most of that time, Columbus's Journal is very short, just brief notes about the conditions; some days have no notes at all, and mostly in the third person. But, now that he had reached the New World, the entries became fulsome and detailed. Best of all, they are often in Columbus's own, first-person, words.

Las Casas stopped paraphrasing, realising that he could not possibly improve on the spontaneity, the richness of the descriptions, nor the enthusiasm and excitement of Columbus himself. These are some of his observations over the subsequent couple of days, as he wrote directly to his Sovereigns, giving his first impressions of the native people as he found them.

FRIDAY, OCTOBER 12, 1492 IN ORDER that they might develop a very friendly disposition towards us, because I knew that they were a people who could better be freed and converted to our Holy Faith by love than by force, we gave to some of them red caps and to others glass beads, which they hung on their necks, and many other things of slight value, in which they took much pleasure. They remained so much our [friends] that it was a marvel, later they came swimming to the ships' boats in which we were, and brought us parrots and cotton thread in skeins and darts and many other things, and we swopped them for other things that we gave them, such as little glass beads and hawks' bells. Finally they traded and gave everything they had, with good will; but it appeared to me that these people were very poor in everything.

They all go quite naked as their mothers bore them; and also the women, although I didn't see more than one really young girl. All that I saw were young men, none of them more than thirty years old, very well built, of very handsome bodies and very fine faces; the hair coarse, almost like the hair of a horse's tail, and short, the hair they wear over their eyebrows, except for a hank behind that they wear long and never cut. Some of them paint themselves black (and they are the colour of the Canary Islanders, neither black nor white), and others paint themselves white, and some red, and others with what they find. And some paint their faces, others the body, some the eyes only, others only the nose. They bear no arms, nor know thereof; for I showed them swords and they grasped them by the blade and cut themselves through ignorance. They have no iron. Their darts are a kind of rod without iron, and some have at the end a fish's tooth and others, other things. They are generally fairly tall and good looking, well built.

I saw some who had marks of wounds on their bodies, and made signs to them to ask what it was, and they showed me that people of other islands which are near came there and wished to capture them, and they defended themselves. And I believed and now believe that people do come here from the mainland to take them as slaves.

They ought to be good servants and of good skill, for I see that they repeat very quickly whatever was said to them. I believe that they would easily be made Christians, because it seemed to me that they belonged to no religion. I, please Our Lord, will carry off six of them at my departure to Your Highness, that they may learn to speak. I saw no animal of any kind in this island, except parrots. All these are the words of the Admiral.

SATURDAY, OCTOBER 13, 1492 AT THE time of daybreak there came to the beach many of these men, all young men, of good stature, very handsome people. Their hair is not kinky but straight and coarse like horsehair; the whole forehead and head is very broad, more so than [in] any other race that I have yet seen. The legs of all, without exception, are very straight and [they have] no paunch, but are very well proportioned. They came to the ship in dugouts which are fashioned like a long boat from the trunk of a tree, and all in one piece, and wonderfully made (considering the country), and so big that in some came forty or fifty men, and others smaller, down to some in which but a single man came.

They row with a thing like a baker's pole and go wonderfully, and if they capsize all begin to swim and right it and bail it out with calabashes that they carry. They brought skeins of spun cotton, and parrots, and darts, and other trifles that would be tedious to describe, and give all for whatever is given to them.

I was attentive and worked hard to know if there was any gold, and saw that some of them wore a little piece hanging from a thing like a needle case which they have in the nose; and by signs I could understand that, going to the S, or doubling the island to the S, there was a king there who had great vessels of it and possessed a lot. I urged them to go there, and later saw that they were not inclined to the journey.

This island is very big and very level; and the trees very green, and many bodies of water, and a very big lake in the middle, but no mountain, and the whole of it so green that it is a pleasure to gaze upon, and this people are very docile, and from their longing to have some of our things, and thinking that they will get nothing unless they give something, and not having it, they take what they can, and soon swim off. But all that they have, they give for whatever is given to them, even bartering for pieces of broken crockery and glass. I even saw sixteen skeins of cotton given for three *ceitis* of Portugal, which is [equivalent to] a *blanca* of Castile. This I should have forbidden and would not have allowed anyone to take anything, except that I had ordered it all taken for Your Highnesses if there was any there in abundance. It is grown in this island; but from the short time I couldn't say for sure; and also here is found the gold that they wear hanging from the nose. But, to lose no time, I intend to go and see if I can find the Island of *Cipango*. Now, as it was night, all went ashore in their dugouts.

On October 14, Columbus set off on a short exploratory trip of the island, rowing up its coast in one of his fleet's small boats. He had not yet tried a dugout, which of course was a canoe, the first recorded sighting of them. (The Indian word for them passed into the Spanish, then the English, language.) He arrived at a likely-looking beach where people rushed to the shore to welcome them, offering food and drink.

MANY CAME and many women, each with something, giving thanks to God, throwing themselves on the ground. They raised their hands to the sky, and then shouted to us to come ashore; but I was afraid to, from seeing a great reef of rocks which surrounded the whole of this island. Inside it was deep water and a harbour to hold all the ships in Christendom, the entrance of it very narrow. It's true that inside this reef there are some shoal spots, but the sea moves no more than within a well. In order to see all this I kept going this morning, that I might give an account of all to Your Highnesses, and also [to see] where there might be a fortress; and I saw a piece of land which is formed like an island, although it is not an island (and on it there are six houses), the which could in two days be made an island, although I don't see that it would be necessary, because these people are very unskilled in arms, as Your Highnesses will see from the seven that I caused to be taken to carry them off to learn our language and return; unless Your Highnesses should order them all to be taken to Castile or held captive in the same island, for with fifty men they could all be subjected and made to do all that one wished.

Moreover, next to said islet are groves of trees the most beautiful that I have seen, and as green and leafy as those of Castile in the months of April and May; and much water. I inspected all that harbour, and then returned to the ship and made sail, and saw so many islands that I could not decide where to go first; and those men whom I had captured made signs to me that they were so many that they could not be counted, and called by their names more than a hundred. Finally I looked for the biggest, and decided to go there, and so I did, and it is probably distant from this island of San Salvador five leagues, and some of them more, some less. All are very level, without mountains, and very fertile, and all inhabited, and they make war on one another, although these are very simple people and very fine figures of men.

Only three days and nights were spent on San Salvador, before Columbus decided to move on. He had been delighted by the cotton they had bartered for, even if he did feel they had perhaps cheated the natives. It was disappointing for him, however, that they had found so little gold, though the Indians were full of tales of how much more there was on the surrounding islands.

The voyage, like the arrival, had been relatively easy, with no dangerous seas or serious accidents. The earlier psychological fears had been overcome, no real mutiny had happened, and Columbus was now vindicated.

The island they chanced upon was green and rich and the natives friendly, open and helpful. Columbus, believing he had landed in the Indies, referred to them as Indians. He considered them to be intelligent but primitive, people who could well be turned into dutiful children of God. He clearly wanted to do his best by them, to be fair and kind.

One can also sense his keen interest in the thought of all that gold. He was obviously excited by the Indians telling him that a king on a nearby island had huge quantities of it. Several times, during those three days, he reports how the Indians are suggesting which islands have the most gold.

Were they perhaps deceiving him? There is a suggestion that the Indians could have been hoping the Spaniards would move on soon. After three days, the novelty of these strange white beings from another world was possibly wearing off; even the thrill of playing with a hawk's bell. The crew had had thirty-six days cooped up on board ship, and many of them had become convinced they would never see land again, never mind food and drink, or naked women. Since their arrival, they had naturally been celebrating rather enthusiastically.

However, as far as Columbus could see, the Indians were as thrilled by the arrival of the Spaniards as he was pleased to have arrived. The first stage of the Great Discovery was over.

Columbus arrives in the New World.

8

Bahamas Today

I WAS on the plane to Nassau, hoping somehow to get myself from there to the little island of San Salvador, one of the many islands of the Bahamas.

I had written to ten different countries in the Caribbean and South America, all associated with Columbus, asking for help in seeing their Columbian monuments and if I could meet any officials involved in their 1992 celebrations, should they be having any. Only two had replied. One of them was the News Bureau of the Bahamas government. They were clearly very excited about the whole world coming to celebrate in the Bahamas in 1992, going to San Salvador and stepping on the actual beach where Columbus first trod.

But did he? On the plane, I picked up a copy of the *National Geographic Magazine*. After five years of study, hiring countless experts, commissioning a new translation of the Columbus Journal, putting all the known nautical facts through a computer, allowing for this, adjusting for that, doing everything you might expect of a well-brought-up American magazine, they had come to the conclusion that Columbus did not arrive on the Bahamian island called San Salvador. Instead, he landed sixty-five miles away on a much smaller, totally uninhabited island called Samana Cay.

The controversy is not a new one. Over the centuries, nine different islands have been suggested as the landing place, most but not all in what we now call the Bahamas. Washington Irving, back in 1828, stated that it was Cat Island. Grand Turk has been put forward many times, and still has its supporters to this day.

Conception Island has also been popular. Other nominations have included Egg, North Caicos, Mayaguana and Plana.

Columbus does not precisely locate his landfall, which is what has caused all the arguments. He left many descriptions, but no settlement on the island, and almost immediately he went wandering round the other islands, most of which look very similar.

Watling Island was first suggested in 1793, but this theory was ruined by Irving, when he said that was simply the source of the light which Columbus thought he saw. However, Watling Island came back into general favour in the 1920s. The Bahamas government decided to settle the matter, and encourage possible tourist trade, by changing its name in 1926 to San Salvador. The great debate seemed to have been settled once and for all when Morison in 1942 pronounced San Salvador, né Watling Island, as correct. Generations of American school and college students have accepted this as gospel ever since. Until the *National Geographic Magazine* intervened.

My first surprise on arriving in Nassau was how American it looked. I walked down Bay Street and every accent, every shop, every fast-food outlet seemed totally American. I came to a break in the street and stood back in alarm as a monster skyscraper appeared to be moving towards me. It turned out to be a cruise liner, leaving its dock, one of the hundreds of cruise ships filled with Americans which steal right into the main street, then hang over the town like vultures. Around half of the three million tourists who come to the Bahamas every year sail into Nassau. Yet Miami is just sixty miles away, so why bother coming? The answer is gambling, which is not allowed in Florida. Almost all those Americans spend their time indoors in Nassau, playing the machines, chancing their luck.

The original inhabitants of the Americas when Columbus arrived were wrongly described as Indians, and the name has lingered on. Hence Cowboys and Indians. Those living in the Bahamas are often called Arawak Indians, though technically Arawak refers to South American Indians. Arawak is also often used for the name of their language, though this is not strictly correct either. The Bahamian Indians should properly be called Lucayans.

The Lucayans had been in the Bahamas for some 500 years, having migrated from the mainland of South America. Before that, who knows? Anthropologists are still arguing, but it is thought they came down from North America. Before that, they possibly came over from Northern Europe. And, before that, they might have been in Asia. So, they could originally have been Indians.

The Spaniards did not colonise the Bahamas, dismissing the islands as too flat and marshy, and they were virtually ignored for the next hundred years after Columbus had left. The next arrivals were the British, not directly from Britain, but via Bermuda. A colony of English settlers under William Sayle set up a religious community in 1647 on what is now called the island of Eleuthera, named after the Greek word for freedom. Nassau was laid out in 1695 and takes its name from King William III, Prince of Orange-Nassau. Most of the islands of the Bahamas have strange-sounding names, the origins of which are hard to guess. Andros, for example, sounds Greek, but comes from the name of a British Governor, Sir Edmund Andros. The origin of Exuma is not clear, but that could be Lucayan. As for the word Bahamas, this is thought to be one of the very few remains of the original Spaniards, taken from the Spanish for shallow seas – las islas de la baja mar.

The Bahamas became a white British colony, ruled from Britain, but gradually acquired a black majority population. During the American Revolution, English colonists who were loyal to the old country fled to the Bahamas, taking their black slaves with them. These were reasonably treated, compared with elsewhere, and together they prospered, with the white minority political party still in power till 1953 when the black Progressive Liberal Party took over. In 1973, the Bahamas became an independent country, but it is still part of the Commonwealth, with the British Queen as head of state.

It was hard to see many signs of those previous 300 years of British rule and influence, or to appreciate the fact that education and law are still run on British lines, until I came to Government House. It did look reassuringly British and colonial. The house, built in 1806, at the top of George Street, is pink and white, with two white-jacketed sentries standing outside, as immaculate as the building itself. It was the home of the Duke of Windsor during the last war, when he was sent to be Governor of the Bahamas.

I was not really looking for Britishness but Columbianism. On the steps in front of the main entrance to Government House I found it: my first statue of Columbus in the New World. He is in a fine position. As you climb the steps, he towers over you, gleaming white, about twice human size, wearing a big Spanish hat, a cloak, a short beard, and with a sword in his right hand.

I looked for a taxi which I was told would take me to Paradise

Island. There are 700 islands in the Bahamas, only twenty-two of them occupied, with a total population of 210,000. Nassau is the biggest town, with some 123,000, and it stands on New Providence Island. Paradise Island is just a little strip off shore, connected by a bridge. The taxi took just three minutes to get me there. On the taxi driver's dashboard hung a notice which said: 'I fight Poverty. I work.'

I had a meeting with Philip Smith, MP for San Salvador, chairman of the Quincentennial Committee. Cabinet Ministers in the Bahamas are full time, but ordinary MPs are only part time. Mr Smith is a personnel officer with a large hotel and leisure company.

'We're looking upon 1992 as a chance to celebrate the introduction of Christianity to the Americas.'

I queried the word celebrate. Several other black nations of the Caribbean were worrying about its use. 'Yes, I know Columbus and the Spaniards destroyed the Indians, but we are not referring to that. We have a nice image in the Bahamas, and we're going to stick to it. We're also celebrating the beginning of our own history. What caused us to be what we are today helps us to see down the road ahead. He who doesn't know history is bound to repeat it . . .' He broke off to answer another telephone call. 'We are all the same really, just that some of the waters got mixed up along the way. We can trace our pedigrees from black Africans, Indians, Spaniards, but in reality we are all now brothers. In my family, for example, six generations ago my ancestors were slaves, no more important than a dog. They couldn't read or write and owned nothing. Baby, look at me now!'

I asked him what was planned for 1992. There is already an annual yacht race from Spain, following Columbus's exact route. The Bahamas were being missed out at first, as Spain appeared to be interested only in Spanish-speaking countries, but after a bit of lobbying the Bahamas are now included. For the big race, in 1992, when three reproduction ships will sail, they expect the first stop to be in the Bahamas. As of course it should be.

For their own internal celebrations, they hope the Pope will grace them with his presence. 'I want to see him come ashore on the beach on San Salvador, as the leader of the world's Christians, and hold a commemorative service, 500 years ago to the day Columbus first landed. We also plan to build on San Salvador itself a new city, "Columbus – City of Peace". It may be ten acres, or a hundred acres. I know it's quite easy to call a place a city. Open a post office, and you can call it Columbus City. But we hope to build hotels, conference centres, and invite the USA, Spain, Italy and other countries to put up statues and monuments to Columbus, and of course hold international conferences there. San Salvador has only a population of 600 at present, and it's still falling, so it would sure help the economy of the island . . .'

But what if it was agreed by the experts that the *National Geographic* was right, and Columbus had not arrived on San Salvador? Wouldn't that be a bit inconvenient?

Mr Smith smiled. The vital factor was that the magazine had not named an island belonging to the Turks and Caicos, the next group of islands to the Bahamas, which is a separate country.

'That would have been a bit different. I would probably have gone out and shot them. So long as it's one of the Bahamian islands, I don't really care. I think the *National Geographic* has done us a favour. The story has been all over the world. Morison's grandson is said to have denied the evidence, saying Morison was right to say it was San Salvador. There are already academics who are finding flaws in the Samana Cay theory. It's a good controversy. I'm pleased by it.'

What he is not so pleased about is the assumption by the rest of the world that the Bahamas is just an offshore bit of the USA. He admits they are totally influenced and overpowered by the USA and that even residents look upon the *Miami Herald* as their national paper, considering the Nassau papers as small-town sheets. 'We have our own TV and broadcasting company, but everyone tunes in to NBC for their national news. It does seem as if we're some sort of suburb of Miami.'

He tries to correct mistakes as he sees them. He served on a parliamentary broadcasting committee at one time and was incensed when he heard a local TV newscaster come out with the words: 'Today, Prime Minister Pindling of the Bahamas met President Carter.'

'It was as if our PM was from a foreign country, and President Carter was our President. I made them change it to "Today, the Prime Minister met President Carter of the USA . . ." I am not anti-American, or anti-anybody. We just have to build up our national identity. When you consider the influence of the USA, it's surprising we have any at all. The Columbus celebrations will help us to establish who we are.'

Next day, I started making plans to get myself to San Salvador, which was more complicated than I expected. I had hoped to sail there, as it is only 154 miles by sea from Nassau, the sort of distance I might be able to stand, and imagine myself arriving like Columbus. There is no regular steamer service, just a mail boat, going round the islands, which takes some passengers and is supposed to land at San Salvador every three days. That sounded interesting. But I had not reckoned on bad weather. It was January, clear sunny spring-like weather to me, coming from London, but at sea it was rough and the boat had not reached San Salvador for the last three weeks. The island was cut off, except by air.

When I investigated the plane service, there was further bad news. None for four days, and then I would have to spend a whole week on the island before I could return. By the sound of it, a week on San Salvador sounded six days too long. Columbus himself only gave it three days.

I changed hotels while I waited, from a grand one to a not so grand one. Nassau is one big hotel, a totally tourist-orientated development, the source of huge wealth. Yet none of the Bahamas islands has any real natural advantages. They never get above 200 feet high. There is no lush scenery. How have they done it?

I went to see Basil Albury, Deputy Director at the Ministry of Tourism. He was beaming at the latest figures. They had beaten their own records by earning one billion dollars from tourism in the previous year. He now reckoned that, per capita, they were the most successful tourist country in the world.

Some of his reasons for this state of affairs were surprising. Columbus and the Spaniards moving on so quickly had been an advantage, as the Bahamas did not become Catholic. That helped, he thinks. Unlike most Latin American Catholic nations, their population has not grown beyond their resources.

Then there was luck. That played a big part, especially Castro's revolution in 1959. Until then, the Bahamas tourist trade was slight and seasonal, with only 40,000 visitors a year, compared with three million today. 'Cuba had been very popular with Americans, especially the sophisticated and wealthy. Once the communists took over, it scared them all off. We're now the number one place for Americans.'

Naturally, they like to think that careful planning has played the biggest part, especially since 1967 when their well-organised black government took over. 'Today, two-thirds of our labour force is in tourism and it accounts for 72 per cent of our gross national product. People say tourism is a fickle industry, and it could all collapse, but is it any more fickle than say argriculture? Sugar was wiped out here in just two years.

'A black looking like me, even just ten to fifteen years ago, could not be living in the area where I live. It was totally white. I can remember when on house conveyances it stated "Only for Caucasians". In fact you needed a white signature to get a bank loan at one time. Now that area is 60 per cent black. We have a black government, with a black cabinet, but the whites are not prejudiced. Those who left in 1967 are now back – and doing better. Some of them were poor whites then. Now they're millionaires.'

My hotel, the Nassau Beach Hotel, was half-empty, as the poor weather had put off even the hardiest Americans. I decided to have a walk along Cable Beach, expecting to have it to myself. I could hear a loudspeaker and then I came to a little grandstand which had been erected on the white sand, with people all around, shouting and cheering. In front of them, on the sea, there appeared to be a swarm of multi-coloured butterflies, swooping back and forward, their wings stretched taut to catch every breeze. I had stumbled across the North Atlantic's biggest windsurfing regatta.

I had never seen so many before, nor realised there are such animals these days as professional windsurfers. About a hundred of them were competing for $50,000 in prize money. It was so colourful and artistic, so clean and healthy, the bodies so tanned and beautiful. It seemed unreal. They could have been making a commercial for Coca-Cola.

I talked to some of the surfers, and learned that the world champion was present, Stefan van den Berg, a Dutchman aged twenty-five. He said he thought there were only a couple of dozen full-time surfing professionals, but the number was increasing all the time. Their money comes from sponsorship, and prizes. Today, the winning man and winning woman would get $10,000 each. His speciality was speed, so he said. He raced at up to 20 m.p.h. But slalom races were becoming more important, and those took different skills, different bodies.

That night, I got talking in the bar to some of the people who had been watching the surfers, most of them residents of Nassau, all of them white. They agreed that the present government had done a great job. There was political stability, economic wealth, no racial tension.

But, after a few drinks, some of their complaints and worries did emerge. One businessman felt that the black government was too keen on rewarding its own supporters. 'You now can't sack certain people, which is why some hotels are not as efficient as they should be. They wouldn't stand for this sort of nonsense in Miami. You'd get the sack on the spot.'

Another feared that the Bahamas were becoming totally material- istic. 'There is no social conscience. Because people don't pay taxes, they think therefore the state and the government have nothing to do with them. Rules and regulations are there to be avoided.'

All of them were most concerned about drugs, muttering about corruption in high places, drug-dealers giving out presents, poli- ticians who have been forced to resign. 'This is the last staging post between Colombia and the USA. A lot of crack comes through the Bahamas because we're so near Miami.'

Two days later, I had some good luck. I heard about a private party going to San Salvador, out on the scheduled flight, but hiring a private plane to return. They were said to be Columbus enthusiasts, had heard about my project, and agreed I could hitch a lift.

I turned up at the airport, as arranged, and met my companions, José Gomez and Paul Bower. José's father had originally come from Spain, via Cuba, working first as a carpenter, then moved to the Bahamas where José was born. He now runs the family tile- importing firm. His American wife Barbara was coming with us, despite being heavily pregnant. They already had a girl, christened Isabella after the Queen of course. If this time they had a boy, he was going to be called Cristobal. José is an active member of the Bahamas Chamber of Commerce and had just been elected chair- man of their Quincentennial Committee, hence his desire to go to San Salvador.

Paul Bower is English, tall and distinguished-looking with an Edward VII beard. He had come to the Bahamas twenty years earlier and stayed on; now he was running a little publishing company, producing guides and tourist newspapers. His wife Erika was also in the party. She is half-Chinese, her family originally coming from Hong Kong, though she was brought up in Jamaica.

The first thing I noticed when we landed at San Salvador's little airport was a large wooden notice saying: 'Welcome to the friendly island of San Salvador, site of Columbus Landings.' It was the plural which intrigued me. The airport was bigger than I expected, the legacy of a military establishment which was set up in the 1950s as part of the US space programme. For a while, it brought work and prosperity to the island and the population doubled to 1,200. No tourists were allowed during this period, as the work was classed as secret. Now they have gone. All that is left is an unnecessarily large air-strip, one road round the island grandiosely called the Queen's Highway, and a few empty army buildings. There is only one hotel, the Riding Rock Inn. The island is just twelve miles long by five miles wide. Most of the interior is as swampy and undeveloped as it was when Columbus arrived.

Our first bit of exploration was along the coast road to the Catholic Church of the Holy Saviour. The parish priest, Father Herman Wind, was in his shorts and a check shirt, mending his satellite dish with a pair of pliers. Outside his church, over one of the windows, there is a plaque of Columbus's head.

Father Wind gets the occasional visitor, in the steps of Columbus, but most of them are Spanish-speaking, from South America. 'I wish I could understand what they say. I'm only from Minnesota.' Then he went back to worrying about his dish. The church is near San Salvador's only town, Cockburn Town, which consists of a huddle of houses along the road, plus a few shops, a school and a clinic with a nurse in attendance. There is no doctor on the island.

Just outside the town, at the end of a long beach called Fernandez Bay, we came to our first Columbus monument, a small, pyramid-shaped white stone. The inscription read: 'Christopher Columbus made the first recorded landing in the New World on this beach, October 12, 1492. Yawl Heloise [a boat on a round-the-world cruise], Feb 25, 1951.' People who put up monuments are very confident: not just the right island, but the right spot on the right beach.

Two miles further south, on Long Beach, there is a much more impressive Columbus memorial: a large white cross, very simple, but dramatic against the bright blue of the sea. It was put up by Ruth Wolper, an American woman who has made Columbus her pet research subject. The inscription this time is more careful: 'On or near this spot, Christopher Columbus landed on October 12, 1492.' There is also a small plaque commemorating the visit in 1960 of Cristobal Colon XVII, the Duke of Veragua, a direct descendant of Columbus, a Spanish admiral and member of the government, who was assassinated by Basque separatists in 1986.

Around the cross are twenty-one poles where on October 12 each year the flags of various nations are hoisted. Nearby is a larger, circular monument, big enough to walk on, with a metal urn which was used in 1968 to contain the Olympic flame on its journey from Greece to Mexico.

The third Columbus arrival monument, and the oldest, is on the other side of the island, at Corab Cay on the east coast. 'On this spot,' so the tablet reads, 'Christopher Columbus first set foot on the soil of THE NEW WORLD. Erected by the Chicago Herald, June, 1891.'

No one seriously believes now that he could possibly have landed on that side of the island, on such a rocky, dangerous part of the first coast. The more likely landfall positions would be near one of the two monuments, on the other coast, where the long sandy beach is safe, with no rocks. There is, however, about a mile out, the inevitable Caribbean coral reef, though there are gaps. Columbus did very well, wherever he landed, to avoid any mishap.

That night, Paul and José and I spent a long time poring over Columbus's Journal for the days he was on San Salvador. Having toured most of the island, I had a much clearer impression than I had gained from looking at Columbus's words on my own in London. If San Salvador really is the landfall island, and his description of his approach and arrival do make good sense, then perhaps other references would be identifiable. Paul and José were particularly keen to establish the bay which Columbus said was big enough 'to hold all the ships in Christendom'.

Next day, we explored the northern coast and came to a dramatic bay beside Grahams Harbour. There were high limestone cliffs at one end, very dangerous, but on the leeward side the sea was calm and peaceful, with a long beach which would make a safe harbour.

We climbed on to the cliffs as Paul wanted to see if he could recognise Columbus's 'island that is not an island'. Sure enough, there is now an island, formed where a bit of the peninsula has broken away over the centuries, separated by a shallow channel, about twenty metres wide. It even has a name, Cut Cay (Cay, pronounced Key, means island in the Bahamas). In Columbus's day, it might have looked easy enough to create this island, with a day's hacking, and a little fort could then have been erected on the resultant piece of land. Was this in Columbus's mind? We all agreed it was very likely. Certainly the geography fitted.

As we came back, I looked down on the wild side, where the Atlantic was roaring and charging, and thought yet again what maritime wonders Columbus performed to get himself ashore safely. Below, there was a most alarming sight, a large tanker impaled on the rocks, half of its long-dead body under water, but the rest clearly visible and apparently intact. Only the blood-red rust on the hull and decks gave away the fact that the disaster had not happened that very morning.

I discovered later that the ship had been wrecked three years previously. Something had gone wrong, either a fire or engine failure, and it had been swept on to the rocks. The crew had abandoned it and disappeared almost at once, never to return. No one had claimed the wreck. It had just been left. Most locals on San Salvador suspect it was on the way from Colombia, possibly carrying drugs.

Not far away, just round the northern tip of the island, is San Salvador's lighthouse, the highest building on the island. On the way to it, Paul's wife Erika saw some wild pomegranates. They were small, very seedy, but the juice was strong and sweet. Then she saw some wild orchids, some ausidium (known locally as Christmas rose), and bay geranium, which is boiled like tea and drunk as a cure for a bad cold. At first glance, San Salvador had seemed to me barren and scrubby, with very few trees, none over twelve feet high, but Erika had continually surprised us, and herself, by discovering different types of cacti, flowers and shrubs. Columbus had enthused greatly over the vegetation, but I had presumed it had all vanished, or suspected he had been exaggerating, to persuade their Catholic Majesties that San Salvador was a better discovery than it really was.

From the top of the lighthouse we could clearly see the interior of the island, which had been hidden from the coastal road, and it corresponded with Columbus's description. 'Many bodies of water and a very big lake in the middle.' I would call them inland lagoons, not lakes, and they appeared very swampy, dark and disease-ridden.

Our last visit was to the island's little museum, part of a modern-looking private house, which we had passed several times, going up and down the coastal road. 'The Museum of the New World', as it is proudly called, is another creation of Mrs Wolper's.

It appeared to be locked up, but we knocked at the side-door and the caretaker emerged. 'I's Bobby Benson,' he said. On Nassau, it had been very difficult to identify a Bahamian accent. To my ears, they all sounded American, or mid-Atlantic. On San Salvador, there was more of a West Indian influence, in the look of the people and in their English. The museum was one large room, dusty and untidy, with show-cases collapsing, the displays wilting, the photographs fading and most of the hand-written captions almost illegible. The objects included some Arawak pottery and an Indian canoe. Best of all was a hawk's bell. Could this be one which Columbus gave to the first Indians he met in the New World? The caption, as far as I could decipher it, said it had been found in a

local cave. The museum is in poor condition, but perhaps it will
be spruced up for 1992. And perhaps there will be a better postcard
for visitors to buy. The current one shows 'The Discoverer' with
thick blond hair, blue eyes, clean-shaven, looking like Robert
Redford's older brother.

Before we left the island next morning, which was a Sunday, we
all went to the Catholic church where Father Wind was celebrating
Mass. His church had looked so bare and simple on our first visit,
but now it was a blaze of colour, absolutely packed, with around
eighty men, women and children. The girls were in silks and
satins, yellow and purple, brightly coloured tights, yellow and blue
high-heeled shoes, their hair in ribbons and braids. Some of the
younger men wore white suits with bow ties. These were the hidden
flora and fauna that I had missed.

Father Wind began by apologising for the lack of hymn books.
The mail boat had still not brought them, though they had been
ordered at Christmas. 'I fear they might have arrived in El Salvador
by mistake.' His sermon was in praise of public servants, a topic
nicely attuned to his audience.

There was no organ or piano and all the singing was unaccom-
panied, but the sound was tremendous, done with hot gospel
fervour. During 'Down by the Riverside' and 'Amazing Grace' they
all clapped and swayed. In front of me, a whole row of women had
taken off their shoes.

We finally checked out of the hotel, shook hands with all our
friends, and went to the airport for our private plane which Paul
and José had hired to get us off the island. It was a six-seater Piper
Aztec, built in 1967, the smallest plane I had ever been in, and
probably the oldest. The pilot got out his map and discussed the
route with Paul and José, as if we were going for a spin round the
block. Then we were up and away. There is no control tower at
San Salvador. You just take off when it looks clear.

Then came a big surprise. Paul and José had not revealed to me
what was in their minds, just in case the weather turned bad. We
were not heading back to Nassau, as I had assumed. The pilot had
been booked for a longer, more unusual trip, which was why there
had been so much map-studying. We were to fly south-east, heading
for Samana Cay, hoping to find the uninhabited island which the
National Geographic claimed as the real landfall island.

Paul soon had his camera at the ready, his notes and cuttings on
his lap, in anticipation of the first sighting. All I had was an
illustrated sheet map of the Bahamas I had picked up in Nassau at

the tourist office. Samana Cay was not even on it, although I knew it was supposed to be only sixty-five miles from San Salvador. I could see from the pilot's speedometer that we were flying at 150 miles an hour, yet we had been going for an hour without seeing it.

Through a gap in the clouds below we could see a large passenger liner. A few minutes later, in another gap, we saw the same liner again. When we came across it for the third time, the pilot very honestly admitted he was lost. He did a few more circles, trying to get his bearings, and decided to fly back the way we had come as we had obviously missed Samana Cay.

We found it, thirty miles back, a fuzzy blur on the horizon at first, which I thought was just another reef; then, as we got nearer, the shape emerged.

We dropped down as low as we could, to around 300 feet, so that the whole island was perfectly clear as we made our first swoop over its entire length. 'Look, look!' shouted Paul. 'That bay. As big as Christendom!' It was as large as the one on San Salvador, but I was beginning to think there must be thousands of such bays, all over the Bahamas.

On our next swoop, we all looked out for 'an island not an island'. We did see one which could fit the description, though it was a totally different arrangement from the one on San Salvador where the chunk had fallen off the rocky peninsula. There were no isolated rocks or cliffs, but we did spot a long flat coral causeway which at first sight, approaching low over the sea, appeared to be the coast, but turned out to be a long tongue of land, with a lagoon behind. It could easily be made into an island, and therefore technically fit the description, but in Columbus's mind he was going to build a fortress on it. No one would build a fort on such a flat strip of land, separated by only a few shallow feet of water. There would be no protection. We felt pleased that we had dismissed one of the so-called pieces of evidence.

After several other swoops, Paul instructed the pilot which way he wanted him to fly us back to Nassau, taking the route which Columbus describes in his Journal, starting from Samana Cay, assuming that was the landfall. This way Paul hoped to check off the descriptions and directions as noted by Columbus during the rest of his exploration of the Bahamas. We went first to Acklins Island, then Crooked Island (called by Columbus 'Santa Maria de la Concepción'), Fortune Island (which he called 'Isabella') and Long Island ('Fernandina'). Most of them looked much the same as San Salvador, with inland lagoons, sweeping white sandy beaches, most of them very flat, except for a few limestone cliffs, plus coral reefs and odd bits which could be islands but which are not.

Paul ticked off all the landmarks, checked the directions, and came to the conclusion, if I understood him correctly, that in some ways a route starting from Samana Cay, round the Bahamas, did fit in better with the route Columbus described after his landfall. However, on due reflection, when we considered all the evidence we had seen on San Salvador, the rocky island not an island, the size and shape of the coast, the finding of the hawk's bell, we came to the conclusion that San Salvador was still the better bet as the first landfall.

Before I left Nassau, I was fortunate enough to make contact and then have dinner with Dr Hoffman, one of the academic experts who had been employed by the *National Geographic* on their investigation. Columbian academics are hard to find, in the sense that the subject is so vast that they tend to study only one localised sliver of the subject, rather than his life as a whole. Charles Hoffman, Associate Professor in the Department of Anthropology at Northern Arizona University, first started digging on San Salvador in 1965, when he was working on his doctoral thesis. He has been back several times since, the most successful dig being in 1983 on Long Bay. On that occasion, they unearthed six glass beads, buckles and pottery, all of which were analysed and found to be Spanish. He even found a Castilian coin, dated 1494. There is strong evidence that San Salvador did have resident Indians at the time of the arrival, a vital point if San Salvador is to be accepted as the landfall; and the Spanish remains indicate their presence around the right period.

The *National Geographic*'s research, using a computer and sea charts, created a sea route which pointed to an arrival at Samana Cay, rather than San Salvador; but naturally, if no remains of any human habitation of any sort could be found on Samana Cay, this theory would fall flat. Dr Hoffman and his wife Nancy Watford, also an archaeologist, were sent to find out.

They were flown to Samana Cay by sea plane, and left to spend most of the next seven weeks living in tents. 'We woke each day at five in the morning, then worked from six till two o'clock. I had a piece of bread for breakfast, some peanut butter and a can of grapefruit juice. At night, we collected firewood, and cooked rice, along with sardines or corned beef.'

They chose two sites, took one each, and started digging. Fairly quickly, they found Indian remains, including some Lucayan pottery and bones from the late fifteenth century. The *National Geographic* considered that proof of Indian settlements mattered most, as there is clearly no doubt that Indians were on the landfall island when Columbus arrived. Finding proof of any Spanish presence was not so vital, as Columbus's men were only visitors, not settlers, and evidence of their arrival could hardly be expected to have lasted to the present day. Even any gifts they handed out would probably not have stayed in the same place. So the *National Geographic* was quite pleased with the results.

Now that the report has gone round the world, been agreed by some and refuted by others, does he sincerely think that Samana Cay was the landfall island? Dr Hoffman smiled enigmatically. He refused to say either yes or no. So far, it was all unproven, whatever the *National Geographic* had said. All he could do was list the pros and cons and let others decide.

San Salvador appeared to have the strongest case as the landfall island. Dr Hoffman agreed that the west coast would be the obvious place, somewhere on Fernandez Bay, but he personally would put the landing site at a spot called Bamboo Bay.

However, as Paul had observed, despite the negative features on the island itself, Samana Cay made good sense if you were coming from it, following Columbus's route, rather than arriving on it.

I offered my opinion which would explain the apparent differences. Columbus did arrive at San Salvador, but then in his log he altered a few of his subsequent directions, just as he altered his mileages, so no one could follow his route. That is how, by chance, Samana Cay appears to fit in better with his later movements.

Either way, the Bahamas still contains the landfall island. Let us hope the Pope does arrive in 1992, to bless it once again.

9

First Voyage – from the Bahamas, via Cuba and Hispaniola, to Spain

ON OCTOBER 14, 1492, Columbus left San Salvador encouraged by tales of bigger islands. What he hoped for above all else was gold. So far, everything he had discovered agreed with his maps. They indicated a large island called Cipango (Japan), off the mainland of China, and a string of little islands. The natives were not black, as in Africa, but did seem Asian, or how he believed Asians might appear. They were not civilised or developed, as the people of the Grand Khan were known to be, but that no doubt lay ahead. At least they were friendly, charming, attractive, dignified, despite going naked and being heathens; he was determined to treat them kindly and gain their help, and he insisted his sailors did the same. Six had been taken on board, fine specimens, to be displayed at the Spanish Court. One later escaped and got away in a canoe. During the next ten days or so, wandering round the islands, Columbus discovered how fast these canoes could move. 'There was never a boat which could catch up with them.' They could also cover enormous distances.

He re-christened all the islands he came to, ignoring their native, heathen names, and creating new ones which were either proudly Spanish, usually aiming to flatter his lords and masters at Court, or decidedly Christian, to appease an even higher deity. While sailing between Santa Maria and Fernandina, they came upon a lone native in a canoe, who stopped when they came alongside. 'As the way was long and weary,' writes Ferdinand, 'he was taken aboard.' Inside his boat, he carried a lump of bread, as big as a man's fist, some water and some mysterious dried leaves. 'They must be much valued,' so Columbus recorded that day in his log for October 15, 'since they offered me some at San Salvador as a gift.'

The Indian's other possessions were more easily recognised – glass beads and coins, all Spanish. Could they really be the first white explorers? Were there perhaps other Spaniards ahead of them, giving out the same sorts of trinkets? On cross-examination, the man turned out to be from San Salvador. He had decided to dash round the islands, showing off his treasures. Ferdinand has a nice explanation for why the Indians 'valued' the trinkets they had been given. 'They were convinced our men came from Heaven, and therefore wished some relic of it.'

When they got to Fernandina, they let the canoeist go, and gave him back all his possessions, plus some honey and a few trifles to give to his friends. It was a public relations gesture by Columbus. At this stage, he was clearly intent on giving a good impression to the natives, and to his royal masters at home. The object, so he writes, is 'that he may give a good account of us when (please our Lord) Your Highnesses send hither, and those who come may be welcome and given all they need'. Columbus is already thinking of colonisers to come, and the need to have friendly inhabitants.

At no time does he wonder where the natives have come from. He describes them very carefully, as he does their habitations, food, ornaments, customs, natural environment, but he never speculates about their origin. This might surprise us today, as we still argue about the origins and movements of the people of the New World. Columbus knew where he was, and who the people were, and he could easily see and imagine how they had spread out, speeding over the waves in their home-made boats, settling all the little islands.

In his log for October 17 he uses for the first time the word 'Indies' about the islands he has discovered. 'And on all these days since I was in these Indies, it has rained more or less. Your Highnesses may believe that the land is the best and most fertile and temperate and level and goodly that there is in the world.'

This matter of rain intrigued him, and Columbus comments on it several times. In European countries, even southern ones like

Spain or Italy, rain is usually associated with cold weather and being uncomfortable. But here the entire crew were delighted at finding it warm, tropical, refreshing rain.

Going round the islands, exploring the little villages, Columbus noted a form of dog which did not bark. It is not clear if these really were dogs, who had just not picked up the idea of barking (it has been said that Eskimos' dogs do not bark until they have encountered outside dogs) or they were not dogs at all, perhaps a form of rabbit or large rodent. References to these 'perros mudos' 'dumb dogs' occur throughout Columbus's explorations, but are still a mystery. Forty years later, Oviedo in his book about the West Indies said they were dying out, but he described them as looking just like dogs in Spain. The Indians bred them in their houses, trained them to capture smaller animals, and they were all mute. 'Even when beaten or killed they did not know how to bark.'

The Indians had a varied diet, meat as well as fish, even if some of it disgusted the Spaniards, such as fat spiders, which Ferdinand called loathsome, white worms bred in rotting wood and fish taken almost raw. They grew maize for their bread and also cotton, using it for 'weaving clouts'. They had all appeared completely naked at first, but as he toured the islands Columbus noticed some of the islanders were better organised, more used to bartering their goods, and that some women 'wear in front of their bodies a small piece of cotton which barely covers their genitals'.

The principal end product of their cotton weaving appeared to be internal furnishings, notably beds. This discovery delighted the Spaniards, and they all remarked on it when they had been in an Indian house. For once, the Spaniards took over the native, Arawak name, 'hamaca', hardly changing it. The hammock is still with us.

The Indians on every island he visited had been telling him about Cuba, the largest of all the places they knew, a land they called 'Colba'. Various other names and pronunciations were given, convincing Columbus that it was in fact Cipango, or Japan. On October 23, he decided to head in that direction.

The three ships landed at the mouth of a river, near a place now called Gibara, in the province of Holguin, on the northern coast of Cuba, towards the eastern end of the island. It was a large river, the first Columbus had so far seen, as all the islands of the Bahamas are riverless, so he began to wonder if perhaps it was not an island after all. He took various soundings by observing the stars and worked out how far from the Equator he was (all his deductions were wrong), still basing his calculations on the theory that in coming 3,500 miles he had reached the East. He now decided that perhaps he had arrived at the mainland of China, not the island of Japan.

The people were certainly not quite as he expected the Japanese to be. There were no signs of finery or exotic buildings. The inhabitants were much less friendly than any previously encountered, some carrying spears and running away when approached. The Spaniards explored down the coast, heading east, and visited several settlements, seeing strange images of women, which might have been objects of worship. They found skulls and a head hanging in a basket, and heard stories about a fierce tribe called Caribs or Canibs who were greatly feared by the locals and said to eat human flesh. (Cannibals and the Caribbean both come from the same root.)

It was on their arrival in Cuba that the Spaniards discovered what the dried leaves were for. They saw them being smoked; even stranger, people appeared to be somehow enjoying the experience. Columbus dutifully recorded the world's first evidence of tobacco, but he does not appear to have indulged himself, or seen much future for this weird habit.

If Cuba really was China, then not too far away must be the capital, the seat of the Grand Khan. At long last, the resident Arabic and Hebrew scholar, Luis de Torres, had something to do. On November 2, Columbus sent him, with another Spaniard and two Indians, into the interior with strings of beads to exchange for food, plus samples of spices, brought with them from Spain, to see if they could find any which matched. By now, they had realised that Cuba would not yield up any gold, so they might as well look for what the East was most celebrated, its spices. They also carried with them letters to the Grand Khan, from their Catholic Majesties, written in Latin, plus a few personal gifts, and instructions to make friends at court and pick up any information about towns and harbours. All this, so Columbus records in his log, had to be done in six days, at the end of which he wanted them back. It was a formidable undertaking.

They returned four days later, with very little to report. They had reached a native settlement, of some fifty huts, where they were welcomed by women who kissed their hands and feet, to check that they were real, and had met the local chief, but there was nothing which could be described as a city, far less a Grand Khan.

On the way back, they came across some men and women, going to a local little town, who were carrying 'firebrands' and 'drinking the smoke'. They had yet to learn the local word 'tobacco', but this time they correctly noted the act of inhaling.

Moving down the coast, exploring all the while, Columbus picked up six young men in a canoe, deciding to take them back to Spain, along with the ones already captured. Next day, he added seven women and three children, explaining that the Indians would do better in Spain with women of their own. That night, an Indian came on board and pleaded to be taken as well. Columbus agreed. He turned out to be the husband of one of the women, and father of the three children. Columbus related this incident as if to show how kind he was, and how happy the Indians were at the thought of being taken to Spain. Ferdinand saw his father's action in a similar light. 'This favour the Admiral willingly granted.' There were no qualms about seizing people, splitting up families, and dragging them off as yet more specimens. They were of course not Christians, therefore different rules applied, and it was anyway the custom of the age. The Portuguese had shown the way.

Columbus was already forming ambitious plans for the future, boasting to the King and Queen about the great trade with these islands that would ensue one day, all for the benefit of Spain. He constantly praised the climate and the scenery, and on one occasion (never repeated) boasted about the crews' good health. 'Praise be to Our Lord,' he wrote on November 27, 'up to the present among all my people nobody has even had a headache or taken to his bed through sickness, except one old man with pain of gravel from which he has suffered all his life, and he was well at the end of two days. This I say applies to all three vessels.'

Almost all the natives encountered so far had been friendly, ideal in other words for trade, and the few who were less welcoming could quite easily be subdued, either by a simple ruse, such as bartering trinkets for their darts, or with an even simpler system – overpowering them.

It is a surprise to find such a thought entering Columbus's head. He was still in the first flush of affection bordering on love for all the Indians, none of whom had shown a trace of hostility, yet he was contemplating war against them. 'Ten Christians could put 10,000 of them to flight,' so he assured the Sovereigns on December 3, 'so cowardly and timid are they.'

The most dramatic occurrence during the six weeks spent exploring the north coast of Cuba was the reduction of Columbus's little fleet of three ships to two. It was not caused by storm or shipwreck. Very simply, they lost *Pinta*.

On November 21, while they were looking for another island, said to contain quantities of gold, *Pinta*, under the command of Martin Alonso Pinzon, disappeared. Columbus's account stresses that bad weather was not to blame, as there was none. He puts it down to Pinzon's avarice. 'He was moved by greed to separate from the Admiral,' says Ferdinand. 'He could have followed if he chose. Instead, his ship being a smart sailor, he drew further and further away, until by nightfall he had completely vanished from sight.'

Apologists for Pinzon – and he and his brothers had many close friends and supporters in the little fleet – suggested it was a mistake. But, if his ship was so fast, why did he not reappear, knowing that Columbus had given strict instructions against separating.

Pinzon by this time was becoming impatient with Columbus. He did not agree with all his decisions, wandering apparently aimlessly in and out of the islands; or with his explanations of where they might be, which ranged from Japan to China, from a large island to the mainland. Nor with sending parties with Latin letters into the interior. The first excitement of the landfall, which had joined them all together in jubilation, was now over. Pinzon, for whatever reasons, had become fed up.

On the other hand, if it was a deliberate act, a form of mutiny, then why had *Nina*, under the other Pinzon, not gone too? Perhaps it was a sudden, spontaneous gesture on the part of Martin Alonso. In that case, surely he would soon turn up, but days passed, then weeks, with no sign of *Pinta*. The mystery deepened. And so did the explanations.

Columbus's first thought, as stated in his log, had been that Pinzon was motivated by greed, rushing off to find the gold first. Now, a more worrying reason entered his mind. What if Pinzon had decided to go straight home, to Spain, to be first back with the amazing news of the whole voyage, stealing all Columbus's glory?

On December 5, Columbus left Cuba and crossed the fifty miles of the Windward Passage, heading for another large island, which again the Indians had vowed was full of gold, and for which, according to Ferdinand, *Pinta* was making before her disappearance. Columbus dropped anchor at a place he named Puerto San

Nicolas, because it was the Feast of St Nicholas. On a map of modern Haiti the name has remained – the first place on Columbus's journeys which, in spite of wars and foreign invasions, has always retained the name he gave it. (Admittedly, San Salvador in the Bahamas is still San Salvador, but only after a long lapse of time.)

Columbus was delighted with his new discovery, saying it was even more wonderful than anything seen before, in fact the 'most beautiful in the world', forgetting that he had already used this phrase. He decided to give it a name which was neither regal nor religious, but simply patriotic – La Ysla Española. The island did seem like Spain; not just in its mountains and plains and river mouths but in the sort of fish they all recognised from their homeland, such as a local form of sardine, sole, mullet, lobsters. Columbus went so far as to describe Hispaniola, as it has been generally called ever since, as 'even better than Castile'. High praise, even from a Genoese.

The two ships moved along the coast of Hispaniola, exploring any likely harbours, looking at the settlements. One day, the sailors brought back a beautiful girl, whom they had captured in a village, wearing nothing except a gold ring through her nose. At every port of call, the thought of finding women doubtless entered one or two of their Christian minds. On this occasion, Columbus ordered the young naked woman to be clothed, and sent back safely.

In the logs and letters, we are constantly told just how naked the Indians were. This was not simply prurience. Spaniards always stayed fully clothed even in the most intense heat, to protect them from the sun. There was also the notion that being naked was un-Christian, wicked and sinful.

One has to read between the lines to decide what really happened when these naked non-Christians were dragged on board, and wonder if Columbus himself condoned such behaviour, or even participated. But his fine moral action over this particular naked girl had a beneficial result, which was his intention. The word went round that these strangers from the sky were good people, wishing no harm, giving out gifts, not abusing their women.

For the first time on his voyage, Columbus was invited to meet a local chief; not quite the Grand Khan, but a cacique, as he refers to him, a tribal leader of great local importance. He laid on a feast, entertained all the Spaniards, and in turn Columbus invited him back to the *Santa Maria* and gave him dinner in his cabin. The Chief ate the meats which were offered, and drank the wine, then told his advisers and courtiers to follow suit. After dinner, the Chief presented Columbus with a belt and two pieces of gold. 'I saw that a sampler which I had over my bed pleased him,' wrote Columbus. 'I gave it him, and some very good amber beads which I wore at my neck, and some red shoes and a bottle of orange water with which he took such satisfaction that it was marvellous.'

It is not known what the Chief did with the red shoes, but we do at least learn that Columbus had a bed on board, and wore beads. The only trouble, presumably, was the language barrier, but Columbus maintained he understood. When the Chief left, he told Columbus that 'if anything pleased me, the whole island was mine to command'.

For the next week, the week leading up to Christmas, it was unalloyed delight, as the entertainments continued and Columbus and the other Spaniards enjoyed themselves, enthusing about the beauties of Hispaniola, the landscape and the women. 'In other places,' Columbus recorded on December 21, 'the men try to conceal their women from the Christians out of jealousy, but here not. The women have very pretty bodies and they were the first to come and give thanks to Heaven and bring what they had, especially things to eat. They are as naked as their mothers bore them. In other lands, the women wear in front some little cotton things to cover their genitals, like a flap of a man's drawers, but here neither girl nor woman wears a thing.'

He exclaimed over the whiteness of their bodies, some as pale as those of Castilian women, and waxed lyrical on the subject of the climate. 'The air was like April in Castile, the nightingale and other little birds were singing as in that month in Spain.' He ordered his men continually to respect the local Indians, 'because they are the best people in the world and above all the gentlest'.

At the same time, in the very same day's journal, Columbus's thoughts were turning again to how easily they might be controlled. 'They bore no arms, and are completely defenceless, and very cowardly, so that a thousand would not dare face three. So they are fit to be ordered about and made to work, to sow and do all else that may be needed; and you may build towns and teach them to go clothed and to adopt our customs.'

It is very hard, today, to reconcile these two opposing attitudes, Columbus at one moment loving their gentleness, the next planning to enslave them. He was of course writing partly for his masters back home, to keep them interested and excited, pointing out the commercial gains. But it was also an attitude of the age: admiring the innocence of the natives, yet considering them hardly human, certainly not on a level with Christians.

Meanwhile, the good times continued, more friendships were established, the women still smiled and offered fruits, the celebrating and carousing went on as Christmas Day approached, with the Spaniards already in a state of rejoicing. On December 23, a huge party started, with all 2,000 of the villagers taking part, fêting the Spaniards with food and drink. In return, selected Indians were invited to visit the two ships, at anchor just off-shore. Columbus estimated that 500 of them swam out to the boats, as there were not enough canoes to go round.

Was it a judgement, the terrible tragedy which happened on Christmas Eve, a punishment for all this carousing and merrymaking?

Columbus retired to bed at eleven, so Ferdinand says, tired out, 'for he had gone two days and nights without sleep'. The sea was calm, there seemed no danger, so the officer in charge of the helm for the night decided he too could have some sleep, and, contrary to all regulations, left the tiller in charge of a ship's boy. The boy probably fell asleep as well, or was unable to understand what was going on, for in the night a swell got up, the boat drifted on to a reef, and Columbus awoke to realise the *Santa Maria* was stuck on the rocks.

Columbus immediately went into action. He ordered some of the crew into the ship's boat, taking the *Santa Maria*'s anchor with them, and told them to row into deep water and drop the anchor, thus making the *Santa Maria* secure. They started to do so – then rowed in the other direction. They were convinced *Santa Maria* was about to go down and had decided to head for the safety of the *Nina*, moored half a league away. It was dark, so Columbus did not know what had happened, but he was furious to discover that they had disappeared. He ordered the main mast to be cut down, so as to lighten the ship, but still *Santa Maria* drifted and bounced on the rocks, now leaning over at a dangerous angle. Eventually, as dawn broke, water seeped in and she began to sink.

On *Nina*, they realised what had happened, and refused to let the crew fleeing from *Santa Maria* on board. They sent their own little boat to the rescue and at last Columbus and the rest of the *Santa Maria*'s crew were safely taken off.

In the morning, it was obvious to all that the *Santa Maria* was finished, so Columbus decided to rescue as many of her stores and fittings as possible. With the assistance of the Chief and his villagers, who made endless journeys in their canoes out to the ship, every single item worth saving was taken ashore, put safely in a store and guarded. During this operation, 'not so much as a lace point went missing'.

Columbus was full of admiration for the Indians, their help and their honesty, but his mind quickly turned to recriminations. He blamed the helmsman in charge that night (he was also the *Santa Maria*'s master) and those crewmen who had fled. He said they were from the same area, all of them Basques, so the whole sequence of events could have been predicted. This is the first we hear of any internal rivalries. He also blamed the people of Palos for making him take the heavy and clumsy *Santa Maria*, which was not suitable for a voyage of exploration.

Eventually he calmed down slightly and stopped looking for excuses. He never blamed himself, as Admiral in charge, for all the communal junketing that had been going on, in which he was involved. The other part of his personality now comes into play, the good Christian, the devoted Catholic. He concluded that it had all been 'meant'. It was a sign from Heaven for him to do something. Especially as all this had happened on our Lord's Birth Day.

His plan, so he reveals in his log, had been 'to discover and not tarry in a place more than one day'. Now, he decided he would build a settlement there, a fortress on the beach, near the precise spot where *Santa Maria* had been wrecked, using her remains, all the wood and materials that could be salvaged. And he would call it Navidad, after the Nativity of our Lord.

To celebrate, the Chief was once more welcomed on board *Nina*, this time for dinner. He arrived wearing a Spanish shirt, an earlier gift from Columbus, and also a pair of gloves, another present. 'Over the gloves he made more rejoicing than anything he had given him. In his eating, by his decency and fine sort of cleanliness, he showed he was of good birth.' It is interesting to note that Columbus must have brought an extensive wardrobe with him. We know that on the first landfall, at San Salvador, they had all got dressed up to go ashore; now it appears he had enough finery to give clothes away.

On December 30, Columbus was invited to a grand reception at which the Chief was also entertaining five other local chiefs. During the ceremonial, which included Columbus being seated on a dais and given the Chief's crown to try on, he handed over some more presents. 'The Admiral took off a cloak of fine scarlet cloth that he was wearing that day and invested him with it; and sent for some coloured boots that he had him shod with, and placed on his finger a large silver ring because he had been told they had seen a silver ear-ring on a mariner and had done much to obtain it.'

During these festivities, two Indians brought some exciting news. They had sighted *Pinta*, just two days' sailing away, towards the east. Columbus's first reaction was not all that joyous. He noted in his log that 'all the evil and inconveniences came from the parting of the caravel *Pinta*'. It is hard to blame *Pinta* for *Santa Maria*'s shipwreck, but it is true that Columbus had been in a dilemma about what to do next. He wanted to explore more of the island, which he said was 'as big as England', but realised that with only one boat this would be dangerous.

The building of the fortress continued, as they waited for further news or sightings of *Pinta*. A party in a canoe went off to try and find her, but without any luck. Ferdinand says that the initial report of a sighting began to be disbelieved.

Meanwhile, they came round to the subject of who would stay behind, to man the fortress. There turned out to be no shortage of volunteers, which at first glance might appear surprising. Why would anyone want to be marooned on this island, with no certainty of ever getting back to Spain, or that supply ships would return with more materials? They had already been on their wanderings for five months, since leaving Palos. Some of the incentives, how-ever, were attractive. Columbus said their task would be to start collecting the gold, which he was sure could be found quite easily, using the pliant Indians to do all the hard work. Then there was the lure of the Indian women. The fact that the Indian men were cowards, as Columbus alleged, must have been persuasive (the Spaniards of course had arms). Just to make the point clear, Columbus exploded a few muskets and lombards at one of the Chief's parties, to amuse the guests, and add a warning hint that these men from Heaven could be warlike, despite their red shoes, silver ear-rings and amber necklaces.

On January 4, Columbus set sail from Navidad in *Nina*. There was still no sign of *Pinta*, but he did not strictly need her, as thirty-nine men were being left behind, roughly equivalent to the crew of the ill-fated *Santa Maria*. Amongst the thirty-nine men mentioned in the log were the King's butler, a marshal, some Court officials, a carpenter and caulker, a good gunner, cooper, physician and a tailor. They were given bread and biscuits for a year, wine, artillery, a barge for coastal or river exploration (presumably *Santa*

Maria's), and goods for bartering with the natives in return for food and gold.

It is not known what the general feeling was on board *Nina* as she sailed away. Were they relieved to be heading for home, or envious of those left ashore, safe in their new fortress, surrounded by friendly Indians, an idyll come true, even an El Dorado, if they found all that gold? Columbus did record his own feelings. He was worried that the crew of *Pinta* might now be on the way to Spain, to 'give false information to the Sovereigns' and escape the punishment they deserved for having gone without permission.

Two days later, on January 6, while anchored off Monte Cristi (now part of the Dominican Republic), they finally met up with *Pinta*. Pinzon came aboard *Nina* and apologised profusely to the Admiral for what had happened, saying it was all a mistake, he had not meant to disappear. Columbus appeared officially to accept the excuses. He forgave Pinzon and there was no mention of any punishments. The matter would seem to be over.

In his own log, however, Columbus is full of bitterness, even hatred, talking of Pinzon's 'insolence and greed, his lies and falseness'. He suspects him of having found gold on his wanderings during the previous six weeks, and divided it between himself and his men. So why did he not make an example of him, speak his mind, punish him in some way? The incident does give a further insight into Columbus's character, veering as it did between strength and weakness when it came to handling his crew. He admits as much, inferring in his log that he avoided a confrontation through fear. 'The whole enterprise could come to ruin,' says Ferdinand, 'since the majority of the Admiral's crew were Pinzon's townspeople and many were his kinsmen.' So he said and did nothing, needing their cooperation for the long voyage home. But he was determined 'to quit their bad company' once he was safely home, 'as he always said they were a mutinous lot'. He vowed to tell the Sovereigns about them, 'their deeds done by lewd fellows, devoid of virtues'.

Before they set off again, Columbus made Pinzon release four Indians and two girls whom he had taken by force and kept on board *Pinta*. He ordered them to be given clothes and set ashore, adding a very sanctimonious note in his log to the Sovereigns, telling them what he had done: 'Men and women are alike subjects of Your Highnesses . . . honour and favour should be shown to the people, because in this island there is so much gold and good lands and spices.'

Columbus seems to have forgotten that he himself had been capturing Indians, ever since they reached San Salvador. Or has he by now persuaded himself that all his Indians had clambered willingly aboard, desperate to be taken to Spain? In which case, why are there several reports of Indians escaping? Perhaps, as Admiral, he was allowed to do such things, on the Sovereigns' behalf of course, but others had to behave differently.

On January 13, while they were still working their way along the northern coast of Hispaniola, there was the first recorded warlike incident between Spaniards and Indians in the New World. It was only a small skirmish, and no one appears to have been killed.

They came across some Indians armed with bows and arrows which Ferdinand describes as being 'made of yew and are as large as English and French bows'. The Indians themselves seemed fiercer than any they had met before. Their bodies were painted and their hair worn long ('as do the women of Castile'), gathered behind the head in nets made of parrot's feathers. At first, the Indians were pleased to swap and barter their bows with the Spaniards, who were greatly intrigued by them, then they decided they wanted them back. They suddenly looked as if they were about to attack the Christians, getting ready to tie them up with ropes. The Christians immediately started lashing out with their swords, wounding several of the Indians, before withdrawing to the boats.

Columbus, in his account, says they could have killed many of the Indians, although they were outnumbered fifty to seven, but the officers sensibly backed off. He thought they were probably Caribs, the man-eating savages, so it was just as well to teach them a lesson, to frighten anyone else on the island who might think of attacking other Spaniards, such as those at the base in Navidad.

In his log, there is beginning to creep in a slight feeling of resentment. Until Navidad, everything had been sweetness and joy, endless exclamations of delight. First there was the disappearance of *Pinta*, and the ill-will between him and the Pinzons, not mentioned before, gradually becomes apparent. Then, when the *Santa Maria* is lost, he blames the people of Palos. On January 14, we learn that the two caravels are letting in water through the keel. He immediately blames this on the caulkers of Palos for not carrying out a proper job. He did reprimand them at the time, he says, realising they were not doing it well, but then they disappeared.

The most unexpected, and in a way dangerous, complaint appears on the same day, when he suddenly lashes out at unnamed enemies back in Castile, who he alleges were always against him and his venture. 'And they have been the cause that the royal crown of Your Highnesses has not hundreds of millions more revenue than it has, since I came to serve you (which was seven years ago on the 20th day of January) and more by which it would be increased from this time forth; but Almighty God will remedy all.' Las Casas adds, in quoting this, that 'these are his words'.

Although he was praising Ferdinand and Isabella for backing him against his enemies, he was clearly suggesting that, if only they had let him go seven years earlier, the treasures would now be rolling in. It was not very subtle, nor very sensible, to criticise his Sovereigns in any way.

On January 16, Columbus finally headed for home across the open seas, leaving the Caribbean. His last anchorage was off the north coast of Puerto Rico, though the Spaniards do not appear to have landed there. They heard tales of its being inhabited by cannibals, and of another island, called Matinino, which contained only women, all large and strong, who were visited once a year by Carib men; it sounds very much like the legend of the Amazon women. Columbus was greatly interested, but realised he must return to Spain, to break the great news, confound his enemies, and get supplies. Perhaps, at some other time, God willing, he would be able to return and explore further.

The two ships turned to the north, and continued to aim in that direction, rather than going east towards the Canaries, the way they had come. Columbus had deduced he would not be able to return by that route, as the trade winds which had blown them across would now be dead against them. It looks from the logs, however, as if there was some controversy about the exact route he was setting, with the Pinzons having their own views.

Nina, on which he was sailing, responded well, but *Pinta* started to drag a bit – which he blamed on Pinzon, for not having fitted a new mast in the Indies, when he had plenty of time, instead of being 'greedy, thinking to fill up the ship with gold'.

Things went well at first, with fairly calm seas, and in one day they managed the astonishing distance of 200 miles. But after a month at sea, around the middle of February, they hit high winds and soon a tempest got up, far worse than anything experienced on the way over.

On February 14, they lost contact with *Pinta*. She seemed to vanish from sight, while wrestling with the storm. *Nina* lit several flares, and for a while they saw *Pinta* lighting flares in return. Then nothing. *Pinta*, once more, had disappeared. This time it was for good, so they presumed, gone down for ever into the ocean.

Only *Nina* now was left, and Columbus feared she would be next. He worried that he would die and his two sons, still at school in Cordoba, would be orphans, 'left friendless in a strange country' (which indicates that in times of stress he still looked upon them and himself as foreigners). But, should he die, he hopes their Majesties will look after them.

They filled the empty water casks with sea water, hoping to make the ship more stable, but that did not help. So they all turned to God for delivery, vowing to go on pilgrimages should He spare them and return them safely to Spain. Each time they were convinced the waves had finally got them, and their little boat could not possibly be thrown around any longer, they made even stronger supplications, promising to go on even more arduous pilgrimages. It started with the promise of a pilgrimage to Santa Maria de Guadalupe (in Estremadura, but the name has been used in many places since, from the West Indies to Mexico). They drew lots with chick peas, to see who should make the pilgrimage, carrying with him five pounds of candles. Columbus was the winner, and considered himself fortunate. 'Henceforth he regarded himself as a pilgrim and bound to go to fulfil his vows.' The next draw was to determine who would go to Santa Maria de Loreto. This time an ordinary seaman was chosen, but Columbus promised to pay his travelling expenses. Then as the storm became even fiercer, they decided on a pilgrimage and Mass at Santa Clara de Moguer, the home church of many of the people of Palos. (The real name of *Nina* was of course *Santa Clara*.) Columbus won again, but insisted they should all make the pilgrimage together, should they survive.

It is easy from the log to imagine these thirty or so bedraggled, terrified sailors, crouching solemnly in the most sheltered corner, while a handful of chick peas is scattered on deck, one of which has been marked with a cross. Columbus meticulously recorded all the promised pilgrimages, adding his own prayers for delivery from the storm. The Good Lord had helped them on the way across, despite all the problems. It then transpired that, even on the voyage out, something Columbus never mentioned at the time, he had enemies on board who were 'making protests and determined to return and to mutiny'. He was revealing this situation at a disturbed time, in a state of fear, so it is hard to decide how real a mutiny it had been.

Columbus decided there was one more action he should take, apart from praying to God, and that was to clear himself with posterity. He therefore wrote out a full account for his Sovereigns of everything that had happened in the Indies, so that they might know the truth. 'This parchment he enclosed in a wax cloth, very well secured, and ordered a great wooden barrel to be brought, and placed it inside, without anyone knowing what it was, unless they supposed it was some act of devotion; and so he ordered it to be cast into the sea.'

His action is rather touching, though it could have been his reputation with which he was most concerned, setting down his account before any of his enemies might have a chance to do so. The thought of it all having been for nothing, that those years of struggle in Portugal and Spain had been in vain, that the astonishing discoveries of the last few months would never be known, must have been as terrifying to Columbus as the storm itself. By committing some written record to the waves, there was a slight chance the world might eventually learn the truth. And so, overboard went Columbus's remarkable story, into the eye of the storm.

In 1891, as the 400th anniversary of the discovery approached, an illiterate fisherman on the south coast of Wales found a barrel. The contents made its way to London, with money changing hands, and a publisher produced a limited edition, printed in Germany, of what he called 'My Secrete Log Boke', claiming it was written by Columbus. The fact that the journal was written in English should have alerted the world to the possibility of a fraud, but copies were sold, people were intrigued. In 1941, it was reported that the Columbus Journal had turned up in a library in Russia, but this was never substantiated. No doubt, around 1992, there will be further sightings and amazing finds. From the care Columbus says he took, his barrel could still be out there, floating around somewhere. In fact there could be two barrels. Ferdinand adds, in his account, that his father placed a similar cask at the stern of the *Nina*, so that if she sank it might float safely on the waves. He also says that Columbus put in a note, addressed to any finder, promising a reward of 1,000 ducats (to be paid by the Sovereigns) when the barrel was safely handed over. He thought that would deter any foreigner from destroying the barrel or the parchment. On a long sea journey, with time to think, time to fear, you also have time to worry about posterity.

On February 15, they sighted land in the distance, and there was much jubilation at having survived the storm, and excitement at the prospect of getting ashore, even if there was some doubt about precisely what shore it was. Some sailors said they recognised the rock of Cintra, which meant it was Portugal. Others thought it was Madeira. Others, ever hopeful, believed they had arrived straight back in Castile. Columbus was ill at the time, not having slept for three days, and his legs were crippled with cold and what sounds like arthritis.

It turned out to be one of the islands of the Azores, Portuguese property, though this fact was not recorded till a day later; Columbus added that he knew it all along, as he had always been heading for the Azores. He had let the crew think they were further on 'to confuse the pilots and seamen in order to remain master of that route to the Indies'. Sea routes were state secrets, and had to be protected, so Columbus was doing his duty. All the same, it is sometimes hard to fathom Columbus's deviousness and it makes one wonder if other lies still remain hidden and unrecognised.

They had arrived on the little island of Santa Maria, an apt name, though the connection was now just a sad memory. The locals were amazed to see them, as the storm of the previous fifteen days had been the worst anyone could remember. A boat came out with fresh food and water, and greetings from the Captain of the island who was elsewhere at the time. They were astounded to hear of Columbus's voyage, that he had been right across the world to the Indies, and rejoiced in his success and safe delivery.

Next morning, Columbus sent half of his crew ashore. One of the many penances they had promised to undergo was to march barefoot, dressed only in their shirts, to the very first shrine of the Virgin they came upon, wherever it might be. They decided to go in relays, the first group being told to find the priest and ask him to say a Mass.

As half the ship's crew walked to the shrine, the Captain of the island suddenly appeared with a company of townsmen. They approached the sailors, and arrested every one.

What followed was partly comic opera, though it might easily have had a tragic outcome. Columbus, anchored in the bay, was unaware of what had happened, but naturally began to be worried when his men failed to return. He sailed round the bay, to a point where he had a clearer view of the shrine his sailors were heading for. He could see men on horseback and some sort of commotion. He sailed nearer. Then a boat came out from the shore towards *Nina*. On board was the Captain of the island, who announced he had come to arrest Columbus and the rest of his crew.

Columbus refused to let the Captain come on board, warning him of the consequences when the King of Portugal found out what had happened. The Captain said he acted on behalf of the King of Portugal, and Columbus and his crew had been acting unlawfully. Columbus reminded him of the friendship between their Catholic Majesties and the King of Portugal. And he brandished his documents signed by Ferdinand and Isabella.

Despite his bravado, Columbus had a sudden moment of doubt. While the Captain was studying the Spanish documents, Columbus wondered if, during his absence, Spain and Portugal were no longer friends. Anything could have happened. They might even be at war. But he decided to brazen it out. It was highly unlikely that this provincial bureaucrat would know what was really happening in Lisbon.

The Captain ordered his boat to draw away, and delivered one final demand. On the order of the King of Portugal, Columbus must come ashore, immediately, and give himself up without further delay. Columbus responded by threatening to capture a hundred of the Captain's men and take them to Spain as prisoners.

For safety's sake Columbus sailed further out into the bay. The next day the wind rose and a storm got up. *Nina* lost an anchor and was forced to run for safety to a nearby island, San Miguel. Columbus, in a rage, waited there while he contemplated his next move.

Over the next two days they made repairs to *Nina*, before deciding to return to Santa Maria. They anchored at the same spot, and waited to see what might happen. At length, a boat came out from the shore, with five Portuguese seamen, two priests and a notary on board. Columbus produced all his insignia and official letters, even the one to the Grand Khan. They were sufficient at least to impress these petty officials. They studied them carefully, pronounced themselves satisfied, and agreed to return all the men who had been arrested.

Later, in discussions with the Captain, Columbus learned that the King of Portugal had indeed given orders for Columbus to be detained. But the Captain worried that, as he had failed to arrest Columbus the first time, and had let him sail away, the latter would return to Europe, as he had threatened, and lodge a complaint with the King of Portugal. So the Captain had decided to avoid a further confrontation.

The rest of the journey, back to the mainland of Europe, was relatively uneventful, apart from several more storms, and several more promised pilgrimages.

On March 4, they found themselves off the rock of Cintra in Portugal. It was not the country they would have chosen, given all the trouble in the Azores, but a storm was still raging and the *Nina* was forced to go for shelter into the Tagus estuary, down river from Lisbon.

As bad luck would have it, there was a heavily armed Portuguese man of war lying in the estuary, and immediately an armed vessel was sent to *Nina*, to find out what was going on and why. Various demands were made, questions asked. Columbus in reply asserted he was Admiral of the Ocean Sea and therefore beyond their control. After some initial suspicion, Columbus displayed his assorted documents to the master of the Portuguese ship, particularly the one requesting help from all nations of the world. The master read them, listened to Columbus's stories, and ended by congratulating him on his discoveries.

By an amazing coincidence, the master of the Portuguese ship turned out to be Bartholomew Dias, who had discovered the Cape of Good Hope and whose triumphal return to Lisbon in 1488 Columbus himself had witnessed. Almost every book on the Columbus story has highlighted this chance meeting between two of the world's greatest explorers.

But the only evidence for it comes from Columbus. Morison hedges his bets by saying it was 'probably the same man'. Columbus, in the logs, spells out his name clearly enough, adding that he was 'Bartholomew Dias of Lisbon'. In Ferdinand's account, strangely, the name of Dias is not even mentioned. Dias was of course a rival, and his success had delayed Columbus's own voyage, so perhaps Ferdinand did not want to write about him. But the dates tie in, as Dias was still in the King's service, as captain of various ships (unlike Columbus, he was never promoted to be Admiral), and appears to have been in Lisbon at the time. (He later went with Cabral to Brazil and died in 1500, at sea, when his ship went down during a storm, ironically off the Cape of Good Hope.)

Next day, news of the arrival of Columbus swept Lisbon. *Nina* was immediately surrounded by a flotilla of little boats. The King, nine miles away north of the city, asked to see Columbus, a command he could hardly refuse. He was welcomed enthusiastically, allowed to keep his hat on in the King's presence, a great honour, and made to sit beside him, and tell the whole saga. Columbus had a few Indians with him, as prize exhibits, and according to Las Casas the King checked the details of the story by getting them to make a map of the Caribbean on a table, using beans for islands. Some slight edge to the conversation crept in when the King suggested that the newly-discovered lands might be Portuguese, as the King claimed everything stretching west from Guinea, but Columbus denied this. It all ended amicably, with the King offering to repair and refit *Nina* and give any other help and hospitality on the journey home.

There is, however, an account in contemporary Portuguese documents, describing the same meeting, but rather differently. Some of the King's advisers suggested that Columbus was an insolent braggart and should be killed, then and there, or at least it should be arranged for robbers to attack him on his way home, so that Spain would not have the secrets of the Indies. The Portuguese Court was notorious for its brutality, and the King himself had stabbed his brother-in-law, who had been accused of plotting against him. Columbus's suspicious mind, and occasional paranoia about Court behaviour, would seem to have had some justification.

Nina arrived back in Palos on March 15, 1493, seven months and eleven days after leaving. Columbus did not stay long, going straight on to Seville, waiting to hear from their Highnesses, ready to accept the congratulations and honours he knew would be showered upon him.

Just hours after *Nina*'s arrival in Palos, who should turn up but Pinzon in the good ship *Pinta*. Neither ship knew that the other had survived. Thousands of miles, countless dangers surmounted, and yet they arrived on the same tide. Pinzon could actually see the masts of *Nina* as he sailed in, and his spirits immediately collapsed.

Pinta had missed the Azores completely and hit the mainland of Europe in the Bay of Biscay, at Bayonne, probably around the same time as Columbus reached Lisbon. He sent a message overland to the Spanish Sovereigns, telling of his safe return and all the discoveries. Two weeks later, the message came back that it was the Admiral they wanted to see.

This must have been disappointing enough, but it was far worse to see *Nina* as he sailed into his home port, knowing that Columbus would get in first with the news, and probably accuse him of desertion and stealing gold. The exact details of Martin Alonso Pinzon's movements are not known, except that he avoided seeing Columbus, and even his own brother, who was still on board *Nina*. He went straight to his house between Palos and Moguer, took to his bed, and died five days later. Was it suicide or a broken heart? Illness or exhaustion? Columbus went on into history, and Pinzon was left to die alone, unsung, unknown, with only his immediate family and crew to protect his name and achievements. And of course the good people of Palos.

Columbus waited a week in Seville, being cheered everywhere he appeared, applauded in the streets as he went to Easter Mass in the Cathedral. It was Holy Week, a good time for a hero to arrive. Local honours were bestowed upon him as he waited for the royal summons from Barcelona, where their Highnesses were in residence.

His arrival in Barcelona was a triumphal occasion. A special dais had been set up outside the palace, so that the whole of the city could watch, not just the King and Queen and their Court. Isabella and Ferdinand greeted Columbus in person, inviting him up to the dais, while the aristocracy applauded and the crowds cheered and waved banners. The Monarchs would not let Columbus kneel or kiss their hands, in the customary way, but made him sit down beside them and Prince Juan, as if he were an equal.

They then retired inside, into the great hall of the palace, where Columbus entertained a choice assembly of the Court to the highlights of his voyage. Servants circulated with trays, exhibiting the gold bars, and wicker baskets containing parrots. The Indians stood around, half-naked, wearing their paint, commanded at intervals to talk in their strange language, much to the amusement and delight of the ladies of the Court. For over an hour, Columbus enthralled the Sovereigns with his description of what had happened. Isabella hung on every word, her support and patronage of Columbus vindicated at last. Witnesses said that she had eyes only for Columbus.

Afterwards, there was a state procession round the streets of Barcelona. 'The Admiral rode on one side of the King,' wrote Ferdinand, full of pride for his father. 'Never before had anyone been permitted to ride with the King, save his very close kinsman.'

All the many titles and honours which Columbus had demanded were awarded to him, plus many more. Ferdinand goes to great lengths to quote and list them all, covering many pages, complete with the signatures of all the witnesses. The phraseology is highly legal and very complicated, but the facts are clear enough. Columbus had had confirmed all that he always wanted from his Sovereigns. 'And it is our will and pleasure that you, and after your days are ended, your sons, descendants and successors, one after the other, shall have and hold the said office of our Admiral of the Ocean Sea . . .'

The news of Columbus's achievement spread almost instantaneously. In fact the speed was remarkable, considering that messages could only go at the rate of the fastest horse. Four hundred years later, news of European wars and calamities were taking just as long to get through, and sometimes much longer. Yet, within two months, Columbus's voyage was common knowledge throughout every major city in the whole of Europe.

There was a ready audience to receive and accept and understand such discoveries and scientific achievements. A letter written by Columbus appeared in printed form on the streets of Barcelona by early April 1493, two weeks before he had even arrived in the city. In the next few months, it had been translated and was appearing in Rome, Madrid, Florence, Antwerp, Basle, Paris. By 1500, seventeen different editions had been printed.

The first edition of this letter is the most valuable of all printed Americana. As published, it was only four folios, containing around 3,500 words, so it was not a huge publishing enterprise. Columbus started to write it when he was on the last leg of his journey, having safely reached the Azores. He finished it the day he arrived in Lisbon. His object was to get it to the Spanish Court as quickly as possible, and he sent it off by messengers the moment he arrived. (Pinzon acted as quickly, though it did him no good.)

It is fairly simply written, a straightforward account of what Columbus did and saw in the Indies. He obviously used the same material as in his daily journals, and there are no new incidents or events of importance. The tone is efficient and in command, no overt complaints, no hectoring or special pleading of the sort which had from time to time poured out in his daily log. He was obviously confident, pleased with himself, trying not to boast too much, just giving the facts, letting the Sovereigns see what a marvellous job he had done. The letter was addressed personally to a friend at Court, Luis de Santagel, the Queen's Keeper of the Privy Purse, but was clearly meant to be rushed at once to both Sovereigns.

He begins by listing the islands he has discovered, using the names he has given them, San Salvador, Fernandina, Isabela, Juana and La Española, knowing that the significance of their names will be understood. Juana (Cuba), he says, is bigger than England and Scotland together, while Hispaniola is larger than all Spain. He saves most of his purple prose for Hispaniola, describing its harbours and coast line as 'beyond comparison with others I know in Christendom'. He lists the palm trees and other varieties of trees, the birds and animals, and then the people. You can sense him working his way neatly through a list of topics he must have made, sitting on deck, looking out for the first glimpse of Europe, recollecting in tranquillity and, so he hopes, with suitable modesty all the wonders he has seen.

He has nothing but praise for all the Indians he has met. 'Of anything they have, if you ask them for it, they never say no.' And there is a hint of self-praise. 'I forbade that they should be given things so worthless as pieces of broken crockery and glass and lace points, although when they were able to get them, they thought they had the best jewels in the world. Thus it was learned that a sailor for a lace point received gold to the weight of two and a half castellanos.' It was that sort of detail which had all Europe buzzing, eager to join the next voyage and get their chance to swap trivial trinkets for lumps of real gold.

Columbus was still convinced he had reached the true Indies, and that he had just missed meeting the Grand Khan. He emphasises all the trading potential and the profits to be made, and suggests that all this should be organised from Hispaniola, the most convenient place, with the best gold mines. He makes the most of Navidad, describing it as a 'large town and in it I have built a fort and defences', leaving enough people to run it, with plenty of food and arms, and the friendship of the local king, 'who took pride in treating me as a brother'.

He lists the materials which can be traded, from gold to mastic, rhubarb to cinnamon, and also of course the Indians themselves. 'Slaves can be shipped, as many as shall be ordered, who will be idolaters.' By this he means that, as non-Christians, it is acceptable to capture and sell them.

Columbus introduces some details which might interest or amuse the Queen. 'In all these islands, men are content with one woman, but to their king, they give up to twenty. It appears that women work more than the men. I have been unable to learn whether they hold private property, but it appeared to me true that all took a share in anything that one had, especially in victuals.'

He states that he personally met no monsters or monstrosities, despite all the legends prevalent in Europe, but he did believe reports he had heard of a tribe who ate human flesh. There was also an island to which these men went once a year, 'to have intercourse with the women', who live there alone, 'using no feminine exercises, but bows and arrows'.

Towards the end, there is a slight hint of complaint, but it is not amplified. 'The truth is I should have done much more if the vessels had served me as the occasion required.'

'In conclusion, to speak only of that which has been accomplished on this voyage, which was so hasty, their Highnesses can see that I shall give them as much gold as they want if their Highnesses will render me a little help.'

Perhaps this was slightly curt, even peremptory. A good and faithful and diplomatic servant should leave it to the masters to come to that obvious conclusion. On the whole, Columbus's tone was good and sensible. It was the contents not the style which were being analysed and marvelled over. The letter was considered astonishing, containing as it did fascinating and totally new material, for the Sovereigns to ponder and for the whole of Europe to wonder at. April in Castile, Columbus's gauge for what made a perfect time and place, had come true for him, in every sense, in that glorious spring of 1493.

Not just titles and fame and personal glory came pouring in, but political influence. Columbus's discoveries immediately had the two greatest powers of the day in deep and long discussions. Finally, the Pope himself stepped in, to arbitrate and decide how Spain and Portugal should divide up the world between them; all thanks to Columbus, and all based on the information he had brought back.

The high-level discussions were resolved in 1494, when the two countries met at Tordesillas, and they agreed to divide up the world. A line was literally drawn down the middle of the Atlantic, following roughly longitude 48 degrees, from about Greenland down to the Antarctic. To the right, or east, of that line, Portugal held sway. To the left, or west, was Spain's. The agreement established what had already roughly been happening, that Portugal would concentrate on Africa and that route to Asia. (By chance, this Atlantic line was soon found to cut across a slice of South America, that corner chunk which we call Brazil. This explains why Brazil became Portuguese, and still speaks that language, while the rest of South America speaks Spanish.)

That dividing line, created by Columbus's discovery, established the West Indies and the Americas as being Spanish and gave Spain the legal and moral authority which they tried to exert for the next 300 years. That one voyage, and the return of one very small ship (if we temporarily forget *Pinta*), led to the creation of one of the most powerful and richest empires the world has ever seen.

Columbus was now approaching his forty-second birthday. He was no longer a young man. He had been ill on the return voyage with the first painful traces of arthritis. His hair was already grey. He had at last fulfilled his ambition, achieved everything he had set out for, justified those decades of struggle and humiliation, proved his enemies wrong, received the praise and privileges he had yearned for. Deservedly so. No one was publicly gainsaying him or his discoveries. He could not have had a more stupendous or magnificent royal reception. He would have money for life, as his share of the trade to come had been agreed, as well as his titles. His two sons would be generously provided for. Already there were plans for both Diego and Ferdinand to be taken into the Court circle. Just after the grand arrival, Ferdinand, aged only five, was appointed page to Prince Juan, heir to the throne.

Why therefore did Columbus not decide to retire gracefully? He was clearly at the top, a winner, after almost a lifetime of failures. He could now enjoy his honours and privileges in comfort, savour the success and acclaim and wealth he had always wanted and had so bravely and resolutely worked for. He had surely earned it. He could marry again, and probably have Europe's finest and most eligible ladies to choose from. Let the younger men go off now, follow the tracks he had created, face the dangers and problems and awful discomforts which he had had to suffer. After all, next time he might not be so lucky.

This thought never seems to have struck him, not for one second. In that letter to the Sovereigns, written before he had even got home, he was already planning his return, wanting royal help for his next voyage. Lesser men, more ordinary mortals, and probably wiser souls, would have called it a day. But it was not in the character of Columbus. He was obsessive, as we saw in those depressing years before he departed, and obsessives do not suddenly cease to be obsessive. He had unfinished business, those other islands to explore, the Grand Khan to meet, the continent proper to conquer or control, and the garrison at Navidad to relieve.

He also knew that in some ways he had not succeeded, though he had disguised this feeling well in his official letter. He had not reached the East proper, nor the mainland, nor had he accumulated anything like the amount of gold he had boasted about, despite the tantalising displays he had arranged. He was convinced it was there, in enormous quantities, just waiting for him to find it, so why should others reap the reward for all his hard work?

Most of all, though, he simply wanted to go back. He so obviously loved the Indies, was passionate for the next excitement, the next island, the next horizon. During that week in Seville, awaiting the royal pleasure, he wrote another letter to Ferdinand and Isabella, this time more of a memorandum, listing all the arrangements that must be made, not just for the next voyage, but for proper colonisation, thousands of people sent out, towns built, magistrates and notaries appointed, trade rules established, with Cadiz becoming the main port of embarkation. By June, once the royal audiences were over, and the ceremonies fully enjoyed, he was back in Seville, making preparations.

As far as Columbus was concerned, the Grand Adventure had only just begun. Only with hindsight can one dare to suggest that it might have been better for him had he cried halt and stayed at home in Seville, basking in his glory, satisfied with what he had so far achieved.

Illustrations from a first edition of Columbus's letter, 1493.
Left, ship of the Santa Maria type. Centre, imaginative
impression of the islands Columbus discovered. Right, even
more imaginative view of Columbus landing, with extra added
oars.

10

Seville Today

I CROSSED the Guadalquivir and entered Seville, hitting the usual urban sprawl and aimless fly-overs which never seem to lead you in the direction you think you want to go. The old part of the city seemed as far away as ever. The river looked grey and sluggish, totally unattractive, like so many famous rivers whose names and history encourage you to think they will sparkle and shine.

Seville played a significant part in Columbus's life. It witnessed part of his triumphal return, which somewhat compensated for the miserable time he had spent as an unknown in the city, hanging around the Court. Seville eventually became headquarters of the New World, with the Americas virtually being run by its officials and politicians based there.

Everywhere I went there were signs and symbols for Expo 92, the World Fair being organised in Seville for 1992, the biggest by far of any of the 500 Columbus celebrations. Spain is determined to do her adopted son proud, and put herself once more on the world map. Over 200,000 new jobs will be created, just preparing for Expo 92, building new roads, bridges, improving rail and air links, and creating a new town on 200 acres of disused land, down by the river. The Spanish pavilion will be centred round an old monastery where Columbus once stayed. Later on it will become a university.

When Expo 92 is all over, Seville will still be the main centre for Columbus research. No one on the Columbus trail can fail to visit its Cathedral, and peer at the Columbus monument, or go to the Columbus Library and see his original books left by his son

Ferdinand, or do research in the massive Archives of the Indies. But would I get in to all of these? Once again, few of my letters had been answered. But this time I had copied Columbus. It was not quite a letter to the Grand Khan from their Catholic Majesties, just an official-looking document, written in formal Spanish, signed by the Director of the Spanish Institute in London, saying how important I was and requesting all possible assistance.

Cervantes spent much of his youth in Seville, and Don Quixote, his most famous creation, was supposedly born in a Sevillian prison. Many European writers have been fond of seeing connections between Don Quixote, tilting at windmills, carried away by his own crazy notions, and Columbus, as if he somehow typifies a certain sort of Spanish mentality. They forget of course that he was not Spanish. You could as well make comparisons with to Don Juan, another fictional hero, also from Seville; or the Barber of Seville, as portrayed by Beaumarchais and Rossini; or even Bizet's flighty Carmen.

I had booked myself into a little hotel very near the Cathedral. I liked its name, the Murillo, after the painter, another famous Sevillian. I knew it was in Seville's oldest district, Santa Cruz, but I had not realised how old. The streets did not seem to have been altered since medieval days. They were about four feet wide, scarcely more than alleys, impossible to drive down. I went round and round, getting nowhere, chased endlessly by traffic police. Eventually I left the car in a little square, pleading with a policeman to give me fifteen minutes' grace, before chucking me in prison, and I ran with my bags down the narrow streets to the Murillo, checked in, then returned. The hotel had given me the name of a car park, a few streets away, across the Avenida, but it was full. In the end, I drove all the way back to the airport, just to find a place to park the car. Then I got a taxi back to town.

It was late afternoon by the time I had unpacked and washed, so I went for a stroll, to get my bearings. In one of the neighbouring narrow streets I found a plaque, high up on a wall, in honour of Washington Irving, the biographer of Columbus. I got to the Cathedral, only to find it closed, but I did find a most impressive Columbus monument in some pretty gardens outside the walls of the Alcázar. Isabella and Ferdinand featured prominently, as did a very arty cut-out of the *Santa Maria*, sticking out of the column. Columbus was at the bottom, half-hidden by a permanent spray from the fountain, doomed to be for ever wet.

The following morning, I set off again for the Cathedral. I

expected it to be white and dazzling, like a bigger Rabida, or multi-coloured and startling, like the Duomo in Florence, but it was rather dour and northern, fussy rather than flashy. It was being built while Columbus was in Seville, on the site of what was once a mosque, till the Moors were thrown out. 'Let us build a church that is so big that we shall be held insane,' said one of the clergy. The result is the third biggest Christian church in the world, after St Peter's in Rome and St Paul's in London.

The Columbus monument is hard to miss as it is just inside the main door. It is a vast tableau, part of a supposed funeral procession, showing Columbus's coffin, containing his relics, being borne aloft by four princelings, all covered in gold and gilt. Columbus would have been both impressed and deeply satisfied. It was designed in 1891, in time for the 400th celebrations.

The Cathedral was dark and gloomy, in the southern European fashion, and there seemed to be no attendants to answer my questions, just hordes of Spanish children rushing around. I was now looking for the Columbus Library, the famous collection which belonged to Ferdinand, containing books his father had personally annotated, one of the primary sources for Columbus scholars. The Library is supposed to be in the Cathedral.

I knocked at the door to a little office and in my best prepared Spanish asked a cleric for directions. He had no idea what I was talking about. I got out my letter of introduction, but he would not even look at it. A very dignified Mexican lady, in eloquent Spanish, came to my assistance, but she was brushed away as well. Then another official appeared and said the Library had moved. The roof had collapsed in the room where it used to be. It was now in the Archbishop's Palace, outside, across the square.

I stumbled down long corridors, in and out of hidden courtyards, opening doors at random. I caught some high-ranking cleric half-dressed, judging by the purple robes he was struggling into, so I quickly closed his door. I tried some more rooms, all empty, and wondered how big a library it would be. It might well be just a large shelf in someone's room, or a hall the size of the Bodleian.

I opened another door, expecting yet another empty room, and was startled to find it full of people. There were eight young librarians, mostly women, sitting at a large rectangular table, all smoking heavily. My first reaction was to cough and jump back. They were just as surprised to find a stranger breaking in upon their meeting in the depths of the Palace. On the table in front of them were lots of dusty boxes and faded index cards.

One of the women jumped up and tried to usher me out, saying it was private, very private. I waved my letter. She stared at me for a while, then sat down and read it, watching my face at the same time. Others came and read it over her shoulder, also studying me carefully. Then one of them, in halting English, said she was sorry, they were closed, no one was allowed in.

I pleaded with them. If only I could just see one of Columbus's books, not to read or use, just to be able to say I had seen Columbus's handwritten marginalia with my own eyes. They all looked puzzled. None of them knew anything about Columbus's handwriting. I tried to explain. They said it was no use. They were working through 70,000 books, the Cathedral's entire stock, re-cataloguing every one. They had not come to the Biblioteca Columbina yet.

I started to plead again, but they said it was impossible, they could never find the right books. What if I give you a few titles, could you not quickly look them up? The first woman sighed. All right, she would look for one, and only one, and, if it could not be found quickly, that would be it, and I would have to leave. I agreed.

I had not expected such an interrogation and had therefore not prepared myself with a list of individual titles. I had read enough about the importance of the Library, and remembered some of Columbus's marginal comments, but not which books they were in, let alone their exact titles and authors and publishers and dates. They would probably be wanting international standard book numbers next.

Seneca, I said, Columbus read a lot of Seneca. Which works? You get the list out, I said, and I'll tell you the exact ones. She extracted some dusty records and turned up twenty cards, each referring to a copy of a book by Seneca. Many of the editions were published too late to be read by Columbus, so I pointed to one dated 1457, thinking that might well have been a copy he read as a young man.

The librarian made me stay in the room, while she left, saying I could not follow her to the store room. I tried to remember when printed books first reached Spain. Gutenberg's Mazarin Bible was 1456, but it took a decade or so for printing to be done in Spain. Could Columbus have used handwritten books?

She reappeared with a beautifully bound volume, very old, but in excellent condition. It was in handwriting, but so uniform and immaculate that it looked like printing. Its title was *Tragedianum Senecae*. A cross-check with the record cards confirmed it was from the Columbus Library, so that was a good sign. Inside the book, there was a handwritten note in ink which said 'debio obtener lo de so padre Tio od de algun amigi herencia o donativo'. With the help of my dictionary, I took this to mean that the book belonged to Ferdinand's father and uncle, and was left as a gift by him. So the chances were that Columbus himself had handled it at some time.

I turned the pages carefully, looking for any marginalia. At first there seemed to be nothing, each page virgin and unmarked, but then I found several short paragraphs, in small handwriting, extremely neatly done in the margins, but very faded. I strained hard to read them. Several librarians came to help me, crowding round. We decided the added words were in Latin. Sadly, there is no record of Columbus being able to write Latin. One librarian thought the notes had been written at the time of the book, in the same hand, by the monk who copied it out. They all shared my disappointment that I had not been able to see Columbus's writing.

I asked for one last favour. Could they possibly find anything by Ptolemy? Columbus relied a lot on his astronomical and carto-graphical work. They looked at the yellowing record cards again and I pointed to a work dated 1513, the oldest I could see, too late for Columbus himself to have used. It apparently belonged to Ferdinand himself, judging by a note in his hand at the beginning. It was printed, large format, full of fascinating maps, showing the discoveries of the Catholic Monarchs in 1513. I noted that Cuba was being called Isabela and Hispaniola was spelled 'Spagnolia' and Jamaica was 'Jamaiqui' while the Virgin Islands were 'Ionizes mil Virgines'. Over Brazil was written 'Terra Icognita'.

I thanked the librarians for their help, and wished them good luck over the next year. I felt envious of those future writers and researchers coming to the Columbus Library who would be able to find the names of the precise books which Columbus owned and annotated. I doubted, though, whether they would be able to handle them. Or the bureaucracy.

Next day, I set off for the Archives of the Indies. I had tried telephoning to make an appointment, but without any success. The Archives are in a large and impressive building, across the square from the Cathedral. It was built in 1572 as Seville's stock exchange, till King Carlos II decided it would make a suitable home for his most precious archives, those referring to the Indies. He considered that the conquest of the Indies was 'the grandest enterprise ever undertaken by a nation' and was eternally proud that his country had done the job of 'discovering, conquering, evangelising, humanising

There are over 70 portraits of Columbus in existence – but not one is
contemporary. This was done in 1519, thirteen years after his death.
*Christopher Columbus by Sebastians del Piombo, reproduced courtesy The
Metropolitan Museum of Art, New York.*

Columbus Portraits:
According to his son, he had
blond hair when young, which
quickly turned grey. There are
no reports of him going bald.
*Portrait of Columbus by
Ghirlandaio reproduced
courtesy the Museo Navale,
Pegli, Genoa.*

His eyes were always described
as 'light coloured', so these are
too dark, but the grey hair looks
realistic. *Private Collection.*

A modern view of Columbus, looking as handsome as Robert Redford. *Reproduced courtesy Ruth G. Wolper, New World Museum, San Salvador, Bahamas.*

Above – Columbus on a roundel, in Paris. *Copyright photo – Musée de la Marine, Paris.* Right – Columbus on a mural in the Capitol, Washington. *Architect of the Capitol.*

Genoa, where Columbus was born in 1451. Its wealth and power in the 15th century stemmed from its magnificent natural harbour.
Reproduced courtesy the Museo Navale, Pegli, Genoa.

Left – Queen Isabella, staunch supporter of Columbus, though she never actually had to pawn her jewellery to finance his voyage. *Reproduced courtesy the Museo Navale, Madrid.* Below – Idealised impression of Columbus arriving in the New World with flags of Spain. *Architect of the Capitol, USA.*

Columbus Arrives:
Above – Italian version, welcomed by
Indians. *Mary Evans/Explorer.*
Right – French version, sighting
land. *Photo J. L. Charnet.*

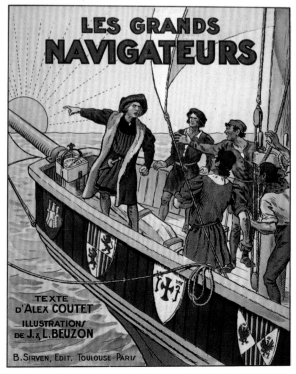

LES GRANDS
NAVIGATEURS

TEXTE
D'ALEX COUTET
ILLUSTRATIONS
DE J. & L. BEUZON

B. SIRVEN, EDIT. TOULOUSE-PARIS

Our Intrepid Author on the Columbus Trail: Hunter Davies arrives on San Salvador, confused by all the landings; in Madeira, posing with a statue; in Genoa, outside the so-called birth place; in Jamaica, on the empty beach where Columbus was stranded for a year.

and populating an empty and silent continent, from pole to pole, from sea to sea'. These words are still being quoted today, in modern guide books to Seville, and Spaniards are encouraged to honour those who 'gave their flesh, their blood, to fill an empty, silent continent with a dark smile and a sweet accent'. I wondered what the black politicians in Jamaica or Haiti might think of that.

I entered by the main door and walked up a steep marble staircase, passing students carrying bulky files. I came to a table and handed over my letter of introduction, asking an official if I could see the Director. I thought I might as well start at the top. A porter would have done, just to point me down a few corridors. The official disappeared with my letter, the top copy, and I thought I would never see it or him again.

I sat for about half an hour, watching the students coming in and out. Then came the surprise. The Director would see me, this very moment. I was taken on a route march, then shown into a room about the size of the Albert Hall, hung with enormous portraits of Spanish royals and assorted grandees. It was more like a ballroom than an office. I recognised Isabella and Ferdinand and the present King of Spain.

The Director turned out to be a jolly-looking, middle-aged woman, dressed like a humble junior clerk, perched at a small desk in the far corner of the vast room. She was beckoning me to sit down on a sofa, while she talked on the telephone. When she finished, I explained my project, and how I would dearly like to look at any original Columbus manuscripts, anything at all, or any material belonging to Ferdinand, or even to Las Casas.

She shook her head. Impossible. They had a new policy. Even the world's most important scholars could no longer handle the original Columbus documents. Everyone had to work from photocopies. They were perfectly adequate. She could order some for me now, whatever I wanted.

I put on my best crestfallen face. All this way from London. Just a quick peep. I promise not to handle. No, she said, terribly sorry, but she could not help. They were just too precious to take out, for anyone. So we chatted a bit, about the running of the archives, problems of conservation, how long she had worked here. From time to time, she took other 'phone calls, making mock-serious faces when it was 'The Minister' on the line.

Then she suddenly got up, took a huge bunch of keys from a drawer in her desk, and walked across her vast office to a wooden cabinet not far behind me. I had noticed two of them, old fashioned tallboys. She took a dusty box from one of the drawers and sat down on the sofa beside me, flicking through the contents, till she came to the bundle she was looking for, the original Columbus documents. The first item she handed me to look at was quite modern, dated 1927 in fact, and was a copy of the cheque paid by the Spanish Government to the Duke of Veragua (Columbus's heir) when he passed over his family's archives to the state. Along with it were various press cuttings and letters, giving details of the purchase. How interesting, I thought, that the top document in the nation's Columbus archives should refer to money. After all, it was gold which spurred him on, and which became the basis of the whole Spanish Conquest.

Then we came to the original documents, many signed by Isabella and Ferdinand – 'Yo el Rey', 'Yo la Reina' – and also by Columbus himself, letters he had written to their Catholic Majesties.

I was particularly thrilled to hold and touch one letter which he had finished off with his mysterious signature. This is a sequence of letters and initials, arranged over four lines in a special pattern. I had first caught sight of it in Genoa, framed in their archives.

Columbus had adopted this strange signature on his return to Seville; it was part of his assumption of lordly importance, now that he was an Admiral and Viceroy, not to mention God's Messenger. For centuries, learned men have struggled to decipher it, looking for Latin allusions, Biblical references, Spanish, Portuguese or Jewish influences. There is still no clear agreement on what it all means, though, as I could see, the letters themselves are easy enough to make out, even 500 years later.

S.

S.   A.   S.

X   M   Y

Xpo   FERENS

The last line stands for Christopher, and might even be a complicated verbal pun on his name, Christo-pher, Christian man of iron. The third-line letters are presumably religious, standing perhaps for Christ, Mary, Joseph, which is what Morison suggested. (While I was in Genoa, the Director of their archives told me he thought XMY stood for Christiams, Moors and Jews) As for the first two lines, they are anyone's guess, though the first S is often taken to be Salva (save me). I feel sure, whatever the meaning, that it reflects considerably on his character, a sign of his wit, his learning, or perhaps just delusions of grandeur.

The Director did not give me much longer to study it. The letter I was holding, one of forty-five known examples of his fanciful signature, is dated 1503 and was written to a cleric. It was heavily creased and the ink rather blotchy. The Director said it would not last much longer, if she allowed many other people to handle it. She put it away, with the other documents, and I thanked her profusely.

I left Seville, impressed by their archives, impressed by their grand preparations for 1992, and with one further thought: Columbus would be pleased, and amused, to think that people are still trying to discover his secrets.

Letter from Columbus to the bank of St George, Genoa, April 2, 1502: note the distinctive signature.

11

The Second Voyage

COLUMBUS'S SECOND Voyage was magnificent. The size and scale of it, the preparations and planning, and then the glorious departure, all of it made people catch their breath in awe. By comparison, those three little ships which had left Palos, just over one year previously, crept out, rather than departed.

Columbus was now based in Seville, and acting like a grandee, not an unknown foreign upstart setting off from a small provincial harbour. He was preparing for a veritable armada to carry a complete civilisation across the ocean.

Their Majesties held back from allowing him complete freedom of the purse, appointing the Archdeacon of Seville, Fonseca, as the overall treasurer and administrator, helped by two other officials. There was some ill-feeling, as Columbus maintained they were penny-pinching, or did not sufficiently recognise that as Admiral of the Ocean he should have the final say in all matters pertaining to his lands, which he had discovered. But there was so much to be done, so much to spend, so much excitement all round, that these little local differences did not really matter.

The ninety who had gone on the first voyage had not been conscripted, and were not criminals, as has often been alleged, but many had been 'persuaded', by Columbus and the Pinzons. This time, everyone was a volunteer, indeed clamouring to go, begging to be included. Most were not contemplating a quick voyage, a brief expedition, there and back, but a long-term commitment, perhaps even permanent settlement. The aim in the summer of

1493 was Colonisation of the Known. In the summer of 1492 it had been Exploration of the Unknown.

The fleet this time numbered seventeen ships which were to carry horses and sheep, seeds and cereals, plants and grapevines. There were farmers ready to train others to start farms; technicians who could create roads, canals, irrigation systems. Over 1,200 men were chosen, picked from the hordes who had applied. Surprisingly, only two were friars, to carry God's message to the heathen and administer to the travelling army of good Catholics. Perhaps Columbus preferred men who would contribute positive trading and commercial skills to the search for El Dorado. (That phrase was still to be coined, but the underlying desire for quick wealth was already apparent.)

The *Nina* was sailing again, though she had changed her name to the *Santa Clara*, and many of her original crew had enrolled, particularly from Moguer, near Palos. But not one Pinzon was on board this time. Columbus's flagship was again called *Santa Maria*, but her name was later altered to *Maria La Galante*, when it was realised how well she sailed. Columbus had proper quarters this time, as befitted a real admiral, with a real fleet. The master of his ship was a well-connected captain called Antonio de Torres, who had friends at Court.

They set sail from Cadiz on September 25, 1493. Palos was too small to supply and launch such a large number of ships, materials and men, so they moved a hundred kilometres down the coast. Cadiz organised a grand display for the departure, with banners and music. Prince Juan himself, heir to the throne, watched from the top of a lighthouse as they left the harbour. Also watching were Diego and Ferdinand, aged thirteen and five, Columbus's sons. Ferdinand gives a total of 1,500 who were on board, though most experts think it was nearer 1,200. He remarks on the large number of 'caballeros y hidalgos', gentlemen adventurers with private means, mixing with the 'peasants and artisans', who were there to do the physical work. It is not clear if some of the gentlemen paid their passage, just for the honour of being there, or for the sport, or whether it was on the understanding that they would have roles to play, once the trading colonies were established.

Alas, Columbus's log of the Second Voyage has not been preserved. He presumably kept one, as he did on the First Voyage, to record the evidence of his triumphs and discoveries. On the First Voyage, he produced several accounts, with copies, out of both panic and pride, fearful that he might never survive, so it is not surprising

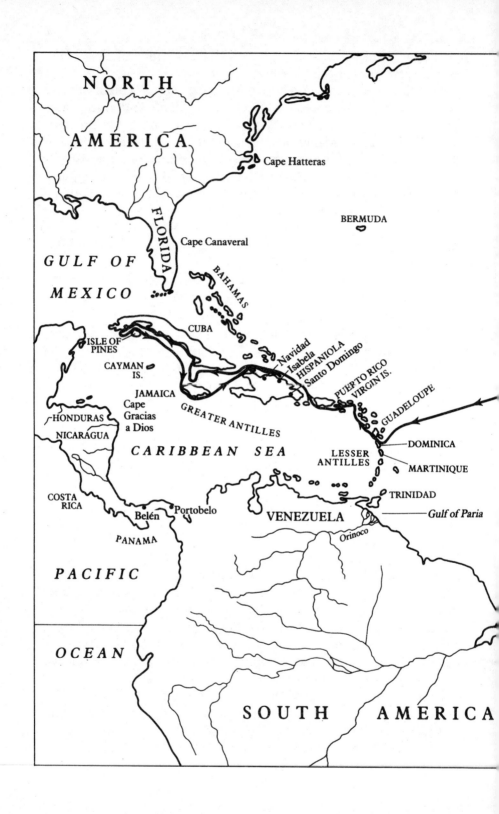

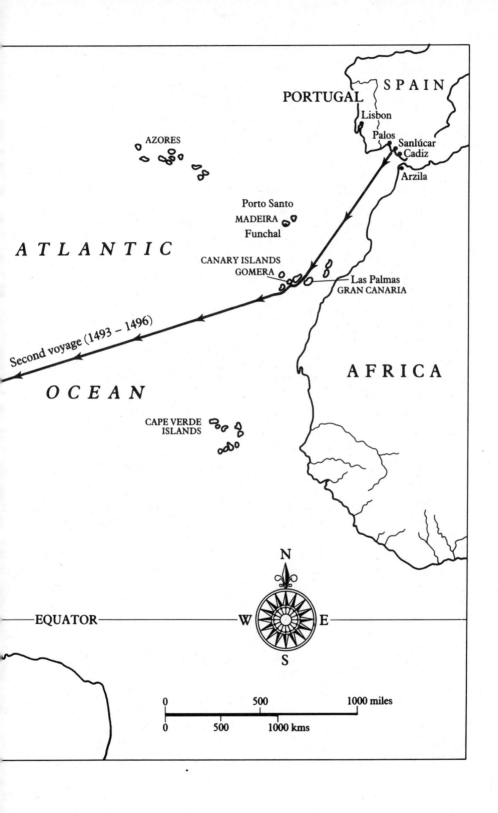

SPAIN

PORTUGAL

Lisbon

Palos

Sanlúcar

Cadiz

Arzila

AZORES

Porto Santo
MADEIRA
Funchal

A T L A N T I C

CANARY ISLANDS
GOMERA

Las Palmas
GRAN CANARIA

Second voyage (1493 – 1496)

O C E A N

AFRICA

CAPE VERDE
ISLANDS

N

W   E

S

EQUATOR

0   500   1000 miles

0   500   1000 kms

that so many of his exact words have survived. However, the fleet
this time contained all those gentlemen, many of them well-
educated. Naturally, several of them wrote long letters which were
later published. Three have survived. One in particular is totally
gripping, providing far better colour than anything from the First
Voyage, giving the real, unexpurgated, inside flavour of the behaviour of the Spaniards, a long way from home.

There are also Ferdinand's biography, carrying on his father's
life story, dutifully covering everything, and the history of the
Indies written by Las Casas, whose own father went on the Second
Voyage. The Instructions from the Sovereigns are also very important; these are in a document which still exists in the Seville archives,
recording, rather formally, all the conditions for the voyage,
explaining Fonseca's role as treasurer, how materials had to be
purchased, who was in charge of what. This document was
partly in reply to Columbus's long letter, setting out his plans for
the next stage.

The most interesting paragraph in the Instructions, a gentle
hint perhaps, but ominous in a way, says that the Admiral to make
sure his men care for the Indians. 'That they treat the said Indians
very well and lovingly and abstain from doing them any injury,
arranging that both peoples hold much conversation and inti-
macy, each serving the others to the best of their ability. If some
persons should maltreat the said Indians in any manner what-
soever, the said Admiral, as Viceroy and Governor, shall punish
them severely by virtue of the authority vested in him by their
Majesties.'

Columbus had acted properly enough on that First Voyage,
particularly in view of the times, in that no Indians had been killed,
and the only minor skirmish ended harmlessly. True, he had taken
some Indians, partly to act as guides and interpreters, and partly
to exhibit back home, but their Highnesses do not appear to have
specifically banned him from doing so again. None the less, the
general instruction was to be kind to them, the ultimate object
being to convert them to the Holy Faith, hence the two friars on
board. Several of the first batch of Indians had already been
converted, and one was on board, returning home, to act as an
interpreter. His new Spanish name, on being baptised, was Diego
Colon.

They made excellent weather on the first lap to the Canaries,
the same initial route as on the First Voyage, getting there on
October 2, just a week after leaving Spain. Once again, they put in

to the little island of Gomera, and this time we have it spelt out in black and white why Columbus tarried there. 'If I should tell you what we did in that place with salvos, lombard and shots and fireworks, it would take too long. This we did because of the Lady of the place, with whom our Lord Admiral in other times had fallen in love . . .'

This is the beginning of a most revealing and colourful letter written by one of the gentlemen volunteers on board, Michel de Cuneo. He was an Italian, from Liguria, and it seems possible he might have known Columbus from their Genoa boyhood days, as his father once sold a house to Columbus's father. He was educated and cultured, interested in fauna and flora and native customs, but most of all interested in enjoying himself, and describing his adventures informally and graphically. Unlike Columbus, he was not trying to impress or keep in with any royal masters, just amusing the friend to whom he was writing. (The original has disappeared, but a copy was done which at first was thought not to be authentic, till it was verified by experts and eventually published in 1885, just in time for the 400th celebrations.)

While Columbus dallied five days with his lady love, the fleet took on more supplies, including eight pigs. They finally left the Canaries on October 13. Before setting sail for the Indies, Columbus gave each of his seventeen captains sealed instructions on how to reach Navidad on Hispaniola. They must not be opened, unless in a dire emergency, such as being separated from the fleet. Columbus had learned a lot from his first voyage.

The route this time was more southerly, as Columbus wanted to hit a string of islands the Indians had told him about, an arc of a thousand islands, so it was said, then to work his way along and between them to Hispaniola. It seems an unnecessary detour, if he really wanted to get to Navidad quickly and obtain fresh supplies and expand the garrison, which was the supposed main object of the Second Voyage. It was also dangerous, going into new waters and round new islands and reefs, this time with sixteen ships in tow, any of which might get lost or go aground. Columbus decided he could manage both aims – to get to his destination reasonably quickly, and at the same time have the excitement of a new route, perhaps with some new discoveries.

The journey was indeed quick, without any dramas, and in just twenty days they hit land, the island of Dominica, named by Columbus as they had arrived there on a Sunday (not after his father, as has often been stated). They moved on to a smaller island nearby, which he named after his ship, Mariagalante. Next they came to a larger island he called Santa Maria de Guadalupe, after the shrine in Spain where Columbus had gone to fulfil his vows made on the First Voyage.

They had now entered Carib territory, islands which the Caribs raided and terrorised, and were soon seeing signs of sacked villages and young men who had been castrated. Cuneo is not sure of the reason for the latter. 'On that island [Guadaloupe], we took twelve very beautiful and very fat women from 15 to 16 years, together with two boys of the same age. These had the genital organs cut to the belly; and this we thought had been done in order to prevent them meddling with their wives, or maybe to fatten them up and later eat them.' Ferdinand, in his accounts, says it was for the latter reason. 'The Caribs castrate them, as we do to fatten capons, to improve their taste.'

Cuneo describes how, when villages were empty, or the locals ran away when the Spaniards arrived, 'we went in and took anything we pleased'. He has a good description of a band of seamen going ashore and getting lost, which must have been a regular occurrence whenever they landed somewhere new. Cuneo himself appears amused at their uselessness.

WE LANDED on this island and stayed there for about six days; and the reason for our staying was that eleven of our men formed themselves into a company for purposes of robbery and went into the wilderness five or six miles, so that when they wished to return they did not know how to find their way, and this in spite of the fact that they were all seamen and looked for the sun, which they could not well see because of the thick and dense forest. The Lord Admiral, seeing that those men were not coming and could not be found, sent 200 men divided into four squads, with trumpets, horns and lanterns, yet for all this they could not find them, and there were times when we were more in doubt about the 200 than for the first ones. But it pleased God that the 200 came back very tired and hungry. We thought that the eleven had been eaten by the aforesaid Caribs, who are accustomed to do that. However, at the end of five or six days, the said eleven, as it pleased God, even with little hope to find us, started a fire on top of a rock; and we, seeing the fire, thought they were there and sent them the boat, and in this way they were retrieved. Had it not been for an old woman who by signs showed us the way, they would have been lost, because on the following day we meant to make sail for our voyage.

In Ferdinand's account of the same incident, he says that Columbus punished those who had got lost, putting some in chains and others on short rations. Ferdinand's descriptions tend to be more prosaic, often ending with a moral or academic point. He takes a whole page, for example, to ponder the discovery one day of an old iron pan. He knows the Indians are ignorant of such things, and suggests that it was probably a piece of flint, mistaken for iron, but then he wonders, if it was iron, where it had come from. Could the Caribs have been robbing the Spaniards on Hispaniola? Could a Spanish ship have been wrecked and the debris swept across the Atlantic? It is a nice problem for an intellectual mind like Ferdinand's to wrestle with.

Sailing on, they came to what we now call the Virgin Islands. Seeing such a vast number of virgin islands stretching all around him, he named them after the legend of the eleven thousand virgins.

On the island of Santa Cruz (now part of the US Virgin Isles) they encountered their first serious battle in the Indies, during which one Spaniard died. Cuneo gives a graphic description, but he also includes what afterwards happened to him personally, an incident not mentioned by Ferdinand. Is this the first recorded sexual encounter in the New World?

WHILE I was in the boat, I captured a very beautiful Carib woman, whom the said Lord Admiral gave to me, and with whom, having taken her into my cabin, she being naked according to their custom, I conceived desire to take pleasure. I wanted to put my desire into execution but she did not want it and treated me with her finger nails in such a manner that I wished I had never begun. But seeing that, (to tell you the end of it all), I took a rope and thrashed her well, for which she raised such unheard of screams that you would not have believed your ears. Finally we came to an agreement in such manner that I can tell you that she seemed to have been brought up in a school of harlots. To that cape of that island the Admiral gave the name Cape of the Arrow because of the one who had died of the arrow.

They left the Virgin Isles – a misnomer if we are to believe Cuneo – and approached Puerto Rico, which some of the Indians on board immediately recognised, helping to guide the fleet round the southern coast. At last, they were heading directly for Hispaniola, and the fort of Navidad.

They anchored first at Monte Christi, about fifty miles away from Navidad, and sheltered for two days in a river estuary, during which time Columbus sent out various parties, to scout the land and river, as he had it in mind that this, one day, might make a good settlement.

During their stay, a terrible discovery was made, according to Dr Chanca, the fleet's doctor, who also wrote an account of the second voyage.

> *'As we went on making our observations, some of our men found two dead bodies by the river's side, one with a rope round his neck, and the other with one round his foot. This was on the first day of our landing. On the following day they found two other corpses farther on, and one of these was observed to have a great quantity of beard. This was regarded as a very suspicious circumstance by many of our people, because as I have already said, all the Indians are beardless . . .'*

What could it all mean? When they arrived in Navidad, there were further worrying signs. A canoe with six Indians came out to meet them, stopped, then went back again. Columbus for the time being kept all his sails set, just in case his ships might have to undertake some speedy manoeuvres. Then they anchored in the bay and Columbus ordered two guns to be fired, waiting for the Spanish garrison to respond.

'When we received no reply,' writes Chanca, 'and could not perceive any fires, nor the slightest signs of habitation, the spirits of our people became much depressed and they began to entertain the suspicion which the circumstances were naturally calculated to excite.'

In the night, the same canoe returned, and one of the Indians, a cousin of Guacamara (the friendly Chief), asked to speak to Columbus. He would not leave his canoe at first, till a light was shone and he could see the Admiral's face, then he agreed to go on board. For the next three hours, he told the story of what had happened, while Dr Chanca and others listened.

All the Spaniards had been well at first after Columbus's departure, though some had subsequently died of fever and some were killed in quarrels amongst themselves. But then the whole region had been invaded by two hostile tribes who had burned the houses and killed many people. In fact Guacamara himself was still recovering from his injuries, otherwise he would be there to greet the Admiral.

That then was the given story. Next morning, none of the Spanish garrison arrived. Some of Columbus's sailors imagined that, in the night, returning to shore, the Indians had been drowned, capsizing their canoe while drunk.

Columbus took a party, including Dr Chanca, ashore and they found that the Spanish settlement had been utterly destroyed by fire. They discovered Spanish clothes on the ground, but no more bodies. 'There were many different opinions amongst us,' writes Chanca. 'Some suspecting that Guacamara himself was concerned; others thought not, because his own residence was burnt; so it remained a doubtful question. The Admiral ordered all the ground which had been occupied by fortifications to be searched, for he had left orders with them to bury all the gold they might get.' According to Ferdinand, they also looked into Navidad's well, but it was empty.

A search was made of the whole area, during which one party unearthed the bodies of eleven Spaniards, with grass already growing over them. Columbus and Dr Chanca, in going round some native huts, found many Spanish belongings, including an anchor from the *Santa Maria*. All the natives told the same tale: there had been an invasion by two other tribes. 'But notwithstanding all this, we began to hear complaints that one of the Spaniards had taken three women to himself, and another four, from whence we drew the inference that jealousy was the cause of the misfortune which had occurred.'

The Chief's brother was found, and he sent gold and other presents to Columbus and the leading Spaniards, but he was still too ill to come himself. Eventually, Columbus and Chanca and a party of officials, all richly dressed and carrying fine gifts, decided to go to see the Chief. He was in his house, resting, stretched out in a hammock, his leg bandaged. He apologised for the fact that he could not get up.

The Chief was told that, by great good luck, the Spaniards had with them someone 'skilled in the treatment of human disorders', who would be only too happy to inspect the Chief's wound.

The Chief agreed, but Chanca said he needed the place cleared first, there was too great a throng which had darkened the room. 'When the wound was examined, it was certain that there was no more wound on that leg than on the other, although he cunningly pretended that it pained him too much. Ignorant as we were to the facts, it was impossible to come to a definite conclusion, so that the Admiral was at a loss what to do.'

There were those, such as the friar sent by the Sovereigns, who said the Chief and all his men should at once be punished, by death, for killing the Spaniards. But Columbus did nothing, deciding that, until they arrived at the facts, they ought to conceal their distrust. They never did agree on the truth about what had happened at Navidad. Columbus exacted no punishment.

The event can be used to show him in a rather humane light, or as being indecisive and weak, depending on one's point of view. We have the benefit of three first-hand accounts which give a good description of the whole incident – by Cuneo, Dr Chanca, and a gentleman called Syllacio, in a letter he wrote in Latin which is a transcript from a report of a friend present on the voyage. There are other contemporary accounts, such as Ferdinand's, based on what eye-witnesses told him. They all point to the fact that the Spanish garrison probably brought about their own downfall – by a combination of greed and sexual excess.

'Bad feeling arose,' writes Syllacio, 'and broke out into war-fare because of the licentious conduct of our men towards the Indian women, for each Spaniard had five women to minister to his pleasure.' Syllacio adds, dryly, a possible explanation of their need for five women each: 'For the sake of progeny, I have no doubt.'

He deduces what the end-result of all this must have been. 'The husbands and relatives, unable to take this, banded together to avenge this insult and eliminate this outrage, no race of men being free from jealousy, and attacked the Christians in great force. Although they resisted staunchly, they were ruthlessly cut down. The truth of these words was demonstrated by the corpses of ten Spaniards which had been found by our men, miserably deformed and corrupted, smeared with dirt and foul blood, hideously dis-coloured, for they had lain out in the open, neglected and unburied for almost three months.'

Cuneo, a man of the world, not the sort one would expect to be taken in, was nonetheless impressed by the Chief's explanation. 'With tears running down his breast, he told us that the lord of the mountains called Caonanbo had come and killed them [the Spaniards] and some of his own people. We could find nothing of what the Admiral had left; and, hearing this, we believed what he told us.'

Perhaps three things happened. The Spaniards upset the Indians by taking their women, and by demanding too much gold. At the same time, there was possibly fighting amongst the Spaniards themselves. Thirdly, an invasion by another tribe might have taken place, for various reasons, perhaps inspired by the behaviour of the Spaniards, trying to expand their territory. The Chief's behaviour does seem suspicious, inventing the leg wound, showering the Spaniards with presents. He also laid on a parade of twelve naked girls, so Syllacio says, when they went to see him. Was it guilt, or just fear that he would be blamed?

Whatever the precise chain of events, thirty-nine Spaniards had been killed. It was Columbus's first serious set-back in the new world. It was also the first recorded bloody massacre in Latin American history.

Columbus gave the bodies a decent funeral, then decided to leave Navidad for ever. He deemed the site anyway too marshy. He moved back along the coast, towards Monte Christi, the way they had come, found a river estuary, explored slightly inland, and began work on a new and bigger and better settlement, a proper town this time, which would have stone buildings, and be called Isabela. Work began on January 2, 1494, and they made a good start to what they hoped would be a good year. On January 6, a full mass was celebrated, the first in the New World. While the masons worked, and the farmers started sowing, several parties were sent into the hinterland, in search of gold.

Cuneo was with the gold-digging party, and he is remarkably blunt on exactly what it was like.

'Not too well fitted out with clothes,' is his first comment. 'On that trip, we spent 29 days with terrible weather, bad food, and worse drink, nevertheless, out of covetousness of that gold, we all kept strong and lusty. We crossed and recrossed two rapid rivers and those who did not know how to swim had Indians carry them swimming. Several times we fished in those rivers but no one ever found a single grain of gold, for this reason we were very displeased with the Indians.

'While we were staying in our fort, many Indians came to see us as if we were marvels, bringing to us some of the gold they had, and they exchanged it with us. There were also exchanges in secret against the rules. As you know, the devil makes you do wrong, and then lets your wrong be discovered. Moreover, as long as Spain is Spain, traitors will never be wanting. One gave the other away, so that almost all were exposed, and whoever was guilty was well whipped; some had their ears slit and some the nose; very pitiful to see.'

While the gold mines were proving a mirage, the building work was also running into problems. The site turned out to be swampy and soon everyone was being bitten alive by mosquitoes. The rains came, the insects became worse, and around 300 men went sick. The food was running low, and soon there was insubordination among several of the Spanish officers. The Indians, being made to do all the hard work, were also growing restless.

On February 2, Columbus decided to send twelve of the seventeen ships back to Spain, under the command of Antonio de Torres. He gave him a personal report for the Sovereigns, and apologies for not so far sending much gold. He asked for new supplies to be sent out urgently, more food and clothing, medicine and animals, as well as a hundred skilled miners.

Columbus himself had fallen ill, so ill, says Ferdinand, that he was unable to keep his own journal for three months (from December 11, 1493 until March 12, 1494). This is the first mention by Ferdinand of his father's state of health on the voyage. Neglecting his journal makes it sound serious.

When he recovered, on March 12, he decided himself to make an expedition inland, to supervise the building of a new fort, and to join the search for gold. He left his younger brother Diego in charge. This is the first mention of him. He had apparently arrived in Spain from Genoa after Columbus's triumphal return from his first voyage, and was invited to join the second.

Columbus found he had a mutiny to put down, so Ferdinand says, which had been stirred up by some of his enemies while he had been ill. They were plotting to seize a vessel and return home. A written list of charges against Columbus was discovered. They were all false, says Ferdinand, and the leaders were punished. But the problems continued. Arguments amongst the Spanish leaders, troubles with the Indians, Spanish workmen turning out to be 'shirkers', according to Ferdinand, not realising that gold needs sacrifice and hard labour. The town of Isabela had started off so well, now everything seemed to be going wrong.

Columbus's bold and imaginative plan of large-scale colonisation had resulted so far in large-scale problems. So he decided to move on, again leaving Diego in charge. At heart, he was turning out to be an explorer, not a coloniser, despite what he had led his Sovereigns, and himself, to believe.

On April 24, 1494, he set off for Cuba. He was in *Nina*, accompanied by just two other ships. He clearly preferred a small fleet, as on the First Voyage, with few men and therefore fewer problems. The new and the unknown were beckoning, giving him a chance for a while to forget the known and the difficult.

They sailed along the southern coast of Cuba for about a week, putting in at various harbours, taking on board any likely-looking Indians. On cross-examining them, they learned that the real gold was over there, in another island they called Jameque. Columbus decided to head for it at once, landing at St Ann's Bay, Jamaica. They sailed along the coast towards what is now Montego Bay, exclaiming at the beauty. Columbus said it was the most beautiful island he had seen so far. But there was no gold. So, off they went, back to Cuba, after just six days in Jamaica.

For the whole of the next month, they continued further and further along the south coast of Cuba, occasionally veering off on minor expeditions to small islands, with Columbus becoming convinced that he was on the continent of Asia, albeit a peninsula. He desperately wanted it to be the continent, proof that he had reached the East. All his maps and beliefs and Biblical quotations indicated to him that he was right. The ancient Greeks had believed there was some sort of peninsula in these parts, hanging down below China. He therefore decided that Cuba was what we now call the Malay peninsula. (If you look, cursorily, at a map of the world, there is a similarity in the pattern of islands in the West Indies and in the East Indies. The Florida peninsula does correspond to the Malay peninsula; and Cuba and Hispaniola are roughly the same shape as Sumatra and Borneo.)

Columbus called a halt on June 12, off Bahia Cortes, feeling he had no need to go any further. They were definitely on the continent. (If only they had gone on for another day, they would have realised their mistake, and seen that Cuba was an island. And, if they had proceeded for a second day, they would have hit Florida by turning north, or Mexico by going straight on.)

To prove he was correct, should the Sovereigns harbour any doubts, he made his entire crew swear on oath that they were in Asia, and that they had come to this conclusion on their own. Anyone who signed and later changed his mind would be punished, either by a fine or by having his tongue cut out. Everyone signed, including Cuneo and Juan de la Cosa, a famous cartographer. (Later, Cosa did represent Cuba as an island, but until around

1516 most map-makers agreed with Columbus, or played safe, and put it on the mainland.)

Columbus's dogged and irrational insistence on this signed document appears bizarre. It could indicate that he himself was not convinced. There was an historical precedent. Bartholomew Dias had made his men sign a similar statement when they rounded the Cape of Good Hope.

Columbus would clearly like to have gone on, as indeed he always did. Ferdinand even suggests that he longed to carry straight on, without ever turning back; in other words, to sail right round the world. 'Had he had plenty of food, he would have gone on to return to Spain by way of the East.'

On the long journey back to Hispaniola, looking at various other islands, they ran into bad weather; and many of the crew became ill and discontented, as Cuneo makes clear. 'Sailed for about 15 days without finding land of any sort. Seeing this we all began to grumble, saying that we are going to be drowned and that the food would fail us.' Columbus, in an attempt at least to cheer Cuneo up, gave him an island. 'The Lord Admiral called it the La Bella Saonese and gave it to me as a present and I took possession of it, according to the appropriate modes and forms, by virtue of a document signed by a notary. On the above mentioned island I uprooted grass and cut trees and planted the cross and also gallows and in the name of God I baptised it with the name of La Bella Saonese. And well it is called beautiful, for in it there are 37 villages and at least 30,000 souls, and this too the Lord Admiral noted down in his book.'

Cuneo records in his letter that he estimated the island of Jamaica, which they sailed round again on the way back, was around '700 Roman miles and Hispaniola to be 600 leagues around, and this is for your own information'. That addition is interesting. He obviously knew that such details were state secrets, and Columbus would not be best pleased if he found out that his friend was scribbling away, passing on private pieces of information.

The whole expedition, to Cuba and back, lasted five months, and was relatively pointless, and at times dangerous. Cuneo amused himself for some of the time by doing word sketches for his friend back home. Many of his observations had been recorded by Columbus during the First Voyage, but to Cuneo it was all new and exciting. He heads this section of his letter 'The Indians'. It makes fascinating reading:

As I have told about the nature and variety of the brute beasts, it now remains to tell something about the people. I must then say that people of both sexes are of an olive complexion like those of the Canaries. They have flat heads and the face tattooed; of short stature; as a rule they have very little beard and very well shaped legs and are thick of skin. The women have their breasts quite round and firm and well shaped. These, as a rule, when they have given birth, immediately carry their infants to the water to wash them and to wash themselves, nor does child-bearing give them folds on the belly, but it always stays well stretched, and so the breasts. They all go naked, but it is true that the women, when they have had knowledge of man, cover themselves in front either with the leaf of a tree, with a cotton clout, or briefs of the same cotton.

They eat all sort of wild and poisonous beasts such as reptiles of 15 to 20 pounds each; and when they meet the biggest ones they are devoured by them; and whenever they wish to eat those reptiles they roast them between two pieces of wood. When we were left without food, we ate some and there are some which are very good and their flesh very white. They also eat dogs, which are not too good. Likewise they eat snakes, lizards and spiders which are as big as chickens. They eat some poisonous insects which breed in the swamps and weigh from a pound to a pound and a half. Likewise for bread they eat some of those big roots which are like our turnips, as I have said above, and their drink is water.

The Caribs and those Indians, although they are innumerable and inhabit an extensive territory, are scattered in distant groups one from the other. Nevertheless all have one language and all live alike, in appearance like one nation of their own, save that the Caribs are more ferocious and more astute men than those Indians. The Caribs whenever they catch these Indians eat them and they say that a boy's flesh tastes better than that of a woman. Of this human flesh they are very greedy, so that to eat of that flesh they stay out of their country for six, eight and even ten years before they repatriate; and they stay so long, whenever they go, that they depopulate the islands. And should they not do that, those Indians would multiply in such a way that they would cover the earth. That happens because as soon as they are of procreating age they procreate, respecting only their sisters; all the rest are common. We wished to hear from those Caribs how they catch the Indians, and they told us that during the night they hide themselves and when day comes they surround their houses and catch them.

Those Caribs and Indians shave their hair and their beard and so do the women. They shave with canes and the hair from the nose they uproot with their fingers. Their knives are stones which cut like real knives, and they make the handles, and with these they cut and work their boats called canoes, which are trees hollowed out with those knives, and in which they navigate from island to island; but they do not use sails, only oars which look like those paddles we use to beat hemp. When those Caribs hunt the Indians, their weapons are very big clubs with a knob on top carved like the head of a man or of some other animal. They also carry very big bows like the English bows. The bowstrings are made of that above-mentioned grass, the arrows of canes, the shaft of very strong wood, made in the shape of a column, inside which they force a pointed cane and bind closely; and the feathers are taken from parrots' wings. With these arrows they do great destruction. Also instead of iron they use fish bones.

We went to the temple of those Caribs, in which we found two wooden statues, arranged so that they look like a *Pietà*. We were told that whenever someone's father is sick, the son goes to the temple and tells the idol that his father is ill and that the idol says whether he should live or not; and he stays there until the idol answers yes or no. If he says no, the son goes home, cuts his father's head and then cooks it; I don't believe they eat it but truly when it is white they place it in the above-mentioned temple; and this they do only to the lords. That idol is called *Seyti*. They take a man whom they have proclaimed holy and who is dressed in a cloak of white cotton. This holy man never speaks, and in their fashion they treat him very tenderly; and they say that in the morning he places himself in the middle of the temple and the first woman who enters it has intercourse with him; and then all the other women go to kiss her as if she was a most worthy object because that holy man has condescended to do business with her.

The said Caribs and Indians, apart from that idol, do not worship anything else nor do they sacrifice in any way to that idol, nor do they know God or devil; they live like proper beasts. They eat when they are hungry, use coition openly whenever they feel like it, and apart from brothers and sisters, all others are common. They are not jealous, and, in my opinion, they are cold-blooded people, not too lustful, which may come from the fact that they eat poorly. According to what we have seen in all the islands where we have been, both the Indians and the Caribs are largely sodomites, not knowing (I believe) whether they are acting right or wrong. We have judged that this accursed vice may have come to the Indians from those Caribs; because these, as I said before, are wilder men and when conquering and eating those Indians, for spite they may also have committed that extreme offence, which proceeding thence may have been transmitted from one to the other.

The Caribs and Indians, in our opinion, live a short time; we have not seen a man who in our judgment would have been past 50 years of age. They sleep mostly on the ground like beasts. Their lords, whom they call cacique, all sleep over cotton sheets. These lords they honour extremely and respect. When they are together to eat, no one would dare to eat if that cacique had not eaten first. The women do all the work. Men only mind fishing and eating. There are plenty of mosquitoes in those countries which are extremely annoying, and that is why the Indians anoint their bodies with those fruits which are red or black in colour, and which are an antidote to their annoyance; but we could not find better remedy than stay in the water.

On the way back to Hispaniola, Columbus became ill once again. Las Casas says the crew were greatly worried. 'The Admiral fell into a pestilential sleep that robbed him of all his faculties and strength, so that it seemed as though dead. Everyone thought that he would not live another day.' He would appear to have been suffering from a combination of gout and rheumatism.

Ferdinand quotes directly from Columbus's own journal, the one which has never turned up. 'I am on the same ration as the others. May it please God that this be for His service and that of your Highnesses. Were it only for myself, I would no longer bear such pains and dangers, for not a day passes that we do not look death in the face.'

They did reach Isabela safely, but Columbus was seriously ill on arrival. He went straight to his bed and stayed there for several weeks.

De Torres had not yet returned with the supply ships from Spain, but the good and surprising news for Columbus was that his other brother, Bartholomew, had appeared. They had always been close and worked together in Portugal, and in Spain, and it was Bartholomew who had gone off to persuade the Kings of

England and France to give their backing. He had been in France when Columbus returned from his first voyage, and had not got to Cadiz in time to join him on the second.

Bartholomew was reckoned to be a good, tough administrator, more decisive than Columbus. From now on he remained at his brother's side, as his chief assistant, which must have been a great comfort to Christopher, though it did not make him very popular. There were hints of nepotism and general bad feeling when Christopher announced that Bartholomew had been appointed 'Adelantado', or provincial Governor, a title he was always given from now on in the various contemporary accounts, just as Columbus himself was always referred to as the Admiral. Columbus maintained that, as Viceroy, appointed personally by the Sovereigns, he could assume their regal rights and make such appointments. His enemies disagreed.

Bartholomew faced several immediate problems. Relations with the Indians had grown worse and there was another revolt involving a group of Spaniards, led by the friar who had been appointed by the Sovereigns, Father Buyl. He maintained from the beginning that Columbus was too lenient with the heathen Indians. The mutineers seized three caravels, the ones in which Bartholomew had arrived, and sailed back to Spain, where naturally they fomented trouble for Columbus, spreading stories at Court about his incompetence as an administrator and his appointment of his brother.

De Torres finally returned in early 1495 with fresh supplies, greatly needed as sickness was widespread amongst the Spaniards and food and materials were dangerously low. The inland fort was proving impossible to run, with constant attacks from the Indians, and disagreements amongst the Spaniards, so in March 1495 Columbus and Bartholomew decided to settle the problem once and for all. Around twenty Spaniards had been killed and the situation could not continue. The result was the first real war, during which hundreds of Indians were killed or captured, and many Spanish lives and vital supplies lost.

To compensate for the costs, and the fact that no appreciable supply of gold had yet been found, Columbus decided to send back a large number of slaves. His theory was that they could be sold, and the proceeds used to replenish the colony's coffers.

Cuneo describes the process of rounding up the slaves (he had elected to go back on the slave boats, and was obviously quite pleased to be leaving Hispaniola). 'Amongst the Indians who were taken on board was one of their kings with two chiefs who it was decided should be killed with arrows on the following day, so they were tied up; but in the night they knew so well how to gnaw one another's ropes with their teeth that they were freed from their bonds and escaped.'

Over 1,600 Indians, male and female, were not so lucky. That is the number Cuneo says were lined up at the quayside, ready to be taken to Spain and sold as slaves. The best were then picked out, men and women, some 550. 'Of the rest who were left, the announcement went around that whoever wanted them could take as many as they pleased, and this was done. And when everybody was supplied, some 400 were given permission to go wherever they wanted. Amongst them were many women who had babies at their breasts. They, in order to escape us, since they were afraid we would return and catch them again, left their infants anywhere on the ground and started to flee like desperate people.'

On the journey, says Cuneo, 200 Indians died, 'because of the unaccustomed air, colder than theirs. We cast them into the sea. When we reach Cadiz, we disembark all of the slaves, half of whom are sick. For your information, they are not working people and they very much fear cold, nor have they long life.'

Cuneo also has a few words to say about 'Master Bartholomew', as apparently his friend, to whom he is writing, is eager for any information. He tells him the news that Bartholomew has been made Adelantado. There is no comment, just an implication that this is a good bit of perhaps damaging gossip.

At the end of his report on what he saw of the Second Voyage, Cuneo does praise Columbus – for his navigational skills. 'There is one thing I wish you to know, in my humble opinion, that since Genoa was Genoa, no other man was born so magnanimous and so keen in practical navigation as the above mentioned Lord Admiral. Only by looking at a cloud or by a star at night, he knew what was going to happen and whether there would be foul weather. He himself steered at the helm; and when the storm had passed over, he hoisted sail while the others were sleeping.' Cuneo then adds some equally complimentary words about his God-fearing nature. But it is noticeable that there are no words or comments, favourable or adverse, about Columbus's administrative abilities.

According to Ferdinand, once the civil war had been successfully brought to a conclusion, things remained calm for the rest of 1495, despite the fact that the Spanish forces were down to only 630, including women and children, many of whom were now sick. 'The Admiral had completely pacified the country without having to unsheath his sword again. He reduced the Indians to such obedience and tranquillity that they all promised to pay tribute to the Catholic Sovereigns every three months.' Ferdinand then goes on to explain in detail how this system works, how every Indian over fourteen has to pay so much gold and in return will be given a token to be worn round the neck, proof that he has paid the tribute. 'Any Indian found without such a token was to be punished.'

Ferdinand clearly thinks Columbus did well to devise this system, and to have brought the whole island under his control, with only '200 poorly armed men, half of them sick, to subdue such a multitude'. He is also grateful to God. 'The good Lord wished to punish the Indians, and so visited upon them with such shortage of food and such a variety of plagues that He reduced their number by two thirds, that it might be made clear that such wonderful conquests proceeded from His supreme hand and not from our strength or intelligence or the cowardice of the Indians.'

Ferdinand has hit on one of the most important, most devastating, truths of the whole Spanish invasion of the New World. It has always been surprising that a handful of Spaniards, both here in Hispaniola and later in Mexico and elsewhere, could have managed to subdue and eliminate millions of Indians. The Spaniards did have arms, but their canons and muskets were primitive, certainly not enough for five or six men to overpower a thousand natives, as continually happened. According to Ferdinand, it was disease, not the brutality of the Spaniards, which was killing off most Indians.

The Spaniards saw in this the hand of God, as Ferdinand states, a theory enshrined in the Old Testament, that God shows his displeasure in pestilence. Even more important, the Indians believed it. It was part of their mythology, that the gods spread disease when they were angry. So the Indians suddenly appeared to give up in the face of negligible opposition. They too believed God was on the side of the white man. And Indian culture was so completely destroyed, as the Spaniards advanced, because the Indians who survived quickly turned to the Catholic faith and the Spanish language.

The Spaniards did not necessarily set out to destroy the Indians. Columbus clearly loved them, when he encountered them during his First Voyage. On the Second Voyage, when the struggle to control the Indians began, he needed them alive – for tax purposes, and also for their labour. They just seemed to die. It was God, therefore, who had the ultimate explanation.

The American historian, William H. McNeill, considering the whole history of the Spanish Conquest, believes it was disease which won America for Spain. Not arms, not God. Smallpox appeared first in Hispaniola, during the war Columbus was fighting. (Later it helped Cortes wipe out the Aztecs.) McNeill says that the Spaniards themselves did not suffer from smallpox to any great extent, because in Europe they had been exposed to it since childhood, along with influenza and measles, two other diseases which acted like plagues in the New World. Indian communities lived enclosed lives, on islands, isolated for centuries, so a brand-new disease swept through them like a forest fire. The Spaniards also succumbed to illness in Hispaniola, but this was put down at the time to poor food and the swampy conditions around Isabela.

Once Columbus had calmed the general situation, he realised that he had probably made a mistake with Isabela, setting up his headquarters in such an inhospitable area. A great deal of work had been completed, such as stone buildings, broad avenues, and the church which only two years earlier Syllacio's letter had described as being fit for the Sovereigns themselves to visit. But Columbus began to look instead for a site for a new city in the south of the country. Meanwhile, though, he had a different sort of worry.

Out of the ocean blue, unheralded, unexpected, arrived a Special Envoy from Spain, Aguado, who said he had been sent from their Highnesses to report back to them exactly what was happening in this far-flung province of their kingdom. Alarming reports of civil war and maladministration had been reaching Spain from those who had returned at the time of Cuneo, and on later ships. Nor was the Queen pleased by the sad state of the Indian slaves.

Columbus was furious and for two months refused to acknowledge the presence of Aguado or of his royal documents. He maintained that, as Viceroy, he need not answer to anyone, except the Sovereigns themselves.

In the end, Columbus decided it was best if he went home to Spain, and explained everything to his Sovereigns in person. 'Because many spiteful envious men were giving the Sovereigns false accounts of what was happening in the Indies,' writes Ferdinand, 'to the great prejudice of the Admiral and his brothers.'

One strange result of the Envoy's arrival was that Columbus took to dressing himself in the simple brown habit of a Franciscan friar. This was not just to show his true devotion and humility, nor out of sympathy with the sick and because of the sad recent events. Las Casas explains that it was to make clear that only he could humiliate himself, not any so-called Royal Envoy.

On the day Columbus was supposed to leave, a hurricane blew

up, and the fleet getting ready was lost, except for little *Nina*, his favourite. He had to wait till a new ship was built, the first in the Americas, which was christened the *India*.

Both ships set off on March 10, 1496, grossly overcrowded, carrying 200 Spaniards and thirty Indians. At night, they had to sleep on deck in shifts, as there was so little room. In Guadaloupe, they were attacked by women firing arrows, but no one was injured. On the high seas, there were storms and consequent fears.

So severe was the lack of food, says Ferdinand, that some Spaniards suggested they should eat the Indians, just as the Caribs did. Others suggested they would save food by throwing all Indians overboard. 'And would have done, if the Admiral had not forbidden it, saying that as Christians and human beings, they should not be treated worse than the others.'

They arrived back in Cadiz on June 11, 1496, almost three years after they had departed. There was no triumphant public reception this time, no honours, no sitting at the right hand of the Sovereigns. It was no longer such a remarkable event to have ships going back and forward across the ocean. Many had now achieved this. And many were not wholly convinced it was worth doing anyway.

The Sovereigns were otherwise preoccupied, as Don Juan was about to be married to the Holy Roman Emperor's daughter (Ferdinand and his brother Diego, as pages to Don Juan, were present at the wedding); but eventually they did give Columbus an audience and Ferdinand records that the Admiral 'was well received by the Catholic Sovereigns'.

But even the ever-faithful, ever-dutiful son Ferdinand could not hide the fact that things were not going so well for his father. The attitude of the Sovereigns was not what it had been. 'Later, because of the lying reports of spiteful and envious men, they changed their demeanour and permitted injuries and offences to be done to him.'

He names as one of the guilty men Fonseca, Archdeacon of Seville, who had equipped the Second Voyage, or 'mismanaged' it, according to Ferdinand. Fonseca had developed a 'mortal hatred' of the Admiral and his projects, 'heading a faction that caused him to lose the favour of the Catholic Sovereigns'.

While Columbus had been away for those three years, a new disease had broken out in Europe, unrecorded and unknown until this time. It was syphilis, soon to be the scourge of Europe, amongst all classes, for the next four hundred years. The first case occurred in 1494, the year after Columbus returned from his First Voyage. The date could have been coincidental, but most people thought not and medical opinion soon agreed that the disease was imported from the Indies by Columbus's returning sailors. Either the Indians passed it on to certain ladies and hangers-on at the Court, which is what some Spaniards alleged, or the sailors themselves were the carriers.

Those three years of hard and thankless labour in the Indies had done Columbus no good at all. His prestige and honour were now less than they had been when he departed. The Sovereigns were not pleased that he had made his brother Adelantado, as they considered he did not have such powers. However, they decided themselves to reappoint Bartholomew, so Columbus was spared some element of disgrace.

Columbus felt he had achieved much in Hispaniola, most of it going unrecognised. He had opened up the island, building the town of Isabela, establishing forts, planting crops and getting many of them to grow in record time, all against terrible odds and ruthless enemies, not to mention bad luck and acts of God.

But he also knew that the Second Voyage seemed ill-fated, from the moment when they arrived back in Navidad. That was the first of many tragedies. After Navidad, the letters and reports show him becoming increasingly convinced that there were enemies against him, that he was running into ill-luck for which he was not responsible.

Compassionate observers might suggest in mitigation that he was forced into actions against his nature and better judgement, by events out of his control. He felt compelled to capture and kill so many Indians, then to send them back as slaves, as the only way to raise finance and save the situation. Other observers, more forthright, might simply say that Columbus made his own mistakes, that he became megalomaniac, out of his depth in situations he was not suited to handle, making political errors, such as appointing his brothers, misjudging other people's feelings, misjudging, most of all, what the Sovereigns might be told and what they might believe.

Columbus had clearly loved everything during the First Voyage, the islands and the people. At that stage, he had only good to say about them and his heart had patently been in the right place. He still thought it was. Alas, others had begun to have their doubts.

His main ambition now was to get back to Hispaniola. It had become the seat of all his troubles, but he believed it was still the source of his power and wealth and success, both in the past and in the future.

12

Haiti Today

Colombo '92

THE PLANE to Haiti was very crowded. I found myself sitting next to a nervous-looking Jamaican woman of about thirty with her head in her hands, fidgeting with her numerous bags. I thought this must be her first flight, no wonder she's worried. So I chatted idly, to take her mind off the flight, saying this was my first visit to Haiti, and I too was worried. Was there still civil war? Would there be any hotels in Port au Prince to stay in? She said I should be fine. She had been to Haiti fifty times in the last two years, and always found somewhere to stay. I felt suitably humbled.

She did the trip to Port au Prince once a fortnight, catching the plane every second Monday, then returning on the Thursday. Most of the people on the plane were doing the same, off for their regular three days in Haiti. Her problem was her stomach. She had picked up something on her last trip.

I looked slowly around the plane and realised that I was the only male on board. It appeared to be full of youngish black Jamaican women, aged twenty-five to thirty, chattering like starlings, their arms and necks dripping with gold rings and ornaments, dressed to kill in silks and satins, high heels in pink and bright green. The woman beside me had on a silver pill-box hat, silver jacket and silver high heels. She could be a show girl, on tour with some musical, but nobody in their right mind would be sending a show to Haiti, not at this point in its history.

As it transpired, they were all entrepreneurs, to a woman, going on yet another buying trip to Haiti. Once there, they would stock up on local crafts, baskets, clothes, souvenirs, all of it incredibly cheap, bringing the stuff back to Kingston where they and their families would sell the goods from street-market stalls. From what my new friend told me, the women were the brains of their respective extended families, the go-getters, doing all the deals. No one was organising them, or telling them what to do. They made the decisions, while their parents back home waited, and the young men in their families sat around doing nothing, smoking ganja. Their erstwhile husbands had mostly moved on, or disappeared, leaving them to cope, which they were clearly doing successfully, even triumphantly. My friend hoped to clear a thousand Jamaican dollars every fortnight, after she had paid her return flight and expenses.

It was chaotic at Port au Prince airport. Everybody was squabbling or fighting, including the rather pathetic little band standing outside the arrival gate. It is a normal sight, in the Caribbean, to have a gaily-dressed ethnic group playing local music, usually 'Island in the Sun', to welcome foreign visitors. This band was refusing to play, being more concerned with some private argument. When they did start, reluctantly, the result was a combination of Caribbean sounds, Latin American rhythm and French provincial bar music.

The Jamaican women were refusing to queue, pushing to get out of the airport as quickly as possible and reach their suppliers. Two younger women ahead of me were literally fighting, squaring up and punching each other, one accusing the other of queue-jumping. It had all been sweetness and laughter on the plane, now they were acting more like street-traders. A Haitian soldier, rather alarming at first sight, with his gun holster and sharply pressed uniform, came over and tried to part them, but half-heartedly, too tired and limp to frighten them, managing only to keep them apart physically, while they continued to trade insults.

I was waiting my turn at the end of what passed for a queue, standing beside one of the older Jamaican women, aged nearer forty than thirty. 'Listen to dem niggers', she said. It was addressed to herself, rather than to me. She was shaking her head sadly. I had never before heard a black person call another black person a nigger.

Over the tannoy, I heard my name being called. Or was I imagining it? I often do think I hear my name being announced in public places. Delusions of importance, or just bad hearing. I pushed my way round the side of the queue, and struggled to the front, explaining to the uniformed passport control official that I was being paged. He took no notice. By this time, several of the Jamaican women were yelling at me, and trying to pull me back. I gave up, returning to the end of the queue, and was the last person to get through customs.

I had written the usual letters in advance, but this time had no hope at all of a reply. There were daily reports from Haiti of civil war, murder and looting, revolts and counter-revolts, a situation which had continued ever since the overthrow of the Duvalier régime. They had better things to worry about in Haiti than a visiting writer on the Columbus trail. My travel agent in London had advised me to check the political situation with the embassy before I left. There was no Haitian embassy or consulate in London. The nearest was in Paris, and they had not replied. Nor had I got a response from a letter to the British Consul in Haiti. My family thought I was mad even to set off.

The information desk directed me to a desk marked 'Tourisme'. Yes, my name had been called, a taxi-driver had been waiting for me, but he had long gone, assuming I was not on the plane. One of my letters had been addressed to the Director of Tourism, Port au Prince, just a shot in the dark, asking for a hotel to be booked, a taxi to pick me up. Some post was clearly getting through.

The airport building looked much like an airport building in any provincial town almost anywhere in the world, though perhaps it was a bit hotter than most. It was passably modern, with the usual concrete and glass, and kept passably clean, but when I left the airport buildings I was totally unprepared for the first sight of Port au Prince itself. The dirty, dusty road, all the way into town, was swarming with people, living in encampments by the road. Families were washing in open gutters, sleeping on the pavements, cooking on makeshift fires, sleeping under rags. Filth and disease were everywhere. They were not refugees, in transit. This was their home. This was where they lived.

In the town itself, there were shanty buildings which gave slightly more protection, but mostly they had breeze-block foundations and walls which would never be finished, corrugated iron roofs slung over piles of rubble. The poverty and filth were just as bad as on the road into town. Many of the side-streets, even those leading off the main road, were unmade-up, dust and rubble and potholes. My eyes could not quite adjust to the vast number of people. Every time my taxi crawled to a halt, there were eyes staring in, hands trying to sell cigarettes or clothes. Despite the poverty, the roads were swarming with cars and lorries, most of them old and battered, overloaded and dangerous, driven fiercely on their horns by drivers who shovelled and jostled humanity aside like fallen branches after a storm.

Amidst all this nightmare of poverty and disease there was one note of brightness and hope – the tap taps. These are the local Haitian buses, most of them created out of old pick-up trucks, then crudely built up with wooden frames and simple seats, yet each one a miracle of art. Every inch of the surface, wood or metal, is lovingly hand-painted, the lettering artistic and inventive, with patterns or tropical scenes, faces and figures, all attractive and colourful. It was hard to believe that people so poor, with such limited resources, could be inspired to produce such beautiful, exuberant creations. How did they even afford the paint?

Most of the tap taps had been individually christened, their names emblazoned at the front, often strangely spelt. I made a note of Couraj, Jistis, Libete, Du Mersi, Bon Dew, and one called Rastman. There were signs and slogans in the street, also spelt in a form of pidgin French. One banner strung right across the street announced Poo Noo Too. I later found out this was an election slogan for a political party, whose official motto is 'Pour Nous Tout' – for us all.

The Hotel Villa St Louis was away from the slums and shanties, on a hillside leading towards the suburb of Petionville, the smarter part of Port au Prince. The streets were empty, but once the taxi stopped a group of sullen youths crowded round, offering to clean the taxi. When that was refused, they offered to guard it, presumably from other groups like themselves. When that too was refused, and the driver had said something threatening to them, they retreated across the road, to stand and watch in the shade of a palm tree.

At the front, the hotel looked like an ordinary suburban villa, simple and rather homely, like a French pension, with potted plants and little bamboo tables in the reception area. A man behind the desk, speaking on the telephone, asked me for my passport, which I handed over. He studied it and gave me a room key, still speaking on the telephone. I realised he was talking to the police, asking them to come as quickly as possible.

I noticed further down the hall a white woman sitting with her head in her hands, crying, while a man stood beside her, trying to give comfort. I took them at first for man and wife but they were colleagues in a computer firm from California, so I learned later, invited by the Haitian Government to bring computer technology to the island. They had been here three weeks, and were due to leave tomorrow, first thing.

'I've been robbed,' she sobbed. 'They've taken all my money, credit cards, passports, air tickets. I'll never get another passport in time. I'll never be able to leave this goddamn country.'

It had happened only minutes earlier, while she was taking a shower in her bathroom. Someone had got into her room, and taken her handbag. 'It must have been an inside job. No doubt about that. Oh my God, what am I going to do?'

The man told her not to worry, another few days wouldn't matter, they would both stay on, but she started crying again, saying it was all her fault. I asked if I could help, lend any money, make any calls for her, but she shook her head. The reception clerk came over and said the police were on the way.

My room was at the back of the hotel, in a new jerry-built concrete wing, arranged like a cheap motel, with open landings. Anyone below could clearly see what was going on above, and watch each person going in and out of their bedroom. There was a pathetic patch of garden, with a very small and very empty swimming pool, and beyond that a low wall and a noisy road. It felt totally exposed.

My bedroom was hot and fetid. I turned on the air-conditioning, to clear the atmosphere, but the noise was overpowering, as if I was in a ship's engine room. I opened the door and walked out on to the concrete landing. Down the corridor, I could hear all the other air-conditioners; each with a plastic washing-up bowl under the exterior air vent, full of stagnant water.

I had a shower and lay on my bed. I could hear voices, low but clear, talking in whispers. I went round the room, found nothing, then traced the voices to a grille in the bathroom. Was there an air-shaft, down to the kitchen, or were people crouching outside, ready to pounce? I could see why the American woman was so frightened.

Haiti has been a dangerous place ever since the days of Columbus. If anything, it has got worse. For the last 200 years, there have been almost continual blood baths, civil wars, violence and poverty.

When Columbus captured the whole island, and christened it Hispaniola, it had around one million Arawak Indians. Within fifty years of the Spanish arrival, the Indians had been worked to death, killed, or mostly died through disease. African slaves were then imported to work the plantations and their descendants form the population today, with ninety-five per cent of them black, the rest mulatto.

Hispaniola is now two separate countries. Haiti takes up the western third, and is French-speaking, thanks to the French pirates and then colonists in the seventeenth century, who took over the areas where Spanish settlements were sparse. The rest of the island, now the Dominican Republic, still speaks Spanish. Under the French, Haiti prospered and became the richest colony in the New World, exporting coffee, cotton, and sugar. A great deal of the wealth of France's Ancien Régime came from their Caribbean possessions.

The Revolution in 1789 not only changed France, but also her colonies, stimulating the black slaves to rebel. Napoleon sent 45,000 men to put down Haiti's revolution, arresting the leader, Toussaint l'Ouverture, who was brought back to France and died of starvation. The battle for independence went on, and was finally achieved in 1804 when Haiti proclaimed herself the first black republic in the world. Her leader, Dessalines, had himself crowned Emperor, but he was soon assassinated and the country became divided, the north having its own leader, Henri Christophe, who built himself nine royal palaces in fourteen years. He committed suicide in 1820, before anyone could kill him, but the pattern from then on was assassination, civil war, dictatorship, assassination, with occasional but short-lived bouts of peace. The arrival of Papa Doc Duvalier in 1957 was greeted in Haiti with delight, as he appeared to have been elected democratically. He was considered to be a good doctor and, as a pure black man, it was felt he would curb the power of the mulatto élite and stop the internal squabbles and battles. He did so, by making himself dictator for life, then surrounding himself with private gangsters, the Tonton Macoute, who terrorised the population and became more powerful than the army. In 1971, his son took over, and continued the repression, until he and his family fled in 1986, leaving Haiti to the military under General Namphy.

I had not chosen a very happy time to arrive, in the middle of this post-Duvalier chaos, but one report had particularly worried me. On the night the Duvaliers finally fled, a group of young Haitians, celebrating, had gone down to the waterfront, picked up a statue of Columbus, and hurled it into the sea. According to an American newspaper, which was where I had read the story, it was an anti-colonial gesture. Columbus was seen as a symbol of all the repressive régimes Haiti had had to suffer.

Next morning, after a nervous night, I caught a plane north. I liked Cap Haitien from the beginning. It was as crowded as Port au Prince, with shanty encampments, but people seemed happier, friendlier, less scared. It was also brighter, with more interesting architecture, most of it still in reasonable condition. Cap Haitien has had its share of bloodshed, as it was here that Napoleon's troops landed to put down the rebel slaves; and then, a hundred years later, the American Marines came, for humanitarian reasons, they said, but in reality to establish a base to protect the Panama Canal. They ended up occupying Haiti from 1915 to 1934.

I booked myself into the Hotel Mont Joli, for the name as much as anything else. There was a telephone in my room, which did not work, but the shower did. I seemed to be the only resident, but it was only mid-afternoon. The manager was a white Haitian. I assumed he must be of French extraction, left over from the French plantocracy, but he said his family were originally German, coming to Haiti via the Argentine. In 1969, he had converted what was his family home into a hotel.

'Things were going quite well till 1982 when an American doctor came out with the news that Aids originated in Haiti. We immediately had a forty-five per cent drop in tourism. Then, when the Duvalier régime ceased and the country was in chaos, we dropped another forty-five per cent. For a year we were practically empty. Now things are picking up a bit and a few cruise ships are coming in. Tonight, we're thirty per cent full, which is very good. The average for all Haiti's hotels at present is eighteen.'

A black Haitian businessman, who was checking in, picked up the reference to Aids. 'That rumour has done us such a lot of harm. It's just not true Aids began here. My theory is that they put three things together because they all began with H – homosexuals, haemophiliacs and Haiti.'

I pointed out that, 500 years ago, there had been a similar theory about Haiti – that it was the source of syphilis. I told him how the early Spaniards picked up syphilis in Hispaniola, then brought it back to Europe.

I explained my Columbus project, and how I wanted to find the site of Navidad, the first settlement in the New World. It meant nothing to him, or to the hotel manager. Then I mentioned the name of Dr Kathleen Deagan of the University of Florida. Her team of anthropologists had been digging near Cap Haitien for the site of Navidad. I knew she was not there at present as in a letter she had told me that 'due to the political situation in Haiti, we have temporarily closed our sites'. I thought the manager might have recognised her name and remembered where she had been digging. Still no reaction.

Then I found her letter to me and read out the name of a local man she suggested I should contact, an amateur archaeologist, called Dr Hodges, who had in fact first discovered the site.

'Oh, everyone knows Dr Hodges,' exclaimed the manager. He described him as their local Dr Schweitzer, a medical missionary doing incredible good works, out in the jungle. 'He works at a hospital at Limbe. They have a phone, but he never comes to it. I'll try and get a message to him, if you like.'

I slept well that night, thankful that I had got out of Port au Prince, and was up early to ask the manager if he had heard from Dr Hodges. Nothing so far. It would clearly take time.

Later, at the reception desk, I encountered a tough-looking farmer in heavy boots and very worn flying jacket talking on the telephone. He was an Englishman called John and I told him of my search for the site of Navidad. 'I know it well. I watched them doing the digging a year ago. It's right beside my plantation. I'll take you there.'

We drove about ten miles out of town, up the coast. Eventually we left the tarmac road and hit a series of dried-out mud paths. His plantation covered 750 acres and employed 300 Haitians, all of them women, except for his overseer. John was the resident manager. They grew sugar, mangoes, three types of orange, grapefruit, bananas, but the big crop that month, which was January, was French beans.

We headed for the Navidad site, adjoining his fields, and the ground got drier and dustier. He said this is what it would all be like, if they did not irrigate. I found a little hut on the Navidad site, where the excavations had been done. It was just a few open bamboo poles, with a sheet of corrugated iron on top. Inside, on a shelf, someone had put up a notice in English: 'Tarantula on Duty'. Near the entrance to the field was a more official notice: 'ISPAN – Institut de Sauvegarde du Patrimoine National. Projet – La Navidad.' It had been painted white, but was peeling badly.

I stood for a long time, thinking about the bones of the *Santa Maria*, underneath these fields somewhere, and the dramas which had taken place, the battles to the death, amongst the Spaniards, against the Indians, the bodies left rotting for the return of Columbus. I scanned the horizon. I could not see the sea, as the surrounding fields were very flat and scrubby, but I estimated it was two miles away.

Why was the site of Navidad here? Surely Columbus had erected his first fort on the beach? I had to see Dr Hodges. Only he could explain the mystery of Navidad.

The hotel manager still had no reply to his message sent to Dr Hodges's hospital. I asked him if he would try again, and spent the rest of the day waiting. Late that night, he told me he had eventually got Dr Hodges himself, on the telephone. 'He says he can't see you. He can't see anyone. He's far too busy. Sorry about that, but I did try.'

I got up very early next morning. I had come all this way, to the site of the first settlement in the New World. I had to make one last attempt to meet the person who had discovered it. From talking to the manager, I learned that Dr Hodges took a half-hour lunch break at 12.30 every day. I got reception to order me a taxi, someone knowledgeable and reliable. An old Landrover eventually lumbered to the front door and I met Louis, a middle-aged, very dour-looking Haitian. I explained I wanted to go to the hospital at Limbe. Did he know it? He nodded, gruffly. The job might take two or three hours, how much? He quoted 40 dollars. It seemed a lot, compared with 1.60 dollars for a woman working a ten-hour day on a plantation. But then life, and salaries, are not fair. So I agreed.

The mud huts in the jungle all looked much the same as we drove past them, then gradually I began to pick out different architectural stages. The most primitive houses were simply a square of plaited bamboo, with no doors or windows, just an opening, and a tin roof. The more elaborate had thatched roofs and wooden windows. The grandest had been plastered over with mortar and lime, then painted, usually in bright blue; nothing as artistic as their tap tap buses, but attempts had been made to decorate some of them. Around these dwellings were scattered modern bicycles and radios. John had said this was how Haitians judge respective wealth, not as in the West by the size and style of their houses.

It took us several false turnings to find the hospital, going down tracks which disappeared into the undergrowth, while we saw a line of people sitting patiently on a white wall, many of them with legs and arms in plaster, their families and children standing beside them. There were three or four modern buildings, low and simple, grouped round a garden area. I looked for the name, 'Hôpital le Bon Samaritain', but could see no signs.

What I did see were two men whom I took to be doctors. I told them I was looking for Dr Hodges and they pointed to a door. He would be coming out in three minutes.

I positioned myself outside the door and waited. Dr Hodges emerged at exactly 12.30; he was a tired-looking man wearing braces over a checked shirt. I fell in beside him as he walked round the building, keeping to the shade of the palm trees. I blurted out that I was from London, and that I had come 10,000 miles to see him and I was very sorry if I had disturbed him with messages and I knew he was very busy with more important things to do but if only he could spare me a few minutes as there was just one thing I wanted to ask him . . .

He kept walking, saying nothing. From time to time he gave me a quick glance, looking into my eyes. I decided it was time to ask my question.

'How did you discover Navidad?'

'Have you eaten?' he said at last.

He led me to what I took to be his own house and into a large family dining area. Around a long table were seated about twenty people, adults and children, mostly American, though a few of the smaller children were Haitian.

Dr Hodges sat down and indicated I should sit on his left. He introduced the people nearest to him, asking me my name again and to explain my project, while he leaned back, saying nothing, eating his bread and watching me, as if waiting for me to say something stupid.

I turned to the man opposite, who said he was working on a Creole dictionary. When published, it would contain 15,200 Creole words, and would be invaluable for all doctors and missionaries. From his researches so far, he had defined two sorts of Creole. There was Real Creole, an Anglo–French hybrid based on the original African roots, and French Fried Creole. This was his own phrase, to describe the artificial Creole used by Creoles when speaking to French-speakers. Over eighty-five per cent of Haitians speak nothing except Creole.

I moved the conversation on to the hospital, and asked how many patients they treated. In the wards, he said, there were 100 to 120 beds, while on any one clinic day they treated 400 to 500 out-patients. Surgical operations were not carried out, as they had no theatre, but most other things were attempted. There were three qualified medical doctors on the staff, including Dr Hodges, two final-year medical students in training, ten nurses, plus ancillary staff. One of Dr Hodges's sons was the hospital's engineer and handyman, a daughter was a nurse, another a laboratory technician, whilst his wife Joanna, also a nurse, was part of the team. They had five adopted Haitian children.

Dr Hodges had listened to all this, adding nothing, so I asked him what were the main ailments suffered by the local Haitians.

'I've looked at them, all day long, for twenty-nine years,' he said, pausing. 'I would say they were a healthy, vigorous people, who can work all day. Most of the problems have stayed the same. I suppose half our work is to do with respiratory problems, pneumonia, meningitis. About a third is to do with veneral diseases.'

I asked about Aids. He sighed. The first case he had seen was not until 1978. Now he was seeing two new cases every day. I asked if he thought it was true the early Spaniards had brought back syphilis to Europe. 'I believe that. We gave them smallpox and measles. They gave us syphilis.'

Dr Hodges pushed back his chair and looked at me again. My name had been troubling him, ever since I had arrived. Then he remembered seeing it on a book about Hadrian's Wall. He had not bought it, but considered doing so as he was interested in all aspects of archaeology. I felt I had passed some undefined test. At last he started talking freely.

He had arrived in Haiti in 1958 as a Baptist medical missionary. From the beginning, he had also been interested in local archaeology and had set himself the task of finding the location of Navidad. First he read all the primary sources on Columbus's life, by Las Casas, Ferdinand, Oviedo and others. Then he moved on to local sources, such as a work published in 1797 by a Frenchman, Moreau de St Méry, who did a parish-by-parish description of the old French colony. He thought he had discovered the site of Navidad, and his evidence included a Spanish coin of Isabella and Ferdinand, which he dated 1476. Dr Hodges retraced the Frenchman's evidence and in 1974, by an amazing coincidence, he came across an identical coin, in the same area. A local farmer had dug it up, while working in his peanut garden. It was in slightly better condition than the first coin and Dr Hodges was able to prove that it was not of the Isabella and Ferdinand period, but had been minted some time after 1518. The Frenchman had got the date wrong. It was examined by professional historians, and it is now agreed that each coin is a 'cuarto', or a piece of four maravedis, the first coins minted in the New World. Dr Hodges started digging in the same area, and found more evidence of a Spanish settlement, Puerto Real, which was established in 1503. It was a very important discovery, but it was not Navidad.

He decided to organise his search for Navidad in three ways. Firstly, he made it known he was in the market for any unusual bits of pottery, coins, stones, glassware, which people might dig up. 'I promised to reward them monetarily in proportion to the importance of the object found.' Secondly, he started tracing any signs of ancient Indian villages, those going back 500 years. There are no such records in Haiti, so this work had to be done on foot.

Thirdly, he started to reconstruct his own geomorphic map of the original coastline. This has been the biggest problem for all researchers over the centuries. Morison believed at one time he had located Navidad on a sand dune at a place called Limonade, but could never prove it. (Dr Hodges says it is in fact an eighteenth-century French fort.)

He discovered that during the French occupation they had drained the shallow and swampy coastline, putting in new channels, changing river beds, reclaiming the coastal strip for agricultural use. The result was that where Navidad had once stood was now two miles inland. He could therefore eliminate many possible sites, as they would have been underwater in 1492. 'I tramped around in my bare feet in the tropical swamps, looking for evidence, but it was those hundreds of eyes of local farmers which helped me find the artefacts I needed.'

One day, a boy dug up an oxbell, the sort of trinket which Columbus's men gave to the Indians to amuse them. 'I gave the boy five dollars, and he nearly fainted.' By 1977, he had found hundreds of items, a lot of them Spanish, but also remains of an Indian settlement which he decided must be the Indian town of Guacanacaric, named after a king mentioned by Columbus.

'I decided to run a trench in the area that seemed most likely from all the evidence. Even before we started digging, I felt sure from the shape of the mounds it was Navidad.' The trench was only eighteen inches wide, as he was working on his own, with just a few friends, and could not cover the whole area. Very soon, he was finding late fifteenth-century Indian pottery and then in an abandoned well he discovered a pig's tooth. 'That was very exciting. There were no pigs on Haiti till the Spaniards came.' He found other clues, which convinced him, but it was not until he called in Dr Deagan from the University of Florida that a proper dig was organised, and finally his discovery was verified.

'Dr Deagan's archaeologists had to leave in the end under a hail of bullets and a lot of harassment. The site has not been touched since they left. I put that sign up. Personally, I would go in quickly now, for the kill, and dig it all up, but then I'm an amateur. The professionals do things very slowly, putting every spoonful through their computers.'

Dr Hodges's work had not gone unrecognised. He had recently been awarded a thousand-dollar prize by Philias, the American Columbian study circle, and invited to the Dominican Republic for a Columbus conference. And he had also managed to create his own museum, near the hospital.

When he casually mentioned the musuem, I thought it might be merely a few personal bits on a dusty shelf in some disused mud hut, so I was amazed to find it was a modern building, architecturally designed, more impressive than any of the hospital buildings. There were wrought-iron gates at the entrance, two large pillars, a formal garden and above the front door were the words: 'Dieu Créa L'Homme À Son Image.'

It was the best museum of Arawak and early Spanish life I had seen anywhere so far, in Europe or the West Indies. It is a shame that so few people ever visit the Musée de Guahaba, as it is called, but then few people these days go to Haiti. As for the locals, out of a population of 15,000 in Limbe, only 225 had visited it in five years, most of those being school parties. But then they have other concerns.

'Things are now worse in Haiti than they have been at any time in the last 30 years. No one is safe. Ordinary villagers now carry machetes to protect themselves. Economically, they are not as badly off as they have been, because the contraband boats have brought down the price of things like rice and bikes, but there is much greater fear and uncertainty. I'm more worried about the future than I've ever been.'

I thanked him for all his help and hospitality, and information. I had intended to fly straight home, pleased that my mission had been accomplished, without stopping in Port au Prince, but Dr Hodges had told me something else I did not know. *Santa Maria*'s anchor is in Port au Prince. I could hardly leave Haiti without seeing that.

On the little plane back from Cap Haitien, I found myself with two very over-excited, bible-thumping preachers from Florida. One of them insisted on taking my hand at take-off, asking me to pray with him to Jesus. He was shaking with fear, but once we were safely in the air, he unclenched me and started boasting about a coup he had just pulled off, securing a hundred acres of jungle land to build a new church and school. 'The Catholics have been after that land for years, but we got it, boy, we got it. Praise the Lord.'

I was better prepared this time for Port au Prince, and had booked myself into a recommended hotel, the Montana, up on the heights of Petionville, well out of the town, which felt relatively safe and was certainly very comfortable. I spent the next morning enquiring about the National Museum, where Dr Hodges said the anchor was displayed. It still existed, and I got the address, opening hours and even the name of the Director.

It turned out to be in the same square as the Presidential Palace, home of the Duvaliers during those decades of dictatorship and corruption. The palace looked triumphant and splendid, a cross between Buckingham Palace and the White House, with landscaped lawns and some neat, very un-Haitian-looking fir trees. I had heard many tales of the torture and killings which had taken place in the ceremonial rooms.

I could not find the Museum at first, or see any building remotely probable, till I almost fell over it. No one had told me it was underground, a bunker in the Hitler mould, carefully hidden under the gardens in the centre of the square. There were two guards beside the entrance to the gardens who waved me back. I could not understand what they were yelling, as it appeared to be in Creole, but I decided to push on, shouting in reply that I had an appointment with the Director, which was a lie.

I rushed down the steps, into the bunker, and came to the entrance hall. A woman at the reception desk barred my way, saying they were closed. Impossible, I said, I've just telephoned, and checked your opening hours. 'No lights,' she said. 'No problem,' I replied. 'I'm not taking photographs.'

She indicated a light switch, then turned it off and on, to demonstrate it was not working. It finally dawned on me what had happened. There was an electricity cut. Naturally, in an underground building, that can be something of a handicap. I asked for a torch, but she said I would have to leave at once, no one was allowed in. When would it open? Tomorrow, perhaps, she didn't know. I asked to see the Director, but she said he was out.

There are two supposed *Santa Maria* anchors, both dug up in Cap Haitien in the 1880s by a Dominican doctor called Alesandro. During his search for Navidad Dr Hodges had spent a lot of time looking for local documents concerned with their discovery, until he found they had all been destroyed in a fire. The other anchor is now in Chicago, and Dr Hodges thinks its history is a trifle murky. But he is convinced the Port au Prince anchor is authentic.

The woman was now on the telephone. I suspected she was ringing the two guards outside, to come and eject me, if not imprison me. The half light inside the museum was not too bad, now that I had got used to it, and I could see that the museum was circular. I decided to make a dash for it.

I raced down the corridor and found myself quickly at the centre. I looked around, decided to try the right-hand displays first, running past them as quickly as possible. I noticed King Christophe's pistol, the one he committed suicide with, and Toussaint's watch. But I was interested in only one thing.

The anchor was on its own, resting on a little bed of pebbles. It was bigger than I had expected, about four metres long. Even relatively small ships like the *Santa Maria* needed hefty anchors. Despite the rust, it looked strong and still usable. I got out my notebook and was making a quick sketch when I heard shouting behind me. The guards were on their way. I dashed round the circle, keeping ahead of them, passed the reception woman who was still on the telephone, up the steps, and out into the gardens.

I had seen Dr Hodges. I had seen the anchor. Haiti, for me, turned out to be a happy place.

Map of Navidad, in Columbus's hand – thought to be the only known example of his map work.

13

The Third Voyage

IT TOOK Columbus over a month after his return to Seville, in June 1496, before their Majesties agreed to see him. His requests for his proposed Third Voyage were relatively modest: only eight ships. And this time he wanted to go much further south and discover many more new territories, perhaps even reach the large land mass which was supposed to be there. His proposal was followed by silence; no decision was forthcoming.

Ferdinand blames Columbus's enemies at Court, of which by now there were a great many. But the King and Queen did have other things on their minds. They were at war with France, and they were also negotiating a double wedding, their son and heir Don Juan and their daughter Juana to marry the daughter and son of the Holy Roman Emperor. They had already married off another daughter, Isabella, in 1490, to the son of the King of Portugal. He had died within six months, leaving her a very young widow, but she had then married his brother, who had subsequently become King. Their fourth and final child, another daughter, Catharine, was supposedly betrothed to the Prince of Wales, Henry VII of England's son.

The main point of all these marriages was a diplomatic one. By making marriage alliances with Portugal, the Austrian Empire and England, Spain was limiting the power and influence of her enemy, France. But the negotiations were tortuous. And, even when political agreements were eventually made, the financial aspects had to be sorted out. Personal preferences, let alone love, did not of course play any part. Queen Isabella herself had been betrothed at the age of six.

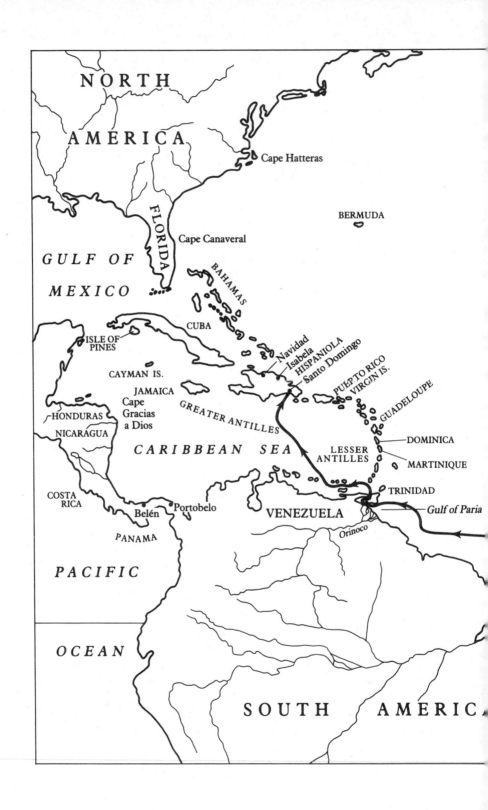

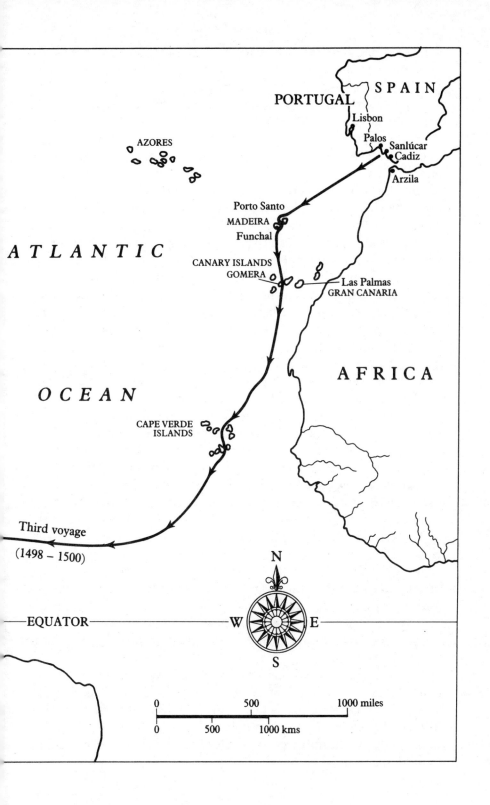

SPAIN

PORTUGAL

Lisbon

Palos

Sanlúcar
Cadiz

Arzila

AZORES

Porto Santo
MADEIRA
Funchal

CANARY ISLANDS
GOMERA
Las Palmas
GRAN CANARIA

ATLANTIC

AFRICA

OCEAN

CAPE VERDE
ISLANDS

Third voyage
(1498 – 1500)

N

EQUATOR

W E

S

0		500		1000 miles

0	500	1000 kms

The double marriage came to pass, in 1496, so there was great rejoicing, but also a great deal of expenditure. Isabella and Ferdinand needed 130 lavishly decorated ships for the two betrothals, escorting their daughter in style to Flanders for her marriage, and bringing back the bride for Don Juan.

In the middle of such dynastic manoeuvring, Columbus could hardly claim centre stage. Indeed, he seems, for a while, to have become almost a figure of fun. People pointed at him in the streets of Seville, muttering, 'There goes the Admiral of the Mosquitoes.' Most people had heard about the political and civil problems in Hispaniola, and also the appalling climate which had to be endured. Columbus was still wearing Franciscan robes, spending most days in the company of friars, pouring out his soul, poring over his problems.

In 1497, Don Juan developed a high fever after a feast in his honour at Salamanca, and died. He was aged nineteen. His mother was distraught. 'It was the first knife of sorrow to pierce her heart,' wrote a Court historian. The tragic death distracted the life of the Sovereigns and the Court for many months. It also meant that the sons of Columbus, young Ferdinand and Diego, were out of a position, as they had been pages to Don Juan; the Queen, however, decided to take them on to her personal staff.

Isabella did not overtly turn against Columbus, but she was beginning to have her worries. The whole matter of the slaves bothered her. Was it morally right to bring back Indians and sell them? Some advisers said, yes, if they had been captured, and anyway they were heathens. But should they not be converted and saved for God? asked the Queen. King Ferdinand and Columbus's enemies were more concerned with the cost. There were 500 men out there in Hispaniola. They all had to be supplied and paid for, with so far very little return.

In 1498, the subject of Columbus's new expedition received serious consideration once again when there were rumours that Portuguese explorers were thinking of straying west. They were said to be looking for fresh lands, rumoured to be below the Equator, possibly on their side of the dividing line agreed by the Treaty of Tordesillas.

In May 1498, Columbus was finally allowed to depart on his Third Voyage, two years after he had returned from his Second. He was given only six ships, not eight; and three of these were later deemed supply ships, to go direct to Hispaniola, while the other three, under Columbus, could explore southwards, before ending up in Hispaniola.

Columbus did something significant before he departed. He made a will. It must have entered his mind that he might never return from this voyage to the deep south. Now that he approached the age of forty-seven, he should have his affairs in good order, and protect his sons, now growing up. All his titles and privileges were to go to Diego, his legal son and heir. There was also an interesting condition, imposed upon Diego, that he should hand over certain sums to a bank in Genoa. This is one of the few written pieces of evidence linking him with his birth-place, and also an indication that he had borrowed heavily from Genoa. If trade with the Indies materialised, perhaps Diego would benefit, and settle his father's debts.

Just before the little fleet left the Guadalquivir, Columbus got news that there were French warships lying in wait off Cape St Vincent, so he decided to take a different route. Instead of heading direct to the Canaries, he made for Madeira, Portuguese territory, but safe now that Isabella's daughter was Queen of Portugal.

His first stop was at Porto Santo. This was when, according to Las Casas, he took on wood, water, fresh provisions, and heard Mass. As far as is known, this was the first time he had returned to the little island where, twenty years previously, he had lived with his wife and baby son, and where all his dreams had begun.

He then followed the previous route, and made for the Canaries, once again putting in to Gomera. Las Casas does not mention the fair lady of the island, Columbus's love of earlier years. After the little fleet left Gomera, the three supply boats went off on their own, direct to Hispaniola. Las Casas observes that Columbus appointed as captain of the supply boats the brother of his mistress Beatrice (mother of his second son Ferdinand), adding that their father had been one of those killed in the Navidad massacre.

Columbus kept his course due south and arrived next in the Portuguese-held Cape Verde Islands. He considered their name a misnomer. 'For he never saw a single green thing,' says Las Casas. 'Everything was dry and sterile.' On one of the islands, Boa Vista, equally badly named, so he thought, being miserable and melancholy, he came across a leper colony. Ferdinand describes how the Admiral wished to find out how the lepers were cured and was told it was firstly because of the temperate climate, secondly a diet of turtle meat, and finally by smothering themselves with turtles' blood. Columbus was immediately led into an investigation of the habits of the turtle: how at night the locals with torches turned them on their backs, so they could not run away, then next day chose the best for eating, and let the smaller ones go.

Throughout Columbus's journals, whether quoted directly or indirectly, there is this constant curiosity about the world. He is so obviously fascinated by every new sight and sensation, and determined, like a good Renaissance man, to investigate and understand. Sometimes he details an assistant to do a proper study and produce a little report, as on Hispaniola where he asks a Father Ramon to investigate the language and rituals of the Indians (the earliest anthropological report on the New World), but more often he does it himself, recording the results in his daily journals. Las Casas and Ferdinand are only picking out the highlights, or important events which take the story forward, but there was clearly much more they could have used, now all lost. Columbus takes such innocent pleasure in new knowledge, despite his lack of formal education, despite his now frequent illnesses, and despite, probably most important of all, the fact that the rest of his crew are eager to move on.

After they left the Cape Verde Islands, they continued due south, as Columbus's plan was to cross the Equator, but they ran into a serious problem: not storms but doldrums. They were becalmed for eight days, during which time they thought they would be burned to death. 'The heat was so excessive,' writes Ferdinand, 'that it scorched the ships. None could endure staying below deck. Many barrels of wine burst, snapping their hoops, and all the wheat and other provisions were scorched.' It seems more likely the wine was inferior or there were no air-vent bungs, as Columbus had trouble before departure with his suppliers, suspecting he was being cheated by the coopers and chandlers. He is said to have punched one of them on the jaw, which impressed his crew, but did not necessarily produce better supplies.

He took many sightings, studied the North Star, observed the strange movements of the magnetic needle of his compass, tried to work out exactly where he was and the relationship between the Equator and the North Pole. He estimated he had reached seven degrees above the Equator, but his measurements are confused, as are his theories and explanations, all of them mixed up with his Biblical beliefs.

Fortunately, we have some of his own comments on this voyage as not long afterwards he wrote a letter to the Sovereigns, reporting on what he had concluded about sailing towards the Equator. 'I have always read that the world, both land and water, was spherical, as the authority and researches of Ptolemy and all the others who have written on this subject demonstrate and prove, but I have seen this discrepancy and am compelled to come to this view of the world: I have found it has the shape of a pear, which is all very round, except at the stem, on one part of which a woman's nipple has been placed.'

It is an engaging theory, the world as a breast rather than a football. In arriving at it, so modern astronomers agree, he did notice and record several astronomical anomalies which had not been known before, but his scientific conclusions become clouded by other considerations. He believed, for example, as he repeats in this letter, that the Scriptures are right and that God did create an Earthly Paradise, that there is a fountain from which the Earth's four main rivers flow, the Tigris, Ganges, Euphrates and Nile. This fountain is at the centre of the Orient, exactly where he is not sure, though it could be in that nipple, which would explain the little bump on an otherwise spherical globe.

Perhaps because of all this mental fervour, added to the equatorial heat, Columbus began to suffer from some sort of fever. Las Casas says it was 'an attack of gout and insomnia, but he did not cease from working and watching with great care and diligence'. In the end, Columbus decided not to cross the Equator and run the risk of being fatally burned, so they turned to the west, heading directly towards the Indies, and the area which Columbus was roughly familiar with.

If they had kept to this route, they would have hit the Amazon, found what is now Brazil, taken it for Spain, and introduced an interesting demarcation argument with the Portuguese. Instead, while just a hundred miles or so off the mainland, they turned north, deciding at last to head for Hispaniola.

Columbus might have made mistakes in his estimates, been confused by the meaning of his own discoveries, been wrong to believe what he thought the Bible said, but there was always a consistency about his sense of direction, based on his own instinctive observations and personal records, which enabled him to head for home. After a period of general wanderings and being technically 'lost', he always seemed to know which direction would bring him to where he wanted to go.

On July 31, 1498, the look-out man sighted land, away on the port side, three peaks rising up on the horizon. There were celebrations on board, 'Salve Regina' was sung, and Columbus named the new island Trinidad, after the peaks, but also in honour of the Holy Trinity. They turned along the south coast, looking for a good harbour, as they needed to stop to get water. A party went ashore, but saw no one, as the Indians had fled their houses, leaving their fishing tackle.

Two days later they came across a large canoe, out at sea, with twenty-five Indians on board, who stared in amazement at the Spaniards, and began shouting to them. Columbus presumed they were proclaiming who they were, in the Indian style, so he decided to appear as friendly as possible. According to Las Casas, he did this by 'displaying some brass chamber pots and other bright objects, coaxing them with signs and motions to approach the ship'. The Indians were unimpressed. Columbus thought he would try entertainment instead, and told the tabor player to give a tune while the ship's boys were commanded to dance. This time, there was a fairly immediate response. The Indians dropped their oars, picked up their bows, and sent a hail of arrows over the Spaniards.

No one was hurt, but Columbus ordered his crossbowmen to fire over the Indians' heads, to frighten them; it had the desired effect and everyone calmed down. One of the Spaniards then went on board the canoe, taking a coat and cap and other presents which he gave to the man he thought was the leader. The Indians invited him, in sign language, to come ashore and visit their village, but he said he must first consult the Admiral. He got back into his own barge, to return to Columbus's ship, but the Indians immediately decided not to wait and so departed. 'They were never seen again, by the Admiral or anyone else,' so Las Casas writes. It was one of those inconclusive episodes, of which there must have been so many, on every voyage, which stuck in Columbus's mind, and intrigued Las Casas.

They did, however, meet some of the residents of Trinidad, and were delighted by both the people and the landscape, the prettiest Columbus had ever seen, with woods leading right down to the water's edge. He was intrigued by bits of other islands he could see, or what he thought were islands, but rather alarmed by the sea itself. It seemed to have a constant tide, on and under the surface, which moved at all hours of the night and day; but, strangely, it was not very salty.

He had wandered into the Gulf of Paria, on the coast of what is now Venezuela, an extremely dangerous area, with conflicting tides, and narrow, rocky channels which appear to lead into the open sea, but can be traps. He called the first channel the Boca de la Sierpe, the Serpent's Mouth.

On August 5, 1498, he landed on the Paria peninsula, though he still thought it was an island. He found an abandoned fire and fish and empty huts, but no people. Next day, moving five leagues on, he landed at another bay, where he was met by friendly natives.

'They have very beautiful figures and are all large, the genital member is bound up and covered and the women are all naked as their mothers bore them. Some of them wear their hair long, others as we do; none of them has sheared hair as in Hispaniola. I gave them hawks' bells and beads and sugar and after they heard of the good treatment accorded to their fellows, they all wanted to board the vessels. Those who had canoes came and they were many and were warmly received. They brought parrots of two or three species . . . They brought bread and water and some beverage like green wine . . .'

All in all, it was a happy arrival, although Columbus did notice that the Indians had bows and arrows, the arrows tipped with poison. He clearly thought highly of the people, and of the land. 'The whole region is full of very beautiful, very populous islands, lands of great altitudes, valleys and plains. The people are much more civilised than those of Hispaniola, they are warriors, and the houses are attractive.'

It was a bit like his first, joyful impressions of San Salvador, on his first landfall, except that this time he was not on an island. Nor were most of the bumps of land which he could see islands. He had landed at long last on the American continent: South America, to be precise.

Paria is on the northern coast of South America. Columbus and his companions were the first recorded Europeans to set foot on this continent, indeed on any part of the mainland of the Americas, if the Norsemen in the eleventh century are discounted.

Perhaps, for a moment, he wondered if some other foreign visitors had not already got there first, judging by some unusual goods the local Indians were carrying. 'They brought kerchiefs of cotton carefully embroidered and woven and workmanship exactly like those which are brought from Guinea. Everyone tied their heads with small kerchiefs which held in place their hair and looked very fine . . . kerchiefs worked in colours that it looked like an almayzar . . .'

An almayzar was a colourful Portuguese handkerchief, imported from Guinea. Columbus was simply commenting on the similarity in style and design, without drawing any conclusions. It is possible, if you dredge through all the journals and contemporary letters, to see little references like these and work up a thesis, however thin, to suggest that perhaps people from Africa had already made connections with America, before the Europeans.

Columbus saw something else worn by the Indians which attracted his attention much more sharply, though at the time he did very little about it. 'Some women came who wore on their arms strings of small beads and among them pearls or baroque pearls of high quality.' He saw these everywhere, as he sailed down and around the Gulf of Paria, and he even collected a few, but his mind was set on other sorts of treasure, namely gold. It was later Spanish explorers who exploited the pearls he had found, thus giving the Spanish Empire a hundred years of highly lucrative trading.

Columbus's main preoccupation, as he worked his way down the coast, was the enormous amount of fresh water. He discovered that he had to go around twenty miles off the coast, before it became true salty sea water. What did it all mean?

His first musings were Biblical in context, as he thought naturally of the Four Great Rivers of the Old Testament, wondering if perhaps he was getting near the fount of all life, all wisdom, not to mention all geography. According to his journal at this stage, as quoted by Las Casas, he was becoming ill again. 'Suffering affliction in his eyes from lack of sleep till they became bloodshot.' Las Casas says this always happened in dangerous waters, as Columbus was unwilling to leave the navigation to the pilots. He also appeared to be hallucinating, which could be linked with his religious theories, most of which do not make sense.

At the same time, Columbus started looking back on his life, on the things which had gone wrong, on his enemies, appealing for sympathy and help to his Sovereigns. 'I spent seven years in Your court and not a few took part in discussions. But finally only the extraordinary daring of Your highnesses decreed that the venture be made, against the judgement of all those who said it could not be done.' He adds, piously, that naturally he did not do any of it with a thought to 'amassing wealth and riches and many other things which we use in this world to which we are more favourable than to the things which can win salvation for us'. Las Casas stresses that these are Columbus's exact words. It was all done for God. There was no mention of the titles he insisted upon, or the hard bargains he made, the large percentages he demanded.

After about a week sailing down the coast, heading east, which was roughly the direction he needed to continue on towards Hispaniola, thinking he was still following an island which he would soon circumnavigate, he suddenly realised he was going completely the wrong way. Soundings showed that the water beneath was getting shallower, down to just two fathoms. He sent the smallest of his ships ahead, to reconnoitre, and they reported a vast gulf, with many openings. They had come upon the delta of the Orinoco. Columbus ordered his little fleet of three to turn round, and proceeded back down the coast of Paria, the way they had come.

The explanation for all the fresh water was now perfectly obvious. They had hit an enormous river.

'The consideration which moved him,' writes Las Casas, 'was that he did not see lands large enough to provide a source for such large rivers, unless, he says, this land is a continent.'

This is the first occasion, some time around August 13, 1498, that the possibility of a new continent is actually recorded. Las Casas then quotes Columbus's own words. 'I have come to believe that this is a mighty continent which was hitherto unknown. I am greatly supported in this view by reason of this great river and by this sea which is fresh, and I am also supported by the statement of Esdras in Book 4, Chapter 6 which says that six parts of the world consists of dry land and one part water . . .'

Even at his moment of greatest geographical discovery, Biblical revelations were still coming into Columbus's mind. Later, on reflection, he became confused again, not knowing what to call his latest discoveries, still obsessed by the thought that it might not be a new continent, but part of the huge continent of Asia, a sort of sub-continent, below China.

Academic arguments still rage about what precisely Columbus thought he thought. The problem stems from the fact that, subsequently, Columbus went back on his own theories, not aware that he really had discovered a new continent. This volte-face has been used to mock him, to make him look stupid. It is clear, however, to anyone studying the contemporary written evidence that, at that precise moment, he did use the word continent, and he meant it, even if he did not know which continent it was.

Columbus finally left the Gulf of Paria by negotiating a further difficult piece of water, which he called the Boca del Dragon, the Dragon's Mouth, a twin horror to the Serpent's Mouth, where he had entered this strange sea.

In his letter to the Sovereigns, there is an interesting phrase: 'And Your Highnesses have won these vast lands, which are an

Outer World.' Until then, he had normally used the words 'the Islands of the Indies'.

Once out of the Gulf of Paria, sailing round the north of the peninsula, this time in open sea, Columbus paused for a while at a new island, which turned out to be rich in pearls. He called it Margarita, as it is still known today, after a Spanish word for pearls.

He wanted to dally longer, explore this vast new region of the Outer World, but he realised he could not and should not. In arguing with himself, he listed six reasons against. Firstly, he was ill and in pain. Secondly, his brother the Adelantado would be waiting for him in Hispaniola. Thirdly, his supplies on board were being damaged. His fourth reason reveals that he had deceived his crew: 'For he had not dared to tell them in Castile that he was setting out with the intention of discovering, lest they set up obstacles and ask more pay than he could give.' Fifthly, his vessels were too big for discovery. Finally, he had almost lost his eyesight, and the men were exhausted. All these were good arguments for hurrying on to Hispaniola, which had always been his main aim, expected by his Sovereigns as well as by the crew. It was two and half years since his departure, and his brother Bartholomew must by now have become desperate for his return.

Perhaps Columbus did not want to hurry, fearing what he might find on Hispaniola. Those many problems he had left unresolved might by now be far worse. It was much more attractive and tantalising and exciting to savour further the virgin pleasures of the Outer World he had just discovered; to make the most of it, while he could, without suffering the troubles of administration and colonisation.

Indians at work, San Salvador: 16th century engraving.

14

Venezuela Today

Colombo '92

VENEZUELA'S CLAIM to world fame today is based on her oil, the source of her wealth and power. Columbus thought it would be pearls, but nature in the end gave up a different resource. The change happened quite suddenly, around 1914, when oil was first discovered near Maracaibo. Over the next seventy years, the oil was used to turn Venezuela from a deprived, overlooked and primitive country into the richest in South America. Caracas and Maracaibo were rebuilt and became booming modern cities, and a network of roads was created which is the best on the continent. By the early 1980s, Caracas was the most expensive city in the world. Then came the collapse.

On the plane to Caracas I sat beside an oil man who talked about it as Black Friday, as most business people in Venezuela still do, that day in February 1983 when the Government devalued by half. Caracas suddenly became one of the cheapest modern cities in the world, with luxury hotels charging under half the European rate and petrol down to 25p per gallon.

'We had about four years of misery in the oil industry. There was the extra worry that the Maracaibo oil was finally going to run out, then they found huge resources in the Orinoco delta. But this is heavy oil, unsuitable for most uses. Now an emulsion has been invented which breaks up the molecular structure of the heavy oil and makes it easily usable. You can even thin it with water, or burn it direct. It means Venezuela's oil reserves are now assured for the next 400 years.'

So Venezuelan oil wealth will come again, this time from the

Orinoco delta, which is where Columbus landed, rather than from the far west, around Lake Maracaibo, which is where Amerigo Vespucci landed. He arrived in 1499, the year after Columbus's landfall on the Gulf of Paria. Vespucci, a Florentine-born adventurer, was on a voyage with Alonso de Hojeda. When his sailors saw the Indian dwellings round Lake Maracaibo, suspended on stilts, they were reminded of the waterways of Venice. And so they called the country Little Venice.

I shared a taxi into Caracas with Carlos, my oil friend, a ten-mile drive from the sea up and over the steep coastal mountain range. As we ascended, the air became cooler, but the traffic more horrendous. The cheapness of the petrol means even the relatively poor can afford to drive. Carlos pointed out the last number on every car's licence plate which signifies the day on which you cannot drive it in Caracas. An 8, for example, means that you are banned on Fridays. This regulation was meant to cut the traffic at a stroke, but all that happened was that most families bought another car, to be driven on the no-go day. The authorities cannot rescind the rule as overnight all the second cars would appear and the traffic double.

Caracas lies in a long, low valley, over the top of the range, surrounded on each side by large mountains, green and lush, now mostly given over to national parks. It was dark as we approached and millions of lights were glistening high up on the mountainsides, as if the more affluent residents had already lit up for Christmas. Carlos said those were the shanty towns. Caracas is unusual amongst the world's cities in that the poor live on the lush surrounding hill-slopes while the rich live down in the valley. The city has a population of over four million, a high proportion of them illegal immigrants from surrounding South and Central American countries. Gangs of these are alleged to come down into the plain at night, looking for pickings.

I had booked myself into the Hilton International. I did not intend to stay long. My aim was somehow to get down to the Orinoco and find the place where Columbus landed. I had a great many telephone calls to make and arrangements to organise, so a modern hotel would be useful. Also safe.

I had a new set of impressive letters of introduction, written personally by His Excellency the Venezuelan Ambassador in London, telling the world and his secretary that I was a 'distinguido escritor británico, que ha escrito más de 30 libros'. Three of the letters were addressed to famous Venezuelan historians and academics, who I was told would be pleased to see me.

I spent the whole of the next day trying to reach these three academic contacts, but not one address was correct, the institutes they worked for had moved or disappeared. I eventually got the secretary of one of the professors, Sr Doctor Moron, President of the National Academy of History, a household name in educated Venezuelan households, but he had gone to Costa Rica for a conference.

In the bar I got talking to an American teacher, resident in Caracas. He said that, being British, I should not have too much trouble making contacts. The British were still quite popular, thanks to the fact that Simón Bolívar had a British ADC in his final battle.

The struggle for independence from Spain began in 1811. It was sparked off, as in so many places, by the French Revolution, but the Spanish fought back and it was not until 1823 that Bolívar finally triumphed. I had to admit that I had always presumed Bolívar was Bolivian. I knew about his extraordinary march over the Andes, but I had never realised he was born in Caracas, in 1783, of mixed white race, with a touch of Indian blood, and that his army of liberation from Spain caused the independence of six countries – Ecuador, Colombia, Panama, Peru, Bolivia and Venezuela. He remains a hero in all of them, but most of all in Venezuela where countless streets, cities, parks and places are named after him; and the currency as well. His portrait is everywhere, dressed impressively if stiffly in Napoleonic uniform, to hide the fact that he was very small.

'The character of the Venezuelan is optimistic,' said the American, 'not very provident, with a sense of humour and a strong sense of personal dignity. We'll probably start in 1991, getting ready for 1992, ten years behind everyone else, but we'll end up spending ten times as much as other countries. That will be very typical.'

Next day, I found a couple of Columbus objects to look at. In the Parque del Este they have a reproduction of *Santa Maria*, moored in what appears to be a large paddling pool. The park was closed, so I could only gaze through the gates. But I did get up close to a large and impressive statue of Columbus, risking my life in the process, as it is on a traffic island, not far from the Plaza Venezuela. I had to race between freelance break-down lorries, looking for accidents, then avoid the street vendors, jumping maniacally at anyone who might be in need of lottery tickets, dolls or straw mats.

Columbus stands on top of a high column, one arm outstretched.

Below him a half-clad woman is climbing up the column, for no
apparent reason, while low down there are two more women, on
either side of the main column, sitting on their own plinths, one
holding a globe, the other a stick. I had become something of a
connoisseur of Columbus statues and this was one of the finest bits
of sculpting I had seen so far, set in a splendidly high position.
Sadly, the finer points of Venezuelan symbolism were wasted on
me. Nor was the inscription much of a help: 'Colon en El Golfo
Triste.' Where is the Sad Bay? Was that what Columbus called his
landing place in Venezuela? Or is that a Venezuelan name for the
Gulf of Paria, where he first sailed?

I decided I had had enough of Caracas. Columbus never got
there and, despite being the capital city, it did not seem very
interested in the country's first European visitor. I obviously had
to get myself down to the Gulf of Paria. Nobody I met had ever
been there, as it cannot be reached by road. Eventually, I found I
could get a local plane going in what appeared to be the right
direction, so I booked a return ticket, costing only £20 for something
like a thousand-mile trip.

I got up at 4.30 the next morning, to catch my taxi, but even at
that hour the roads were busy. Caracas's airport, inevitably called
Simón Bolívar, but known locally as La Guaira, which is where it
is located, was already crowded, with queues snaking round the
departure points, all good-humoured. I was making for a place
called Guiria which I was finding very hard to pronounce; I was
worried I would never get there, but spend all my time at La Guaira
airport instead. The airport bus went round and round the tarmac,
looking for our little local plane which was the propeller variety, of
uncertain age. It seemed to be stuck together with black sticky tape
and was shaking rather violently.

Porlamar, the first stop, is on the island of Margarita, round
which Columbus sailed, though he does not appear to have landed
there. Just forty years after he left, the Spaniards were exporting
the local pearls back home and Courts throughout Europe competed
for the best specimens which were said to be as big as pigeon's
eggs. Today, Margarita is Venezuela's booming holiday island,
billed as 'The Pearl of the Venezuelan Caribbean', attracting one
and a half million tourists a year, thanks partly to the fact that it is
duty-free. Visitors now come for the cheap alcohol as much as
for the beaches and hotels. The island also boasts cock-fighting,
dog-racing and a giant roller-coaster. There are fake Indian adobe
huts on the beaches, with palm-leaf thatch, and also reconstructed

Spanish castles. So the Venezuelans have not completely ignored their own history.

Our final stop was Guiria, the end of every line, either by road or air. The rest of the Paria Peninsula, which stretches for another fifty miles or so, till it comes to a point opposite Trinidad, is impassable by land, with no roads at all, and is mainly equatorial jungle and rocky mountains. This was the coast that Columbus sailed down and then up, realising he had reached the shallows of the Orinoco delta at one end.

The airport was just a strip in the jungle. I managed to commandeer the only taxi. On the way into town the track turned into a fast-flowing stream and we got bogged down in some deep red mud holes. There had obviously just been a fierce tropical downpour. It was almost Christmas, and the winter rains should have been over by now. The town appeared completely jerry-built, a grid pattern of low concrete blocks, very like the shanty towns in Caracas. Here, in Guiria, it was considered civilisation, compared with the jungle beyond.

I had the name of one hotel, taken from a Venezuelan guidebook I had bought in Caracas, which did have the decency to make it clear it was only fourth class. Even so, when the taxi pulled up outside, I was convinced it was either closed or abandoned. I told the driver to wait, just in case.

I got out of the car. The heat and humidity was intense. Every movement was an effort. There were insects everywhere. As I crossed the empty street, I could see poverty stricken locals sitting motionless in the shade of boarded-up doorways, watching me, wondering where this stranger had come from, and why.

I found the hotel door, just a hole in the concrete, and walked upstairs along an open landing, feeling I was still being watched by the street below. I came to a little reception area. Two men were slumped in old-fashioned straw chairs, one black and wearing sunglasses and a baseball cap, the other younger, Mexican-looking, in need of a shave. They stared at me coldly. I asked a plump girl behind the desk if she had a room for the night. After much jangling of keys and studying of lists, she said yes, and asked to see my passport. She also wanted the money in advance, 150 bolívars, about £2.50 for the night. The key was tied by a piece of string to a lump of wood, big enough to carve into a model of *Santa Maria*. I was beginning to regret my journey. How could I possibly find anyone to talk to about Columbus in this god-forsaken place? Haiti, despite being frightening, did have a sort of culture, going on beneath the bloodshed and poverty. Guiria felt totally abandoned.

My room was clean, that much can be said. I could smell the disinfectant and saw a cleaner scurrying out with her bucket as I approached. But it was threadbare, a primitive bed and a chest of drawers. There was one little window and I found myself staring into the backyard of what appeared to be a slum, with sinister alsatian dogs growling around the debris and a half-naked child eating a bone. On top of a derelict fridge there was a large, unattended ghetto blaster. It was blaring out George Harrison's 'Got my Mind Set on You'. I went back down to reception and enquired in my appalling Spanish if the girl could put me in touch with any English-speakers, a local teacher or priest for example. No reaction. I asked about historians, anyone who knew about Guiria. Silence. Then perhaps she could tell me the way to the harbour. Nothing.

'Take it easy,' said a voice behind me. It was the unshaven Mexican-looking young man. I almost jumped for pleasure. They turned out to be his only words of English. He kept on repeating them, grinning inanely, just to cheer me up. Every time he said them, I forgot and replied in English, and he would say, once again, 'Take it easy.' He was willing and keen and friendly. With a Spanish dictionary and a lot of pointing and sign language, I eventually explained I wanted to get to the harbour. Did he know the way?

He jumped up, got his keys, and went off to his room. He appeared about half an hour later with his wife, a young mulatto woman, clutching a red-haired chubby baby. He then sat down beside me and opened up some massive maps. I realised they were all deep-sea maps, showing currents and sand-bars and off-shore rocks around the Paria Peninsula, what Columbus would have found invaluable 500 years ago, but not essential for me.

He was a fisherman, with his own boat, based normally further down the coast at Puerto la Cruz, about 400 kilometres away. He had been fishing the Gulf of Paria when his boat had been damaged. He had been forced to leave it in Guiria while it was being repaired, and had now returned to pick it up. Only it wasn't ready. So he too was stuck in this god-forsaken place, along with his wife and baby.

'Take it easy,' he said for the umpteenth time, standing up, clapping me on the back, indicating that I should follow him. The burly black man in the baseball cap got up as well. He had been reading a comic and I had not realised they were friends. He took the baby's pushchair and carried it downstairs.

Outside, we got into an old Landrover, driven by the man in the baseball cap, all of us squeezing on to the front seat. I had no idea where we were going, but it turned out not to be far. We went once round the block, waving at people in the shade, and pulled up outside a café. It was time for breakfast, my fisherman friend explained.

Eventually we got back into the Landrover and this time we reached the harbour, which was much bigger than I had expected, with several massive cargo boats unloading. In the early decades of Spanish settlement, Guiria became their first port on the continent. Perhaps I should just stay here and soak up the atmosphere. After all, Columbus did sail up and down this very coast, and probably stopped at Guiria, as an obvious place to shelter.

The actual beach where Columbus landed is at Macuro, some thirty miles away, into the depths of the peninsula, and totally unreachable by land. I could see no possible way of getting there. My fisherman friend had shaken his head when I asked about boats. There are regular steamer services from Guiria across to Trinidad, but trips along the coast have to be organised privately.

I suddenly noticed a little motorboat which had on the side the name VENCEMOS. I had seen a reference to this company, which makes cement, as having a quarry not far from Macuro. It is still known as Macuro to everyone in Paria, despite the fact that the Government on its latest maps is trying to call it Puerto Colon.

A rather severe-looking black man in a pith helmet and sunglasses was standing on the deck of the motorboat, folding a rope, obviously getting ready to leave. I blurted out a few words of Spanish, asking if he was going to Macuro. He carried on working, so I turned to a few men standing on the quay, and asked if anyone spoke English. The pith helmet suddenly replied, 'I speak English.' He said he was originally from Trinidad, many, many years ago, but never spoke English these days. If I talked slowly, it should all come back to him. He was leaving for Macuro, in ten minutes, but he could not take me without permission. I pleaded with him, but he shook his head, then he turned to a boy on the quay and in Spanish gave him some instructions.

The boy ran towards an old car so I followed him and we drove along the waterfront to a tumbledown house. An old woman in an apron met us in the hall, looking fierce, but after the boy had gabbled something to her she led us into a front parlour which contained a dusty desk, some old shelves and a wind-up ship-to-shore telephone. The old woman wound it up and started screaming into it, all the time watching me closely as she yelled.

She was trying to contact someone called Señor Rubio, apparently manager of the quarry, whose permission was needed for me to be taken on a company boat. All I could hear was a lot of shouting. She finally hung up, and shook her head.

Back at the boat, the pith-helmeted captain said he should not take members of the public without authority. However, he was prepared to give me a one-way lift, but I would be on my own, and I would have to find my own way back. And he was going now. Take it or leave it.

I had no baggage or clothes with me. It was at least twenty-five kilometres by sea, according to the map. There was no hotel accommodation. I could be stuck there for days, even weeks. Yet it all seemed 'meant', arriving at the harbour, just as this little boat was leaving for the precise place I wanted to go to. I knew how Columbus must have felt when he decided something was 'a sign'. So I jumped in.

As we left the harbour, I tried to take a couple of photographs, but I was practically swept off the deck. At the end of the harbour wall, where we hit the open sea, all hatches were battened down and I was ordered below. The little motor launch was picked up, thrown high in the air by mighty waves, then sent crashing down again.

Beside me, cowering below round a little bench table, were three other passengers, all presumably connected with the cement company, probably well used to the journey, but none of them looked very happy. There was an old woman shaking her head. A girl of about eighteen, very fat, who sat staring at me, and a workman in his mid-twenties. He had a filthy bandage completely covering one arm, which looked gangrenous, while with his free hand he was turning over the pages of a sex comic. The old woman started muttering in Spanish, either to God or to me, neither of whom was doing her much good. The fat girl picked up an old newspaper from the floor and pointed out a cartoon to me. I could not understand it, but I gave a wintry smile, which seemed a suitable reaction.

I could feel my stomach churning and sea-sickness coming on, mixed with fear that we were going to be smashed to pieces. I wondered how Columbus survived year after year of this. And we had a motor, though it did not seem to be helping.

No one knows I am here. They don't even know who I am, my

name or address, where I'm from, where I'm going, why I happen to be on this stupid little boat. I'll be a mysterious body, found drowned at sea, unable to be identified. Would they eventually match it up with some baggage left behind on a hotel bed by some strange person who just arrived, then disappeared?

I tried to take my mind off a watery grave by scanning the coast through a port-hole, a difficult operation, as we were going up and down so violently and the spray was like a cloud. There was as yet no rain, but the black sky and the tremendous waves and wind were warning us that the worst was yet to come. The coast-line seemed to be sheer rock, red in parts, then mostly granite. Beyond, towered the jungle and the misty mountain-tops. Occasionally there was a little sandy bay, and through the trees I caught glimpses of some huts, no doubt belonging to fishermen.

It took two hours to reach Macuro, a battle all the way. I staggered off the little boat just as the rain began to fall like warm concrete bullets. The captain, still in his pith helmet and sunglasses, and looking as severe and schoolmasterly as when we had set off, said he would take me personally to Señor Rubio. We had tied up at a small cast-iron pier, which led to a huddle of concrete, modern buildings, to the right of which was the beach, hazy in the rain, but completely unspoilt; there was no sign of life, either past or present, though as we walked along the iron gang-plank I could see a few primitive huts in the distance.

We came to a one-storey bungalow, white-washed with a red-tiled roof. The captain looked hesitant, as if he was trespassing, as if I had pushed him already too far, making him do things he did not want to do. A woman came to the door, short and stocky, aged about thirty, and looked at us warily. The captain apologised and asked if Señor Rubio was in. The woman disappeared.

Señor Rubio at length appeared. He was also short, but very athletic-looking, tanned and fit, in shorts and tee-shirt. I stumbled through my explanation. He looked blank for a few moments, as if wondering how to react. Then he opened the door, told me to come in out of the rain, change my clothes, sit down, have a beer, stay for lunch. His hospitality was quite overwhelming, without knowing who I was or what I was doing. He just seemed to gaze at me for a moment, look me over, then say, welcome. Without him I would have been completely stuck, forced to sleep on the beach in a thunderstorm, and with no obvious way of getting back to Guiria.

Jesus Rubio was born in Pamplona, Spain. When he was thirteen his parents left to look for work. Jesus remained at home, in charge of two younger brothers. Two years later, his parents sent for him and his brothers, and they set off on a fifteen-day trip on a cargo steamer across the Atlantic. 'There were so many immigrants, all in the same position. It was like a democracy, all equal, there was a community spirit.'

His parents had originally intended to go to Canada, but had changed to Venezuela, being told there was more opportunity there, as they were Spanish. This was a typical situation in the 1950s and '60s. Venezuela had few European immigrants in the nineteenth century, compared with Brazil or Argentina. The population explosion has been post-war.

Jesus is now a Venezuelan, and proud to be so, thankful to his country of adoption for the opportunities he has been given. They started in one room in Caracas, shared with three other Spanish immigrant families. 'Every day at school was a fight. I was teased all the time. They laughed at the way I spoke. I couldn't understand them. I wanted to leave, but my father said no, you must go to school, I have come all this way for a better life, and that means you must be educated to get on. You can't do that in Spain, but here you can go to college if you pass the exams.'

Jesus went to a Catholic college, La Salle, and then after graduation to the University of Texas to read for his Master's in Marine Geology. He came back to Venezuela and eventually joined Vencemos. The name stands for Venezuelan Cement, a nationalised company, but also, rather neatly, it means 'let's go', 'let's get moving', in Spanish.

Four years ago, Jesus was moved to Macuro as manager of the gypsum mine. There were problems with the quarry which needed an expert geologist to solve, and someone with social skills to look after the local community. Vencemos, being the only employer within a radius of thirty miles, is like a feudal estate, the boss having powers like those of an old-fashioned village squire. The native village has 240 houses and a population of 800. Some manage to scrape a living off the land by farming, mainly cocoa and tobacco, but the returns are uncertain and irregular, as they are so far from all markets. 'Young people don't like going to work on the haciendas. They don't like waiting three months for any money, so they try fishing, which is much tougher, but can give quick money.'

In the end, most able-bodied young men leave for good, to work elsewhere, abandoning a surplus of young women, who have no work at all, and a lot of children. Half the population is under fifteen. The older men often end up looking after three families, to all intents and purposes with three wives. 'There are not the sexual hang-ups here you get in towns.'

Vencemos, in their little quarry, have work for only nineteen full-time workers and six part-time, but Jesus rotates the vacancies so that in the end most able-bodied men in the village get a few days' work and acquire some sort of training. He sees it as part of his job, as the quarry manager, to look after the village. 'I love it here and I've tried from the beginning to be involved in the community.' His two children go to the village school. It takes them only up to the age of ten, but has 200 pupils.

When I awoke the following morning in my room in the company's guest house, the storm had stopped.

As it was a feast day, the quarry was closed, and Jesus offered to show me around in his old Landrover, the only car in the whole of Macuro. We drove along the beach for a few hundred yards, past an army security post, manned by National Guard soldiers. They are there officially to guard the quarry, as Vencemos is a state company. In the village itself, there is a police station, but it has little to do. Thieving was unknown till 1983 when Black Friday came along and people overnight found their money worth half.

We splashed along a muddy path, past a few overgrown fields. Jesus said one of these, behind a wall, was the cemetery, but it looked as uncultivated as everything else. Eventually we came to the village proper. The quarry and its associated buildings are all fairly modern, concrete and white-washed, gathered at one end of the bay. The village is in the middle of the bay, slightly obscured by trees, with a few fishing boats on a white sandy shore and a small wooden pier. The mist from the mountains seemed to hang over everything.

There were no cars of course, and the streets were muddy and unmade-up, with pigs and donkeys and other animals roaming free, but there was a sense of township, with broad streets and houses laid out on a grid pattern, all rather pointless with no traffic, but quite impressive. The actual buildings were all one-storey, with tin roofs and high doorways. Many had been painted pale yellow and green. There was a certain faded attractiveness about them, which was a surprise, certainly more charming than Guiria.

No one knows what happened to the original Arawak communities Columbus saw, as later Spaniards settled much further round the peninsula, and records of Macuro do not begin till 1735 when some missionaries arrived. The name Macuro is thought to have come from the word 'marcouri', meaning pale face, or whites, though the villagers today are almost totally black. Could it have been the arrival of Columbus and his men which caused the name?

In the late nineteenth century, Macuro sprang into life when the Government turned it into a military and excise base. It became a thriving customs post, with a garrison of 300 soldiers. This was when the streets were laid out and some large warehouse buildings erected. Fine ladies paraded in their carriages up and down the broad boulevards, according to some blurry photographs in the Museum of Macuro.

This prosperity came to an end in 1935 when the customs work was moved elsewhere. Since then, Macuro has completely stagnated, except for the minor fillip given it in 1951 with the arrival of Vencemos to open their little gypsum quarry. (Cement contains around five per cent gypsum.)

Jesus pointed out some interesting tall doorways and windows, with further openings above them, very typical of what is known as Antillean-style architecture. We went down to the shore to explore the old warehouses, now in ruins, and an old stone court-house. Everywhere we went, people came to the front door to wave and say hello. Jesus seemed to know everyone by name and he insisted I was introduced properly. For days to come, he said, he would be admonished by villagers who had missed me. They do not get a lot of visitors, certainly not from Europe.

I met the chief of the military station, tall and moustachioed, who came out at a crossroads, as if about to apprehend us for some motoring offence, despite ours being the only car around for thirty miles. We had proceeded round the town at about five miles an hour, thanks to the pot-holes and to give the children a chance to run after us. He was indeed angry. Jesus had forgotten to sign me in officially in his station record book. We promised to do so on the way back.

Then I met the Judge, which was how he was constantly addressed, a white Venezuelan. He was standing drinking outside a bar, in the shade, with two other men. One of them passed round a bottle of sweet-smelling liquor. The Judge had been there four years, looking after matters like marriages, deaths and legal documents. I wondered what he did for company, in such a place. Jesus said there were four bars, each with a juke box, so you could spend an evening going round them all, which was what most people did, when they had any money.

I did meet one English-speaking resident, but she was too shy to say much. This was Amada, the village's unofficial midwife, who delivers every baby, an almost full-time job. They normally have a village doctor, but were waiting for a new one to come. Amada had the most beautifully smooth complexion and I was amazed to find she was sixty-three, mother herself of sixteen children. She had been born in Trinidad, hence her good English.

The residents I talked to did not seem to mind the total isolation of life in Macuro. They would not want a road over the mountains to Guiria, even if anyone had the necessary billions to spend. The company launch or the local boat was enough. The only real complaint was about the lack of a proper sewage system.

Our triumphal tour had taken us so long that it was suddenly getting dark. The streets had become full of long lines of young boys, humping sacks and boxes on their backs. It is their job to unload the village's supplies from the boat. They always wait till the evening, when the heat has receded.

We got home quite late, after Jesus had remembered to take me to the military post, where we disturbed a soldier, slumped over a television in a little office. I signed his records, trying without success to see how many other visitors the village had had in recent weeks, or recent years.

I went to sleep quickly that night, but the tropical noises woke me early. I could hear parrots and what sounded like monkeys in the trees outside. The equatorial mist was still draping the mountain-tops, hanging in thin curtainy clouds over the beach and the village.

After breakfast, Jesus took me first to the statue of Bolívar. It was small and insignificant, as was the little scrubby square in which it was set. Then we went round the corner to see the Columbus statue, larger and grander in a rather handsome setting. Jesus thinks Macuro is the only place in the whole of Venezuela where the Plaza Bolívar is smaller than the Plaza Columbus.

At one time, there was only a simple wooden cross on the beach, marking the landfall, but a previous president of Vencemos, a keen historian, had managed to spirit away a large Columbus statue from Caracas and get it re-erected in Macuro. It is tall and grey, in need of a clean, but Columbus himself looks very handsome, in a fur-collared cloak, rather a hot garment for the Tropics, though it gives him an aristocratic appearance. He has a sword at his waist, left hand resting lightly on it, while with his right hand he is pointing, as ever, into the middle distance.

'When he arrived,' said Jesus, 'he fell into the water as he was being unloaded from the boat. The tip of his little finger got broken. The first thing that happened when he was set up straight was that he peed water, out of his broken finger.'

There is another Columbus monument in Macuro, a little white-washed bust on a plinth near Jesus's house. That makes two sites to look for, should there be a sudden flood of tourists in 1992.

Jesus arranged for the company launch to take me back to Guiria. The sea was now totally calm and the sky a clear blue. I asked him what the weather would normally be like in August, when Columbus landed.

'Very hot, very humid, probably quite rainy. The sea out here can be very dangerous, but it depends on the tides. I should think his sailors would have been very scared at times, wanting to stay here and shelter. What all sailors have to face round here is the build-up of fresh water, coming straight from the Orinoco.'

It was of course the fresh water itself, not just the amount, which perplexed Columbus.

'When the tide is going out, and the current is running fast, then boats travel exceedingly quickly, even to this day, when we have motors. Once you hit the open sea, at the place still called the Dragon's Mouth, then the winds hit you from the other direction, the north-east. That's when it's really dangerous. You are running so fast and have no control, then wham, huge waves and winds suddenly hit you. Local fishermen never go out there at that time of the tide. They wait for the tide coming in, back towards the Orinoco, when the Gulf is filling up. That way you go more slowly, and you can control your speed.'

I looked out towards Trinidad, just visible on the horizon, and noticed a large, rocky island halfway between, another difficult obstacle, easily hit in a storm. How had Columbus managed it all, in such primitive boats, going up and then down this unwelcoming coast, not knowing the dangers and tides and traps ahead, looking for routes and places that did not exist? Yet he managed all this complicated navigation blind, without losing a boat, without mishap. Five hundred years of scientific progress have hardly made sailing in these waters much easier, as I know only too well.

15

The Third Voyage: 1498–1500

Colombo '92

COLUMBUS ARRIVED in Hispaniola from Venezuela on August 20, 1498, slightly annoyed with himself for having allowed strong currents to push his three ships further west than he had intended. He hit the south coast of the island, as planned, but about a hundred miles from where he had expected. All the same, it was first-class navigation, considering that for the last three months he had been in uncharted seas, meeting no other ships since they had left the Cape Verde Islands, seeing no known landmark, relying on his instincts and his own rough measurements and maps. He had left his brother Bartholomew, now officially and regally confirmed as Adelantado, to explore the south in his absence, find a good river, and then a suitable site on which to build a new capital.

This was now, technically, the end of Columbus's Third Voyage. Once again he had successfully crossed the Ocean Sea, and added this time a few deliberate wanderings and explorations on the Outer World, going down and around the heat of the Equator, possibly to the edge of the Earthly Paradise. The aim had always been to get back to Hispaniola, relieve his brothers, find out what they had been doing since he had left three years previously, then take charge once again, establishing Hispaniola as the centre of all Spanish dominions in the Indies.

The first signs were somewhat puzzling. He sent a party ashore to find some Taino Indians, as the inhabitants should be called, who could carry an urgent message to Bartholomew. Six came out to his ship. 'One of them carried a crossbow complete with cord and bolt and rack,' writes Las Casas, 'which caused him no small surprise, and he said, "Please God that nobody is dead."'

Indians, if they were armed, carried simple bows and arrows, with or without poisoned tips. The Spanish crossbows were mightily superior weapons which used the latest technology. In the space of only three years had the Indians advanced several centuries, from the Dark Ages to the sophisticated late fifteenth century? Or had this particular Indian just stolen the crossbow, perhaps from a dead Spaniard? Columbus received no explanation, but the six Indians did as they were directed, and hurried off with Columbus's message to his brother.

Bartholomew soon arrived, and there was a touching fraternal reunion. Columbus, though, was quickly given some very disturbing news. Things had not gone well. There had been a revolt. The colony was now split, with a large band of rebel Spaniards, under Francisco Roldan, whom Columbus had left with the position of mayor of Isabela, having set up their own province, over on the west.

Columbus's party made its way to Santo Domingo. It was his first sight of the new capital. They had chosen well. The Spanish town was on the left of the river bank, just inside the estuary, sheltered from the open sea, well clear of the native settlement on the other side of the river. A fort had been built, a strong barricade erected round the town, and work was in hand to replace the original wooden houses with good local stone which was now being quarried. The new capital had been named Santo Domingo by Bartholomew, in memory of their father.

Life in the city, however, was far from satisfactory, and the atmosphere depressed Columbus at once. 'Entering Santo Domingo almost blind from his continual vigils,' writes Ferdinand, 'the Admiral hoped to rest after the difficult voyage and find his people at peace, but he found unrest, for all the families were infected with a disorderly and rebellious spirit.'

Many were also infected with something else. 'More than 160 were sick with the French sickness [syphilis].' Perhaps the Spanish women, sent out from Castile so that proper family life would be encouraged, had introduced the disease. There is a theory, proposed by a professor in Florence, that women sent from Spain were in the main prostitutes.

Even worse news was the fact that the three supply ships, which Columbus had sent on ahead, to sail directly from the Canaries, had not been seen.

Gradually, Columbus was told the full details of the Roldan rebellion. Ferdinand devotes four chapters to it in his biography all about Roldan's men refusing to do any proper work, a plot to steal a boat, then a plot to kill Bartholomew himself (which was luckily discovered and the men punished), then an armed uprising, the rebels plundering and stealing and disappearing into the jungle with vital supplies and goods. Ferdinand's main point is that the rebels were shirkers, disloyal and wicked, who preferred an easy life instead of doing their duty as chaste, loyal Christians. 'They chose to settle in a province that was the most fertile in the island, with the most civilised natives, and especially the best looking and best natured women in the country. This last was their strongest motive for going there.'

It is possible, using the same facts which Las Casas and Ferdinand provide, to put another gloss on the rebellion. Roldan's men had simply made a break for freedom, wanting to live in peace amongst the Indians, treating them as human beings, disgusted by the materialism and brutal rule of Bartholomew. They had merely taken their share of the supplies, and women, and gone off to start their own settlement.

While Columbus was trying to make sense of all the dramas and alleged crimes, working out a suitable punishment for the rebels, the three supply ships turned up. But, as ill-luck had it, they landed in rebel territory. Roldan gave them a warm welcome, told them he was working under direct orders from the Adelantado, and commanded them to unload all the supplies at once. One of the three captains eventually did suspect that something untoward had happened, but Roldan had already persuaded a great many of the crew members (whom Ferdinand dismisses as ex-convicts) to join him in the good life.

If Columbus had seriously ever wanted to punish the rebels, it was now going to be almost impossible to do so. He had only around a hundred able-bodied men fit enough to fight, while the rebels numbered at least eighty. It would be a long-drawn-out struggle, possibly without a resolution, so after much soul-searching Columbus opted for peaceful discussions. He sent a message that he would like to meet and talk to Roldan.

Roldan naturally demanded safe-conduct, and many meetings, over the course of several months, ensued, with agreements made and then broken, while Roldan slowly began to realise that he in fact had the upper hand and could demand anything. He did so. Finally, Columbus gave in completely. All rebels were to be pardoned, allowed to live in their province, free of taxes, while anyone who wanted to leave the island would have a ship provided and could return to Spain, a free man, not accused of rebellion, taking with him any woman or slaves he chose. This is precisely what Columbus hoped they would do, thus ridding him of potential trouble-makers; the next supply ships might bring a better type of settler. But most decided to stay, though Roldan did at least promise his future loyalty.

Peace amongst the Spaniards does appear for a while to have been established, leaving the Columbus brothers free to organise the Indians in the gold mines. When that was done, they made plans to return to Castile, to report that all was now well in Hispaniola. But just as they were about to embark, in September 1499, another enemy appeared on the scene, a gentleman called Hojeda, arriving with four ships.

Hojeda had been on Columbus's Second Voyage, and had served him well in the early explorations of Hispaniola, but now he had turned against him. According to Columbus, he had somehow stolen or gained access to his map of the Gulf of Paria, which had been sent back to Spain, over a year earlier, when Columbus had first arrived in Santo Domingo. Hojeda had then set up his own little expedition, getting Fonseca to authorise it, something which Columbus maintained was not legal, and had sailed directly to the Gulf of Paria, in the company of Juan de la Cosa, the cartographic expert, and the Italian adventurer Amerigo Vespucci. They had explored the continental coast but, most important, they had gathered a great quantity of pearls: yet another illegal act, so Columbus maintained.

Columbus was furious when he heard where they had been, as he had authority, vested in him by the Sovereigns, over all lands he had discovered. No doubt he made his point abundantly clear, since de Hojeda at once started making trouble, siding with some of those former rebels who were still opposed to Columbus. De Hojeda also spread rumour, which may or not have been true. 'He attempted to cause a new revolt,' writes Ferdinand, 'by giving out that Queen Isabella was at death's door and that on her death the Admiral would be without a protector.' Many people believed this, and agreed that Columbus's days were numbered.

Queen Isabella, however, was not on the point of dying, though she had lapsed into a period of depression and illness, stemming from a series of tragedies within her family. In 1498, just a year after the death of Don Juan, her daughter Isabella, the Queen of Portugal, also died, in childbirth. The child, Prince Miguel, survived, becoming heir to both the Spanish and the Portuguese thrones, but then died, aged two. All the lines of succession were thrown into confusion.

The new century dawned dimly for Queen Isabella, and for Columbus, still beset with conflicts among the settlers, finding that the position of Viceroy and Governor was proving increasingly difficult. He was now entering his fiftieth year; his eyes were worn, his limbs weak, his patience beginning to tire as his enemies continually fomented hatred and revolt against him and his two brothers. His forgiveness of the first rebels seemed to have solved nothing. Bartholomew, the tougher and more determined brother, had always advocated a more brutal handling of any opposition.

Queen Isabella was receiving constant reports of the troubles from the ships which were regularly going back and forward, bearing tales of disaffection from those who had chosen to go home. Columbus's son Ferdinand, then aged twelve and still a page in the Queen's retinue, remembers Isabella being warned that, unless she intervened, there would be total ruin in the Indies. 'And that even if ruin was avoided, the Admiral in time would rebel and form an alliance with some foreign prince, claiming the Indies were his possession because he had discovered them by his own efforts and industry.'

Ferdinand recalls being with the court in Granada, at the time of the death of the Queen's baby grandson, Prince Miguel, and witnessing poor people who had returned from the Indies complaining in public to the Sovereigns.

'More than fifty of these shameless wretches brought a quantity of grapes and sat down to eat them in the court of the Alhambra, loudly proclaiming that their Highnesses and the Admiral had reduced them to that pitiful state by withholding their pay, and adding many other insolent remarks. They were so shameless that if the Catholic King rode out, they would crowd round him, shouting "Pay! Pay!" And if my brother and I, who were pages of the Queen, happened by, they followed us crying, "There go the sons of the Admiral of the Mosquitoes, who discovered lands of vanity and illusion, the grave and ruin of Castilian gentlemen." Adding so many other insults that we took care not to pass before them.'

The King had never personally been a supporter of Columbus, and now even Isabella herself was forced to agree with him that the situation in Hispaniola was extremely serious. No man could have so many enemies, or have created so much opposition, without there being some truth in the allegations. She still admired Columbus greatly as an Admiral, but as a Viceroy and Governor she was beginning to believe the general wisdom at Court that he had turned out to be a failure. He had formed a clique consisting solely of himself and his two brothers, all of them foreigners; they were disliked as much for that as for their apparent lack of leadership skills.

On August 23, 1500, there arrived in Santo Domingo a certain Francisco de Bobadilla, a high Spanish grandee, well connected at Court, well thought of by the Sovereigns, a respected judge by profession. Isabella had finally agreed that someone should be sent out to Hispaniola, with the royal authority, to find out what was going on, and if possible to sort out the problems, once and for all. Columbus himself, in an earlier letter, had suggested that a complete outsider, someone with judicial experience, should come and see for himself what he, Columbus, was facing. But he never thought that his advice would be acted upon, still less could he imagine the subsequent chain of events.

At the precise moment when Bobadilla arrived in the harbour at Santo Domingo, there were seven bodies hanging from the gallows, all of them Spanish. 'They were still fresh,' writes Las Casas, 'having been hung just a few days before.' There had been another revolt and Columbus himself had ordered the death sentences. Unfortunately for him, he was not in residence in Santo Domingo at that moment. With Bartholomew he had once again gone inland, to investigate yet more troubles.

Bobadilla was horrified. It seemed at once to confirm all the worst stories he had heard back in Spain. Diego Columbus, the third brother, had been left in charge, and Bobadilla immediately ordered him to release several Spaniards who had been imprisoned. Diego at first refused to acknowledge Bobadilla, saying he took orders only from the Admiral, but Bobadilla produced his royal credentials and took over control of Santo Domingo.

Columbus's own house and personal possessions were confiscated and then auctioned. Friendly letters, written under the signatures of the Sovereigns, were sent out to the rebels, pardoning them. Permits were given out at random, without fee, contradicting all the regulations Columbus had so painfully established. Diego, still refusing to take such orders, was arrested and put in chains.

Bobadilla sent off a messenger with a letter to find Columbus, addressing him simply as 'Admiral of the Ocean Sea', with no mention of any viceregal position; his own title read 'Governor of the Islands and Mainland of the Indies'. He was therefore Columbus's superior.

Columbus maintained he never received that letter, or any written accusations. Naturally, he was horrified on his arrival back in the harbour at Santo Domingo. He denied that Bobadilla could be his superior, refused at first to look at any of his credentials, abused Bobadilla for what he had done, saying that he should be receiving orders, not issuing them. Bobadilla's response was to clap Columbus in irons.

Two Columbus brothers were now incarcerated in the fort's tower. When Bartholomew eventually returned, he joined them. They had not as yet been convicted of any crime, but Bobadilla quickly convened a series of legal sittings, hearing only complaints from Columbus's enemies and the rebels. Perhaps no one would speak in favour of Columbus, or Bobadilla simply refused to call them.

Early in October 1500, the caravel *La Gorda* set sail from Santo Domingo. On board were all three Columbus brothers, being taken back to Spain to be properly tried and convicted for their alleged misdemeanours. They were all still in chains. Columbus refused to take his off during the whole of the voyage, although the captain, once they had left Hispaniola, offered to release them.

'He had been placed in chains in the Sovereigns' name,' writes Ferdinand, 'and he said he would wear them until the Sovereigns ordered them removed, for he was resolved to keep those chains as a memorial of how well he had been rewarded for his many services. And this he did, for I always saw them in his bedroom, and he wanted them buried with his bones.'

On the voyage home, Columbus did at least have the use of his hands because he wrote a long, rather tortured, very self-righteous letter to a friend at court, Donna Juana de Torres, pouring out his heart to her, knowing the contents would be passed on to the Queen.

'I have now come to such a pass that there is none so vile as to dare not abuse me. Had I despoiled the Indies, or the land which lies towards them, and given it to the Moors, I could have been shown no greater enmity in Spain. Who will believe such a thing of a country where there has always been such magnanimity?'

He then gives his account of what had actually happened in Santo

Domingo. The rebellions are described in detail, the guilty men are named. Then he moves on to the arrival of Bobadilla.

'The day after he arrived, he made himself governor, performed executive acts, issued permits for gold, remitted tithes and all other obligations. He announced he had come to pay everyone, even those who had not served properly up to that day. Without reason or necessity, he had granted to vagabonds privileges of such extent that they would have been excessive for a man who brought out a wife and children.'

Columbus had instituted a system whereby the Spaniards had to pay tithes on any lands they settled, and also a third of any gold they found. Bobadilla said all such things should be free, which was what the Sovereigns had always wanted for their citizens, that in fact Columbus had been robbing them. No wonder the residents so quickly took Bobadilla's side. He also rescinded Columbus's ruling that Indian women were not to be bought and sold.

'A hundred castellanos are paid for a woman, and this has become common practice; there are many merchants who go looking for wenches – those of nine or ten years old are now at a premium, but a good price can be obtained for women of all ages.'

Columbus also accuses Bobadilla of pocketing gold for his own use, illegally, and of stealing Columbus's possessions from his house. The constant accusation is that Bobadilla was trying to curry favour with the populace, at the expense of the good of the Sovereigns' lands, and to make money for himself.

Ferdinand, in his description, adds extra colour by saying that the rabble were encouraged to shout insults at Columbus and his brothers, and they were allowed to 'post scandalous handbills on the street corners'.

When the ship carrying the Columbus brothers finally left Santo Domingo, insults were still being hurled after them and horns blown in derision.

On board, Columbus was consumed with self-pity, but he did try in his letter to remind himself, and his Sovereigns, how in the past he had overcome so many slurs and slanders heaped upon him.

'I think your Grace will remember when the storm drove me into Lisbon without sails, I was falsely accused of having gone there to the King, to sell out the Indies. Their Highnesses learned to the contrary and that it was all malice.' That is a new and interesting piece of information, not mentioned by Columbus at the time, seven years before, on his return from his first triumphal voyage.

Had Columbus changed? Had events simply swung out of his

control, beyond his talents, forcing him to act against his true nature? In this letter there are no regrets or admissions of guilt about any of his own actions. It is all the fault of others. An outsider, or an insider at Court, might well read it and come to somewhat different conclusions. But he appears hopeful, still trusting to the good sense and good nature and friendship of the Queen, confident that she will accept his account and see him for the loyal servant he believes he has always been.

Meanwhile, as the ship neared Spain, Columbus's chains were still intact, his own form of self-flagellation. But would they remain to be buried with his bones, or would they soon be removed at his forthcoming trial? That was clearly Columbus's expectation, once more defying all his enemies, and with one mighty bound, the Great Discoverer would be free and proved right, yet again.

Columbus being arrested and chained by Bobadilla.
(Theodore de Bry, 1594)

16

The Dominican Republic Today

Colombo '92

THE PLANE was shaking as we neared Santo Domingo; everyone was silent, most of the passengers were crossing themselves. We could see nothing out of the windows except thick dark clouds. For most of the way there had been the usual chatter and clatter, in a variety of languages, but all talk stopped completely once it was realised that we had hit a violent tropical thunderstorm.

When we landed, we discovered that the airport was flooded and the tarmac outside had become a lake. Chaos reigned inside the airport. Nobody could move. Nobody could find anything. People were wading ankle-deep in water and mud even inside the concourse area. On the way into town, I could see abandoned cars everywhere, stopped by the floods, some just left in the middle of the road.

Such storms are not often mentioned in the travel brochures for the Caribbean, but they happen all the time between June and September, even though they are not as fierce as the real hurricanes, the famous 'named' ones, which can be utterly devastating. Columbus, as he was very fond of boasting, taught himself to understand the Caribbean weather and was able to predict when a bad storm was on the way. The most famous occasion happened in Santo Domingo. He prophesied an imminent storm, which no one else believed, and an entire fleet set out. They were all lost, dozens of boats and countless lives, but Columbus and his boat were able to shelter.

The day after my arrival the sun was out, the sky was blue, and the heavens were pretending that nothing at all had happened. Only the steam rising from the earth hinted at what had happened, as did the mud on every road. On the shore, the waves were enormous, pounding over the rocks, and as I walked into the town I came across two large boats, both wrecked in the night, stout iron-built cargo vessels. One had been in dock for repairs, been badly tied up, then had blown free and been smashed to pieces.

Hispaniola figured in every voyage which Columbus made. After the débâcle at Navidad, the headquarters of the Spanish West Indies moved to what we now call the Dominican Republic, and eventually to its capital, Santo Domingo, the city which was established by Bartholomew Columbus. (In due course Diego Columbus, Christopher's son, became Governor.) The Dominican Republic boasts the first cathedral, first university, first monastery and first hospital in the New World, as well as the first street, the Calle de las Damas.

The Spanish conquest and control lasted for less than a hundred years. By 1550, most of Hispaniola lay neglected, left to pirates and marauders, such as Francis Drake who attacked Santo Domingo in 1586. The Dominican tourist literature makes no bones about describing him as a 'pirate', but I noticed in *Fodor*, the American publication, mindful of UK sales, they call him an 'explorer', thus giving no offence.

For almost the next 400 years, the country was overrun by seven different invaders, including England, France, Spain, and the USA. French claims to the western part of the island led to the formation of Haiti as a separate country ruled from France, and in turn Haiti decided to take over the whole island, though the Haitians were driven out during the Napoleonic Wars and for a time Spain took control again. There is an ancient piece of verse, by a Father Vasquez, which says: 'Yesterday I was born a Spaniard. In the afternoon I was French. At night I was Ethiopian. I don't know what will become of me.'

It was not until 1844 that the Dominican Republic became independent. Then followed the inevitable sequence of dictators, the worst perhaps being the most recent, Trujillo, who took over in 1930. He was not assassinated till 1961. Since then, the Dominican Republic has been a fairly stable, fairly successful democracy.

Like many people, I had confused the Dominican Republic with Dominica, thinking they might be one and the same. Both were discovered by Columbus, but there the similarities cease, as the little island of Dominica has been resolutely British for almost the last 200 years, part of the Commonwealth till it became independent in 1978. The Dominican Republic, despite all its different rulers, has remained Spanish-speaking. Unlike Haiti or Ḉuba, it has rarely made the world's political headlines in the last thirty years, nor has it become known as a tourist trap, like the Bahamas or Barbados.

I half-expected the Dominican Republic to resemble Haiti in appearance and character, though I knew they are deadly rivals and hate any comparison. But I felt as if I was in a different century, not just a different country. Santo Domingo reminded me of a modern American town, with its smart hotels and new public buildings. The old quarter, which is what I had come to see, had obviously had a fortune and a lot of love expended on it, getting it ready for 1992. But perhaps the biggest and most obvious difference is the safety factor. They boast that you can walk anywhere at any time without fear. I did not believe this, until I saw the explanation: the vast number of security police or soldiers.

I was in the Plaza Colon when a boy came up to me. He kept pointing at his badge, which I thought was purely ornamental until I noticed his photograph on it and a proper stamp. He was an official street guide, he said, licensed to trade from the Parque Colon, outside the Cathedral, available to take me anywhere I wanted for a sum set down by the authorities, forty pesos for two hours. It sounded reasonable enough. His English was quite good and he had a nice smile and I liked his name, José Ivan Lusiano.

The Cathedral was closed, so I said he could take me down the Calle de las Damas. I asked what he thought about Columbus, what he had picked up at school. 'Columbus loved it so much,' he said, smiling and slapping me on the back, 'that he wanted to be buried here. It must be true he's buried here, that's why we're celebrating the 500.'

But had he not heard stories about Columbus and his men ill-treating the natives, was that really a cause for celebration?

'It wasn't him. It was the ninety-five other people on the ship, not Columbus. He came here to discover, not to kill.'

We walked the whole length of the Calle de las Damas. At first sight, it seems a fairly plain, empty, cobbled avenue, very straight, quite broad, very quiet, with no remarkable or dominant buildings. This is because the mainly two-storey fronts give little away. It is only when you get inside that you discover the hidden cloisters and courtyards, towers and gardens, palaces and museums.

The Alcazar stands out because it is a separate building at the end, in its own square, overlooking the river. This was the imposing palace built by Diego Columbus, which he wanted to reflect his dignity and importance as Governor, and was much criticised by his enemies for its ostentation. Architects from Spain were brought over to design it and 1,500 Indians did the heavy work. From the outside, it looks rather like a fortress, almost a prison with its light grey stone walls, but inside it is richly furnished. It is not enormous, just twenty-two rooms, but was considered enormous at the time, in 1510, in a new colony, a long way from home. It has been carefully reconstructed in recent years, and none of the fixtures is Columbian, nor are the furnishings; they date from the Spanish colonial period, so there is a feeling of an authentic Spanish grandee's house.

It is always a surprise in far-flung old colonial countries to see how the early European settlers took almost every detail of their homeland with them, even when they were deep in the tropics. The typical English country churches of Barbados make you blink when you first see them, surrounded as they are by palm trees. The little Portuguese churches in the Azores even smell like those in Lisbon or Lagos. The early craftsmen had been trained to build churches or houses in a certain way, and their early clients expected them to look as they did back home. Getting stone and other materials caused huge problem. At the Alcazar they did manage to find stone, but you can see traces of coral in it, which was present when they dug it out of the river. They also had no nails in 1510. All seventy-seven doors and windows still turn on pivots.

Back in my hotel, there was some good news. The Honorary British Consul had replied to my letter and was willing to see me. I expected some mysterious figure from a Graham Greene novel but she turned out to be an elegant English woman, Maureen Tejeda. She had lived in Santo Domingo since 1961, moving there when she married a Dominican businessman. The appointment as Honorary Consul came when the British Government gave up having an ambassador and a proper embassy, deciding they could run matters from Caracas. 'The retiring Ambassador said there was no work, really, just occasionally I'd have to go and get some Brit out of jail.' There was no salary involved, but she could put CD plates on her car and would be invited to diplomatic functions.

Maureen Tejeda arranged several appointments for me, to help me along the Columbus trail, firstly a Museum in the Plaza Cultura, 'the most impressive cultural area in the Caribbean', so the Tourist Board states. It must have cost a fortune and is a typically grandiose scheme beloved of dictators, but it was being well used, judging by the crocodiles of well-dressed schoolchildren. It took me some time to find the specific building, the Museum of Dominican Man, and as I wandered around I suddenly recognised the name on one of the statues. It was Bartolome de Las Casas, the first time I had seen his name in the Caribbean. He richly deserves to be commem- orated, not just because of his services to all Columbus scholars, but because he was the first to expose what the Spaniards were really doing in the Indies, from his own first-hand experiences. He settled in Hispaniola in 1502, took advantage of the land grants, then became a priest, rising to become a bishop.

Inside the Museum, I met one of the academic staff, Dr Fernando Perez Memen, a black Dominican with a fine Spanish name, one of nine brothers and sisters. He is the author of several books on the Church and State in the Spanish West Indies. I asked him what the man in the street knew about Columbus. Not a lot, was his answer. Most people were not interested, except to say 'Azarosa', which means bad luck, whenever they hear the name Columbus. It was the first time I had heard this in any Caribbean country, and thought it strange that in Santo Domingo, the richest city of the Spanish period, Columbus should be remembered for his ill-luck.

'Firstly, he brought bad luck, because all the Indians died. He then suffered here himself, as you know, being put in chains. Today, he still brings bad things. Three aeroplanes took off from Cuba to retrace his route, but they crashed and were never seen again. There have been monuments to him which never got built and ended in disasters. So that's what most people think of, when they hear his name.'

But what were his views, speaking as an expert? 'He was caught between two periods, the Middle Ages and the Renaissance. One moment he was religious and interested in mysticism, the next he was being very greedy, obsessed by the search for gold. It was typical of the period. He was a man who made extraordinary discoveries and was a truly great navigator, but he was a bad conqueror and a bad governor. He did not properly understand the modern state, the absolute power of his King and Queen. He tried to be independent, forgetting their power, and the power of the Court around them.'

Did he deserve what happened to him? 'He made the King and Queen angry, which shows he wasn't clever enough, not clever enough to play politics, so in that sense he didn't do his job well as

Governor. He was not a good diplomat. What happened to him was unjust, because his enemies had won. He did discover a new continent, but the fact he thought he had arrived in India was always held against him. And he always insisted he was right. Then his mental state deteriorated, he became obsessed by the Biblical prophecies.'

Maureen's major triumph was to invite me to dinner with Bernardo Vega. Everyone in the Dominican Republic I spoke to had heard of him, and was in awe of his many talents and the important positions he had held; he is a literary figure as well as an economist, an author and publisher who has also been Governor of the Central Bank and an Ambassador.

When he arrived at the restaurant, he looked totally English, in a pin-striped suit, white shirt, neat tie, tall and very distinguished-looking, greying at the temples, aged about fifty. His English was very English, with no trace of an American accent. At first he hardly seemed to concentrate, because he was continually being pestered by people at other tables waving and smiling.

At length, he relaxed, and I began to ask him about himself, and his impeccable English. I should have guessed. His father had been the Dominican Ambassador in London, sending him to Downside, not to improve his English but his Latin. 'It was in the early fifties, and rationing was still on, and my father used to send me extra sugar, which I swapped for sweet coupons, till I'd cornered the market. My housemaster told me to stop it, as it was disrupting the school. In 1953, on the death of your King George VI, I was invited to the funeral, with my father, but the school wouldn't let me off for the day because I was a foreign boy and it wasn't fair I should be the only boy in the school going to the King's funeral. I was rather picked upon for being foreign. I was called a dago and sometimes a bullfighter. I'd never seen a bull in my life, or been to Spain.'

I asked about his time as Governor of the Bank, from 1982 to 1984, but he merely made self-deprecating jokes about it, in a very English way. 'Being an economist is very much like being Columbus. You don't know where you are going, when you will arrive, and you don't recognise it when you get there, but it's all paid for by the Government . . .'

We talked about Columbus and I asked about Isabela, the site of the first proper town in the New World, after the fort of Navidad had been destroyed. It is up on the north coast, about an hour from Puerto Plata. It was at one time thought to have been built on the site of an Indian village. 'You'll remember that the Spaniards complained of being ill all the time and they had endless trouble with mosquitoes, which should have given a clue. They did not in fact build their settlement on the same site. That's why they had mosquitoes. The Indian site has now been found – up on the hill, well away from the coastal mosquitoes.'

Was it worth visiting? 'In the 1930s, the President of the day decided to make a visit to the site. "The President is coming," they all cried. "Let's make it clean and tidy for him." So they got a bulldozer out. It's now like a baseball field.' That answered my question. There is nothing now worth seeing at Isabela, though by 1992 there should be a few recreated remains on display. The other major plan is for the Columbus lighthouse, out on some rocks, down the coast from the river estuary, near Santo Domingo's airport. I thought it already existed, one of the Dominican Republic's greater glories, judging by the way it has appeared on coins and on the country's postage stamps. Vega sighed. It was a very long story.

In 1910, a proposal was put up to move the so-called tomb of Columbus to a newly built lighthouse. The light inside, over the body, would be practical and symbolic, lighting the way to the New World, as Columbus had done originally. There was an international appeal for money, but nothing came of it. In 1934, there was a competition, won by a British architect, and work was begun, but never completed.

'Today, it's back on the agenda for completion, but look at the price of oil. You'd need to make it light up the whole sky, all night long. And think of the danger to pilots who might crash their planes. The new idea, wait for it, is laser beams.'

'I hope they do finish it,' said Vega's wife Cynthia, 'and move the Columbus tomb to the lighthouse. He lies in the Cathedral at present, and he ruins everything. It's just too dominating. I want my daughters married in the Cathedral, but not while that monster is there.'

It was obvious that, despite being such a cultured man of the world, Bernardo Vega, like everyone else, considered Columbus unlucky. 'I was given the Order of Christopher Columbus by the President. When it was mooted, I said I'd rather not, thank you, there's a jinx on him, and the President said come on, you're an intelligent man. So I received it, but in the official ceremony I put my underwear on the wrong way round, just to counter his bad spell.'

The next day was my last day. I decided to visit the Cathedral. Outside it, dominating the square, is a statue of Columbus. He stands on a high pillar, pointing of course, and there are some clever bits of sculpture in the shape of the prow and stern of a ship. Just below him is a naked Indian woman, with a feather in her hair, who is climbing up towards him. It is not clear if this is in supplication, or whether she is about to write his name. She does appear to have a pen in her hand.

At one side of the square is Santo Domingo's Cathedral, famous throughout the New World. I could see the main door, very impressive, tall and ornate, flanked by decorated columns. And yet, as I stood back, I found it hard to accept it as the greatest glory of the Catholic Church in the Americas. For a start, it does not look particularly Spanish, not in the highly-coloured, highly-decorated sense. There is no spire, not even a clock tower. It could be just another civilian building, some nobleman's palace.

In May 1510, when a Royal Order decreed it should be built, an eminent architect, Alonso Rodriguez, was sent out from Spain, along with thirteen masons. Don Diego Columbus, still Governor, laid the cornerstone. As work progressed, it became clear that Santo Domingo was losing its importance as the centre of Spain's New World. It was still the capital, still the seat of power and administration, but all the gold and money was over on the mainland, the Spanish Main, as it became known. The conquistadores might still be setting out from Santo Domingo, but the centres of activity had shifted to Mexico, Peru and Colombia. That was where the adventurers were going, followed by the priests, the settlers, the hangers-on, and the humble workmen.

The masons and craftsmen who had come out from Spain to work on the Santo Domingo Cathedral decided to break their contract. The architect took the plans with him, and went off to Mexico where he eventually worked on the first stages of the Cathedral in Mexico City, begun in 1525.

Meanwhile, back in Santo Domingo, visiting bishops from Spain were complaining that the Cathedral was little more than a hut. So work began again, in 1521, when another symbolic cornerstone was laid. This time the Cathedral was completed. In 1546 Pope Paul III elevated it to Metropolitan status, making it the Primate Cathedral of all the Indies, thus giving it an ecclesiastical superiority over all other churches in the New World, including Mexico.

It is of course the Columbus monument which all visitors want to see, and it is impossible to miss. The main structure is of white marble, towering up to the ceiling, with below two black lions. Inside is the tomb itself, containing a black casket and a small trunk-like coffin. Over it hangs a silver chalice with the words 'Cristobal Colon, Descubridor de America.'

No argument there about Discovery, no fudging the words or the issues. If they ever move the tomb to the lighthouse, perhaps they may rewrite the words and soften the claim, in line with the present day sensitivities of the Latin American nations towards Columbus.

I had arranged to meet Maureen, the Honorary British Consul, near the Cathedral, to say my last farewells. As we walked along, with me telling her all the things I'd seen and thought in the Cathedral, she suddenly wondered if her brother-in-law the Bishop might be at home.

We went down a street opposite the Cathedral, in the Old Quarter, amongst the ecclesiastical premises, and knocked on a door. I could hear in the distance some banging and crashing and bells ringing, then this jolly, rather plump, very bright and energetic looking Bishop appeared and welcomed us in. What a stroke of luck, I thought, meeting someone in direct line to Bishop de Las Casas and all those early clerics who played such a vital and humanising role in the settlement of the New World.

Monseñor Priamo Tejeda, the brother of Maureen's late husband, is not the Bishop of Santo Domingo, but Bishop of Bani, a provincial see. He is, however, a very important Latin American cleric, for ever travelling round the world to conferences. He'd just been to Europe on an Aids symposium. Before becoming a priest, he was a medical doctor.

We sat in a spacious but simple entrance room. I could still hear the clattering behind us, the sounds of dishes being washed, or perhaps even thrown around. He stopped and shouted to a maid, ever so nicely, to desist.

He talked first of all to Maureen, swapping family chat, but eventually I managed to get in my question. As a cleric, what did he think about Columbus?

'In order to get anywhere in this life, you have first of all to dream. Secondly, you have to believe in your dream, and that is what Columbus did. While others did not believe in his dream, he did, and he never gave it up, which was why he came here so many times.'

He then returned to family chat, as if he had now dealt with me and the matter of Columbus. We came back to the topic when

Maureen happened to mention how everyone in Santo Domingo had been telling me about the Bad Luck of Columbus.

'Oh, I heard that myself, in the Vatican. The Dominican Ambassador to the Vatican told me the legend. I never knew it before, but since then I try not to use the words Christopher Columbus.'

'As a cleric,' I said, 'what do you think of Columbus? I mean, was he a good Catholic or not?'

'I don't know enough history to answer that properly. He did his devotions. They all prayed on the boats. But if you are asking if it was external piety as opposed to a convincing reality, who can tell?'

The Bishop gave another throaty laugh, his tummy wobbling. 'I know some people, including Bishops, and it is often hard to tell if they are good Catholics. . .'

I wasn't really getting very far, but then I was an uninvited guest. He was being urbane and polite enough, but it was really his sister-in-law he wanted to chat to.

The Inquisition, I said, how can you really equate that with the Catholic Monarchs?

He began with a reference to Theresa of Avalon, which I didn't quite get, except the point that her grandfather was a Jew, then he leaned back, concentrated on me, and spoke nicely and slowly, almost at dictation speed.

'It is a big mistake to judge the past by the present, which is why all historical judgements are so difficult to make. Things, and events and actions, at the time, seemed historically right to them. There was no awareness in those days of human rights as we see them, of the equality of races, of the value of every human life. You must therefore be very careful when making any judgements.'

I had a final walk down the Calle de las Damas, went into the fortress and climbed the medieval tower to look out over the river. Was it here that Columbus and his brothers were chained up? Probably on this site, but in an earlier fortress. The present tower was constructed between 1502 and 1507.

Down by the river itself, not far from the Alcazar, is a tree which the locals say Columbus was chained to, while he waited to be led on board his prison ship. My view of the river and the sea beyond was obscured by old warehouse buildings. When he set sail from here, in early October 1500, Columbus's view of his future was equally obscured.

17

The Fourth Voyage

COLUMBUS ARRIVED back in Cadiz at the end of October 1500, after a quick and relatively calm voyage, something of a relief for anyone doing the trip in chains. Columbus went straight to Seville, defiantly, almost proudly, dragging his chains after him through the streets. He was convinced that the unbiased would consider him to be a martyr, a wronged but still dignified man. Most onlookers thought otherwise. Here was a failure. Here was a fool.

He had no money, no clothes, no possessions. They had all been taken from him in Santo Domingo by Bobadilla. His only hope was to take shelter in a monastery, which he did, accepting help from the Carthusian friars at Las Cuevas in Seville. His life in Spain had come full circle; monastery to monastery, in just fifteen years. A great deal, however, had happened in between. And Columbus had ample time to reflect on these vicissitudes. During the next two years, the monastery remained his main place of refuge.

On his return, Columbus naturally hoped to see the Queen and King as quickly as possible, and have his case heard, but as usual they had other things with which to concern themselves. The annoyance, perhaps even the tedium, caused by all those reports from Hispaniola, appeared to have been settled when they sent Bobadilla to sort out the situation. It was some months before they realised that Columbus was not just back, but in chains. The Queen was upset. She had wanted the Hispaniola problem solved, cleanly and fairly, but reports suggested that Bobadilla had possibly gone slightly too far, humiliating her Admiral, her once noble servant.

So, in December 1500, the order went out for the chains to be removed and for Columbus to be given a royal audience.

The Court was still on the move but Columbus caught up with it in Granada and he appeared before the King and Queen at the Alhambra. Ferdinand's account of what happened is fairly short and describes the royal welcome as 'friendly and affectionate', with the Queen assuring Columbus that his imprisonment had not been their wish or command, and that certainly they would 'restore his privileges'. Other observers say that Columbus was unbearable, bursting into tears, self-righteously defending all his actions, launching an emotional tirade against Bobadilla, even demanding his head.

It was not true, alas, despite what Columbus himself believed, that the Sovereigns had promised him everything back, that life would go on as before. The Sovereigns had simply promised to look into the matter of his privileges. They had agreed he was still the Admiral, but nothing had been said about returning his power, as Governor, or his possessions, confiscated or sold off in Hispaniola, or his supposed large income to come from the Indies trade.

Columbus went back to Seville, reasonably pleased, reasonably happy that the Sovereigns had at least been kind to him, that the Queen was his ally once again, that no trial had taken place, and that he had convinced the Sovereigns about the true nature of his enemy, Bobadilla.

'I cannot absolve the Catholic Sovereigns,' writes Ferdinand, 'for selecting for the post of Governor such a bad and ignorant man as Bobadilla. It may be urged that if the Sovereigns had unfavourable reports about the Admiral, they should not have given Bobadilla such unlimited powers. On the other hand, in view of the many complaints against the Admiral, it is not strange they did so.' So even Ferdinand, that most loyal of sons, was admitting that the Sovereigns had to act in some way against Columbus.

Nothing else happened. Months went by, royal life at Court went on while Columbus continued his monastic existence at Las Cuevas. There was no more news or any announcements about his possessions or his position. He was still destitute, still clearly out of favour, and if he could have read the signs properly and sensibly he would have realised that the Sovereigns simply wanted to hear nothing more about or from him.

Columbus occupied his time during his enforced monastic confinement by composing a Book of Prophecies. (It is now kept in the Town Hall in Genoa.) It consisted mainly of passages collected from the Bible, complete with his own annotations, proving that his discoveries, nay his whole life, was divinely inspired and that he had fulfilled Biblical predictions in almost everything he had done. A great deal of it is incoherent and confused. He bombarded the Sovereigns with similar rantings and tortured appeals, and the indications are that no one bothered to read them. Columbus was now being dismissed as mad, not just a fool and a failure.

In September 1501, it was announced that Nicolas de Ovando was to be appointed Governor, Viceroy and Chief Justice of the Indies. Columbus's fond hopes, or mad fantasies, of a triumphal return were immediately dashed. On the other hand, it did mean that Bobadilla's days were over. Then, a few weeks later, it was officially announced that Bobadilla was returning.

On September 27 came better news. The Sovereigns had instructed Bobadilla to give back everything he had taken from Columbus. The details were contained in a long legal mandate, listing Columbus's restitutions. 'We command that there should be returned and restored to him all the furniture of his person and household, and provisions of bread and wine, which the Comendador Bobadilla took from him, or their just value, without our receiving any part thereof.' Bobadilla was also punished for taking gold and jewels which did not belong to him. Columbus was allowed to have a representative, out in Hispaniola, to make sure that all his possessions were correctly transferred back.

All in all, it was a handsome apology. Columbus was pleased of course, but not remotely satisfied. His fantasies were becoming wilder rather than wiser with age, his paranoia was more intense, his feelings of being unfairly treated were now eating into his heart and mind. Such strong emotions and convictions had always been his strength, the clue to why he had kept going during all those years of rejection in Portugal and in Spain, and during all those long and dangerous voyages into the unknown. His self-belief had made him. Now it looked as if it would destroy him.

Consider, then, what fury and jealousy he must have felt in February 1502, when Ovando, the new Governor, set sail for Santo Domingo, taking with him a truly colossal fleet. Thirty ships and over 2,500 men and women were departing for the New World. His New World. His discoveries. Morally and legally they were all his.

Columbus's reaction to Ovando setting off was predictable – he wanted to do the same. He immediately put forward his own proposal to the Sovereigns and, in a surprisingly short time, he was given permission. In fact in the official Royal Instructions for the Voyage, to be Columbus's Fourth, they advised him 'to leave at once without any delay'. The implication was clear. They wanted him out of the way.

Why Columbus wanted to go is also clear. He wished to prove himself, make more discoveries and force the Sovereigns to restore all his privileges. In particular, he wanted to explore the Western Caribbean, what we now call Central America, looking for a strait which would lead him through towards India.

With the Royal Instructions, the Sovereigns enclosed a letter from them to the Portuguese captain, Vasco da Gama, recently departed on his second voyage to India. They might not have been entirely clear on the geography, but they understood the diplomatic niceties. The King of Portugal had done them a similar courtesy, informing them of da Gama's voyage, so it was felt he should be told of Columbus's.

Columbus therefore had a basic object, albeit very much like the original one of 1492: to reach India. Most of all, he was attracted by a desire to get back to sea, to start exploring again, to reach new lands. This had always been his first love. It was even more attractive now after almost two years of humiliation since his arrest. His little fleet was ready to sail just three months after the departure of Ovando.

In the Instructions, the Sovereigns commanded him not to go to Hispaniola. 'We have already told you that you are to choose some other route,' though he could, if necessary, visit that island on his return voyage, 'for a short time'.

They also instructed him not to bring back any slaves, though there was a rider: 'Unless someone wishes of his own accord to come with the intention of learning our language and returning again.' These would be America's first cultural exchanges, in other words, though it could quite easily be turned into a form of slavery, no doubt, with some subtle psychological persuasion.

The Sovereigns agreed to Columbus's request to take his younger son Ferdinand, now thirteen, on the voyage. And they assured Columbus that his personal title and privileges would be secure and would pass to his elder son. 'All this can be attended to after you have sailed; we therefore pray you not to delay your departure . . .' Were they hoping that he would never come back?

The fleet set off from Cadiz on May 9, 1502, a modest little flotilla scarcely in the same class as Ovando's, with just four ships and 140 men. By chance a valuable document survives which lists

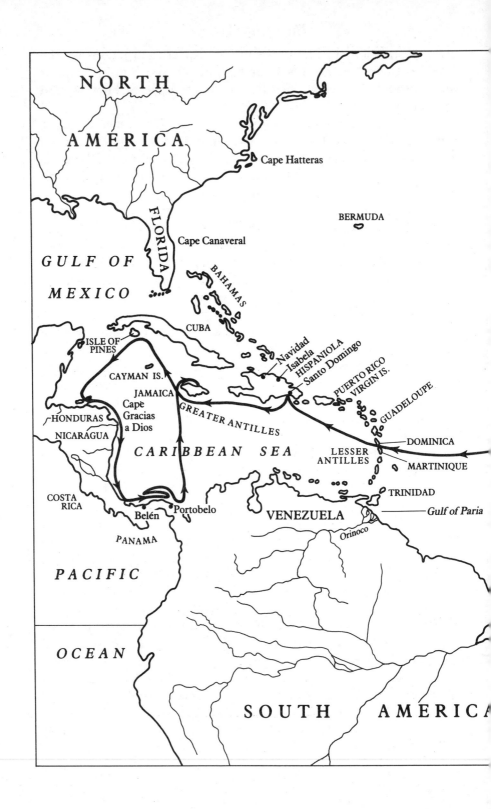

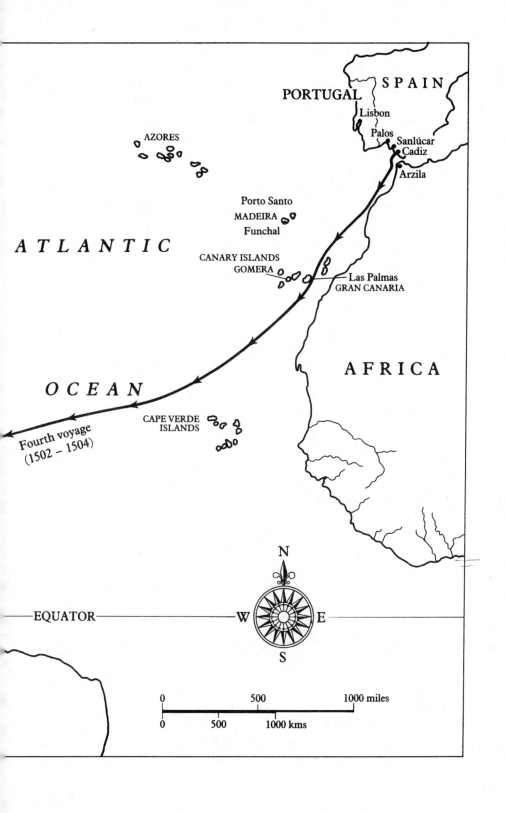

SPAIN

PORTUGAL

Lisbon

Palos

Sanlúcar
Cadiz

Arzila

AZORES

Porto Santo
MADEIRA
Funchal

CANARY ISLANDS
GOMERA

Las Palmas
GRAN CANARIA

ATLANTIC

AFRICA

OCEAN

CAPE VERDE
ISLANDS

Fourth voyage
(1502 – 1504)

N

EQUATOR   W   E

S

| 0 | 500 | 1000 miles |
| 0 | 500 | 1000 kms |

the names and positions and salaries of every single person on board, giving the fullest account of the crews on any of Columbus's voyages. The document starts by recording that the entire crew got six months' pay in advance, which seems surprising until it is remembered that Columbus's previous three trips lasted between one and three years. On board were a larger number of grumets, or boys, than previously, many of them listed as being only twelve or thirteen; so young Ferdinand would not be too isolated, should he need friends of his own age. There were also quite a few men of Genoese extraction, including Bartholomew Fieschi, listed as a gentleman volunteer, who was a close friend of Columbus's.

Only one person, to judge by a careful examination which has been made of all Columbus's known crew lists, was joining him for the fourth time. This was Pedro de Terreros. On the first three trips he had been a steward, personally attending Columbus, but now he was captain of one of the vessels, the *Gallega*. On the *Capitana*, the little fleet's flagship, were listed two trumpeters, Juan de Cuellar and Gonzalo de Salazar. Perhaps they were hoping for more impressive music this time. On the same ship one of the grumets was put down as 'Diego el Negro'. Was he a real Negro, from Africa, or a former slave from the Indies, or was it just the nickname for a darker than usual Spaniard?

They headed once again for the Canaries, but this time they took on supplies at Las Palmas, sparing no more than four days, and there is no mention of a visit to Gomera.

We owe most of the details of this Fourth Voyage to Ferdinand. He had his own memories to draw on, as well as the letters and documents written by his father. His uncle Bartholomew was also on board, perhaps originally not as enthusiastic a voyager as he had been previously, but persuaded by Columbus that he needed him. Young Ferdinand, a bookish boy, never crossed the sea again, so this voyage remained clear in his mind all his life.

The ocean crossing, from the Canaries to Martinique, where they landed, took only twenty days (from May 25 to June 15, 1502), the fastest passage of all four. Five hundred years later, it compares well with that of any modern yacht. They sailed on towards Puerto Rico but ran into bad weather, and one ship, the *Santiago*, had problems. Ferdinand says she was a dull sailer, and that when her sails were hoisted the side of the ship sank almost under the water. She had caused trouble from the beginning, so Columbus decided to make for Santo Domingo and have her replaced. Ferdinand does not comment on the fact that Columbus was not supposed to go there (if indeed he knew of the Royal Instruction). He says Columbus had been heading for the coast of Paria, but was forced to go to Santo Domingo for a new ship.

It so happened that, as he arrived, twenty-eight ships were getting ready to leave Santo Domingo for Spain: the return trip for the fleet which had brought out Ovando, three months previously. And on board one of the ships was Bobadilla, Columbus's sworn enemy, though Columbus was unaware of his presence as he sailed towards the harbour.

He sent a message ashore to Ovando requesting assistance in providing a new boat, and added that he needed to shelter as he could tell that a great storm was on the way. Ovando, fully aware of the Royal Instructions, refused him permission to land at Santo Domingo. He also ignored the warning about a cyclone, dismissing it as one of Columbus's tricks. He was too occupied anyway with the fleet's departure to be concerned with this new, annoying arrival.

Columbus and his four ships sailed round the coast and found shelter of a sort a few miles away, where they waited, making themselves as secure as possible. Sure enough, the storm struck. It was a major cyclone, which completely wrecked Ovando's departing fleet. Over twenty boats went down, with all hands lost. Three managed to limp back to harbour. Only one got safely to Spain.

Amongst those who died was Bobadilla. Even more ironic, another victim was Roldan, Columbus's enemy who had organised the mutiny. He was about to return to Spain an innocent, free man.

Ferdinand knew exactly who was behind this terrible tragedy. 'God was pleased to close the eyes and minds of all those who did not heed the Admiral's good advice. I am certain that this was Divine Providence, for had they arrived in Castile, they would never have been punished as their crimes deserved.'

Ferdinand goes straight on from his graphic account of the fateful storm to a description of a strange fish he remembers seeing, during the time they sheltered and repaired their faulty ship after the storm had finished. Years later, he still 'recalls it with amusement'. Some of the crew of the caravel *Vizcaina* were idly fishing from their ship's boat when they saw a huge ray fish, sleeping on the surface, 'half as big as a bed'. They harpooned it, and it immediately dashed away, pulling their boat behind. 'It drew the boat through the harbour as quickly as an arrow. The men aboard the ship, not knowing what went on, were astounded to see the boat running about without oars. Eventually, the fish died and was hauled aboard with tackling gear used for raising heavy objects.' Ferdinand veers between describing dramatic events and the more humdrum sights and objects of the Caribbean, which of course he is seeing for the first time.

They reached Central America, on the coast of what is now Honduras, at the beginning of July 1502, after sailing along the southern coasts of Jamaica and Cuba. Ferdinand is astounded by an enormous hollowed-out canoe they come across: 'Eight feet wide and as long as a galley with a palm leaf awning like the Venetian gondolas carry. Under the awning were the children and women and all the baggage and merchandise.'

Ferdinand's description of the merchandise is interesting, and new. There are cotton shirts and mantles embroidered in many designs and colours; hatchets made of copper, not of stone as they had seen elsewhere; swords which were as sharp as steel; wooden objects fastened together with pitch; and a fermented wine which he says 'tasted like English beer'. The last does not sound very exciting, but the other references indicate that these mainland Indians, thought to be part of the Mayan empire, were much more advanced than the Caribs and Arawaks of the islands. They had skills in metalwork and weaving and did not go completely naked, like the noble savages elsewhere. 'I should add that they displayed admirable modesty, for if one had his breech clout taken from him, he would immediately cover his genitals with his hands; and the women covered their faces like the Moorish women of Granada.'

The finding of this canoe, and its contents, says Ferdinand, made the Admiral realise they had reached a much wealthier civilisation, but alas he decided to turn south, to explore the coast of what is now Nicaragua, Costa Rica and Panama. If he had gone in the other direction, he would have reached Mexico, or the 'wealth of New Spain', as Ferdinand describes it. Ferdinand is writing his account some years later, so he knows by then what lay round the corner. He calls the decision a mistake, Columbus's search for a sea passage through to India, but defends it by explaining the confusion over the meaning of 'strait'. Columbus was looking for a sea strait, not realising that he should have been looking for a 'land strait'.

The first part of the journey south is slow, but not too dangerous, and Ferdinand keeps up his descriptions of interesting things seen along the way, as they go into the various river estuaries, with Columbus hoping each time the river will turn out to be a sea

channel. The local Indians are still friendly and bring food, such
as chicken, 'that were better tasting than ours'. He notes their
elaborate clothes, their dyed shirts and quilted cotton jerkins worn
like breast-plates for protection against darts. He observes their
practice of embalming dead bodies and is greatly intrigued when
one day they come across a stone building, the first Indian one
anyone had seen in the New World. 'It was a great mass of stone
and lime. The Admiral ordered a piece to be taken as a souvenir of
antiquity.'

Ferdinand is rather surprised when the presents given to the
Indians are either returned or left on the beach. He concludes that
they were perhaps frightened. 'The fact that they refused to take
anything of ours was evidence that they suspected us of being
enchanters, confirming the adage that says a rogue sees himself in
every other man.'

They come across various animals, not seen before, such as
monkeys. One of the Spaniards brings a monkey down from a tree
with a crossbow, then cuts off one of its legs to stop it escaping.
He brings it on board ship, where it terrifies a dog. One of the
ship's pigs, which has previously frightened everyone when it
rushed around, cowers in fear at the sight of the one-legged monkey.
The Admiral orders them to be put together, the monkey and the
pig, to see what happens, and in the ensuing fight the monkey gets
his tail round the pig's snout, his one leg over the pig's head, and
proceeds to bite it. Victory to the monkey; and an early example
of the Spanish liking for blood sports.

By November, things were beginning to go wrong. They hit
storms and fearful currents and for twenty-eight days hardly made
any progress, averaging only six miles a day. The sails were damaged, anchors lost, provisions swept overboard. Las Casas, in his
account, quotes directly from Columbus. 'What wrung my heart
the most were the sufferings of my son. I was sick, at death's door
on several occasions, but still I gave orders from a little cabin that
the sailors had built for me.' He probably had malaria, which would
explain his delirium and ravings. In his journal, he returns again
to Biblical prophecies and medieval legends to prove that he has
really arrived at the doors of Cathay.

They finally reached what is now Panama, but still with no sign
of a channel. Ferdinand is clearly less cheerful. 'In this harbour we
stayed nine days, with miserable weather. At first the Indians came
peacefully to trade, but later, when they saw the sailors sneaking
ashore from the ships, they withdrew to their huts, for the sailors,

a greedy and dissolute set of men, committed innumerable outrages . . .'

This is Ferdinand's first criticism of the crew, after almost eight months at sea with them. He does not detail their exact outrages, but they can be guessed at. It is the beginning of what becomes a series of attacks by the Indians upon the Spaniards, doubtless provoked by their behaviour.

Colourful descriptions of harmless monkeys give way to frightening accounts of sharks which surround the ships, scaring young Ferdinand. 'We made carnage among them with a chain hook until we could kill no more, and still they followed us, making turns in the water. So voracious are these beasts that not only will they eat carrion but one can catch them by simply attaching a piece of red cloth to the hook. Out of one shark's belly I saw a turtle taken that afterwards lived in the ship, and from another they took a whole shark's head that we had cut off. It may seem strange that an animal should be able to swallow the head of another animal of the same size, but their heads are very elongated and the mouth extends almost to the belly.'

They saw in the New Year of 1503 while sheltering from yet another dreadful storm, blown into a harbour by the winds, where they cowered till January 3. Their stocks of food were now so affected by the heat and the tropical rains that even the dried biscuits had become full of worms. 'By that time we had been over eight months at sea and had consumed all the meat and fish we had brought from Spain,' writes Ferdinand. They were forced eventually to swallow the biscuits, despite the worms. 'I saw many wait until nightfall to eat the porridge made of the biscuits so as not to see the worms; others were so used to eating them that they did not bother to pick them out, for fear they might lose their supper by being so fastidious.'

On January 9, they entered a more hospitable river estuary, which they called Belen, after Bethlehem, where the Indians were helpful and willing to barter for fresh food and materials. The river was wide and calm and they explored inland, not this time hoping to find a channel, but encouraged by stories of vast gold mines not far away, in a region they called Veragua, gold which was said to be easy to work, easy to cart away.

From then on, gold became Columbus's main obsession, as he hoped it would make up for the disappointments, recompense them for the hardships, and pay for their losses and expenses so far. All the boats by now were beginning to let in water and show signs of wear.

The *Gallega* was almost destroyed when sudden flood water rushed down a river where they were sheltering, smashing its cables.

Bartholomew was sent ashore with a party of sixty, to look for the gold, get to know the Indians, investigate the terrain. They did find some gold, and the locals seemed friendly, so Columbus decided that a permanent settlement of eighty men should be established, on the banks of the River Belen.

On their explorations inland, they met a cacique, or chieftain. He and the leading men of his tribe had something in their mouths all the time they were talking. 'They never stopped chewing a dried herb,' writes Ferdinand. 'Sometimes they also put in their mouths a powder they carried, together with the dried herb. It seemed a dirty habit.' It is not clear what it was, either tobacco, cocoa leaves, or some other drug. 'The natives of Veragua and its vicinity turn their backs when they speak to each other; and even while they are eating, they are always chewing a herb. We decided that must be the cause of their rotten teeth.'

Step by step, however, as the new settlement is being constructed and the gold mines exploited, using Indian labour, hostilities break out, just as they had in that first settlement at Navidad. One day, the Spaniards hear of a plot against them, so they ruthlessly make an example of a few Indians. This leads to a full-scale rebellion by the Indians and there are various bloody and dramatic incidents. It all becomes very complicated, in Ferdinand's account, and it ends in the deaths of several of the Spaniards.

The worst battle occurs after the river level suddenly drops, leaving only two feet of water at the entrance to the estuary, marooning one of the ships up-river, and cutting off the new settlement, which is then attacked by the Indians. Diego Tristan, captain of the *Capitana*, the main ship of the fleet, is one of those butchered. Their bodies are tossed into the river and seen floating down-stream by the other Spaniards. Diego Mendez, one of the gentlemen volunteers on the *Santiago*, bravely manages to bring the remains of the garrison to safety on a makeshift raft which he negotiates over the sandbanks.

On April 16, Columbus decides to leave Belen, abandoning one of his four ships, the *Gallega*, at the river's mouth, as it is by now too damaged to be used any further. Their hopes of El Dorado have gone, and so had Columbus's ambition to find a sea channel through to the Pacific.

Almost at the spot where Columbus gave up lies the present Panama Canal. There are two towns at its entrance, named Colon and Cristobal. If only Columbus had known he should have been looking for a short isthmus of land, not a channel of water, he might have achieved his life's ambition and reached the Pacific. But by now his supplies and ships and his energies have all been depleted. It was left to Balboa, just ten years later, in 1513, to be the first to spy the Pacific from the top of a mountain.

On April 23, Columbus was forced to abandon another of his ships, the *Vizcaina*, its hull so eaten away by worms that water was pouring in through hundreds of holes. The two remaining ships were also badly affected. They limped slowly towards Cuba, the pilots arguing amongst themselves about exactly where they were, what they should do next, wondering how long it would be before the remaining two ships finally sank. Columbus himself was sick and totally exhausted. 'Since the ships were so riddled by shipworm, day and night we never ceased to work three pumps in each of them. For all our efforts, the water in our ship rose so high that it was almost up to the deck.'

On June 23, they staggered into a bay on the north coast of Jamaica, St Ann's Bay, the two caravels literally unable to proceed any further, bashed and broken by the waves and the storms, the woodwork eaten alive by the worms. They had hoped to make Hispaniola, and help, but Santo Domingo was still at least 500 miles away.

'Since we were no longer able to keep the ships afloat,' writes Ferdinand, 'we ran them ashore as far as we could, grounding them close together, board to board, and shoring them up on both sides so they could not budge; and the ships being in this position, the tide rose almost to the decks. Upon these we built cabins where the people could lodge, making our position as strong as possible so the Indians could do us no harm.'

Columbus realised he had to keep his crew together, so that they could protect themselves in the event of an attack. He knew quite well what would happen if he allowed any of them to wander off ashore on their own explorations. 'Our people being disrespectful by nature,' writes Ferdinand, 'no punishment could have stopped them from running about the country and into the Indians' huts to steal what they found and commit outrages on their wives and children, whence would have arisen disputes and would have made enemies out of them.'

Columbus solved that particular problem, for the moment, by confining all men to their quarters. They were allowed out only with permission, and after signing their names. The next problem was food. 'So much had been spoiled and lost in the haste and disorder of the embarkation from Belen.'

However, the local Indians proved friendly, arriving in their canoes. Columbus ordered that everything should be bartered for, not taken, which meant swapping any little trinkets they had left, such as a few hawks' bells and lace points, in return for which they received cassava bread.

But how were they to get off the island? That soon became the major problem. The two wrecked ships were beyond repair. Food was running out. As the months went by, the Indians became less friendly. There was a growing unease amongst certain of the Spaniards.

The chance of their being rescued was non-existent, for the simple reason that no one knew where they were. Even if they had known in Santo Domingo what had happened to Columbus, they would not have cared. He had been warned to keep away. There was little chance of the castaways being sighted by any passing Europeans. Jamaica was off their route. It had no gold, as Columbus himself had made clear ten years previously.

Columbus's Fourth Voyage appeared doomed to be his final one, ending inconclusively, ignominiously. He and his men were being left to perish slowly, if they were lucky not to be killed quickly.

During the previous fourteen months, since their departure from Cadiz, little had been achieved anyway. Half the fleet had been lost and nothing new of note discovered, not compared with the glories and excitements of the first two voyages. Even the Third Voyage, though it had ended with Columbus in chains, had resulted in the discovery of the mainland of America and the establishment of Hispaniola. It was as if the Fourth Voyage had been a mistake from the beginning.

Spanish ships being attacked by Indians.

18

Jamaica Today

Colombo '92

THE DAY I arrived in Jamaica something interesting happened in
St Ann's Bay; interesting to me, as it took place not far from the
beach where Columbus was shipwrecked, but fairly routine to the
local Jamaicans. According to the *Daily Gleaner*, a plane had
nose-dived into the sea, about three miles off the coast. By chance,
a passing British destroyer, HMS *Cardiff*, was in the vicinity, and
went to help, but there were no survivors. All they could find was
the dead body of the pilot, floating amongst the wreckage, a body
which would be hard to identify, as he should not have been doing
what he was doing. With him was a package containing 1,575
pounds of ganja, with a street value of around five million dollars.
HMS *Cardiff* took everything aboard, and steamed away. The
Daily Gleaner did not say what the destroyer did with her surprise
haul, but added, matter-of-factly, that the pilot was presumably
American, a Vietnam war veteran, on one of the many daily missions
which pilots make from Jamaica for a fee of 10,000 dollars a trip.

Jamaica has ended up English-speaking because the Spaniards
never considered it of importance. There was no gold on the island,
and then of course came Columbus's dreadful experience. For the
next 150 years or so, it was part of the Spanish Empire, but
they neglected it, concentrating their search for El Dorado on
the mainland of Central America, while Jamaica was used for
cattle-ranching and as a supply base.

Spain got the gold elsewhere, but paid a price for being first in
the Indies. When either England, Holland or France was at war
with Spain in Europe, Spanish treasure ships coming back from

the Americas were vulnerable to attacks by freelance buccaneers.

The English arrived in 1655 when a military party, having failed to capture Hispaniola, was looking for somewhere easy to attack. Jamaica was England's first colony to be captured in battle, or by theft, which was what some Spaniards called it, notably the heirs of Columbus who maintained that, under his original agreement with Isabella and Ferdinand, rights in the island still belonged to them.

The French tried to invade not long afterwards, but they were repelled, and Jamaica remained British. In 1944, all blacks got the vote and in 1962 the island became independent, though remaining part of the Commonwealth. Today, with a population of two million, it is the biggest English-speaking island in the Caribbean.

I had landed at Montego Bay, named after the Spanish for lard or butter, and was heading for the St Ann's Bay area, not merely to find the shipwreck beach but because this was the area where Columbus first landed, on his Second Voyage. The Jamaican Tourist Board is still excited by his first description of Jamaica and uses it all the time in their brochures: 'The fairest isle eyes have ever seen.' Columbus thought up such glowing phrases many a time, often repeating them word for word about different places. He later had cause to change his feelings about Jamaica.

The first impression given by Jamaica is of the extremes of life, despair or squalor one moment, then round the corner an air of exuberance and vibrancy. I sensed a richness, culturally and socially, in the music, language and life, which I never felt in the Bahamas or Venezuela, despite their much greater wealth. The Dominican Republic seemed stifled. Haiti felt finished. Jamaica is exciting.

My first points of call were Discovery Bay and the nearby Columbus Park. Discovery Bay was hardly worth discovering. It has been ruined by grimy industrial buildings and the ugly machinery of a bauxite works. Out in the bay, ready to load up, was a Russian cargo boat. The bauxite firm has at least tried to put something back into the environment and the community, by creating the nearby Columbus Park, which has no real connection with Columbus, never mind any Columbus artefacts, though it is an interesting attempt to create an open-air museum.

I asked the woman in charge of the park's little souvenir shop if she got many visitors, but she said no, people were not interested in history, nor was she, she added with a laugh.

'I work here seven years, but I still know nothing about history. But I do know one thing – Columbus is dead. An American woman asked me yesterday if Columbus still come here and I say yes, ma'am, he often come up from the beach to use our rest rooms.'

She laughed and slapped her thighs. 'You have a good time now.'

Whether or not Discovery Bay is the precise bay where Columbus first landed is still in some doubt, partly because it depends on how you define 'landing'. According to the documents on the Second Voyage, he anchored in Santa Gloria (St Ann's Bay) on May 5, 1495, having looked at another bay, possibly Puerto Seco, but rejected it through lack of water. A recent academic article in the *Jamaica Journal* agrees that St Ann's Bay was the first anchorage, but argues that Columbus actually landed at the entrance to the Rio Bueno.

I eventually made contact with a local Columbus expert. There always is one, if you look hard enough, someone who has devoted their spare time to the history of the immediate area. Sometimes, though, they are extremely hard to locate, as was Dr Hodges in Haiti. I was fortunate in Ocho Rios to meet Sam Hart, a retired solicitor, and his wife Lee who comes originally from New York. He is from an old Jamaican family who arrived from England in the 1740s. They are stalwarts of the Jamaica Trust and active locally in the 1992 celebrations.

They live high above Ocho Rios, as many of the richer permanent residents do, where the air is cooler and the noise less pervasive. Their house is filled with glass cases of Arawak pottery and other remains, collected from beaches, Arawak middens and caves. For tea they gave me cassava bread, which was what the local Arawak Indians used to eat, a dry, hard-baked type of biscuit. It saved Columbus's life at one time, when he and his crew could get nothing else. After tea, they said, they would take me on a tour of the real Spanish remains.

We went first to the Seville Estate, or La Sevilla Nueva as the Spaniards originally called it, the site of their first capital in Jamaica, built in 1509. This is slightly inland from the beach where Columbus was shipwrecked and stranded in 1503. It is assumed that, when the Spaniards returned to found a proper settlement, one of Columbus's sailors directed them back to the same spot. Around eighty Spaniards, including whole families, then built a small town with a sugar mill and an abbey. It lasted only twenty-four years, when it was abandoned, and the capital moved south, but it is one of the earliest colonial settlements anywhere in the New World.

Over the centuries, all traces disappeared as it became part of a large sugar plantation, but in 1937 the overseer of the estate was riding along when his horse caught its hoof in a hole and stumbled. The hole turned out to be the top of a well, twenty feet deep. With a local amateur archaeologist, Captain Cotter, the overseer started excavating, and over the next couple of decades almost 6,000 items, some early Spanish and some later, were found. Since then, professional archaeologists from the USA and Spain have pronounced it a site of great historical importance.

There is not a lot for the casual visitor to see, apart from some low stone walls and foundations, covered with a large tin roof. But the well is there. I noticed that it was brick-lined and observed to Sam that surely those early Spaniards hadn't managed to build their own brick factory. His theory is that the bricks were ballast, brought from Spain, carried in the holds of those two ships which Columbus beached.

The actual shipwreck beach is very near, or only a 'few chains away', as Lee put it: an archaic expression, but still used in Jamaica. It is undeveloped and untidy, with plastic debris floating at the edges, coconut husks, stagnant pools, muddy lagoons. About half a mile out I could see the coral reef, and a clear gap in the middle which Columbus managed to limp through, with his two wounded ships. Out in the bay were some marker buoys, bobbing away, indicating where recent underwater exploration had taken place, soon to begin again.

Unlike Cap Haitien, where the *Santa Maria* went down and Navidad was built, the coast here has not been drained and has stayed much the same. So surely there should be some signs of those two tragic ships, under these sands, or in those shallows. That is what many people imagine. For the last twenty years, an assortment of divers and archaeologists have been searching for remains, or any clues. An American diver did find one wreck, which he maintained was Spanish, till a Spanish professor arrived and said it was English. It is hard to believe that there could be any wooden remains, after all those centuries, but perhaps an anchor or two might be found, as happened in Haiti, in time for the 1992 celebrations.

There was no plaque on the beach, to tell the world that this was where Columbus spent the longest time anywhere in the New World, nor is the beach named on local maps. You have to leave the coastal road at the signpost for Seville, look for the notice saying 'To the Seville National Park', then walk through it to the beach behind.

The only statue of Columbus in Jamaica is not far away, just along the coast road, beside a roundabout. It was erected in 1958 by the City of Genoa and done by an Italian sculptor. I expected something grand, a symbol of Genoese glory, but he looked more like Peter Pan, a boy sailor, standing on a lump of rock, clutching his little rolled-up chart.

Next day, I set off for Kingston, capital of the island, where I hoped to discover the nation's 1992 plans, and to hear any official thoughts about Columbus today.

I went firstly to visit Jamaica's National Heritage Trust, in their handsome colonial-style offices in Duke Street, and talked to their Executive Director, Carey Robinson. He is a tall, distinguished-looking black man in his sixties. He started as a reporter on the *Gleaner*, moved to the radio, then on to Government work, serving as a diplomat in Washington, then in the Prime Minister's office. He is the author of several books on Jamaican history.

The Trust has big plans for three major sites in 1992 – Spanish Town, Port Royal harbour in Kingston and Seville. The hopes for Seville were particularly ambitious. They would like to build an Arawak village, showing what life was like when Columbus arrived; a Spanish caravel, of the type Columbus sailed; a reconstructed plantation, showing fields of cotton and tobacco being worked, a zoo, museum, cinema and other attractions. Like every other country connected with Columbus, they are turning his celebrations into a celebration of themselves. The only problem is the cost – 50 million Jamaican dollars.

Carey Robinson sees education for 1992 being just as important as celebration. Jamaicans will be taught to be aware of themselves and their history. 'We are starting work now on new text books for schools, so that the nation will fully understand what 1992 is all about.

'Since we became independent in 1962, it has been necessary for the first time to reassess our own history. Until 1962, we all learned British history, about Nelson and Admiral Rodney, British sailors and soldiers being brave and daring, fighting battles, surviving the seas. It was all terribly swashbuckling. We imagined Henry Morgan, the pirate, must have looked like Erroll Flynn. We never learned Jamaican history, about our own culture. In fact there was no hint at all that we had any culture. If our ancestors were mentioned, which was rare, they were doing something illegal, such as revolting.

'We are no longer British subjects. But what are we? 1992 will give us the chance, the excuse, to find out about ourselves. The British, in their history, only looked at one side. We'll have a slightly different perspective.'

So will the British this time emerge as the villains, along with Columbus and the Spaniards?

'I don't say that all Spaniards were villains. Life was grim for everyone in those days. We'll have to strike a balance. What we have to make clear to our people is that our country was founded on a system of human bondage. Our history is the story of our struggle for freedom and human dignity. As for Columbus, I don't see him as a saint. I see him, well, let me think, as a very eccentric man.

'I'd like to see a new statue of him for 1992, different from the one you saw outside the Catholic Church. That's far too young. When he was stranded here, he was in his fifties, a much older man, tired and sick. I'd like him to appear as he was in Jamaica.

'He was important to us. His arrival was the beginning of the modern Jamaican state.'

I decided on one last visit, to the Institute of Jamaica in nearby East Street, to look at their Arawak remains, said to be amongst the best in the Caribbean. I wanted to get a feeling of local life when Columbus was there.

After I had finished my tour, I left the Institute by a different door to the one I had come in by, and found myself looking down a narrow street towards the sea. I had been warned by everyone that the two areas to avoid in Kingston are Trench Town and the Waterfront. I soon realised I was lost.

I hurried down a narrow street, with boarded-up cafés and people mending broken-down motor cars on the pavement. Two youths in a doorway shouted something at me, but I ignored them, hurrying on, knowing it would either be an insult or an offer of ganja.

Suddenly, one of the youths was standing in front of me, blocking my way, fumbling in his pocket. I wondered at first what he was doing, till a flick-knife appeared in his hand, and he was slashing at my shirt pocket. He could clearly see I was carrying a little red wallet which contained my credit cards.

I pushed the youth away, saying the cards were no good to him, nor was there any money in the wallet. My main worry was that his companion was behind me, and that he might also have a knife.

Then I heard the sound of clothes ripping and realised my assailant had turned his attention to my trousers. There was a huge hole, about two feet long, down the side of my trouser leg. At the same time, he put his hand in and grabbed the cash out of my pocket. I started to shout, and he backed off, looked around, then dashed across the road and disappeared into a doorway. I ran as fast as I could.

I was terribly lucky. It had all happened in a few minutes. I think the youth was nervous, probably dared to do it by his friend. He had not cut me, only my clothes, and all he had taken was twenty Jamaican dollars.

On my entire Columbus trail, I had survived totally unharmed, until the last day, of my last visit, to my last Caribbean country.

It had to be Jamaica, I suppose. That was where Columbus had his worst experience, the one from which he was convinced he would never return.

Indians enjoying a smoke, as Columbus observed them.

19

The Death of Columbus

A TOTAL of 140 men and boys had set off from Spain with Columbus on his Fourth and final Voyage. By the time they ran ashore in Jamaica on June 25, 1503, to find themselves stranded, their ships wrecked and their spirits sinking, there were only a hundred remaining. Ferdinand, who was one of them, never mentions the exact number, but that would appear to be the maximum possible, to judge by the deaths along the way.

In that original, detailed account of the crew members were listed trumpeters, coopers and caulkers. Only two seamen were described as carpenters, though there could have been others with some carpentry skills. It is not clear, therefore, why no attempt seems to have been made to salvage some of the timbers from the two remaining caravels, the *Capitana* and *Santiago*, and improvise some sort of sailing boat. Perhaps every inch of wood was too-far-gone. Perhaps the carpenters had gone too, left rotting somewhere in Central America.

Ferdinand simply says they had neither the implements nor the artisans, and the idea of a new vessel was quickly dismissed. It seems that the Spaniards were not enthusiastic about hard physical labour, hoping Indians would do the rough work of house-building, the making of drains, digging for gold. There is no evidence either, in Ferdinand's account, that they tried to be self-sufficient by attempting any form of farming. All the pigs had been eaten by now and the seeds long lost or ruined.

Instead they skulked on the beach inside their makeshift huts, erected on what was left of the decks of their ships, depending on the Indians for food, arguing about what to do next.

There was one obvious solution; someone should set off in an Indian canoe, since they had no vessels of their own, get to Santo Domingo and bring back help. No volunteer was forthcoming at first, then Diego Mendez, who had shown such courage in Belen, said that if no one else would do it, he was willing, as before, to risk his life in Columbus's service.

Mendez set off in a canoe, with six Indians paddling. Not far along the coast they were attacked by natives and forced to return. It was the end of the first attempt.

This failure did teach them a few lessons. More meetings were held and this time, around July 17, 1503, two canoes set off. Diego Mendez was in one, with ten Indians, while Bartholomew Fieschi, Columbus's Genoese friend, was in the other, also with ten Indians. To avoid the chance of their being attacked, Bartholomew Columbus took a party of armed men as protection down the coast, accompanying them as far as the end of the island, ready to wave them goodbye and good luck, in their hazardous journey across the open sea towards Hispaniola. 'They had to wait for perfect calm before starting to cross that great space in such frail craft,' says Ferdinand. 'By God's favour, this calm soon came.'

Almost six months passed. Not a word was heard of them, no hint of any rescue boats, but on the other hand no signs of any dead Spanish bodies, floating ashore. Had they got there? Or had they all drowned without trace?

Meanwhile, many of the remaining Spaniards, unable to survive on the Indian diet, were going down sick. Rumours and theories abounded. According to Ferdinand, someone put forward a really disagreeable explanation for the long silence: the rescue party had not after all gone to bring help from Santo Domingo, but had headed straight back to Castile. Columbus had sent them there to plead his case once again for the restitution of his privileges. It proved what many of them feared, that Columbus cared more about his titles than their safety.

Small stories and tittle-tattle turned into major grievances. Illness and deprivation made people desperate. A party of men, led by the Porras brothers, one of whom had been captain of the *Santiago*, became determined to take matters into their own hands. They vowed to help themselves, as Columbus clearly had failed.

On January 2, 1504, Captain Porras stormed into Columbus's

cabin, where he lay sick, and shouted at him in an insolent tone, so Ferdinand reported. 'What do you mean by making no effort to get to Castile? Do you wish to keep us here to perish?' Turning away from the Admiral, he cried out to the rest of the Spaniards, 'I'm for Castile! Who's with me?'

Some forty-eight of his henchmen, around half of the crew, were waiting for this agreed cry. Immediately, they started running about, waving their swords and guns, occupying all the makeshift cabins. Bartholomew Columbus attacked the mutineers with his sword, but was overpowered and thrown into a cabin, along with his brother. A few servants protected the Admiral, pleading with them not to murder Columbus, or they would answer for it.

The mutineers then jumped into some canoes, tied alongside, which Columbus had gone to great trouble to buy and barter from the Indians, and they paddled off in high good humour, singing and yelling, so Ferdinand says, as if they had already landed in Castile.

Columbus's life had at least been spared, but he was now left with the weaker members of his crew. Ferdinand adds, rather mournfully, that many of them would probably have gone with the mutineers, if they had been fit enough. 'If all had been well, I doubt if twenty of them would have remained with the Admiral.'

Over the next few weeks, most of the remaining Spaniards recovered from the worst symptoms of their illness, except for the Admiral, who was still weak with arthritis. Then the local Indians, tired of supplying food, and encouraged by the mutineers to believe that Columbus was an evil man, turned against them. 'They knew very well how to bargain with us and that they had the advantage over us, so we did not know which way to turn.'

God again came to Columbus's aid, according to Ferdinand. The Admiral called all the local caciques together and said that God was angry with them for not supplying food to the Spaniards. Some laughed, dismissing this as an idle story. But Columbus told them to watch that night. As the moon rose higher and higher, clear and bright in the sky, it suddenly seemed to disappear, as if into a hole. The Indians were all frightened, crying out in alarm, begging Columbus to plead with God, rushing to bring food. Columbus said he would see what he could do. He waited till the moon had totally gone, then announced that he had indeed spoken to God, and he would forgive them, this time. And out the moon came again.

It was a clever trick. Eliot Morison has pointed out that there were medieval documents which predicted there would be a total eclipse of the moon on that particular night, February 29, 1504. It was the sort of natural wonder which Columbus loved to study and observe. But he did have to have the skills to work out the date, to make allowances for his longitude, and the cunning to make the facts work to his advantage.

The mutineers were not proving to be nearly so ingenious. They had paddled off full of hope, then they ran into bad weather and began to panic when they got out into the open sea. The waves crashed over their canoes, so they started throwing Indians overboard to make the boats lighter. The remaining Indians could naturally not paddle as quickly, so the Spaniards as a punishment cut off a few hands. This helped even less. In the end, they were forced back to the land. Ashore, they went on the rampage, working their way across Jamaica, pillaging villages, raping and looting.

So we now have three separate narratives. There is Columbus and his weaker party, still on the beach. The mutineers, running riot. The third, by now almost forgotten, is the rescue party, still alive, led by Diego Mendez. It is now seven months since they set off.

The two canoes left the coast of Jamaica and reached the open sea safely enough, but then their progress became very slow. The currents between Jamaica and Hispaniola were all against them, and for days on end they seemed to be stationary. One Indian died of thirst and was thrown overboard. The others were convinced they too were about to perish through lack of water, when in the distance they sighted a small rocky islet. They managed to reach it and clamber ashore, but there was nothing there, no vegetation, just rocks.

Amongst the rocks they found small pools of rain-water and immediately several of the Indians started gulping it down. They all died. The remaining members of the group sheltered on the islet for the night, managing to make a fire as Diego had brought a flint with him. (Today, the islet is known as Navassa and is a well-known navigational point in the Windward Passage, containing a lighthouse run by the USA.)

Next morning, when they awoke, they discovered that Hispaniola was on the horizon. Thus reinforced, in body and spirit, they got back into the two canoes and struggled on the final few miles, landing on the westernmost point of Haiti.

Further adventures and obstacles ensued, as Diego went on

ahead, overland, to reach Santo Domingo and plead with the new Governor for help. This led to delays and prevarications, as no one seemed very interested. In the end the Governor agreed that Diego could buy and equip a ship, using the money which Columbus had lying in Santo Domingo, the proceeds from his repossessions. Diego then went straight on to Spain, not back to Jamaica, under instructions from Columbus to tell the Sovereigns in person what had happened. So the mutineers were right in their suspicions, that the Admiral was mostly concerned with his own position.

During the delays and discussions, while the Governor of Hispaniola was apparently trying to decide what to do about Columbus, he sent off a small ship, a caravelon so Ferdinand calls it, to go to Jamaica, locate the stranded mariners, and verify what Diego had been telling them.

This small ship arrived late in the evening, towards the end of March 1504, and anchored in the bay, within sight of the two wrecked caravels. Again, this sudden twist in the drama came at an opportune time. At that moment, some of Columbus's remaining Spaniards, now recovered from their illness, were just about to launch their own mutiny, led by the ship's doctor.

The sudden appearance, as if from heaven, of a Spanish boat, after they had been marooned for nine months, seeing no other ship, naturally stopped them in their tracks. But it also mystified them. The captain came ashore in a barge and presented Governor Ovando's compliments to Columbus. He handed over a cask of wine and a side of salt pork, and then went back to his caravelon. That same night, he departed for Hispaniola, leaving them unaided, unrelieved, and very little the wiser. He even refused to take back any letter from Columbus.

The mutineers decided this was a bad sign, in spite of the wine and pork. The Governor obviously did not want Columbus on Hispaniola. Perhaps it was a spying mission, to see how weak they were, so that soldiers could be sent to finish them off. Columbus persuaded them they were reading the signs wrong. They clearly meant that Diego Mendez had got through, so real help would not be long in coming. They would be sending a larger boat soon, so that they could all be taken to safety, even the mutineers.

Thus encouraged, if only by his own words, Columbus decided to send an olive branch to the mutineers. He dispatched two trusted men to find them, to pass on the news about the arrival of the caravelon, to say that Diego had got through and help would soon be at hand. It was a most magnanimous gesture, not wishing to exact revenge, forgiving them as he had forgiven Roldan. The mutineers were not impressed. They dismissed the arrival of the caravelon as 'a phantom ship made by the art of magic which the Admiral knows so well'.

The mutineers resolved to march on Columbus, to have it out with him once and for all; the leaders told their men and the Indians that Columbus was cruel and wicked, and that anyway they had more influence with the Court in Castile.

As they neared the encampment, Bartholomew was sent out to meet them. The Porras brothers refused this peaceful gesture, believing Columbus's men were still weak and most of them cowards. They unsheathed their swords and charged Bartholomew. A bloody battle ensued. Bartholomew and all the loyal Spaniards fought gallantly and the mutineers were finally put to flight. Bartholomew was restrained from killing those he had taken as prisoner.

Despite all the blood-letting, and the death of a couple of mutineers, few of the loyalists were seriously wounded, apart from Bartholomew in the hand and Columbus's steward in the hip. One of the pilots, on the side of the mutineers, received some severe wounds which Ferdinand describes in detail.

'He fell down a certain cliff and lay hidden that day and the next evening without anyone but the Indians knowing about it or giving him aid. The Indians, now knowing how our swords cut, were amazed; and with little sticks opened his wounds, one of which was on his head and through which one could see his brains and another on his shoulder so large his arm hung loose. Notwithstanding all these wounds, when the Indians bothered him he would cry, "Let me be, or when I get up, I'll fix you!' And at these words they would flee in terror. When this was known, the ship's people carried him into a thatched hut nearby. Instead of turpentine, which was the proper thing, they cauterised his wounds with oil, and his wounds were so numerous that the surgeon who dressed them swore that for the first eight days he went over him he found new ones. Yet at length he recovered, while our steward, whose wound nobody thought to be serious, died.' This steward, Pedro de Terreros, was the one who had been on all four of Columbus's voyages.

The mutineers begged for mercy, which Columbus was pleased to give, granting them a general pardon, but keeping their leader, Porras, in chains, as a precaution. As Ferdinand observed, it would have been difficult to imprison them all. Columbus's concern was to keep all the Spaniards together and relatively happy till the arrival of a rescue ship, which he was convinced would not be long coming.

Five weeks after the battle, a boat did appear and took them all off the island on June 29, 1504. They had been marooned for exactly a year and four days. Perhaps it was not surprising that young Ferdinand never went on another expedition.

At Santo Domingo, Governor Ovando made a great fuss of the survivors. He invited Columbus to rest in his own house, but Ferdinand maintains it was a pretence. 'This was only the peace of the scorpion, for on the other hand he set free Porras, leader of the mutiny, and tried to punish those who had a hand in capturing him. With such endearments, he treated the Admiral with deceitful smiles and dissimulated in his presence.'

On September 12, Columbus set sail for Spain, along with his brother, son, close servants and the more loyal of his crew, just twenty-five of them in all. Oddly, all the others stayed behind, so Ferdinand reports. After what they had gone through, they still preferred the New World to the Old. They had little reason to go back to Spain, which would suggest they were the rootless, low-quality sort of people Ferdinand had always maintained they were. Or perhaps they were simply glad to be free of Columbus.

The voyage home was rough, and the mast was broken in four pieces. The Admiral, still suffering from arthritis, rose from his sick-bed and supervised the patching of the mast, using planks torn from the stern.

They arrived back in Seville on November 7, 1504, two and a half years after they had set out. Columbus had nothing much to show for his troubles and tribulations, except his wounds, physical and mental. He was in a state of physical collapse, hardly able to move, weakened and crippled, and was helped by servants to a rented house in Seville. Emotionally and mentally he appears to have collapsed as well.

We have in all three first-hand accounts of that last voyage. Ferdinand's is by far the longest and most detailed and colourful. Then there is a shorter account, but in parts dramatic, the description by Diego Mendez of his journey by canoe from Jamaica to Santo Domingo, one of the most remarkable sea trips of all time. He did not set this down until 1536 (so Ferdinand did not have access to it when he wrote the Admiral's biography) but Mendez stayed with the Columbus family as a retainer, so the family must have known of his exploits.

Then we have Columbus's own account of his Fourth Voyage. This takes the form of a long letter written to the Sovereigns, the one which Diego Mendez took back to Spain. It is highly convoluted and incoherent, which is not surprising, considering he was ill and despairing, surrounded by mutineers and sickness, convinced this time he was going to die. The lucid parts are full of self-justification.

'I have won little profit from twenty years' service, rendered amid so many hardships and dangers. For today I have no roof over my head in Castile. If I wish to eat or sleep, I have no recourse except to an inn or a tavern, and most of the time I have no money to pay the bill. Another sorrow rents my heart. That was for Don Diego, my son, whom I had left in Spain, an orphan and dispossessed of my honour and my estate, although I was confident that, being just and grateful princes, you would restore everything to him, and more.' The use of the word 'orphan' shows he expected not to return.

Columbus describes the exploration of Panama, what went wrong, and all the storms which they managed to survive. 'Our Lord came to my aid. I know not if any other man has ever suffered more.'

He also reveals what was clearly some sort of mental breakdown, when they were in Belen, the ships worm-eaten, the Indians drawing closer, fever raging. 'There was no hope of escape. I climbed painfully to the highest part of the ship and cried out for help with a fearful voice, weeping to your Highnesses' war captains, in every direction, but none replied. At length, groaning with exhaustion, I fell asleep and heard a compassionate voice saying "Oh fool, and slow to believe, and serve thy God, the God of every man! What more did he do for Moses or for David His servant do for thee . . ."' He goes on at some length about this religious experience, which happened to him, he says, in a 'swoon'.

Later, he becomes almost mystical about gold. 'Oh most excellent gold! Who has gold has a treasure with which he gets what he wants, imposes his will on the world, and even helps souls to paradise.'

The last section contains a paragraph asking the Sovereigns to pay all those who have served with him, and been through so much. Finally, he returns to himself, and how badly he has been treated.

'For seven years I was at your royal court, where all with whom this Enterprise was discussed pronounced it to be fantastic. Now even the tailors clamour for an opportunity to make discoveries.' He argues that great wealth has come the way of Spain, thanks to his discoveries, but all he has got in return has been to be shackled in chains, naked in body, without being tried or convicted. 'Who will believe that a poor foreigner would dare revolt against your Highnesses in such a place without reason?' Calling himself a 'foreigner' is unusual, as he liked to forget his origins, once he had achieved his Spanish title.

'I came to serve you at the age of twenty-eight and now I have not a hair on me that is not white and my body is infirm and exhausted. All that was left to me and my brothers has been taken away and sold, even the cloak that I wore.'

He concludes with a final, desperate, cringing plea for the restoration of his privileges. Again, this shows the mutineers were correct in believing that was what he most cared about.

'I implore your Highnesses. I am ruined, as I have said. Hitherto I have wept for others, now Heaven have pity on me, and earth, weep for me! Of things material, I have not a single blanca to offer; of things spiritual, I have even ceased observing the forms, here in the Indies. Alone, desolate, infirm, daily expecting death, surrounded by a million savages full of cruelty, how neglected will this soul be if here it part from the body. Weep for me, whoever has charity, truth and justice. I did not come on this voyage for gain, honour or wealth. I came to your Highnesses with honest purpose and sincere zeal. I do not lie. I humbly beseech your Highnesses that, if it please God to remove me from here, you will help me to go to Rome and other pilgrimages.

'May the Holy Trinity guard and increase Your lives and high estate. Done in the Indies, on the Island of Jamaica, 7 July, 1503.'

These are amongst the last written words of Columbus which have survived. It is a sad note to end on, full of pathos, anger, hurt pride, yet hoping his dear Queen will once again come to his help.

She probably never even read the letter. Isabella died on November 26, 1504, just a couple of weeks after Columbus returned home. 'Her death caused the Admiral much grief,' writes Ferdinand. 'For she had always aided and favoured him, while the King he always found somewhat reserved and unsympathetic to his projects.'

Isabella had been ill with fever for most of that summer, brought on, so it was said, by grief as much as anything else. The tragic early deaths of so many of her family had weakened her will to live. Prince Juan, her only son and heir, had died in 1497, followed by her daughter Isabella, the Queen of Portugal, in 1498. Their third daughter, and youngest child, Catharine, had married Prince Arthur of England, son of Henry VII, in 1501, but he had died the following year. She then became betrothed to his younger brother, Henry, but tensions between England and Spain stopped their wedding till he had become King, as Henry VIII.

The family drama which occupied her mind in 1504 concerned her second daughter, Juana, married to the Archduke of Austria. Since 1501, she had been showing signs of insanity. The Courts of Europe now referred to her as La Loca (the madwoman).

Isabella did not recover and in the autumn of 1504 arranged for her last will and testament to be drawn up. She signed it on October 12, the twelfth anniversary of her Admiral's landfall on San Salvador. There was, alas, no mention of her once-glorious Admiral. Almost all her possessions went to her beloved husband, to whom she had been totally faithful. She wanted a simple tomb, and the money which would have been otherwise spent used to provide dowries for twelve poor girls. She instructed that Gibraltar was necessary to Spain and must never be given up. She also enjoined her successors to show the greatest kindness to the Indians in the new possessions overseas. 'The world has lost its noblest ornament,' wrote Peter Martyr. 'I know none of her sex, in ancient or modern times, who in my judgement is at all worthy to be named with this incomparable woman.'

In many ways, they had grown up and suffered together, Isabella and Columbus, contemporaries in age but with totally different lives, achieving great triumphs, but in the end brought down by personal sadness. Though she had grown distant from Columbus, aware of his faults and failures, she had stayed a friend, aware that deep down, however exasperating he might have become, there had been some mark of genius about him, which she had noticed from the very beginning. It was not an opinion shared by the Court.

Columbus spent the winter in Seville, nursing his health, bombarding the King and the Court with his letters and documents. Diego, his older son, now twenty-four, carried most of the burden. He was a member of the King's guard, kept on after the Queen's death, and his father expected him to secure a proper hearing for him and his cause. It was the old complaint: he had never received the positions and privileges and monies which had been promised when he had set out on his First Voyage.

The controversy grew complicated, full of legal arguments and precedents and supposed evidence. On the matter of titles, he maintained that he had been made Governor and Viceroy of

Hispaniola, for him and his successors, in perpetuity, not just Admiral of the Ocean Seas. But the Sovereigns had already given this position to someone else, so he had no hope in that quarter.

As for the monies, his letters to Diego are all about his 'tenths', 'fifths' and 'thirds' out of which he had been cheated. These were his various shares of the trade between Spain and the Indies, which he had been legally promised under the Capitulations of 1492. He did have some justification for these claims, to which the Sovereigns had been unwise enough to agree, but the King was determined to deny them, and probably always had been. It was a paradise for lawyers. Columbus, being stubborn, refused to accept their interpretations, so nothing was agreed and the letters and appeals to His Majesty continued.

It was suggested to Columbus, through intermediaries, that if he accepted an estate in Castile, which would give him a fairly reasonable income, then all the unpleasantness and arguments and paperwork could be forgotten. Columbus would have none of that either. He was desperate to reach the King personally, in order to put his case. There was always the chance that the Porras brothers, still unpunished for the mutiny, might get in first, with their version of what had happened on the last voyage.

At Court, he had several friends working on his behalf, apart from his son Diego. Amerigo Vespucci, just back from another South American trip, was there, giving the King the benefit of his wisdom on navigation. Columbus, in his letters to Diego, says that Vespucci has promised to help. 'He is a very honourable man and always desirous of pleasing me. See what he can do to profit me there and try to have him do it.'

The court was in Segovia, and during the winter of 1504–5, when he was feeling rather better, Columbus worked out a plan to go there, without an agreed audience, travelling by hearse. He made approaches to borrow the stately catafalque, an ornate coach used by Seville Cathedral for the funerals of important noblemen. It is hard to understand all the symbolism in this gesture. Presumably he saw it at some sort of ironic self-abasement, on a level with his hair shirt.

In the end, he was granted an audience and did not need to hire the hearse. In May 1505 he travelled to Segovia – by mule. Even this was a complicated gesture. Mule-riding had been officially banned, thanks to the bloodstock lobby who had had it ordained that all riding must be by horse. The King, however, made a special dispensation for Columbus to come by mule, the only privilege

Ferdinand ever granted him. A mule was suitably humble, and of course had Biblical overtones.

The King listened courteously, but made very few comments, gave nothing away, except to promise that Don Diego would certainly inherit the title of Admiral. Columbus harangued him further, trying to make him promise that in due course Diego would also become Viceroy and Governor of Hispaniola. The King made no reply. After all, Diego was scarcely twenty-five, too young for such a position. Columbus was now concentrating more on his successors having the titles and privileges he had lost; perhaps beginning to doubt that he himself would ever get them.

The Court moved to Salamanca and thence to Valladolid, with Columbus still in pursuit. An arbiter was suggested, which shows that the King might have been unsympathetic but he was not harsh. Columbus was allowed to name his own choice, and selected the Archbishop of Seville, believing he would take his side. It turned out that the king wanted not only the monies to be arbitrated, but Columbus's titles, including that of Admiral, which he had already had back. Columbus refused to consider this.

In 1506, Columbus was still in Valladolid, in a small rented house, becoming weaker and weaker. He was continuing with his appeals directly to the King, at the same time instructing his brother Bartholomew to try a rather different tack.

There had been further dynastic developments. Just a few months after Isabella's death, King Ferdinand married the young niece of Louis XII of France. His intention was to produce a son and heir, as quickly as possible, so that La Loca, his mad daughter Juana, would not be able to inherit the throne of Castile, to which she had become heiress on the death of her mother. That part of the plan succeeded, and Ferdinand quickly had a son, but he died.

Columbus hoped that Juana might remember sitting, as a little girl, beside her mother on Columbus's triumphal return after his First Voyage, entranced by his exotic tales. He wanted personally to throw himself at her feet, and beg her help, but he could not face the journey. So he sent Bartholomew instead, but with no result.

By May 1506, Columbus's strength was fading fast. On May 19, he signed the final codicil of his last will and testament. Once again, he complains that he gave the Indies to the Sovereigns, and in his 'privileges' is due 'tenths, thirds and eighths' of the returns, but at the time of writing has not yet received anything at all. None the less, he expects millions of maravedis to be coming in soon, and he wants his son Diego to get most of them, as well as his title and privileges and properties, with directions to pay off some debts in Genoa. He wishes presents given to certain people who helped him when he lived in Lisbon, such as a Genoese shopkeeper and a Jew who lived near the Jewry Gate, and to give money to support a chapel in Santo Domingo. Diego also must help Beatrice, the mother of Ferdinand.

It is noticeable that he had had no contact with Beatrice, his former mistress, on his return to Spain. Now clearly he was feeling guilty for those years of neglect. 'Provide for her in such a manner that she may live in dignity, being a person who weighs heavily on my conscience. The reason for this I am not permitted to write here.' He was by now being tended by friars from a monastery in Vallodolid, and doubtless did not wish them, or posterity, to know of this relationship.

He died the next day, May 20, 1506, in the rented house, aged fifty four. From his own statements and pleadings, he died in poverty, with unpaid debts, cheated out of all his wealth and earnings, with not even a cloak to his name, or so he alleged. His money from Hispaniola had still not come through. His son Ferdinand gave orders, behind Columbus's back, for any proceeds there to be used to pay off his debts.

Did Columbus die in total poverty? Las Casas also states that Columbus was penniless when he died, but some scholars suspect he was not quite as poor as he had pleaded, certainly not destitute, and that he might have brought some gold back with him from his last voyage. They also point to the fact that Diego was soon living the life of a gentleman, possibly on the proceeds of his father's estate, though he did have a very good position at Court.

There is little doubt, however, that he died poor; and, even more tragically, he died in relative obscurity. There were no local nobility from Valladolid present, nor was his death announced in the local register, which normally recorded notable local births and deaths and marriages.

The last witnesses were family and friends. By the bedside were his two sons, Diego and Ferdinand, and two brothers, Bartholomew and Diego. His two most loyal seamen were there, Diego Mendez and Fieschi, and some domestic servants. In front of this small circle, a priest from the monastery celebrated Mass. Afterwards, Columbus's body was taken to the crypt of the monastery. He was fifty-five.

His final words, according to Ferdinand, were: 'In manus tuas,

Domine, commendo spiritum meum.' It was not a death scene fit for a temporal lord with the grand title and aspirations of the Admiral of the Ocean Seas, but there were echoes in those final words of the last utterance of the Lord Himself, who Columbus was convinced would judge him higher than his contemporaries had done.

Columbus's coat of arms.

20

Spain Today – Gomera and Valladolid

MANY TOWNS and cities in Spain today are claiming connections with Columbus, especially in view of 1992 and all the tourists who might be brought in, and there are indeed many places he visited during all those years when he was wearily following the Court. Each has its Columbus statue, or the church where he supposedly prayed, the room where he met the Monarchs, the shrine where he gave thanks, even a house where he lodged. Cadiz, Barcelona, Cordoba, Salamanca, Santa Fé can all make such claims, and are worth visiting, but compared with Palos and Seville they are not really vital to the Columbus saga. After Palos and Seville, the next most important pilgrimage place on mainland Spain is undoubtedly Valladolid, but I was saving that for the end of my investigation.

First, I went overseas, to one of the islands of Spain, Gomera in the Canaries. Little islands played a big part in Columbus's life, from Porto Santo to San Salvador, but Gomera was of particular relevance to Columbus. He visited the Canaries and left from there on all his four voyages, with Gomera being his final port of call on the first three trips. It is still very isolated, the hardest to reach of all the seven islands of the Canaries as it is the only one without an airport.

I flew to Tenerife, which Columbus never visited, as it was still in the hands of the Guanches, the original inhabitants of the Canaries, a pale-skinned aboriginal people from North Africa. And I left as quickly as possible. Tenerife is not for sensitive souls. Mass tourism from Northern Europe has totally taken over, providing packaged pleasures for the masses. Almost one million Britons go there every year.

Gomera has been spared all this. It has a population of some 18,000 and only two hotels, both discreet and tasteful, neither of them high-rise blocks. The island is roughly circular, some twenty miles across, and on the map it appears easy to move around, till you realise the island is really a volcano, rising to almost 5,000 feet. Every journey is a switchback. The island is basically one steep chunk of rock, most of it bare, though in the north the vegetation is rather lusher and in the valleys you can see signs of former cultivation. Thousands of farmers left after the war, giving up the unequal struggle, and emigrated to Venezuela.

I caught the new fast hovercraft ferry from Los Cristianos in South Tenerife, just a thirty-five minute trip and extremely expensive. (The big ferry boat, taking cars, is much slower, but cheaper.) The island looked very forbidding, with the mist-covered volcanic peaks hanging over the capital, San Sebastian. It has a fine natural harbour, and was clearly a perfect last stop for Columbus, at safe anchor, to take on supplies of fresh water.

San Sebastian has a population of 6,000 and a surprising amount of fifteenth-century buildings. Many of them are associated with Columbus, such as the Church of Assumption where he prayed, a well where he drew water and a Casa Colon, where he stayed. This is a two-storey building with stone floors and wooden rafters, cool and shaded, which has been recently converted into a museum, but not with a great deal of success. Most rooms were totally empty, apart from a few garish colour prints of Gomera. The moustachioed man selling tickets and little souvenirs knew nothing about the building and was more interested in listening to his monster ghetto blaster and pursuing some children who had stolen his supply of souvenir felt pens.

Near the harbour is another fifteenth-century building, the Torre del Conde, the Count's Tower, where Beatriz de Bobadilla sheltered when the natives were intent on murdering her. I bought a few locally written and published pamphlets on the history of the Canaries, and discovered a rather different image of Beatriz from the one I had picked up from the Columbus diaries. There is today a renewed interest in their pre-Hispanic history, and research is being done on the Guanches, long dismissed as ignorant cave-men. Beatriz and the early Spaniards in general do not emerge in a very good light.

Beatriz had been at the Spanish Court, as a maid-in-waiting to Isabella, until she was seduced by Ferdinand. In 1481 Isabella arranged for her to be married off to the Governor of Gomera. He turned out to be a cruel tyrant, ill-treating the natives, who eventually rose up against him after he had seduced the daughter of one of their leaders. He was killed in the uprising, but Beatriz managed to barricade herself in the Tower till Spanish troops arrived from Gran Canaria and she was rescued. She took over command of the island, proving strong and resolute, but became almost as cruel as her late husband, and untrustworthy, according to the Guanches.

Perhaps she was making use of Columbus, just as much as he was making use of her? When he arrived with his royal letters and insignia, he was obviously in favour with Isabella. Beatriz might have hoped for him to put in some good words on her behalf at Court, to redeem her position.

There are no direct Columbus connections with Madrid, unlike Gomera, and there are no relevant archives of any importance, despite Madrid being the nation's capital, but the chief officials of the country's National Commission for 1992 are there, so I thought I would try to see some of them.

Their offices in the Avenida de los Reyes Catolicos sounded interesting, worth visiting for the name alone, and they were indeed splendid, with sumptuous furnishings and well-manicured secretaries. I had sent letters in advance, as ever, and made an appointment on the telephone the day before with one official, but when I arrived he was not there. I asked for two other names, but one was working at home and the other was out of town. I waited an hour, but still no one could talk to me, so I left, armed with about half a ton of high-sounding prose, top-quality paper, glossy photographs, splendid printing, telling me about the deeply meaningful events organised for 1992, putting Spain well and truly on the world map once again.

I sat in the station, wondering how they ever managed to run that massive empire. They were so efficient and well-organised, during all those centuries when they controlled the Indies.

I got off the train at Valladolid, 200 or so kilometres north of Madrid, and jumped in the first taxi, asking him to take me to Casa Colon. According to a brief reference in a guide book, it was once the home of the Columbus family, but now appeared to be some sort of museum. I had failed to get a telephone number, so I wanted to establish its existence and the opening hours, before I found a hotel for the night.

Outside the station was a large statue of Columbus, on a globe-shaped pedestal, with naked nymphs at his feet, various heraldic animals and a cross at the top, which appeared to come out of his head.

Isabella and Ferdinand were married in Valladolid, in 1469, when it was the capital of Castile. Many kings and queens were born there and for a while it became capital of all Spain. It has an ancient university, dating back to 1479, and some fine churches. Napoleon was sufficiently aware of its historic importance to make it his headquarters when he invaded Spain in 1809. Today, it has a population of some 325,000 and the reduced status of a local capital, of the province of Meseta Central. It struck me as a decidedly provincial town, rather worn and grey, cut off and remote, stuck out on a flat plateau, deep in the hinterland of Spain, well away from the normal tourist trails.

The taxi took me to the Calle Colon, just a short street, drawing up outside a low, modern-looking building, the Casa Colon. The brickwork looked so new I feared I had got the wrong address. I made the driver wait while I ran to investigate. The building seemed deserted, then I noticed a woman in an apron sitting knitting inside a little ticket office. I asked in my pidgin Spanish if there was a curator, a director or some official I could talk to, but she carried on knitting. I asked if the building was open, and she pointed to the opening times. There were still a couple of hours to go, so I got back in the taxi and asked to be taken to a local hotel.

We found something in the end, modest but clean, the Hostal Lima. I booked in, left my bag, and returned to the Casa Colon. Only then did I finally pay off the driver. It had taken me four years of arriving in strange, out-of-the-way non-tourist towns, making requests which the locals could not quite understand, to realise that the secret is to spend money. Otherwise, you can get dreadfully stuck, with days passing, nothing being achieved.

I paid my entrance fee for the Casa-Museo de Colon, as my ticket officially described it, and walked round, their only visitor. The impression given by the various notices was that this was where Columbus died. I noticed a door marked 'Library' and, when the aproned woman was not looking, I opened it. It was hard to see anything at first, then I spotted a man at a far table, reading with a desk light, and a younger woman beside him. I asked if either spoke English. They shook their heads. I closed the door.

I spent over an hour in the little two-storey museum, studying every exhibit, amusing myself at the various liberties taken with the Life and Death of the Great Discoverer. Pride of place was a massive deathbed mural, covering a whole wall, with the figures life-size. Columbus is in the middle, with long white hair and a white night-shirt. On his right-hand side are six hooded monks, solemnly holding candles, with another two kneeling at his feet. On the other side are thirteen members of his family, plus friends. I was not aware, from the documents, that his deathbed had been so crowded. It was almost like a public meeting. A key to the mural listed the thirteen people present who, surprisingly, included Amerigo Vespucci.

I enjoyed the other exhibits, some old, pre-Columbian pottery and figures from Mexico and Peru, and some fairly new, primitive paintings from Haiti. It was most interesting to see early editions of Columbus's first Letter, the so-called Carta, written on his arrival home after his First Voyage, the one which was immediately pirated round Europe. They had copies printed in Rome, Florence and Paris from 1493, and a Valladolid edition, printed in 1497.

One room was filled with flags from the various countries the Spaniards 'discovered' which made an impressive list – Texas, Uruguay, El Salvador, Cuba, Puerto Rico, Chile, Paraguay, Brazil, Nicaragua, Mexico, Guatemala, the Philippines, the Dominican Republic, Peru, Ecuador, Venezuela, Colombia, Panama, Bolivia, Argentina.

Before I left, I popped my head once more into the library. An hour earlier it had appeared like a morgue, but now it was very lively, with about half a dozen young students, standing around chatting. This time I got out my vintage letter of introduction in diplomatic Spanish, last flashed in the Dominican Republic, and explained my project. One of the girls, who spoke some English, said the older gentleman was Angel Sanz, Professor of American History at the University. This library was part of his department. She and the others had all been his students and had come in to see him as they had just graduated. Would I like to join them and have a drink in a bar?

As we walked down the road, the Professor asked the first girl who I was, what I was doing, and they conferred quickly in Spanish. I could make out the name Samuel Eliot Morison, then lots of laughter. In the bar, he bought drinks for all his students, who seemed very fond of him. He had no English, which made me less embarrassed about my lack of Spanish, so I tried Portuguese and

French, without any luck. Then I remembered he was Professor of American History. Wasn't it a bit of a handicap, teaching American History and not speaking any English? Not at all, he said. He specialised in Spanish American history, so all the documents were in Spanish.

He asked me more about my project, so I explained, with one of the girls translating. 'Why don't you do a biography of Mrs Thatcher?' he asked. 'I would read that. We have too many biographies of Columbus.'

I argued there was a great need for something up-to-date in English. The last so-called standard one was now fifty years out of date, written by Morison. They all laughed again. This was obviously a running joke I was missing, presumably the Professor's pet hate.

The students all soon dispersed, while the Professor and his assistant returned to the library. I went with them, as he had offered to prove to me there were far too many books about Columbus. He took me to the Columbus biography shelves and we counted up around 200, almost all in Spanish. I noticed that Taviani was there, and said what a shame his masterwork finished at 1492. Morison, whatever some people might think of his 1942 two-volume biography, *Admiral of the Ocean Sea*, did cover the whole life. More laughter. I asked him what he thought was the best modern biography, of use to the general reader. He searched the shelves and produced a two-volume, very academic-looking work by Antonio Ballesteros, which was new to me and has not, to my knowledge, appeared in English. I looked at its date: no more recent than 1945. See, I said. The world needs a new biography.

Before I left the Professor and his assistant, working hard into the night, I asked about Columbus's house. Surely it wasn't genuine? No, it had been recently rebuilt, though it was on the site of a house traditionally owned by later members of the Columbus family. If I remembered rightly, Columbus's body was laid out in a monastery. Where had that been situated? To find it, he said, I should head for the Plaza Mayor, then look for the Zorilla.

After breakfast next morning I set off to find the Plaza Mayor and the old part of the city, looking out for buildings which were there in Columbus's day, such as the University. The main part was very ornate, heavily baroque, with decorated columns stretching out over the pavement.

There was a service on in the Cathedral so I stood and admired the nearby San Pablo church, also from the fifteenth century. The whole of the front façade is carved in elaborate figures, from top to bottom, as if some mad sculptor had been working with wet sand and allowed it to trickle through his hands into weird and wonderful shapes. The church's guide describes the style as 'Isabelline Gothic'.

The Plaza Mayor is the largest square in the city, and also houses the Town Hall. In Columbus's day, the central square was always a forum. It still retains its sixteenth-century shape, and there are several fine churches and other ancient buildings. One side has been completely rebuilt with modern blocks. This is the side where Columbus died, and where the monastery once stood.

I walked round the square, wondering what Zorilla might be, and was delighted to come across a row of neat little market stalls set up in the middle of the square, all of them selling books. On one stall, the name Zorilla jumped out at me. It was a biography of José Zorilla, born in Valladolid in 1817, one of Spain's most revered poets.

I crossed the square to have a proper look at the new buildings, the usual glass and concrete modern blocks, with at ground level several arcades, shops, cafés. It was only when I sat down on a chair, looking around, that I saw beside the café entrance, almost obscured by its chairs, an awning saying 'Teatro Zorilla'. I went inside to investigate, and discovered it was a cinema, not a theatre, about to open for the afternoon performance.

I found a door, unlocked, and was about to go in and start imagining Columbus's death scene, when a spotty-faced young man in a bow tie and a worn suit pulled me back. He was trying hard to be authoritative and bossy, despite his tender years and tender moustache. I tried to explain I just wanted to look inside his cinema, not enjoy his film, but he pointed towards the ticket office. Maybe Columbus died at the ticket office. I could just as well imagine the scene here, as a few yards inside the door, amidst the cinema seats. On the other hand, after 50,000 miles round the world, or whatever it is I have done, it seemed perverse not to buy a ticket and enter the actual building.

The cinema was small, totally ordinary, very hard to conjure up any atmosphere. There were a few old men scattered along the back row, perhaps left over from the previous day. The film was just starting and I was surprised to hear English accents. It was 'My Beautiful Laundrette', subtitled into Spanish. What on earth would the old men make of that?

As I left, the manager was putting in the poster for the next day's film. It was entitled, 'America Loco.' I did not recognise the names of the stars, but it was clearly some low budget American campus comedy. 'Mad America' seemed very apt for my final Columbus site. A similar observation must surely have gone through his head as he lay here dying, thinking back on what he had Discovered and all that had happened to the New World of the Americas. A sort of madness had taken over his Life, and over his Discoveries.

Santa Maria, on a 1930 Spanish postage stamp.

21

Columbus Today

Colombo '92

WHAT HAPPENED after Columbus's death is worth a book in itself, in fact two books. There is the mystery of his body, which proceeded to move round the globe over the next four hundred years, so that no one today is quite sure where it lies. Then there is the mystery of his fame. Why was it, for three hundred years or so after his death, that his name and achievements were as good as forgotten?

His mortal remains first. They lay for the first three years after his death in the modest crypt of that Franciscan monastery in Valladolid, where the cinema now stands. Then around 1509 his son Don Diego decided he wanted a more suitable setting. After all, there were no real family or historical connections with Valladolid. Diego was a gentleman, going up in the world, and there was by then some money coming in from his father's estate.

Columbus's body was moved to Seville, the headquarters of the Indies empire, to the Carthusian monastery of Las Cuevas, on the banks of the Guadalquivir, where he had taken refuge and rested between his Third and Fourth Voyages. In his will, he had left the monastery certain of his personal belongings and documents. (Las Cuevas ceased to be an active monastery in the nineteenth century, and later became part of a tile factory. Now it is being revitalised for the 1992 Seville World's Fair.)

The second move came thirty-two years later, around 1541, after the death of Don Diego. One of his last wishes had been for his own body, and that of his father, to be buried in Santo Domingo. This would be the most suitable place of all, the spiritual home of the Columbus dynasty, their hearts lying in the heart of the New World Columbus had discovered. His widow asked permission from the King of Spain, Charles V, for both bodies to be taken from Seville, a request which was quickly granted.

In Santo Domingo, there was some argument at first as it was maintained Columbus had not been ordained, and so could not be buried in the Cathedral. Instead, he was buried in a crypt, under the Cathedral. The two bodies were later joined by those of Columbus's two brothers, Bartholomew and Diego, and also by his grandson, Don Luis.

This then became the Columbus family grave for the next 250 years. It does not appear to have been considered particularly notable, or worth pointing out to visitors. The occasional traveller who did want to find it was told it was somewhere under the paving stones, but no one quite knew where. There had been an inscription, but this had been removed in 1655 when it was feared an English expeditionary force under Admiral Penn (the father of William Penn) was about to besiege the city.

The third move came in 1795 when France occupied Hispaniola. Columbus's direct descendant, the Duke of Veragua, asked for the body to be quickly dug up and transferred to the nearest Spanish-controlled island, which happened to be Cuba. And so, for the next hundred years, Columbus lay in Havana.

The fourth move was in 1899 when in turn Cuba suffered a civil upheaval. The Spaniards were ejected, with the help of US troops who then occupied the island. The Admiral's remains crossed back over the Atlantic and were laid to rest, in great state this time, in that marble monument in Seville. Later, as a good-will gesture, some of his ashes were passed on to Genoa, his birthplace.

In Seville to this day, as I discovered, they proudly boast that they have the body and that their Cathedral was and is Columbus's final resting place. Yet, when I was in Santo Domingo, they too boasted that they had the body, and that their tomb was the true home. Which is correct?

During most of these movements, Columbus's body was part of a private family grave, not deemed nationally important. It was family or local priests who organised the various changes, often in troubled times. None the less, the orders were carried out. Or were they? The Santo Domingo authorities maintain that Columbus was in fact never moved to Cuba. The workmen in 1795 who were told to dig up his body from under the pavement found the wrong one, possibly his brother or son. Columbus himself remained there, and their proof is the fact that in 1877, when building work in the Cathedral was being done, a vault was found, containing bones and dust, with the letters CCA on top of a lead casket. This stands for Cristobal Colon Almirante, so they assert. Columbus therefore never moved. It was his son and brother who went on to Havana and subsequently to Spain.

Various learned papers have been produced over the last hundred years, arguing the case either way, based on inscriptions and historic documents. Since the last war, we have moved into a more scientific age and modern methods are now being used to solve the puzzle. In 1960, an eminent Yale University surgeon was allowed to photograph and measure every bone in the Santo Domingo tomb. He confirmed that the remains belonged to a man of five feet eight inches, who died aged between fifty and sixty, and had suffered from arthritis. But he also maintained that the skeleton had more than the usual number of limbs, yet was missing other parts, which naturally indicated the presence of two bodies, if not more. The theory of one body, Columbus's, staying in Santo Domingo, while his son's was moved, began to look suspect. Instead, it would appear that various parts, willy-nilly, depending on what the workmen happened to dig up, went off in various directions. This solution might have made both Seville and Santo Domingo happy, establishing that some of their remains were genuine, but neither was persuaded. Each has continued to assert it has the whole and real body.

As I write, there is a new investigation being planned by some scientists at the University of California who believe they can help to settle the argument. They applied for permission to the Santo Domingo authorities to take a portion of Columbus's teeth back to their laboratory to be analysed. By examining the strontium content, they hope to be able to identify whether the body belonged to someone brought up in Europe. All seemed to be going well, then permission was not granted. It appears Santo Domingo either did not want to embarrass Spain by being right, or to lose credibility and a lot of tourists by being proved wrong.

The matter of Columbus's fame, the progress of his spiritual body, will never be settled by scientific means. Reputations go up and down, for reasons which are not always clear.

His public eclipse, for almost 300 years, stems from the nature and the circumstances prevailing at the time of his death. In his last gasp, he was still complaining that he had been cheated, that the Sovereigns had kept all his money and denied his glory. For the next fifty years, his sons and heirs maintained this campaign, issuing endless petitions and engaging in constant legal battles. King Ferdinand had never liked Columbus, never agreed with his claims, and continued to ignore or disprove all the arguments. When the cases did come to court, rival claims were encouraged, rival explorers were praised, his old enemies gave witness, and Columbus was generally dismissed as a foreign upstart and pretender who had lived in a fantasy world. This was to the advantage of the royal Court, enabling them to avoid paying any of the supposed debts.

It also explains why the Pinzon brothers, not heard of since the First Voyage, came back into prominence. Their case was brought forward and their claims were established. Witnesses appeared who said that Columbus had stolen the whole idea from an old man who had a secret map, and anyway the voyage would have foundered but for the Pinzons. This became an official view, believed by many people, at least by those who were interested enough to follow the case as it dragged on and on. They certainly believed it in Palos, because it concerned locally-born sailors, still heroes there to this day.

While Ferdinand disliked Columbus, his personality and his pretensions, he treated his son, Don Diego, with fairness. Diego continued at Court, married well (a niece of the Duke of Alba), and in 1509 he was made Governor of Hispaniola, in succession to Ovando. It was Diego who built the grand Governor's palace in Santo Domingo, the Alcazar. He held the post till 1516, when Ferdinand died.

Diego's son Don Luis inherited the title of Admiral, and kept up the family campaign for the return of all the privileges, but finally gave in in 1556, accepting in return some land in Spain and a new title, the Duke of Veragua, which commemorates that area of Panama where Columbus was convinced he had found real gold. The title remains to this day in the Columbus family. There is still a Duke of Veragua, who can also call himself Admiral Colon of the Ocean Seas.

The first reason for the public eclipse was therefore a combination of legal problems and royal disapproval. Secondly, life moved on, especially in the Indies. There were far more exciting adventures and adventurers being talked about and discussed. Unlike Columbus's voyages, they were bringing in real and enormous wealth. Hernando Cortes began his conquest of Mexico in 1519 and very soon Mexican gold was pouring into Spain. Another Spaniard, Francisco Pizarro, moved into Peru in 1532 and conquered the Incas. The era of the conquistadors had begun. There were also navigators achieving great success, pushing back the barriers and frontiers. Ferdinand Magellan, Portuguese but sailing on behalf of Spain, was in command of a small fleet of five ships which left the Guadalquivir in 1519 and managed what no one had achieved before, and which Columbus had failed to do – to sail round the world. He went west, to reach the East. He was killed before the ships returned home, in 1522, but his was the first expedition which circumnavigated the globe.

Then we come to the matter of Amerigo Vespucci. Vespucci was a Florentine, three years younger than Columbus, educated and well-connected, who came to live in Seville as a banker. It seems likely he was present in Seville after the First Voyage, and observed all the celebrations. He then met and became friendly with Columbus. As a banker, he was involved in financing some of the ships for the Second and Third Voyages. Typical of a certain type of Renaissance man, he then became an explorer, went on a series of voyages, either as a navigator or just as a gentleman passenger. There is still argument today about the precise date of his first voyage to Central America, but most experts believe it was in 1499, after Columbus had got there.

His next voyage was more important. Sailing on behalf of Portugal, going much further south than Columbus ever had, he reached Brazil. It was this voyage which convinced Vespucci that South America was a new continent, or a 'New World', which is what he called it in his letters.

Vespucci's accounts of his voyages were published, and received a great deal of attention. He naturally made many grandiose claims for what he had done, but then so had Columbus. He organised the publications himself, in Latin and Italian, and sent copies to his notable friends in the various Courts of Europe.

In 1507, it so happened that a mapmaker in Lorraine called Martin Waldseemüller was about to bring out a new edition of a book about cosmography. He had read Vespucci's voyages, in a copy given to him by the Duke of Lorraine, in which Vespucci stated that he had found 'a continent more densely populated than our Europe . . . and we may rightly call this continent the New World'. Waldseemüller decided to go one better and give it a real name. Who better to name it after than the talented, cultivated explorer, Amerigo Vespucci? As all the continents so far had female

names, Europa, Asia and Africa, he called it America, rather than
Americo.

Waldseemüller probably knew little about the voyages of
Columbus, living as he did in the little Duchy of Lorraine. By this
time, Columbus was dead, half-forgotten or discredited in his own
country, at least the one he had adopted. Within ten years, this
new map and the new name 'America' were circulating throughout
Europe. In another ten years, America had entered common par-
lance. The Columbus heirs were still preoccupied with their legal
arguments over the privileges. Only Las Casas defended Columbus,
writing that it was 'manifest that the Admiral Don Cristobal Colon
was the first whom Divine Providence ordained that this our great
new continent should be discovered . . . and that Amerigo Vespucci
has done him injury and injustice'. Alas, these writings, probably
done in the 1520s, had not yet been published. Nor had Ferdinand's
biography.

Vespucci therefore received all the popular credit. He returned
to the service of Spain, gave up his voyaging and in 1508 was
appointed an official of the new Indies Office, looking after navigation and maps, and serving there with distinction. He later took
Spanish citizenship.

The name America at first referred simply to South America,
and only gradually spread to cover North America as well. North
America, as a place, was not considered of great interest anyway
by Europe for the next two hundred years. The battles and rivalries
for wealth and power in the New World centred round Central and
South America.

It was only in the late eighteenth century that a consciousness of
North America came into being, of a real power, a proper nation
beginning to establish itself. Until then, it was generally considered
little more than a primitive land, there to be exploited.

Philosophical discussions about North America began. Was it
beneficial, the creation of this New World, and what had the Old
World to learn from it, if anything? Within America itself, with the
rise of nationalism, emerged a desire for a deeper understanding of
where they had come from, how had it all begun? Americans started
looking at Americans, investigating and writing their own story.
Yet, even into the early decades of the nineteenth century,
Columbus was still virtually unknown, still unsung. Humboldt,
the great German scientist and explorer, made a lengthy tour of
the Americas between 1799 and 1804, and remarked on the absence
of any Columbus statues or mementoes.

Washington Irving first put Columbus on the map, as far as Americans were concerned. He was travelling in Europe in the 1820s when a friend, who was the US minister in Spain, drew his attention to the publication, in Spanish, of some recently-discovered Columbus documents. He suggested to Irving that an English version, using the material, might be useful. Irving attached himself to the US legation in Madrid where he did the research and his biography was published in 1828, to great success, running into many editions. (In the second edition, he replied to readers who accused him of not having given enough credit to the Spaniard who had made available to him the newly-discovered Columbus documents.)

Irving set the tone for Columbus as Hero, reinforced later by Samuel Eliot Morison, which survived intact in America until recent times. King Ferdinand was the villain, according to Irving, cheating Columbus of his due rewards. He denies that Columbus was mercenary and considers his desire for rank was understandable. 'Not from a mere vulgar love of titles, but because he prized them as testimonials of his achievements.' He praises Columbus for the 'grandeur of his views and the magnanimity of his spirit' and for being 'devoutly pious'. There is only one element of criticism, and that concerns the slaves, which Irving admits was a sin, 'but he was goaded on by the mercenary impatience of the crown and by the sneers of his enemies at the unprofitability of his enterprise'. Irving adds that it would have been much better if all later Europeans had had the same 'sound policy and liberal views'.

In Spain, Philip VI ordered a proper collection of the new Columbus documents to be made, and they were gradually published. The two vital books, upon which I have leaned so heavily, took a long time to appear.

Ferdinand, Columbus's son, after he returned from that voyage, devoted a lifetime to books and study. He secretly wrote his father's biography, knowing that at Court his name was still not to be mentioned. He was incensed by the accusations against him, especially in a book on the Indies, by Oviedo, which gave Columbus no credit. Ferdinand wanted to set the record straight, using the first-hand documents and letters given to him by his father. The existence of this biography was unknown until 1571, thirty-two years after Ferdinand's own death, when the manuscript was sold to a Genoese merchant by the impecunious Columbus family. It was translated, rather badly, and published in Venice. The first English version appeared in 1744. Irving appears to have used a Spanish edition, judging by his footnotes.

The equally invaluable *History of the Indies*, by Las Casas, which he finished by 1550, took even longer to appear. It was not published till 1875.

In South America, the process of Columbus-worship was established in the 1850s when his face began to appear on postage stamps, a sure sign of fame. Chile portrayed him from 1853 on all their stamps for the rest of the century, despite the fact that he never got to Chile. Other South American nations used him as a national emblem, picking the portrait which they thought most suitable and regal.

The Catholic Church then decided he was not just a super-hero but a veritable saint, worthy of beatification, and official proceedings to sanctify him began in 1866. His cause was supported by many cardinals, but in 1891 it all collapsed. Too many of his human faults were becoming apparent, such as producing an illegitimate child, transporting slaves and cheating Rodrigo de Triana out of his little reward for spotting the first land.

In 1892 Columbus's modern status as a world hero was confirmed, when the 400th anniversary of the Discovery was celebrated in style with a World's Fair: not in Genoa, or Palos, or even Seville, but in Chicago. It was officially called the World's Columbian Exposition, organised in honour of Columbus, whose massive statue dwarfed the entrance to the Administration Building, and thousands of visitors gaped in wonder at reproductions of his three ships in an artificial lake. It was in fact mainly a trade fair, showing the wonders of electricity, manufacturing, mining, agriculture, and gave countries from all round the world a chance to show off their progress.

To tie in with the Fair, the US Government brought out a series of Columbus stamps, the USA's first commemorative issues. They appeared a year late, in 1893, and have been greatly prized ever since by collectors. There are eleven in all, showing scenes from the Columbus story. On the one cent stamp, which is captioned 'Columbus in Sight of Land', he is shown as being smooth-chinned. On the two cent, 'The Landing of Columbus', he has a handsome full beard. The gap, in reality, was no more than twelve hours. On the one dollar stamp, the caption is 'Isabella Pledging Her Jewels', a story which first appeared in late nineteenth-century popular books about Columbus, and still reappears to this day. As we know, there is no evidence she sold or pawned any of her jewels to finance Columbus's First Voyage. But she has always been considered the heroine of the Columbus saga. In 1991, there was a campaign to make Isabella a saint, and it was hoped the Vatican would grant it by 1992.

King Ferdinand has had his critics, notably Washington Irving, but today he is no longer dismissed as a wicked king, simply as a peripheral figure, not a supporter of Columbus, but equally not an enemy. The popular enemy today, judging by most of the luridly printed picture books put out in Spain and South America, is Bobadilla.

Samuel Eliot Morison's great works on Columbus, which first appeared in the 1940s, stressed his navigational brilliance, and were based on Morison's own sea expeditions over some of the same routes (he was an admiral, before turning to history). But he also accepted most of Irving's views about Columbus's character, his deeply religious feelings, his upright motives. Several generations of American students have been brought up on this interpretation. There is still a feeling, even amidst college-educated Americans, that Columbus was the first all-American hero, as wonderful as George Washington, who could never tell lies or do anything wrong or mean. The average American thinks he did land somewhere in the USA. Technically, he did reach the USA, if you consider Puerto Rico and the US Virgin Isles as part of the commonwealth of the USA, which they legally are.

In the 1960s and '70s, there was a move to diminish the Columbus-as-Hero image, to counter all the myths and legends, and put Morison in his place for whitewashing him. Several younger, left-wing historians ridiculed the idea of his 'Discovery', as America was already there. His arrival was a disaster, leading to enslavement and several centuries of persecution. Columbus himself was cruel and uncaring. Hans Koning, in his 1976 study (*Columbus: His Enterprise*, Monthly Review Press, New York), specifically attacks the notion of Columbus as a 'grade school hero' and asserts that the 'Columbus Day image of Columbus is false'. His explanation of Columbus's voyages is very simple: greed. 'The motivating force was the search for profits.'

In the 1990s, Columbus will no doubt be reinforced as an all-American hero, an example to all. Even more than Spain and Italy, the United States has always had a special affection, nay adoration, for Columbus.

In 1791, the founding fathers of the brave new republic, Thomas Jefferson and James Madison, linked Columbus with George Washington, giving them equal prominence, when they created the City of Washington, in the District of Columbia. Around the same time, the first Columbus Day was celebrated in the USA, in New York and Boston, and the first monument to Columbus was built, in 1792 in Baltimore. (Columbus Day, October 12, became a legal holiday in New York in 1908, and nationwide in 1934.) The 1792 celebrations were, however, relatively quiet and sedate, compared with those of 1892, and the World's Fair in Chicago.

The 1992 celebrations will be the USA's third centenary party to mark Columbus's arrival, and it should outdo the previous ones. In 1985, President Reagan set up the Christopher Columbus Quincentenary Jubilee Commission. His short official proclamation to the nation said it was to 'honor the courage, faith and vision of the Admiral of the Ocean Sea' and finished with 'God bless you'. The Chairman was an interesting choice, John Goudie, born in Havana, Cuba, in 1946, emigrating to the USA when he was fourteen.

There are certain problems and prejudices to be faced when bringing the USA together, as one nation, to celebrate their favourite hero. Firstly, the Italians have traditionally considered Columbus, quite rightly, as their own true son, and made October 12 their day, a symbol of their ethnicity, before the rest of the nation joined in. The Italian community, however, has to allow some scope for the Hispanic community, now enormous in America, who see 1992 as a chance to proclaim their 300-year ethnic heritage in the USA. Other ethnic groups have also to be considered. Why should the blacks see Columbus as a hero when his arrival led to African slavery in America? Why should the Jews be pleased, when one remembers how Spain treated their forefathers? And what will be the reaction of those groups currently defending what is left of the native Indians and their culture, all but destroyed by the Spaniards?

'The Commission's recommendations,' so Mr Goudie has announced, 'are therefore eclectic. They provide something for everybody, even those who approach the quincentenary with a relatively narrow view.'

The major events in the USA include a new Museum of the Americas, aimed at bringing together pre-Columbian artefacts as well as materials relating to the entire sweep of native American life. It sounds suitably uncontroversial. There are scholarships and exhibitions, special stamps and a 500-year time-capsule, full of messages from Americans now to those alive in 2492. A new opera, *Cristobal Colon*, had its American première in New York in 1988. In 1992 there will be a large-scale floral exhibition in Columbus,

Ohio, a tall ships race arriving in New York, and a special ceremony on the spot where Columbus arrived on 'US soil'. This is called the Columbus Landing National Historic Site, and is beside Salt River Bay on St Croix, US Virgin Isles.

One of the events planned for Washington will not cost a cent, but will be heavy with significance. This concerns the famous Columbus Door in the Capitol, considered the nation's most tasteful Columbus monument. It was installed in 1858 and shows Columbus landing, plus eight other episodes from his life, and honours the parts played by Italy, Portugal and Spain. It will be ceremonially closed on October 12, 1991, staying shut for a whole year. Congress will then take part in a ritual reopening on the 500th anniversary day, October 12, 1992.

Several pressure groups, not from ethnic or political backgrounds, have for some time been working hard to turn 1992 to their advantage. One such is the nation's geographers. They are concerned that Americans have lost interest in their subject, dropping it in high school and college, and want more funding and attention. A recent survey, for example, revealed that, when given an outline map of the Western Hemisphere, twenty per cent of American students identified Brazil as the USA.

One of the first surveys the Commission itself carried out was to discover how many settlements in the USA today are named after Columbus. The answer is twenty-six villages, towns, cities and districts using the name Columbus, including Columbus Circle, Columbus City, Columbus Junction and Columbus Grove; forty-one using some variation, such as Columbia, Columbiaville or Columbiana. That makes a grand total of sixty-seven. Not all of them were named directly after Christopher Columbus. Columbus, North Dakota, was named after a man called Columbus Larsen. Columbus, Texas, was rather lamely named after Columbus, Ohio. Some are the result of name changes. Columbus, Mississippi, used to be called 'Possum Town', while Columbus, Montana, was formerly 'Sheep Dip'. One can understand their desire for change. In 1992, all these sixty-seven places are expected to have their own special plans.

The academics have been busy for some time, doing what academics enjoy best, which is firstly organising conferences, secondly attending other people's conferences, and thirdly producing papers and literature based on these conferences. Local ones, to discuss matters of Columbian research, have been held in Florida and the Bahamas for the last ten years, becoming more global as 1992 approaches, attracting their opposite numbers in Spain, Italy and Central and South American countries. There is even a semi-annual newsletter called *1992*, published by Brown University. It has been appearing since 1984 and lists and reports on all scholarly matters to do with 1992 academic research.

The politicians, of course, will in the end probably dominate public attention with their own views on the Columbus centenary, ascribing to him all the known virtues, at least the virtues they happen to be appealing to in their speeches. Michael Dukakis, as Governor of Massachusetts, inaugurated Boston's five years of Columbian events with a speech on October 12, 1987. He called Columbus 'our first immigrant'. Perhaps he believes that, like his own parents coming from Greece, Columbus not only got to the States, but settled there. 'He had to leave his own native land to find opportunity elsewhere.' This suggests he opened a shop. 'He contributed more to the world – to the New World he found and the Old World he left – than he would reap himself.' This is at least true, though of course some cynics might say he gave the New World very little that was good. 'Columbus is a symbol of opportunity. Opportunity to contribute. And a symbol of how that opportunity extended to one individual came back to benefit all of us so much.' Pretty words, but they could be said of so many people, and still not mean much. But Mr Dukakis's main conclusion was clear and uncontroversial. 'Fundamentally, I see Columbus as very much an American hero.'

Each age can derive from the Columbus story what it wants, pointing up what it approves of, or playing down what might be considered reprehensible. Irving made much of Columbus the visionary, his religious feelings and dreams, and gave serious attention to his prophetic writings, which today many people would skip, or dismiss as ravings. There is still some academic support, from Catholic scholars, for considering him as a mystic, arguing that he was inspired by God and that his real and only aim was to enlarge Christianity. So we may have Columbus, the Religious Hero, in 1992.

The arguments over whether he got to America 'first' seem to have died down, after the dramas of the Vinland map (supposedly done in 1440, showing a big island in the West Atlantic, but exposed as a forgery in 1974). Few people now seem concerned to diminish this aspect of the 'Discovery', acknowledging that Columbus was responsible for the first recorded voyage, and the beginning of European settlement. Other people might well have crossed the Atlantic earlier, but nothing came of it. The written History of America begins with Columbus. Before that, we must call it Archaeology.

There have been regular governmental meetings for the last ten years between most of the countries involved in 1992, as they got ready to celebrate the Discovery. At the first meetings, there was much discussion about the use of the word 'Discovery'. How could you discover something which was already there and contained twenty million people? So, the next year, the offending word was changed to 'Arrival'. They then got down to discussing how to 'Celebrate Columbus's Arrival'. But, someone said, do we want to celebrate an event which resulted in ten million Indians being wiped out and an alien culture being forced upon us? So out went the word 'Celebrate'. In most Central and Latin American countries the correct wording is now 'Columbus's Arrival is being Commemorated'. What they are celebrating is themselves.

Nations such as Haiti and Jamaica are now reconsidering Columbus's position as hero, despite what their nineteenth-century stamps and their colonial history books might once have indicated. They are beginning to see him simply as a factor in their history, someone to be studied, not necessarily a figure to be admired. Some people however, see him as an evil figure, the starter of colonial oppression. In 1992, there will probably be attacks on him as an ecological villain, bringing the horrible Europeans to bespoil virgin landscapes.

It has to be pointed out that the Caribs were killing and oppressing the Arawaks before the Spaniards arrived, and in turn the Spaniards were killed or ejected. That, sadly, appears to be the nature of the human race. Nothing much has changed in five hundred years. Death and destruction, of people and landscape, very often in the name of religion, are still with us. The oppressed can turn oppressors. Man's inhumanity to man continues.

Even in Europe and North America, the days of the complete hagiographical approach to Columbus's life and work are now over. That was the tradition in the nineteenth century, setting up heroes to be admired, drawing moral examples from their marvellous deeds and endless virtues, ignoring or excusing any mistakes or weaknesses. The complete warts-and-all biography, which most famous historic figures have had to suffer in recent years, has not really happened to Columbus, apart from those left-wing studies. The subject is too big, the cast list too long, with such a wealth of material, spread around so many places, that it is a very hard to grab hold of his life and explain it simply. The scholars tend to concentrate on one strand, spending their life studying Columbus in San Salvador, or the influence of the Toscanelli letters, re-translating his first log, analysing his prophecies.

After four years on his trail, I naturally like to think I know something of Columbus's character. I am of course seeing him from the point of view of 1992, with all today's preconceptions of what makes a hero, rather different from those of 1892, and certainly 1492, but I think I can identify three areas of real weakness, as well as three sources of remarkable strength.

Firstly, he lacked 'Management Qualities'. He was politically and diplomatically naive, unable to see the results of his actions, even on a minor scale. One almost winces to see in his letters how he is handling and haranguing the Court. In man-management, even on board his beloved ships, there were so many incidents of discontent and uprising, not uncommon at that time (some of the best explorers suffered mutinies) but so frequent that one begins to doubt his leadership skills. As a Governor, setting up communities, forts and then towns, establishing order and trade, he was never a success. There were several reasons why Navidad, Isabela and Belen all failed, but he chose the sites and must take the blame.

He was never happy in these administrative situations, always looking for a chance to go off and explore new places and forget his organisational problems, but he wished this upon himself. He wanted to be a Governor and Viceroy. He felt he had to do this, to make it work, to prove his explorations had been worthwhile, and to finance the next trip. He might have been better remaining an explorer and navigator, like Bartholomew Dias, or Magellan, or Vasco da Gama. He took too much upon himself, beyond his talents.

On the other hand, he did manage to organise those four voyages, to come from nowhere, with no money and no connections, and overcome all obstacles. That does take organisational skill. But it was his magnificent obsession which helped him there, the power of his personality, persuading people, against the better judgement of better experts, to give him a chance. He had charismatic qualities rather than managerial.

Secondly, Columbus was Greedy. It is impossible to deny this, if one looks at those ridiculous demands he made before he had achieved anything, which so upset people and worked against him. He was greedy for gold, for power, for glory, and for position. He would deny, as he did, that it was personal, and argue that he needed such worldly possessions in order to do his job, to compete at Court. People still say this today. They maintain they accept honours and position for their family, their work-force, the good of mankind. Such people are usually deluded. They do it firstly for themselves.

What is wrong with greed? In this materialistic age, when greed is encouraged, there will be those who would put Columbus's greed in a list of his virtues, not his vices. It is accepted as a commendable and understandable motivation, especially in people who come from nothing and achieve so much. Would he have done anything if he had not been greedy for success and wealth? This is hard to deny. You can see it in his calculations, even before he has achieved anything.

The irony is that he never personally achieved great wealth, though he loved flaunting his titles, and creating that pretentious signature for himself. He did live fairly humbly, but this was perforce. And he often wore that hair shirt, but that was symbolic. Who knows how he would have lived if his metaphorical boat had come in?

His greed can be excused and explained away, but it was there. In the beginning it simply made him enemies, when they heard his preposterous demands, and in the end it blinded his judgement, leading to many disasters and bad decisions, from taking slaves to pointless expeditions for gold. His final years were clouded, ruined even, by his passion to retrieve his privileges. Claiming that small reward for sighting land was ungenerous and unfair and undiplomatic. And greedy.

Thirdly, there was a smaller, less important vice which grew stronger as he got older. Columbus was Self-righteous. He was always right, so anyone who criticised was against him personally, an enemy. This led to paranoia. He also believed he was persecuted for his foreign blood. Being a foreigner had not stopped his rise, so there was no real reason to blame it for his fall. Paranoia led to the appointment of his brothers to high positions. Another mistake.

It is virtually impossible in any of his writings to find him admitting mistakes or faults, although he is always willing to go back and score petty points, long after an event is over. He is ever-ready to lecture people on his own triumphs, to justify what he has done, rather than let his discoveries speak for themselves. His final note is a whine, complaining that he has been cheated and not given enough recognition.

In real life, I fear, he must have struck many people as intolerable, whether humble sailors in his fleets or the King himself. A couple of his crewmen did remain loyal to him to the end, but it is noticeable that by his death there is an absence of any influential friends. In his letters, it is rare to find a hint of praise for anyone.

Now, let us consider his virtues and strengths. The facts of his life do speak for themselves, down the centuries, and everyone knows his successes, what he discovered, and what happened as a result, so there is no need to rehearse, yet again, his importance in history. We are now thinking of his personal attributes, as a man.

Firstly, we must applaud Columbus the Navigator. At the time, it was remarkable, but today, with so many modern aids to sailing and automatic pilots to smooth the way, we find it verging on the incredible to look back and see how much he did, working with so little. How did he manage those four enormously dangerous voyages, overcome all the disasters, yet not once did he lose a boat through his own faulty seamanship? (*Santa Maria* was the boy's or the pilot's fault. In Jamaica, it was woodworm.) And each time he found his way home again. There can have been few humans with such a natural instinct for the wind, the sky, the stars, the waves. He did have his compass and charts, such as they were, but his true genius came from his mind, not from any machines.

Secondly, one must mention his Obsessive Perseverance. In the past, it was more customary to acclaim him as a visionary, as did Washington Irving and scores of others, to say he had some sort of religious experience, and that gave him the goal which guided him through life. The notion of a visionary makes a neat moral story, an example for us all, but in these less religious times we look for more mundane explanations. I do not believe Columbus did it for God. He said he did, and in his old age he certainly betrayed a religious mania, but his motivation was much simpler.

His prime intention was not to spread Christianity, and convert the heathen, though that was a useful justification when dealing with Queen Isabella. Columbus had what he thought was a factual, scientific plan, not a vision. (It turned out to be wrong, as he never arrived in China and the world was far bigger than he believed.) But once he had formulated this plan, it obsessed him, and he had one aim: to get out there and prove it. There was no ultimate philosophy, no religious concept. He thought as a sailor, not as some sort of saint, though he might bring in Biblical evidence to prove what he wanted to do anyway.

Once he became a man obsessed, he needed iron-willed, totally blinkered perseverance. It is astounding that he kept going for all those years, in Portugal and Spain, when everyone ridiculed him. And equally remarkable that he organised each of those voyages. The fact that he launched the Fourth Voyage demonstrated perhaps perseverance gone mad.

Thirdly, Columbus was always Curious; not just curious about navigational and scientific subjects, like any good Renaissance man, but he had a boundless interest in all the new places he came upon in the New World. I greatly enjoyed reading his early joyous descriptions of the Bahamas, Cuba, Hispaniola, and shared with him the natural wonders he so marvellously described. Above all, there was a genuine passion for the people, to study them, observe their habits, language, traditions, clothes, to understand and be-friend them. I believe he began with a real love for the Indians, and a concern for their welfare, despite what happened afterwards. This is not to excuse his later actions, as Washington Irving tried to do, just to remind ourselves of his original good intentions.

I have not mentioned Bravery. All heroes should be brave, physically and mentally. That is taken for granted in the best stories. Columbus certainly was brave, though towards the end he was inclined to list all the blows he had received. Nor have I praised him for being magnanimous, as many have done. It is true he was often quick to forgive rebels, perhaps foolishly so. The mutinies and uprisings might have been better dealt with by decisive if cruel punishment, in Hispaniola and on Jamaica. As for being a model of piety, yet another of the attributes some commentators have bestowed upon him, who can tell how deep that really was? His daily devotions were normal for the time. One laughs almost at his hair shirt and Franciscan robes, his plans to travel in the cathedral hearse. Today, they strike us as calculated gestures, rather than genuine genuflection.

By 2092, the world may consider Columbus's character in a rather different light, valuing other attributes, understanding and explaining his weaknesses in a new way, perhaps with the benefit of new material, not just new interpretations. There will always be mysteries and puzzles to keep us fascinated, in a life during which so much happened that was dramatic and unexpected.

The importance of Columbus's life seems unlikely ever to be diminished. What he did in 1492 matters just as much in 1992. For Columbus introduced the New World to the Old World.

Bibliography

ORIGINAL DOCUMENTS AND LETTERS

There are two main centres for Columbus letters and related documents.

1) Seville: a) Archivo General de Indias. The most extensive collection, though the originals cannot normally be studied, only as photocopies.

b) Biblioteca Columbina, Seville Cathedral. Columbus's own books, collected by his son Ferdinand.

2) Genoa: a) State Archives (Archivio di Stato di Genova) – 63 letters and documents, on display.

b) Town Hall (Palazzo Tursi) – three letters, Codex of Privileges.

PRIMARY SOURCES

The following are printed books, but count as primary sources because they are contemporary, first-hand accounts, as written by Columbus and others, endlessly translated and reprinted over the centuries.

Most of them include all or selections from Columbus's Log of his First Voyage, his Letters to the Sovereigns, the biography of Columbus written by his son Ferdinand, the *History of the Indies* by Las Casas, Dr Chanca's letter about the Second Voyage, Cuneo's letter about the Second Voyage, Diego Mendez's will, Oviedo's *History of the Indies*.

The Spanish Government is reissuing all these primary sources, in Spanish, for the 1992 celebrations.

These are some recommended editions, in English:

Cohen, J. M. *The Four Voyages of Christopher Columbus*, Cresset Library, 1988.

Collard, André, *History of the Indies by Bartolome de Las Casas*, Harper, 1971.

Fuson, Robert H., *The Log of Christopher Columbus*, Ashford Press, 1987.

Keen, Benjamin, *The Life of the Admiral Christopher Columbus by his Son Ferdinand*, Rutgers University, 1959.

Major, R. H., *Selected Letters of Christopher Columbus, With Other Original Documents Relating to his Four Voyages to the New World*, Hakluyt Society, 1847.

Morison, Samuel Eliot, *Journals and Other Documents of the Life and Voyages of Christopher Columbus*, Heritage Press, New York, 1963.

BIOGRAPHIES

Bradford, Ernle, *Christopher Columbus*, Michael Joseph, 1973.

Collis, John Stewart, *Christopher Columbus*, Macdonald and Jane's, 1976.

Fernandez Armesto, Felipe, *Columbus and the Conquest of the Impossible*, Weidenfeld, 1974.

Granzotto, Gianni, *Christopher Columbus*, Collins, 1986.

Irving, Washington, *Life and Voyages of Christopher Columbus*, John Murray, 1828.

Koning, Hans, *Columbus: His Enterprise*, Monthly Review Press, New York, 1976.

Landstrom, Björn, *Columbus*, Allen and Unwin, 1967.

Madariaga, Salvador de, *Christopher Columbus*, Unger, New York, 1967.

Mahn-Lot, Marianne, *Columbus*, Grove Press, New York, 1961.

Markham, Clement R., *Life of Christopher Columbus*, George Philip, 1892.

Merrien, Jean, *Christopher Columbus, the Mariner and the Man*, Odhams, 1958.

Morison, Samuel Eliot, *Admiral of the Ocean Sea*, two vols., Little Brown, Boston, 1942.

Morison, Samuel Eliot, *Christopher Columbus, Mariner*, Faber, 1956.

Taviani, Paulo, *Christopher Columbus, The Grand Design*, Orbis, 1986.

Young, Filson, *Christopher Columbus and The New World of his Discovery*, Grant Richards, 1906.

GENERAL

Castlereagh, Duncan, *The Great Age of Exploration*, Aldus, 1971.

McNeill, William H., *Plagues and Peoples*, Blackwell, 1976.

Mandeville, Sir John, *Travels*, Dent, 1928.

Morison, Samuel Eliot, *A History of the American People*, OUP, 1945.

Pendle, George, *A History of Latin America*, Penguin, 1980.

Penrose, Boies, *Travels and Discovery in the Renaissance*, Harvard, 1960.

Polo, Marco, *Adventures*, John Day, New York, 1948.

Walsh, T. W., *Isabella of Spain*, Sheed and Ward, 1931.

FICTION

André, Marius, *Columbus*, Knopf, 1927.
MacNeice, Louis, *Christopher Columbus*, A Radio Play, Faber, 1944.
Marlowe, Stephen, *The Memoirs of Christopher Columbus,* Cape, 1987.

TRAVEL

Blume, Helmut, *The Caribbean Islands*, Longman, 1974.
Crewe, Quentin, *Touch the Happy Isles*, Michael Joseph, 1987.
Fodor's Caribbean Guide, Hodder and Stoughton, 1989.
Naipaul, V. S., *The Middle Passage*, Penguin, 1969.
Parry, J. H. and Sherlock, P., *A Short History of the West Indies*, Macmillan, 1987.
South American Handbook, published annually, Trade and Travel Publications, Bath.

'*This could be great! They could do all the menial jobs no one else will do.*'
(*Punch, 1987*).

Chapter Notes

Further details on each of the present-day chapters, for those desirous of following the Columbus Trail today.

Chapter 2: Genoa

- 1992 Celebrations Committee: Colombo '92, Via Sottoripa 5, Palazzo Serra Gerace, 16123, Genova, tel: 28 41 71.
- Regional Tourist Board – Regione Liguria, via Fieschi 15, 18100, Genova, tel: 54 851.
- Casa di Colombo, Via Porta Soprana, Piazza Dange. (No telephone.)
- Genoa Town Hall – Commune di Genova, Palazzo Tursi, Via Garibaldi 9, Genova, tel: 20981 (Three letters from Columbus, his Codex of Privileges, urn containing some of his ashes).
- Columbus Archives: La Sala Colombiana dell'Archivio di stato di Genova, Via Reggio 14, Piazza Matteotti, tel: 201992. (63 letters and documents on show.)
- Columbus Statue: outside main railway station, Stazione Principe.
- Hotels. Nothing in Genoa worth recommending. Why not lash out and stay on the coast at the Splendido, Portofino, tel: 269551.

Chapter 4: Portugal

Lisbon: National Board for the Discoveries: Comissao Nacional para as Comemoracoes dos Descobrimentos Portugueses, Casa dos Bicos, 1100, Lisboa. (Portuguese Discoveries, of course.)
Lagos: Statue of Prince Henry the Navigator.
Sagres: Prince Henry's School of Navigation, and Castle. Open all the year round.

Madeira: Regional Tourist Board – Secretaria Regional do Turismo e Cultura, Av Arriaga, 18, Funchal, tel: 29057.

Columbus Homes: While in Funchal, he lived in Rua Esmeralda, house now demolished. In Porto Santo, Casa Colomba is next to the church, Nossa Senhora da Piedade, in Vila Baleira, open to visitors.

Statues: Madeira – in the Santa Catarina gardens, Funchal.

Porto Santo – in the gardens, near the pier.

Books: *Madeira* by John and Susan Farrow, Robert Hale, 1987; *Porto Santo, Ilha Morena* (in Portuguese only), Guido de Monterey, 1982.

Hotels:

Madeira-Reid's, Funchal, tel: 23001.

Quinta da Penha de Franca, Rua da Penha de Franca, 2, tel: 29080.

Porto Santo-Hotel Porto Santo, 9400, Porto Santo, tel: 98 23 81.

CHAPTER 6: SPAIN–PALOS

La Rabida Monastery – Monasterio de Santa Maria de La Rabida, Palos de la Frontera, Huelva, Andalucia.

Palos: Church of St George, plus monument outside to the crews of the three ships; statue of Pinzon in village square; La Fontanilla (fountain) just outside village.

Statues of Columbus: outside La Rabida, Palos; beside the causeway, outside Huelva.

Hotel: Hostaria La Rabida, Palos de la Frontera, Huelva: tel: 953 350312.

CHAPTER 8: BAHAMAS

Nassau: Ministry of Tourism–Bahamas News Bureau, PO Box N 3220, Nassau, Bahamas, tel: 322 7505.

Statue – outside Government House.

'92 Celebrations: Quincentennial Committee of the Bahamas, Newsletter *Encounter* published by Star Publishers, PO Box N 8455, Nassau.

Book: *The Story of the Bahamas* by Paul Albury, Macmillan Caribbean, 1986.

Hotels: Royal Bahamian Hotel, tel: 327 6400; Nassau Beach Hotel, tel: 327 7711.

SAN SALVADOR

Internal flights – Bahamasair, tel: Nassau 327 82223.

Museum – New World Museum, San Salvador.

Monuments – three 'Landfall' monuments; Long Bay; Fernandez Bay; Chicago Herald monument, Crab Cay.

Publications: *National Geographic*, Landfall article, vol. 170, no. 5, November 1986.

Hotel: Riding Rock Inn, San Salvador, tel: 1492.

CHAPTER 10: SEVILLE

Archives of the Indies: Archivo General de Indias, Antigua Casa Lonja, Sevilla. (The old Exchange Building, next to the Cathedral), tel: 211234.
Columbus Library: Biblioteca Columbina, Seville. Cathedral. (Should return there in 1992, after re-cataloguing.)
Columbus Tomb: containing his 'body' – Seville Cathedral.
Columbus Statue: Catalina de Ribera gardens, near the Alcázar.
World Fair – 'Expo 92'. Exposición Universal Sevilla, Avda. de la Palmera, 43, 41013, Sevilla. Tel: 629311.
Regional Tourist Board – Avenida de la Constitución, 21, tel: 228990.
Hotel: Residencia Murillo, Lope de Rueda, 7, Barrio de Santa Cruz, tel: 216095.

CHAPTER 12: HAITI

Hôpital le Bon Samaritain, Limbe, Haiti – letters c/o Jet Center Bldg, 7001 US Hwy 301 N, Sarasota, Florida, 34243.
Navidad-site is near Cap Haitien.
Santa Maria anchor – National Museum, underground building, opposite Presidential Palace, Port au Prince.
Tourist Board: Office National du Turismo, Avenue Marie Jeanne, Port au Prince, tel: 21720
Hotels: Hotel Montana, PO Box 523, Port au Prince, tel: 1920.
Hotel Mont Joli, PO Box 12, Cap Haitien, tel: 20300.

CHAPTER 14: VENEZUELA

Columbus Statues: Caracas, near Plaza Venezuela; Macuro – one in square near beach, one outside cement works residence.
Santa Maria replica – Parque L'Este, Caracas.
Tourist Board: Corporación de Turismo, Torre Oesta, Parque Central, Caracas, tel: 507 8816.
Macuro: Also called Puerto Colon, Columbus landing place in South America, 30k from Guiria, no transport available. Address of Vencemos Cement works is: Yemarco, Macuro, Sucre, 6122, Venezuela.
Hotels: Hilton International, Avenida Libertador, Caracas, tel: 574 1122.
Hotel Gran Puerto, Calle Pagallos, Guiria, tel: 81343.

CHAPTER 16: DOMINICAN REPUBLIC

Columbus's Tomb – Santo Domingo Cathedral.
Columbus Statue – outside the Cathedral.
Columbus House – Alcazar de Colon (Diego Columbus's mansion).
Oldest Street in New World – Calle de las Damas.

Museum – Museo del Hombre Dominicano, Plaza de la Cultura, tel: 687 3622.

92 Celebrations – La Espanola 92, Instit. Dom.de Cultural Hispanica, Santo Domingo; tel: 682 8351.

Isabela, site of Columbus's town – near Puerto Plato.

Tourist Board: Estado de Turismo, tel: 687 5537.

Hotel: Nicolas de Ovando, Santo Domingo, tel: 687 3101.

Chapter 18: Jamaica

Columbus arrival beach – Discovery Bay.

Columbus Park open air museum – Discovery Bay.

Columbus shipwreck beach – behind New Seville site, St Ann's Bay.

Columbus statue – beside Catholic Church, St Ann's Bay.

Arawak Museum – Institute of Jamaica, 12 East St., Kingston.

92 Celebrations – National Heritage Trust, 79 Duke St., Kingston, tel: 92 21287.

Books: *Keeping Company with Jamaica* by Philip Sherlock, Macmillan, 1984. *Signpainting in Jamaica* by Dr James Lee, 1986.

Tourist Board: 21 Dominica Drive, Kingston 5, tel: 92 99200.

Hotels: Plantation Inn, PO Box 2, Ocho Rios, tel: 974 2501; Sans Souci Hotel, PO Box 103, Ocho Rios, tel: 974 2353; Jamaica Pegasus, PO Box 333, Kingston, tel: 92 63691.

Chapter 20: Spain – Gomera and Valladolid

Canaries

Gomera

Casa Colon – Calle de Medio, San Sebastian.

Church – Nuestra Señora de la Ascuncion, San Sebastian.

Torre del Conde – near the Harbour.

No statue of CC in Gomera. (Nearest is Tenerife, Puerto de Colon in Playa de las Americas.)

Books: *Gomera*, photographs by Krisine Edle Olsen, Thames and Hudson, 1989; *The Guanches Survivors* by Jose Luis Concepción (publisher and author), Tenerife, 1988.

Hotels – two excellent ones on Gomera. Hotel Tecina, tel: 89 50 50; Parador Conde de la Gomera, tel: 87 11 00. (Look out for the portraits of Columbus and Beatriz on the landing.)

Gran Canaria

Columbus Museum in Las Palma.

Valladolid

Columbus House – Casa Museo de Colon, Calle Colon. tel: 291353.

Columbus death-place – on site of the Teatro Zorilla, Plaza Mayor, 9. tel: 221530.

Columbus Statue – Plaza Colon, outside the railway station.

Tourist Board: Paseo de Zorilla 48, Valladolid, tel: 337585.

Book: *Cristobal Colon y el descubrimiento de America*, Beretta Ballesteros, 2 vols, Salvat editores, Barcelona, 1945. (In Spanish only.)

Hotel: Hostal Lima, Tudela 4, Valladolid, tel: 20 22 40.

Spain's National Commission for Commemoration of the Discovery of America: Avda de los Reyes Catolicos, 4, 28003, Madrid, tel: Madrid 2430428.

Chapter 21: Columbus Today

Columbus Celebrations in USA:

United States Government: Quincentenary Commission, 1801 F Street North West, Washington, DC, 20026, tel: 202 632 1992. This is the US's official body, set up by Congress in 1984, to plan and coordinate the major 500 events. Publishes a free monthly bulletin, *Commission News*. There is also an official glossy bi-monthly magazine, *Five Hundred*, price $3, published from 1550 Madruga Ave, suite 503, Coral Gables, Florida, 33156, tel: 462 1992.

Other Publications: *1992 - A Columbus Newsletter*, semi-annual, academic digest of Columbus matters – Editor Foster Provost, Box 1894, Providence, Rhode Island 02912, USA.

'Ah well, there goes the neighbourhood'
(Private Eye, 1988.)

Index

Admiral of the Ocean Sea (Morison), 276
Adrian V, Pope, 5
Africa, 26, 32, 37, 55, 91, 118, 200, 242, 284;
    colonisation of 141; exploration of, 28, 40, 44,
    62, 68, 81
Agosto, Dr Aldo, 22
AIDS, 182, 186, 234
Albury, Basil, 108–9
Algarve, 10, 25, 45–46, 73
America, 71, 141, 200, 234, 249, 251, 278,
    284–85, 287, 291: *see also* Indies, New
    World, Central, North and South America
Andalucia, Spain, 71, 72, 75
Andros, Sir Edmund, 105
Aragon, Kingdom of, 3, 9, 26, 58
Arawak Indians, 113, 180, 188, 213, 244, 252,
    254, 255, 291
Archives of the Indies, Seville, 145, 148–51
Aristotle, 36
Asia, 37, 118, 141, 165, 201, 284
Atlantic ocean, 25, 28, 33, 44, 112, 141;
    crossing of, 35, 91, 93, 212, 290–91
Azores, 28, 42, 91, 134–35, 136, 137, 139,
    229

Bahamas, 105–6, 108–11, 120, 228, 251; and
    Columbus, 103, 106–7, 111–12, 116, 289,
    295; native people of, 98–102, 104–5, 113,
    116, 117, 118
Balboa, Nunez de, 248
Ballesteros, Antonio, 276
Barbados, 228, 229
Barbeito, Manuella, 54–55
Barbeito, Ricardo, 55
Barcelona, Spain, 138, 139, 271
Barreto, Mascarenhas, 55
Belen, 246–7, 249, 258, 264, 292
Benson, Bobby, 113
Bermuda, 105
Bible, the, 37–38, 64, 165, 172, 196–97, 200,
    201, 238, 245, 294
Bobadilla, Beatriz de, 60, 92, 157, 272–73

Bobadilla, Francisco de, 222–23, 224, 236, 238,
    143, 287
Bolívar, Simón, 205, 206, 215
Borsodoli, Dr Luigi, 19, 20
Bower, Erika, 110, 113
Bower, Paul, 110, 112, 113, 114, 117
Brazil, 141, 148, 197, 212, 275, 283, 289
Buyl, Father, 170

Cabral, Pedro, 44, 136
Cadiz, Spain, 68, 71, 85, 143, 153, 171, 174,
    236, 239, 249, 271
Caldeira, Captain, 54
Canary Islands, 28, 60, 88, 91, 92, 98, 156–57,
    167, 195, 218, 242
Cap Haitien, Haiti, 182, 188, 189, 253
Cape of Good Hope, 62, 136, 166
Cape St. Vincent, 10, 25, 27, 195
Cape Verde Islands, 94, 195–96, 217
Capitulations, the, 67–68, 69, 76, 267
Caracas, Venezuela, 203, 204–6, 207, 212, 215,
    229
Caribbean, xii, 103, 112, 121, 131, 136, 177,
    181, 226, 229, 230, 239, 244, 251, 255
Caribs, 121, 130, 131, 158, 159, 167–69, 244,
    291
Carlos II, King of Spain, 148–49
Casa Colombo, Genoa, 12, 13, 14, 18–19, 20
Castile, 71; council of, 65; Kingdom of, 26, 42,
    57, 58, 93, 100, 101, 124, 125, 130, 141, 218,
    220, 243, 258–59, 264, 268, 274
Cat Island, Bahamas, 103
Cathay: *see* China
Catherine of Aragon, 59, 191, 266
Catholic Monarchs: *see* Ferdinand of Aragon,
    Isabella of Castile
Catholicism, 58, 61, 108, 127, 172, 286, 290
Central America, 204, 239, 257, 283; Columbus
    reaches, 244–48, 291; conquest of, 250
Cervantes, Miguel de, 145
Chanca, Dr, 160–62
Charles V, King of Spain, 280

China, 38, 39, 62, 118, 121, 123, 201, 245, 294

Christianity, 37–38, 40, 58, 84, 118, 122, 124, 150, 290; conversion to, 99, 106, 156, 194, 294

Christophe, Henri, 181, 190

Christopher Columbus: The Grand Design (Taviani), ix

Christopher Columbus: Portugese Spy in the Service of King John II (Barreto), 55

Colombo, Dominico, 3–4, 6, 14, 18, 21

Colombo, Susanna, 3, 4

Colon, Cristobal: *see* Columbus, Christopher

Colon, Cristobal, Duke of Veragua, 111, 150, 280, 282

Columbus Bartholomew, 3, 28, 34, 57, 61, 62, 169–71, 175, 222, 268, 280, 293; on Fourth Voyage, 242, 247, 258, 259, 262, 263; and Hispaniola, 202, 217–18, 219, 221, 223, 227

Columbus, Christopher, vii–viii, 1–2, 7–8, 79, 231; arrest of, 223–25, 230, 235, 236–37, 265; burial of, 232, 279–81; and Catholic Monarchs, 59–61, 66–68, 69, 81, 89, 91, 98–101, 113, 118–19, 122, 125, 131, 135, 138, 150, 236–39, 261, 264–68, 282, 286, 294; character of, viii, 23, 142, 175, 196, 230, 237, 287, 292–95; death of, 268–70, 275, 278, 294; documentation, viii–xi, 2, 20–22, 30, 32, 149–51, 239–42, 273, 279, 285; early life of, 2, 3, 5, 6–10, 30–31, 32, 34, 42; as explorer, 33–42, 56–58, 60–63, 164–66, 227, 239, 244, 280, 284, 292, 294; fame of, 139, 279, 281–82, 284–92; First Voyage of, 2, 68–70, 73, 80–102, 112, 113, 115, 118, 120–31, 139–42, 153, 158, 166, 170, 175, 275; Fourth Voyage of, 238–43, 244–49, 257–65, 295; health of, 141–42, 164, 169, 200, 202, 221, 259, 263, 264, 265; as Hispaniola's governor, 164, 217–24, 227, 230–31, 237, 238, 292; honours and titles of, 66, 67, 137, 138, 141, 142, 222–23, 237, 258, 265, 266–67, 269, 282; as merchant, 8–9, 10, 29–30, 32, 40; monuments to, 44, 49, 54, 55, 77–78, 105, 107, 111–12, 144, 145, 181, 205–6, 215–16, 233, 254, 271, 274, 286, 288–89; and native peoples, 98–102, 106, 113, 118–19, 122, 124–30, 136, 140, 156, 170, 172, 174, 198–99, 228, 259, 285, 295; navigational skill of, 8, 10, 24, 25, 34–35, 42, 89–91, 93–96, 171, 216, 226, 230, 259–60, 294; in Portugal, 11, 25–26, 28–29, 44, 46, 49, 55, 64, 69, 75, 91, 93, 133–37, 169; religious motives of, 171, 173, 194, 196–97, 200, 201, 230, 231, 235, 237–38, 245, 264, 287, 290, 292, 295; Second Voyage of, 142–43, 152, 153, 156–63, 169, 173–75; in Spain, 55–57, 59–63, 65, 68, 94, 122, 133, 169, 223, 238, 285, 287, 289; Third Voyage of, 191, 194–202, 206, 207, 209, 210, 213, 216, 217–25; *see also* First, Second, Third and Fourth Voyages

Columbus, Diego (brother), 3, 164, 175, 222, 223, 269, 280, 293

Columbus, Diego (son), 31, 42, 43, 54, 56, 61, 65, 132, 142, 153, 174, 221; and father, 195, 266–67, 269, 279–80; as governor of Santo Domingo, 227, 229, 233, 268, 282

Columbus, Ferdinand, 60–61, 83, 132, 142, 144–45, 146, 148, 149, 174, 194, 195, 221, 269; as father's biographer, x, 1, 3, 6, 7–8, 9,

10, 29, 30, 186, 284, 285; of First Voyage, 84, 85–88, 92, 93, 94, 97, 119, 122, 123, 126, 128, 129, 133, 136; on Fourth Voyage, 239, 242–46, 257–59, 262, 263; of Grand Design, 32–33, 35, 36, 38, 39–42, 62–63; of Second Voyage, 153, 158, 159, 162, 166, 169, 172, 173, 174; of Third Voyage, 191, 195–96, 218, 219, 237

Columbus: His Enterprise (Koning), 287

Columbus Library (Seville), 144, 146–48

Columbus, Luis, 280

Commonwealth, British, 105, 251

conquistadores, 233, 283

Cordoba, Spain, 59, 60, 61, 65, 132, 271

Cortes, Hernando, 282–83

Cosa, Juan de la, 68, 74, 165, 220

Costa Rica, 244

Cotter, Captain, 253

Cuba, 108, 110, 120–23, 139, 148, 165, 228, 230, 244, 248, 275, 280, 295

Cuneo, Michel de, 157, 158–59, 162, 163–64, 165, 166–69, 171

D'Ailly, Cardinal Pierre, 38

Daily Gleaner, 250, 254

Deagan, Dr Kathleen, 182–83, 187–88

Dias, Bartholomew, 44, 62, 68, 136, 166, 292

DiNegro family, 9, 29

Dominica, 157, 227–28

Dominican Republic, 129, 181, 188, 227, 231, 251, 275; and Columbus, 227, 230–34

Drake, Francis, 227

Duvalier, "Papa Doc", 181

Duvalier regime, 181, 182, 189

Eanes, Gil, 25, 28, 46

England, 6, 15, 26, 128, 139, 227; colonies of, 251, 254–55; Columbus and, 57, 61, 62, 63, 170; fights Spain, 250, 266

Enriquez, Beatrice, 60–61, 83, 195, 269

Equator, the, 44, 64, 121, 194, 196–97, 217

Europe, 37, 47, 84, 135, 200, 250, 283, 284, 291

Ferdinand, King of Aragon, xi, 58–60, 63, 66, 84, 135, 145, 149, 186, 191–94, 266, 273, 287; and Columbus, xi, 81, 89, 91, 98–101, 113, 119, 122, 121, 135, 138, 150, 236–39, 261, 264–65, 266–68, 282, 294; and New World, 142–43, 148, 172, 173, 200, 201–2, 221–22, 224

Fieschi, Bartholomew, 242, 258, 269

First Voyage, 2, 73, 88–90, 153, 156, 157, 158, 166, 266; crew for, 68–69, 76–77, 80, 81, 83–84, 94–97, 101, 102, 122, 152; first landfall made, 97, 103–4, 116, 117, 123, 127; lands discovered on, 98–102, 118–29, 139; preparations for, 68–70, 80–85; return, 128–37, 139, 170, 275; route of, 91–96, 117, 156

Florida, 96, 104, 165, 188, 289; University of, 182, 187

Fonseca, Archdeacon, 152, 156, 174, 220

Fourth Voyage, 238–39, 242–49, 279, 295; crew for, 242, 245–46, 248–49, 257–59; mutiny on, 259–60, 262–62, 264, 265, 267; and shipwreck, 248–49, 250, 251, 253, 256, 257–63

France, 6, 15, 44, 54, 170; colonies of, 181, 127; war with Spain, 191, 195, 250
Fregoso family, 3–4
Funchal, Madeira, 31, 32, 48–52, 54

Gama, Vasco da, 44, 46, 239
Genoa, 12–14, 19, 24, 25, 30, 32, 34, 47, 72, 73, 157, 164, 171, 242, 254; and Columbus, vii, viii, 1, 2, 12, 13, 14, 18–19, 20, 23–24, 150, 280, 285; history of, 3–6, 9, 15–16, 29, 39, 63, 195
gold, 100, 102, 121, 123, 125, 129, 140, 142, 161, 233, 249, 250, 283; greed for, 172, 200, 230, 246, 264, 292; mining, 128, 163–64, 220, 224, 247, 257
Gomera, Canaries, 92–93, 157, 195, 242, 272, 273
Gomez, Barbara, 110
Gomez, José, 110, 112, 114
Goncalves Borges, João, 49–50
Goudie, John, 288
Granada, Spain, 71
Granada, Kingdom of, 26, 57, 58, 59, 60, 63, 66, 67, 221, 237, 244
Grand Khan, 38, 40, 62, 84, 118, 121, 124, 135, 140, 142, 145
Grand Turk Island, Bahamas, 103
Greek philosophy, 29, 33, 34, 36
Guacamara, Chief, 160–62, 187
Guadalquivir, Spain, 195, 279, 283
Guanches, 271, 272–73
Guinea, 32, 69, 137, 199
Guiria, Venezuela, 206, 207, 211, 213, 215, 216
Gulf of Paria, 198–201, 204, 206, 216, 220
Gutenberg, Johann, xi, 147
Guttierrez, Pedro, 83, 97, 128

Haiti, viii, 12, 149, 176–80, 182, 188, 190, 207, 228, 251, 252, 260, 275; Columbus and, 123–24, 180, 182, 253, 291; history of, 180–81, 182, 187, 227
Harana, Diego de, 83
Hart, Lee, 252–53
Hart, Sam, 252–53
Havana, Cuba, 280, 281, 288
Henry the Navigator, 25, 26–27, 28, 31, 32, 34, 40, 44, 46, 49, 50, 62
Henry VII, King of England, 57, 63, 191
Henry VIII, King of England, 59
Hispaniola, 124, 125, 139, 148, 157, 165, 166, 169, 175, 180, 182, 194, 197, 200–1, 237, 238, 251, 269, 295; division of, 181, 227, 280; native people of, 124–27, 173, 195, 217, 219, 228–29; rebellion on, 218–24, 235, 295; Spanish settlement of, 128–29, 159, 160, 164, 170, 175, 182, 194, 202, 217, 227, 239, 248, 249, 260
History of the Indies (Las Casas), x, 85, 156, 286
Hodges, Dr, 183, 184, 185–88, 189, 190, 252
Hoffman, Dr Charles, 116–17
Holy Roman Emperor, 174, 191
Hojeda, Alonso de, 204, 220
Honduras, 244
Huelva, Andalucia, 57, 71, 72, 77–78, 84
Humboldt, Alexander von, 284

Iceland, 29, 34
Imago Mundi (d'Ailly), 38, 62

Incas, 283
India, 37, 231, 239, 244
Indian Ocean, 62
Indians, 104, 113, 116, 117, 120, 138, 140, 159–64, 166–69, 183, 258, 266; Columbus and, 98–102, 113, 118–19, 122, 124–30, 136, 156, 174, 198–99, 228, 259, 295; destruction of, 106, 172–73, 230, 260, 288, 291; enslavement of, 140, 170–71, 173, 175, 194, 224, 285, 287; as labourers, 125, 128, 220, 228–29, 247, 257–58; rebellion of, 245–47, 248, 259, 262, 264
Indies, 36, 38, 56, 62, 96, 134, 137, 139, 140, 142, 173, 197, 223, 242, 268, 282, 285; colonisation of, 175, 217, 221, 228, 230, 250, 273, 279; conquest of, 148–49, 150, 153, 282; trade with, 195, 237, 267: *see also* New World
Innocent IV, Pope, 5
Inquisition, the, 58, 235
Irving, Washington, 2, 103, 104, 145, 285, 287, 290, 294, 295
Isabela, 163–64, 173, 175, 231–32, 292
Isabella, Queen of Castile, xi, 58–59, 110, 149, 186, 273, 274; children of, 174, 191, 194, 220–21, 265–66; and Columbus, 59–60, 63, 66–67, 69, 81, 89, 91, 98–101, 113, 118–19, 122, 125, 131, 138, 150, 236–39, 261, 264–65, 286–87; death of, 265–66, 268
Isabella, Queen of Portugal, 191, 220–21, 265
Islam, 26, 27, 33, 58, 84, 97: *see also* Moors
Italy, 6, 9, 15, 107, 120; and Columbus, xii, 287, 288, 289

Jamaica, 148, 149, 250, 254–55; and Columbus, 165, 166, 244, 248, 250, 251–54, 256, 257–63, 265, 291, 294, 295
Jamaica Journal, 252
Japan, 37, 39, 41, 91, 95, 100, 118, 120, 121, 123
John I, King of Portugal, vii, 26–27
John II, King of Portugal, 28, 32–33, 39, 40–42, 55, 61–62, 93, 135, 136–37
Juan, Prince, 138, 142, 153, 174, 191, 194, 220, 265
Juana, Princess, 191, 194, 266, 268
Judaism, vii, 3, 27, 50, 58, 150, 235; converts from, 66, 84, 85

Kingston, Jamaica, 254, 255–56
Koning, Hans, 287
Kubla Khan: *see* Grand Khan

Lagos, Portugal, 10, 25, 26, 27–28, 45–46, 47, 69, 229
La Rabida: *see* Santa Maria de La Rabida
Las Casas, Bartolome de, x, 9, 30, 31, 39, 41, 42, 49, 54, 59–60, 66, 85–88, 92, 93, 98, 131, 136, 149, 156, 169, 173, 186, 195, 198, 200, 201, 217–19, 222, 230, 245, 269, 286
Las Cuevas monastery, 236, 237, 279
Latin America: *see* Central and South America
Limbe, Haiti, 183, 184, 188
Lisbon, Portugal, 26, 27, 28, 29, 30, 31, 32, 39, 42, 46, 47, 52, 62, 63, 74, 135, 136, 137, 224, 229, 269
l'Ouverture, Toussaint, 181, 190
Lucayans, 104–5, 117
Lusiano, José Ivan, 228

Macuro, Venezuela, 209–11, 212–16
Madariaga, Salvador de, vii
Madeira, 28, 29, 31–32, 47–48, 54, 91, 134;
    Columbus in, 48–49, 50, 55, 195
Madrid, Spain, 59, 273
Magellan, Ferdinand, 44, 89, 283, 292
Marchena, Father Antonio, 57, 65
Margarita Island, 202, 206
Marinus, 36
Martins, Canon, 39, 40
Mayans, 244–45
McNeill, William H., 172
Medina Celi, Duke of, 59, 63, 68
Mediterranean sea, 4, 15, 26, 27, 29, 37–38, 69,
    91
Mendez, Diego, 247, 258, 260–61, 263–64, 269
Mexico, 111, 132, 165, 233, 244, 275; Spanish
    conquest of, 282–83
Miami, Florida, 104, 107, 110
Miami Herald, 107
Moniz Perestrello, Felipa, 30–31, 32, 42, 195
Monte Christi, 160, 163
Moors, 6, 26, 46, 58, 59, 60, 68, 150, 223, 244;
    defeat and expulsion of, 66, 71, 146
Morison, Samuel Eliot, ix, 7, 81, 88, 93, 94, 96,
    97, 104, 107, 136, 150, 260, 275, 276, 285,
    287
Morocco, 31
Moya, Marquesa de, 65
Musee de Guahaba, Limbe, 188
Museo de Colon, Valladolid, 274–76

Napoleon, 181, 182, 227, 274
Nassau, Bahamas, 103, 104, 105–9, 113–14, 116
National Geographic Magazine, 103, 104, 107,
    114, 116, 117
Navarre, Kingdom of, 26
Navidad, 127, 128, 130, 140, 142, 157, 175,
    253; destruction of, 160–63, 183, 227, 231,
    247, 292; site of, 182–85, 186–89
New World, the, 71, 105, 113, 119, 163, 197,
    253, 280, 283, 290, 295; conquest and
    settlement of, 173, 182, 227, 231, 233, 238,
    253; discovery of, vii, xii, 55, 75, 97–98,
    111–12, 234, 278, 284; *see also* Indies
Nicaragua, 244, 275
Nina, 81, 83, 84, 89, 92, 93, 95, 96–97, 123,
    126, 128–29, 131–32, 133–37; on second
    voyage, 153, 165, 174
1992 Columbus Celebrations, xii, 12, 17–20,
    23–24, 53, 103, 106–7, 110, 114, 252–55,
    272, 273, 279, 286, 287–91
Nino, Juan, 82
Norsemen, 35, 199
North America, 104, 284, 291

Orinoco River, 201, 203–4, 207, 216
Ottone, Dr Piero, 23
Ovando, Nicolas de, 238, 239, 243, 261, 263,
    282
Oviedo, Gonzalo Fernández de, 35, 120, 186,
    285

Pacific Ocean, 247, 248
Palos de la Frontera, Spain, 56–57, 65, 67, 79,
    83, 84, 127, 128, 130, 132, 138, 153, 271,
    282; First Voyage and, 68–69, 70, 76–77, 80,
    91, 137, 152; modern, 71, 72, 75, 77

Panama, 244, 245, 264, 275
Panama Canal, 247
Paria Peninsula, 207, 208, 243: *see also* Gulf of
    Paria
Paul III, Pope, 233
Peirotti Cei, Lia, 20
Perestrello, Bartholomew, 31, 32, 34, 53
Perestrello family, 34, 39, 50
Perez, Father Juan, 58, 59, 63, 65, 75
Perez Memen, Dr Fernando, 230–31
Peru, 275, 283
Philias, 188
Pinta, 81–82, 84, 88, 89, 91, 93, 95, 96–97,
    131, 137, 141; loss of, 123, 128, 129, 130,
    131–32
Pinzon, Martin Alonso, 68–69, 74, 75–76, 82,
    88, 95, 98, 152; quarrels with Columbus, 123,
    129, 130, 131, 137–38, 282
Pinzon, Vincente Yanez, 69, 74, 75–76, 82, 98,
    123, 130, 137, 152, 282
piracy, 9, 10, 25, 62, 63, 227, 251
Pizarro, Francisco, 283
Pliny, 36
Polo, Marco, 5, 38–39, 41
Porras brothers, 258, 262, 267
Porras, Captain, 258, 262, 263
Port au Prince, Haiti, viii, 176, 177–79, 182,
    183, 188, 189
Porto Santo, 31, 52–53, 54; Columbus lives, vii,
    32, 34, 35, 39, 42, 50, 53, 195
Portugal, vii, 6, 10, 15, 26, 31, 44–45, 47, 67,
    195; Columbus and, 11, 25–26, 28–29, 44,
    46, 49, 55, 64, 69, 75, 91, 93, 133–37, 169;
    empire of, 28, 31–32, 40, 45, 47, 48, 54, 122,
    141, 197, 229; exploration by, 27–28, 45, 81,
    85, 90, 194, 283
Prester John, 40, 62
Ptolomy, 36, 62, 148, 197
Puerto Real, 186–87
Puerto Rico, 131, 159–60, 242, 275, 287

Quintero, Cristobal, 88

Renaissance, the, 6, 29, 36, 39, 56, 196, 230,
    283, 295
Robinson, Carey, 254–55
Rodriguez, Alonso, 233
Roldan, Francisco, 218, 219–20, 243, 262
Rubio, Jesus, 210, 211–16

St. Ann's Bay, Jamaica, 165, 248, 250, 251
St. Augustine, 38, 64
St. Brendan, 35
Sagres, Portugal, 27, 34, 46
Salamanca, Spain, 65, 194, 268, 271
Samana Cay Island, 103, 107, 114–17
San Salvador, Bahamas, xii, 104, 107–8,
    110–11, 113–14, 115, 116; Columbus
    landfall, 98–101, 103, 108, 111–12, 115, 119,
    124, 127, 130, 139, 266, 292
San Sebastian, Gomera, 272
Sanchez de Segova, Rodrigo, 83, 97
Santa Cruz Island, 159
Santa Maria, viii, 68, 72, 74, 80–82, 83, 89, 92,
    93, 95–97, 124, 128–29, 145, 161, 205;
    anchor of, 183, 188, 189–90; wrecked,
    126–27, 130, 253, 294
Santa Maria Island, 134–35

Santa Maria de La Rabida, monastery of, 56–58, 59, 63, 65, 68, 72–75, 88

Santagel, Luis de, 66–67, 68, 139

Santo Domingo, 226, 228–35, 269, 279–81, 282; colonisation of, 218, 220, 222–24, 236, 238, 242–43, 248, 249, 258, 261, 263

Sanz, Professor Angel, 275–76

Sardinia, Kingdom of, 9, 15

Sargasso Sea, 95

Sayle, William, 105

Second Voyage, 142–43, 156–57, 173–75, 220, 251, 283; colonisation attempts, 163–64, 173, 175; crew for, 152, 153, 156, 158–59; and Indians, 160–64, 166–69, 170–72; mutiny, 164, 170, 171, 173

Seneca, 36, 147

Segovia, Spain, 267–68

Seville, Jamaica, 252–53, 254

Seville, Spain, viii, 71, 94, 137, 138, 142–43, 191, 194, 283; and Columbus, 144–51, 152, 156, 236, 237, 263, 271, 279–81

slavery, 28, 99, 105, 106, 140, 239, 286; African, 180, 181, 288; Indian, 170–71, 173, 175, 194, 224, 285, 287

smallpox, 173, 186

Smith, Philip, 106–7

South America, 72, 103, 104, 108, 111, 141, 199, 203, 204, 234, 267, 283, 286, 287, 291

Spain, vii, xi, 6, 15, 26, 44, 107, 120, 123, 125, 128, 131, 139, 243, 246, 274; and Columbus, 55–57, 59–61, 63, 65, 68, 94, 122, 133, 169, 223, 238, 287, 289; colonies of, 45, 60, 71–72, 106, 141, 143, 181, 197, 200, 205, 209, 217, 227, 229, 250, 255, 266, 273, 275, 282–83, 288, 291; court of, 58, 118, 138, 139, 142, 144, 191, 200, 221, 225, 230, 237, 261, 262, 267–68, 271, 273, 282, 292–93; unification of, 65–66; war with European powers, 191, 195, 250, 266

Spanish Conquest, 150, 172, 227

Spanish language, 71, 72, 105, 106, 118, 172, 181, 228

Spanish Main, 233

Strabo, 36

Syllacio, 162–63

syphilis, 174–75, 182, 186, 218

Taino Indians, 217

Talavera, Archbishop, 64–65, 67

Taviani, Paolo Emilio, ix, 4, 7, 18, 21, 29, 47, 57, 60, 276

Tejeda, Maureen, 229, 231, 234

Tejeda, Monseñor Priama, 234

Tenerife, Canaries, 271–72

Terreros, Pedro de, 262

Third Voyage, 191, 194–200, 204, 206–7, 216, 279, 283; discovery of mainland, 201–2, 231, 249; rebellion, 218–20, 221–22, 224

Torres, Antonio de, 153, 164, 169

Torres, Juana de, 223

Torres, Luis de, 84, 121

Toscanelli, Paolo, 39–40, 292

Travels of Sir John Mandeville, The, 38

Treaty of Tordesillas, 141, 194

Triana, Rodrigo de, 97, 286

Trinidad, 197–98, 207, 209, 215, 216

Tristan, Diego, 247

Trujillo, Rafael, 227

Turkey, 5, 15, 26, 34, 39

Turks and Caicos Islands, 107

USA, vii, 107, 182, 227, 253, 280, 285; and Columbus celebrations, xii, 286, 287–89

Valladolid, Spain, 268, 269, 273–74, 276–78, 279; Casa-Museo de Colon, 274–76

van den Berg, Stefan, 109

Vasquez Dias, Daniel, 73

Vega, Bernardo, 231–32

Vega, Cynthia, 232

Venezuela, 203–4, 205, 212, 251, 275; and Columbus, 198, 206, 207, 209, 210, 213, 216, 217

Venice, 4, 5, 38, 39, 88

Veragua, Duke of, 111, 150, 280, 282

Veragua, Panama, 244, 245, 282

Verissimo, Dr Nelson, 50

Vespucci, Amerigo, 204, 220, 267, 275, 283–84

Virgin Islands, 148, 159, 287, 289

Waldseemüller, Martin, 283–84

Washington, D.C., 287, 289

Watford, Nancy, 116–17

Watling Island, Bahamas, 104

Welsh, Mrs Georges, 50–52

West Africa, 40, 41

West Indies, 132, 141, 165

William III, King of England, 105

Wind, Father Herman, 111, 114

Wolper, Ruth, 111, 113

Zarco, Fernando, vii, 55: *see also* Columbus, Christopher

Zorilla, Jose, 276, 277

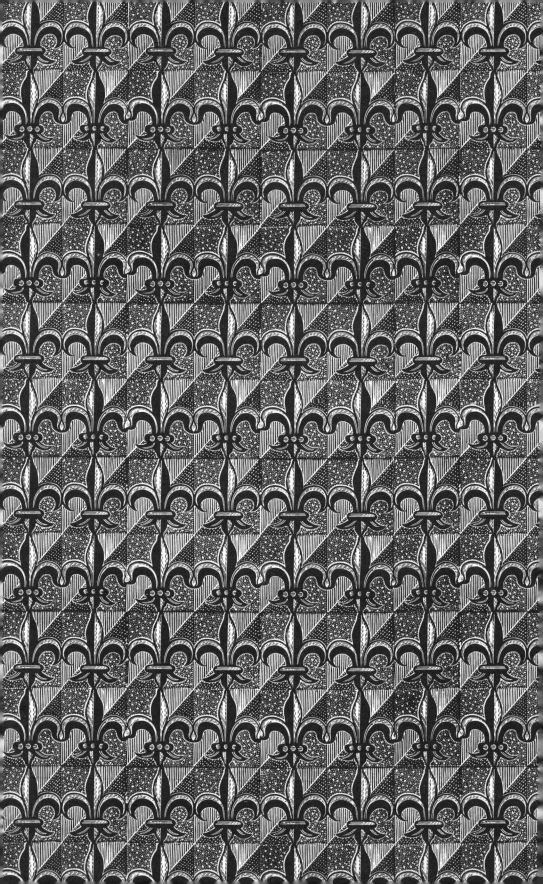